B+T

5

W9-BBM-062

THE
CREATIVE
BALANCE

Elliot Richardson

THE
CREATIVE
BALANCE

Government, Politics,

and the Individual

in America's Third Century

Holt, Rinehart and Winston

New York

Wingate College Library

Copyright © 1976 by Elliot Richardson
All rights reserved, including the right to reproduce
this book or portions thereof in any form.
Published simultaneously in Canada by Holt, Rinehart
and Winston of Canada, Limited.
Library of Congress Cataloging in Publication Data

Richardson, Elliot L.
The creative balance
Includes bibliographical references.
1. United States—Politics and government—1945-
I. Title.
JK271.R454   320.9'73'092   75-5455
ISBN 0-03-013706-3   7-15-96

First Edition
Designed by Mary M. Ahern
Printed in the United States of America
10 9 8 7 6 5 4 3 2 1

To Anne

067939

Contents

Acknowledgments

IN THE CASE of some things, like cooking an omelette or painting a watercolor, I have learned to let well enough alone. Not so with this book. Lacking comparable experience in book-writing, I have found it hard to resist the impulse to keep on amplifying, revising, readjusting, and tinkering. But the book as it stands reflects not only my own best efforts but the suggestions and criticisms of many generous friends and loyal associates. I would like to be able to implicate these friends and associates in the final outcome. In fairness, however, I can charge them only with responsibility for suggestions and criticisms that have greatly improved its quality.

Friends who have read the manuscript from beginning to end—and in the case of some, more than one version—include Richard G. Darman, Concetta Leonardi, Jonathan Moore, Helene K. Sargeant, J. T. Smith, and Donald M. D. Thurber. I wish it were feasible to render a properly appreciative account of their individual contributions. Dick Darman's critical analysis, Cetta Leonardi's stylistic precision, Jonathan Moore's perceptive insights, and J. T. Smith's balanced judgments have severally and in combination corrected, supplemented, and strengthened the exposition. I am equally obligated to Helene Sargeant's sensitivity and Don Thurber's thoroughness—and, in Don's case, for his giving an entire week in London to a careful review of the chapters thus far completed.

A number of other friends, all former colleagues in various government departments, have made significant contributions to portions of the book. These include Russell Edgerton, Wilmot R. Hastings, Laurence E. Lynn, Jr., David B. H. Martin, Richard E. Mastrangelo, George Marshall Moriarty, and J. Stanley Pottinger.

SINCE BECOMING my research assistant in June 1974, Janet Huidekoper Brown has been enormously helpful, not only in all the ways implied by the word "research," but as a resourceful draftsperson of original portions of chapters and as an unfailingly constructive (though frequently astringent) critic. Jeffrey L. Mayer, first as my research associate in the state and local government project at the Woodrow Wilson International Center for Scholars and since then as a friend, has given me valuable suggestions in the whole range from philosophical coherence to editorial clarity. Anthony Ripley, who came to London as my special assistant in March 1975, has been a persistent and constructive challenger of obscurity, turgidity, and shallowness.

A special note of thanks must go to my secretary, Helen Hangemanole. With unflagging cheerfulness, dedication, and unremitting attention to detail, she has from the beginning (more than two years ago) been the efficient coordinator and typist of every successful draft as well as the faithful keeper (and finder) of the files.

THERE REMAIN two important institutional credits. The first is to the Woodrow Wilson Center. It would be hard to imagine a more hospitable environment for serious thought and stimulating discussion. I am grateful to James H. Billington, its Director, as well as to its Trustees, for the privilege of working there during most of the interval between my resignation as Attorney General and my appointment as Ambassador to the United Kingdom.

I am also grateful to the Kennedy School of Government

at Harvard University, and especially to Don K. Price, its Dean, for the opportunity to build the Godkin Lectures for 1975 around the material which has since become Chapters III, IV, and V of this book.

All those who have given me suggestions and criticisms have also given me encouragement, and this in many ways has been even more important. But the encouragement that has meant the most to me has been the encouragement of those from whom the book has demanded the most—my wife Anne and my family. They understood and appreciated that it was something I had to do, and without their extraordinary patience and support during these past two years, I could not have managed it.

December 1, 1975

Introduction

THIS BOOK is concerned with the cumulative forces threatening to submerge the dignity and self-esteem of the individual and with the ways in which governmental policies could more effectively be directed toward coping with these forces.

Although I began to think about writing a book on this general theme almost exactly ten years ago, various offers I could not refuse kept getting in the way. I owe to Watergate the unpremeditated interlude of unemployment which enabled me to get started. But this is neither a Watergate book nor a personal memoir. It draws on my observations and experiences of Watergate, as it does on other observations and experiences, to illustrate or reinforce some aspect of its broader subject.

My point of departure is a set of beliefs which seem to me not only fundamental to the values of our own society but implicit in a valid perception of what it is to be a human being. Foremost among them is the belief that every individual seeks a sense of personal identity and worth. Each person gains this partly through the development and exercise of individual capacities, partly through the sense of belonging and sharing that comes from participating in the society of others. In both cases, freedom to choose is indispensable to the opportunity to become a complete person. It is also essential to our self-esteem that we feel able to exert some control over the forces that affect our lives.

An affirmation of personal worth and freedom was implicit in the truths unanimously declared to be self-evident by "the thirteen united States of America" in Congress assembled on July 4, 1776: "that all men are created equal, that they are endowed by their Creator with certain unalienable Rights, that among these are Life, Liberty and the pursuit of Happiness." To secure these rights was proclaimed as the very purpose of government, whose just powers must derive from the consent of the governed. It followed, and was also declared, that the people retain ultimate power, including the power to alter or abolish any government that becomes destructive of their rights.

For Americans, the Declaration of Independence put to an end the assumption that the sovereign or the state can have purposes distinguishable from the well-being of the individuals constituting a self-governing society. This was the true significance of the American *revolution* as distinguished from the new *independence* for Britain's former colonies. As John Adams wrote to the Baltimore publisher Hezekiah Niles on February 13, 1818, "But what do We mean by the American Revolution? Do we mean the American War? The Revolution was effected before the War commenced. The Revolution was in the Minds and Hearts of the People."[1] The ideas reflected in the great Declaration, however, had by no means spent their force before the war commenced or while it was being fought. In the years between 1776 and 1787 these ideas underwent a continuing process of refinement and adaptation. Wrought in the intense heat of rational debate—and demonstrating as no other people or period ever has that debate can be both heated and rational—the conceptual innovations that took shape in those years were even more revolutionary than those which inspired the revolution itself.

During the years of triumph and tumult separating 1787 from 1776, three ideas, different but mutually reinforcing, reversed the most basic assumptions underlying three hundred years of debate about the design of a durable and benign government. The first of these ideas—a federal structure allocating powers between the national government and the states in such a way that some powers are exclusively national, some are concurrent, and the rest reserved to the states—stood on its ear the previously unquestioned dogma that two governments cannot both exert power in the same territory. Once this dogma had been abandoned, it was no longer necessary to assume that the national government must retain supreme sovereign power, permitting to subordinate governments only such powers as might for the time being be delegated to them from above. It became possible instead to create a limited national government by transferring to it only some of the powers of the constituent governments, which, except for the powers transferred, remained sovereign within their own territories.

The second idea embodied a novel approach to curbing the abuse of power. Rather than attempting to suppress natural tendencies toward the accumulation of excessive authority, a way was found of converting them into the generators of countervailing reactions against arbitrariness and oppression. This invention at the same time harnessed private selfishness to the general welfare and factional strife to forward progress.

The third idea cast aside earlier notions of a contract between governors and governed and made all the institutions of government representative of the people and continually accountable to them. The people thereby acquired a permanent stake in the management of power for the advancement of their own interests.

These innovative concepts became the solid triangular underpinning of the new Constitution for the United States of America which emerged on September 17, 1787, from sixteen weeks of intense debate. It was an extraordinary achievement. As Madison wrote to Jefferson in October, it was "impossible to consider the degree of concord which ultimately prevailed as less than a miracle."[2] John Adams, writing to Rufus King from London just after Christmas, hailed the new Constitution as, "if not the greatest exertion of human understanding, the greatest single effort of national deliberation that the world has ever seen."[3] But even the framers could scarcely have predicted with confidence that the result of their deliberations would survive without fundamental change for nearly two hundred years and assimilate meanwhile a seventyfold increase in population, a fourfold expansion of territory, a transformation from a rural and agricultural to an urban and industrial society, and a transition from isolation to global power and responsibility.

The structure created in Philadelphia was indeed remarkably coherent and comprehensive. Not only has it worked, but it has worked in accordance with the principles so powerfully articulated by its designers. And yet one of its most basic premises was scarcely even mentioned at the time: the role and responsibility of the individual citizen. One can only suppose that this was because the attention of the Constitution-builders was so much absorbed by the erection of barriers against the resurgence of tyranny. Their concern with the citizen focused on his rights, not his responsibilities.

It was apparent, nevertheless, that the structure depended on the citizen for the performance of essential functions—functions so vital, indeed, that it is not a mere exercise of rhetoric to call citizenship a "public office."* The most fundamental of these functions was assertion of the very rights which the framers were intent on guaranteeing to the citizens. These guarantees are worthless unless individual citizens are willing to speak up, to petition, to go to court, to protest, to demonstrate. By insisting on his own rights, one citizen vindicates the rights of all his fellow citizens. And by voluntarily yielding on occasion to the rights of others, the citizen contributes to building a civilized community.

A second function of citizenship, of course, is that of participating, through exercise of the right to vote, in selecting those who will wield the powers delegated to the government by the people. The citizen must be willing to take the trouble to

---

* Like (I suppose) most politicians, I have given many speeches dilating upon the "office of citizenship." I assumed that the phrase was current in the era of the framers and in common use among nineteenth-century orators. It was not, however, until I began this book that I thought of trying to find out where it came from. To my surprise, I have been unable to find any use of it earlier than by Louis D. Brandeis, cited in Alfred Lief, *Brandeis: The Personal History of an American Ideal* (New York, 1936), p. 72.

appraise the views of the candidates as well as to gauge their character and qualifications.

A third function of the citizen is to influence the shaping of the policies of government. And while no one person can have an informed opinion about everything, people can—and if the system is to succeed, they must—be capable of contributing to an intelligent consensus about basic choices. "What is above all important," wrote the late Alexander M. Bickel in a brilliant essay on the legal order, "is consent—not a presumed, theoretical consent, but a continuous actual one, born of continual responsiveness."[4]

There is, finally, the need for integrity: to achieve and maintain a self-governing society, its citizens must feel some attachment to its free institutions and humane values and be capable of resisting any attempt to betray them.

Although the framers did not spell out the role of the citizen, we can infer the importance they attached to it from the indirect manifestations of its impact on their thinking. One of these manifestations was their belief that competition among diverse interests will advance the general interest. In emphasizing competing interests rather than "public virtue" as the key to the workability of representative institutions, the framers recognized that it was unrealistic to assume that the people would be a homogeneous body uniformly activated by a shared perception of the public good. They would inevitably, as Madison pointed out in *The Federalist* No. 10, be grouped into parties and "factions." The question was how to cope with the "instability, injustice, and confusion" resulting from the struggles among factions, for these had always been the "diseases under which popular governments have every where perished." The cure was not to be found in "destroying the liberty which is essential" to the existence of factions; this would be "worse than the disease."[5] As *The Federalist* No. 51 more fully explained, the solution lay in a "multiplicity of interests" which tended to make a "coalition of a majority of the whole society" unlikely "on any other principles than those of justice and the general good."[6]

There could be no clearer acknowledgment of the power of the people. But it must be power tempered by a sensible regard for the general welfare—which is to say, a sense of responsibility. Although too realistic to attempt to banish factions, the framers were also too realistic to overlook either the fact or the necessity of a larger view. In *The Federalist* No. 55 Madison acknowledged that there are "qualities in human nature which justify a certain portion of esteem and confidence." Moreover,

> Republican government presupposes the existence of these qualities in a higher degree than any other form. Were the pictures which have been drawn by the political jealousy of some among us, faithful likenesses of the human character, the inference would be that there is not sufficient virtue among men for self-government; and that nothing less than the chains of despotism can restrain them from destroying and devouring one another."[7]*

Consciousness of the degree to which they had made the success of the system depend on the sovereign power of the people also explains the framers' caution in granting the right to vote. The framers restricted the franchise—or, more precisely, permitted the states to do so—not because they were hostile to democracy but because, having chosen to rely on the people, they wanted to hedge the bet. Some, to be sure, were readier than others to trust the people. On one side was the faith in them associated with the name of Jefferson. On the other was the more skeptical attitude shared by Adams, Hamilton, and other Federalists who, in Hamilton's words, believed that the "turbulent and changing" masses "seldom judge or determine right."[8] But the difference between the two points of view was never more than a matter of degree. Both were aware that the Constitution reposed greater trust in the capacity of the electorate to act responsibly than had ever before been risked in a society of comparable scale.

---

* Benjamin Franklin, full both in years and wisdom (he was then eighty-two), had already made essentially the same point in his address to the final session of the Constitutional Convention. The form of government about to be established, he warned, "can only end in Despotism as other Forms have done before it, when the people shall become so corrupted as to need Despotic Government, being incapable of any other." Daniel Boorstin, ed., *An American Primer* (New York, 1966), Vol. 1, p. 97.

Madison, addressing the Virginia Convention that ratified the Constitution, expressed confidence that this trust was justified:

> But I go on this great republican principle, that the people will have virtue and intelligence to select men of virtue and wisdom. Is there no virtue among us? If there be not, we are in a wretched situation. No theoretical checks, no form of government, can render us secure. To suppose any form of government will secure liberty or happiness without any virtue in the people, is a chimerical idea. If there be sufficient virtue and intelligence in the community, it will be exercised in the selection of these men; so that we do not depend on their virtue, or put confidence in our rulers, but in the people who are to choose them.[9]

The knowledge that the success of the whole venture in self-government would depend on the ability of the electorate to "select men of virtue and wisdom" seems to account for the universality of the opinion that the franchise should be restricted to adult males who owned some minimum amount of property. This restriction was prompted not so much by the notion that property gave the citizen a stake in society as by the belief that property owners were in a position to exercise independent judgment. Sir William Blackstone, whose *Commentaries* was the standard text for American lawyers at the time of the Constitutional Convention, authoritatively expressed the prevailing view: "The true reason of requiring any qualification, with regard to property, in voters, is to exclude such persons as are in so mean a situation that they are esteemed to have no will of their own."*

A continuing awareness of the weight of the responsibilities

---

* Sir William Blackstone, *Commentaries on the Laws of England*, 3rd ed., rev. (Chicago, 1884), Vol. 1, p. 170. Professor Jack P. Greene, to whom I am indebted for this point, has argued that similar considerations explain the exclusion from the right to vote of wives, children, servants, tenants, aliens, and others deemed dependent upon the wills of others. This premium on independence is the more understandable in light of the circumstance that ballots were still cast in the open in those days, and any citizen could see how his fellow citizens voted.

entrusted to the citizen accounts, I think, for the deliberateness with which the franchise has been extended. Step by step over nearly two hundred years, the extension has reached group after group in the order of its presumed capacity for independent judgment: first adult males without property, then black males, and after them women, reservation Indians, and young people between eighteen and twenty-one. The inheritors of the "Jeffersonian" tradition were no doubt readier at any given time to see the franchise extended than the inheritors of the Federalist tradition, but both became less cautious toward the people and more trustful of them at about the same rate over about the same period. Both were attacked by a new surge of doubt about the wisdom of representative democracy in the years between 1840 and 1870 when the cities were filling up with immigrants easily subject to boss rule. Indeed, the Jeffersonian optimists were more deeply shaken during those years than the Hamiltonian pessimists. Even Walt Whitman, viewing "the shallowness and miserable selfism" of "the masses," worried about "the appalling dangers of universal suffrage."[10] In the century since then we have virtually ceased to think of any portion of the people as "the masses."

Concurrently with the extension of the franchise, those who won the right to vote also made other gains. The significance of the franchise was expanded by provision for the direct election of United States Senators and by abandonment of the attempt to give the Electoral College an independent voice in the selection of Presidents. Enactment of the Voting Rights Act of 1965 did all that legislation can do to protect the right to vote against obstruction or interference. And as a consequence of the Supreme Court's 1962 decision in *Baker* v. *Carr*, the "one man–one vote" case, each person's vote now counts for as much as another's.[11]

Gradually, therefore, in the years since 1787, the duties of the office of citizenship have been more widely and more equitably shared. Why has this happened? Some steady, persistent force must have been behind this evolutionary process. What force? It adds nothing to answer, "The demand for the right to vote." Whose demand? Not, surely, that merely of idealists and ideologues dedicated to the moral and theoretical beauty of the democratic principle. No, there can be only one real answer: those who in the beginning were denied the franchise *wanted* to be admitted to full citizenship. Some—especially women— fought for it. But this leads to another question.. Why did they care so much?

Madison seems to be the only one of the framers who even hinted at an answer. In *The Philadelphia National Gazette* for December 19, 1791, he wrote: "The larger a country, the less easy for its real opinion to be ascertained, and the less difficult to be counterfeited. . . . This is favorable to the authority of government. For the same reasons, the more extensive a country, *the more insignificant is each individual in his own eyes. This may be unfavorable to liberty.*"[12] In this brief reference to the link between a sense of individual significance and the enjoyment of liberty is summed up an insight as ancient as Aristotle and as modern as the literature on the relationship between political efficacy and political alienation.

Here we come back to my point of departure—the indispensability to individual fulfillment of the freedom to choose, and the relationship between self-esteem and the ability to exert some control over the forces that affect our lives. Since those forces are influenced by the decisions of government, the more pervasive the role of government becomes, the more essential it is to individual self-esteem to have a voice in governmental decisions. It is in our capacity as citizens that most of us exercise such a voice. Discharge of the obligations of citizenship is thus important not simply to the successful functioning of representative democracy but to the self-realization of the individual. This, I believe, goes a long way toward explaining why throughout history individuals have fought so hard to gain and enlarge the office of citizenship.

As to the other link alluded to by Madison—that between the extensiveness of a country and the individual's sense of significance—we have no way of knowing what he would have regarded as the maximum limits of size and population compatible with a sense of significance. It is scarcely conceivable that he would have put these limits as high as the area and population embraced by the United States in, say, 1950. And yet feelings of insignificance had not then emerged as a cause of malaise sufficient to become the subject of widespread notice. In the quarter-century since 1950 the country's population has increased by only 40 percent and its territory not at all. During that period, however, the belief that we suffer from a sense of insignificance in our own eyes—and each other's—has become the most widely accepted diagnosis of our social malaise.

What has been happening to us during the past quarter of a century? The answer, I believe, is that Madison was essentially right in seeing a correlation between individual self-esteem and the scale of the social environment. This assumes, of course, that the perception of scale is affected by factors more complex than "extensiveness," since a sense of insignificance was not a visible problem during the 150 years of the country's greatest growth in size and population. The factors that have made a difference must, on the face of it, have had a larger role in the third quarter of the twentieth century than in our previous history.

One group of factors that has affected our sense of scale has done so simply by forcing on our attention how many of us there are. Urbanization, for example, has done this by crowding us together. Jet travel has done it by making us seem closer together. Television has done it by annihilating completely the distances between us.

Another group of factors diminishes us in our own eyes by diminishing our sense of effectiveness. Big, remote government has this effect, and the results of size and distance are compounded by complexity, which makes processes that ought to be responsive to us hard to grasp and to influence. The growing impersonality and indifference of nonpublic institutions also demean us. And because it undercuts confidence in our creative capacity, so too does the deadly monotony of degrading work.

Together with the feeling of being overwhelmed by numbers and a diminishing sense of effectiveness there has been a weakening in the dependability of things. This has affected our sense of place if not of scale. We feel less confident that we possess a secure role in an ordered and predictable world. The speed of technological change has disrupted our sense of continuity. Official lying, government secrecy, and the abuse of government power sow distrust, suspicion, and fear. The growing gap between government promises and government performance reinforces these reactions. Other institutions, meanwhile, have been losing the authority and credibility which used to contribute to the stability of the social structure.

The demand for fairness—a greater measure of equality and social justice—has also created strain on the established order. Thus, while this demand expresses the legitimate claims of many individuals, it simultaneously threatens all those who feel comfortable with things as they are. The increased pressure of the demand for fairness is manifested in a number of interrelated developments among which it is difficult to distinguish cause and effect. One, I think, is a level of expectations raised both by the actuality of affluence and by the widespread impression that we now possess resources sufficient to overcome age-old causes of suffering and deprivation. Another is the perception of limits on the foreseeable rate of sustainable growth: whatever the ultimate limits may turn out to be, the belief that the available pie may not grow much larger is bound to generate increased pressure for a larger slice on the part of all those whose present share is small.

For many people self-esteem has been eroded by the loss of community and the slackening of purpose. A community can be repressive and unforgiving, but even at its worst it supplies a sense of place and identity; at its best it makes possible the satisfactions of sharing and belonging. The disintegration of the extended family, mobility (20 percent of American families move in any given year), poor physical planning of neighborhoods, and the diminution of the opportunity for political participation have all had a part in breaking down the structure essential to these satisfactions.

No adequate substitute has yet been found for the faith in purpose, and the affirmation of purpose, that used to be basic to America's religiously oriented, deeply patriotic communities. The decline of the institutions which until recently have been able to transmit from generation to generation an accepted set of values and beliefs has also contributed to the weakening of the individual's sense of purpose. The habit of questioning everything has the merit of exposing the meretricious and the shoddy;

it has the defect, at the same time, of tending to discourage the creation of alternatives to the institutions which are being challenged. To lack a sense of purpose is, for most people, to feel incomplete—and with the need for completeness we once more come back to the link between individual significance and personal freedom.

But the question persists, why was it not until the second half of the twentieth century that these factors brought about a pervasive feeling of malaise? It certainly was not because they had burst upon the scene for the first time. On the contrary, each had gradually been gathering momentum for decades. Even jet travel and television had earlier counterparts in the form of prop planes and radio. The explanation, I believe, has three parts, none sufficient in itself but in the aggregate persuasive. The first is that some of these developments have been growing at a compounded annual rate. Air passenger miles almost tripled between 1955 and 1965 and doubled between 1965 and 1970. Suburban growth reflects the same trend. Between 1960 and 1970, the population in center cities increased 6.4 percent while suburban population increased 26.7 percent. In the second place, each of these developments reinforced the others: urbanization *and* the weakening of established institutions *and* the frustration consequent upon complexity *and* all the rest would, multiplied together, have an impact many times greater than any one by itself could have had. And third, all of them converged on the individual. Even had they not tended to reinforce each other as parts of an interacting process external to the individual, their internal impact on the human psyche was bound to be cumulative. No wonder, in the circumstances, that their effect was to diminish the sense of significance and identity and to stimulate feelings of malaise, alienation, and anomie.

The same forces are still at work. It is not essential to be able to quantify their individual compounded rates or estimate their multiplied product. Whatever their quantity or degree, they will continue to wear away the individual's self-esteem so long as they operate unchecked. Our society, instead of coming closer to what it set out to achieve, as it did for so long, will fall shorter and shorter of its goal—the creation of a setting within which every individual has equal opportunity to fulfill his potential.

To brake this slide and start back up our historic path, the first essential is to decide that it has to be done. This in turn requires the recognition that the order of priorities now facing government is new. To meet these new priorities, we must, in Lincoln's phrase, "disenthrall ourselves" from old conceptions. Forty years ago in the wake of massive economic disasters, New Deal efforts to invoke the powers of government on behalf of the general welfare provoked bitter controversy. The country had long succeeded remarkably well under a weak central government, and it was understandable that there would be resistance to measures which, like Social Security, unemployment compensation, and wage and hour regulations, necessitated major new assertions of government authority. The resulting controversy centered on issues of enormous urgency and difficulty. The outcome was a profound shift in the political center of gravity from the states to the national government and from a passive to an active governmental role in meeting social problems.

The classifications and clichés which first gained currency in that era of upheaval still dominate political debate. In the intervening years, however, two things have happened to make these formulations obsolete. The first is that there now exists wide acceptance of the need for government to respond to the demands of the general welfare. This was true at least as early as 1958, when I was in the Eisenhower administration as Assistant Secretary of HEW for Legislation. The recession of that year brought a sharp rise in unemployment, and many wage earners had exhausted their unemployment compensation benefits. The federal government began to make temporary advances to state unemployment insurance systems for continued payments to these wage earners, but the numbers of those exhausting even the extended benefits became substantial. As the second quarter of 1958 began, it was uncertain whether the recession would bottom out or deepen. At that point, I was asked to draft legislation providing federally funded benefits for all needy, unemployed families—in essence, a dole. At a quiet meeting in the office of former Governor Sherman Adams, President Eisenhower's chief of staff, the legislation was pronounced acceptable by the Republican "conservatives" there assembled. There was no dissent, no significant debate.

As matters turned out, the next report of the Council of Economic Advisers correctly forecast an upturn in the economy, and the legislation never went to the Hill. But to me the incident demonstrated that the only remaining issues with respect to government responsibility toward the general welfare were issues of how, not whether, to deal with a visible need.

How far we have come is even more clearly illustrated by public attitudes toward today's major social measures—national health insurance or welfare reform, for example. None of these raises serious questions about the necessity for government action; they give rise, rather, only to issues of method; whether to rely on premium payments or a payroll tax, whether to rely on state or national administration, and so on. The point is not that these issues of method are easy or inconsequential; on the contrary, most of them are both complex and important. To continue to debate them, however, as if they fundamentally affected the future of our society is to misconceive the character of our present predicament.

The second thing that has happened is that a whole new set of issues has now acquired the urgency which "program" issues once had. These new issues are "process" issues: how to preserve a place of dignity and significance for the individual in the midst of the forces threatening to submerge us; how to give each of us a stronger voice in shaping the policies of an increasingly complex and impersonal government.

Programs are directed toward our most basic needs—food, shelter, health, employment. Processes are directed toward enabling us to live with each other on a footing of mutual respect and appreciation. Program issues center on what government should do for people. Process issues center on how government should relate to people. Liberty, democracy, the protection of individual rights, citizen participation—all these are matters of process. They are what the Declaration of Independence is about. They are what the revolution was fought over. They are the central concern of the Constitution and the Bill of Rights. This is what we mean by a "government of laws and not of men."

Although most political commentators, perhaps merely out of reluctance to abandon their comfortable stereotypes, continue to sort issues and personalities into "liberal" and "conservative" cubbyholes, these categories have become almost completely irrelevant to the genuinely significant problems of the present and future. Concerns about what is happening to the individual and the community, about fairness and honesty, about the responsiveness and responsibility of government, are shared in equal measure—and voiced with equal force—by people whose views on "program" issues cover the whole range from left to right. "Liberal" professors like Alan Westin and "conservative" Congressmen like Barry Goldwater, Jr., share the same concern about the dangers to privacy posed by automated personal data systems. Advocates of the dispersion of government power have sprung from all points of the "programmatic" spectrum; as Irving Kristol has said, "We are all decentralists now."

This book represents an effort to transcend labels and look at substance—to describe the developments that trouble us most, to discern their antecedents, and to suggest ways in which we can take corrective action. These suggestions are moderate, although the times, in many respects, are not. And, some may argue, our immoderate troubles demand immoderate remedies. I cannot agree. We live in a period of ill-tuned response—of over- and underreaction, of counterintuitive effects. We have been frequently surprised, of late, at the extent to which systems we thought or pretended we understood—the domestic economy, the energy system, relations with the natural environment, for example—are not in fact under rational control. There is a growing awareness that the pattern of bold and confident action that contributed so much to our development may now be inducing unintended harm.

I do not, in saying this, mean to endorse inaction. I do mean, however, to suggest the need for a more thoroughly considered approach to change—a perspective that sets the attractions of potential benefits against the background of potential harm, an approach that seeks a creative balance between innovation and conservation.

Just such a creative balance, indeed, is demanded by all the most important goals of our society. For a goal is not a resting place but an optimal relationship among components of a dynamic process. The checks and balances of our Constitution seek an optimal relationship among the thrusts and counterthrusts of competing social and economic interests. Power is constrained by accountability; freedom implies the necessity for choice; individualism flourishes in community; equality requires liberty. Only by the constant pursuit of balance among the elements of change can we induce the flow of events to bring us closer to where we want to go: a society in which all of us can be and become our whole selves—a society which enhances individual dignity and self-esteem, the ultimate values for whose sake our political processes exist.

THE
CREATIVE
BALANCE

I

Abuse of Power: The Mahogany Coffin

"GOD LOOKS after fools, drunkards, and the United States of America." The old saying was fulfilled again in the case of Watergate.

Beyond its own sordid confines, Watergate has been redemptive—a disguised stroke of good fortune for the United States of America. That good fortune may yet turn to ashes, but I am one of those whom H. L. Mencken called the "optimists and chronic hopers of the world" and I see gain for this country in the reassertion of old ideals and the renewal of governmental processes.

America was also fortunate in the extraordinary and improbable chain of events which brought to light the evils of Watergate while it was still possible to correct them. The abuse of power is a corrupting precedent for those who later hold it. For those who are subject to it, its continuing abuse can come to seem like the natural order of things. For both, the effect is addicting. And if the abuse of power goes that far, discovering the habit may come too late to cure it.

1

In dealing with and even drawing new strength from Watergate, our system of government has shown its basic soundness. Watergate can fairly be regarded as demonstrating the failings of men and the resiliency of a constitutional system. John Adams, who drafted the language of the Massachusetts Constitution of 1780 declaring that separation of the powers of government is "to the end it may be a government of laws and not of men," later wrote:

> . . . that law proceeds from the will of man, whether a monarch or people; and that this will must have a mover; and that this mover is interest; but the interest of the people is one thing—it is the public interest; and where the public interest governs, it is a government of laws, and not of men: the interest of a king, or of a party, is another thing—it is a private interest; and where private interest governs, it is a government of men, and not of laws.[1]

The Watergate revelations arrested a process which was beginning to substitute the interest of a President for the interest of a people. We saw how vulnerable to the abuse of power is even our system of checks and balances. And once again, though in starker terms than ever before, we were warned that eternal vigilance is essential to the survival of liberty.

Although this is not a book about Watergate, two Saturdays in 1973—one in April and one in October—gave me considerable occasion to think about the implications of Watergate for the problems that are the concern of this book. Among these concerns is the need for more adequate safeguards of "the interest of the people" against the abuse of power. That need, and the steps that can be taken toward meeting it, are the subject of this chapter.

THE FIRST of the two Saturdays was April 28, 1973. I was then a spectator of Watergate from across the Potomac River at the Pentagon—an outsider absorbed in military affairs. In the middle of a Father's Day morning at my daughter Nancy's school, my friend and former chief, Secretary of State William

P. Rogers, got through to me by telephone. His first words were, "Are you sitting down?"

The President, he said, wanted me to leave the Department of Defense and take over the Department of Justice.

Almost a year had passed since the break-in at Democratic National Headquarters. It had been a long time since anyone tried to laugh it off as just another political caper. The press was filled with reports that John N. Mitchell, the former Attorney General, had authorized hush-money payments to the Watergate burglars and that the money had come from funds held at the White House by H. R. Haldeman, President Nixon's chief of staff. Some reports had it that the burglars themselves were linked to still another burglary—that of the office of Daniel Ellsberg's psychiatrist in Beverly Hills, California—which had taken place after Ellsberg was indicted for releasing to *The New York Times* a secret report on the Vietnam war. The President's counsel, John Dean, had announced darkly that he did not intend to be a scapegoat in this ramifying affair.

Bill Rogers told me that Attorney General Richard G. Kleindienst was about to resign, not because of any personal involvement in Watergate, but because others with whom he had been closely associated—Mitchell, Dean, and Robert C. Mardian —were implicated. The President was also about to accept the resignations of Haldeman, Dean, and John D. Ehrlichman, his principal assistant for domestic affairs. It was urgently important to find a new Attorney General who could restore public confidence in the leadership of the Department of Justice. The President had turned to Rogers for advice. Rogers had proposed me. He said the President had agreed that I was the best possible person in the circumstances.

I had been sworn in as Secretary of Defense on January 30, only three months before. I was deeply immersed in my Defense Department job and had no wish to leave it. The prospect of having to take over the Watergate investigation was not pleasant. I said I would go home, talk to my wife Anne, and call back after I had had a chance to think about it.

I told Nancy that an emergency had arisen, apologized to

the headmistress, and went directly back to my home in McLean. Anne and I agreed that I should avoid the assignment if I could but that this might prove impossible. I then telephoned two of my oldest friends. We concluded that the objective of restoring confidence in the Department of Justice would be better handled by bringing in a new Attorney General who had not been part of the Nixon administration. But we were aware that there were time pressures on filling the job. The President might consider it essential to announce a replacement for Kleindienst as soon as possible. A talent search for an outsider—for a person who was qualified and independent and in whom the President had confidence—might well involve an unacceptable delay. Because of this, and despite my reluctance, I decided that if the President insisted on naming me, I would acquiesce. But the first thing to do was to let the President know my belief that I was not the right person for the job.

Rogers relayed this concern to the President, then called back to say that both he and the President were convinced that despite my long association with his administration, I would be universally regarded as capable of independence. Despite my misgivings on this point, it was left that I would discuss the matter with the President at Camp David early the next afternoon.

Sunday, April 29, 1973, was a beautiful spring day. The Maryland countryside was gentle and serene below the helicopter which took me to Camp David. The President greeted me on the terrace of his lodge. He seemed strained and depressed. He had just asked Haldeman and Ehrlichman to resign—"the toughest thing," he said, "I have ever done in my life." Kleindienst had left only a few minutes before I arrived. The President, visibly holding himself under tight control, told me that I was more needed at Justice than at Defense. As Attorney General I would have full control of the Watergate investigation; it would be my "specific responsibility to get to the bottom of this. Anybody who is guilty must be prosecuted, no matter who it hurts." It would be up to me whether I appointed a Special Prosecutor; he suggested the following as possibilities I might consider: Wilmot R. Hastings, who had worked with me in the Attorney General's office in Massachusetts, at State, and as general counsel

of HEW; John J. McCloy, a distinguished New York lawyer
and public servant; and J. Edward Lumbard, former Chief Judge
of the General Circuit Court of Appeals. He would like me to
remain a member of the National Security Council. And, he said,
I *must* believe—and here he leaned forward and looked me
straight in the eye—that he had not known anything about
White House involvement in Watergate until he began his own
investigation in March. "Above all," he concluded, "protect the
Presidency—not the President if he's done anything wrong."

Department of Defense issues had been taking all my time,
and I was too unfamiliar with the details of Watergate to know
what follow-up questions to ask. I did, however, say to the President that I hoped he would call on me in the future on matters
of judgment even though they did not directly involve my
department. Feeling, I suppose, that he now needed me as he
never had before, I added, "And I hope you will respond to the
crisis of confidence that Watergate has created by opening up
your administration and reaching out to people in a more magnanimous spirit." I had said much the same thing to him before
both in person and by memorandum, and it was a point I had
made several times in conversations with members of his staff.
I now found the courage to express the other half of this thought.

"Mr. President," I continued, "I believe your real problem
is that you have somehow been unable to realize that you have
won—not only won, but been reelected by a tremendous margin.
You are the President of *all* the people of the United States.
There is no 'they' out there—nobody trying to destroy you.
Even the people who didn't vote for you want you to succeed."

His expression did not change as I spoke. I do not recall his
saying anything at all.

BELIEVING THAT my own perspective on the abuses which
came to a head in Watergate might help to prevent anything like
them from happening again, I have tried to understand what
brought them about. Knowing all that I now know, I think I
can discern three principal contributory ingredients. One was
Richard Nixon's own distrustful style, a compound both of his
personal insecurity and of his reaction to the reality of bitter

attack. A second was the amoral alacrity to do his bidding of a politically inexperienced, organization-minded staff obsessively driven by the compulsion to win. A third was the aggrandizement of Presidential power and the tendencies toward its abuse that had already been set in motion before Nixon took office.

Only dimly perceiving that I might be touching on a fatal flaw of character, I alluded to the first of these ingredients when I said to Richard Nixon at Camp David, "There is no 'they' out there." I had, it is true, from time to time caught glimpses of a suspicious and manipulative streak in him, but I had no way of knowing how deep it ran or how much it widened out below the surface. What I saw bothered me enough, however, to lead me to appeal to him from time to time to display greater magnanimity and openness. I was troubled by his unwillingness to trust senior civil servants who would gladly have given him their full loyalty if he had but shown that he was ready to meet them halfway. Similarly, I felt that he was wrong in failing to communicate to the press the awareness that they too have a job to do— and that that job is not to puff the President, right or wrong, but to expose and criticize whenever exposure or criticism is justified. His instinct for the manipulation, rather than the education, of public opinion bothered me, as did his assumption that his relationship with the Congress could never be genuinely consultative. I resisted, sometimes with success, his tendency in dealing with Presidential appointments to apply a narrow test of loyalty to himself and his ideas in preference to encouraging diversity and debate among people whose devotion to the larger public interest could be taken for granted. This tendency was given full rein during the months immediately following his reelection when top-level appointees were being promoted, transferred, and dismissed. The effort to keep good people absorbed a large part of my time during that period. But I saw these things not as unforgivable sins but as excusable shortcomings. In this I was no doubt influenced by the desire to think well of the President I served, a fact which instinctively made me want to give him the benefit of the doubt. So far as my own perception of the man was concerned, it took such revelations as the "enemies" list, the attempt to coopt the Internal Revenue Service as an instrument for punishing political opponents, and the neurotic self-delusion of the tapes to make me fully aware of his deep-rooted insecurity.

A disposition to think of opponents as enemies is a self-fulfilling attitude: the surest way of making enemies is to treat people as if they were enemies. Richard Nixon, in any case, was not lacking either in real enemies or in people who simply did not like him. Hypersensitive as he was to the attitudes of others, he must certainly have been aware that in many people he inspired Thomas Brown's feeling about Dr. Fell: "I do not love thee, Dr. Fell. The reason why I cannot tell." Others actively hated him and thought they knew why; he was aware of that too. Nor did Nixon merely imagine the bitterness of the hostility aroused by his Southeast Asian actions; lacking Lincoln's magnanimity, he writhed under attacks unsurpassed in ferocity by any since those on Lincoln. To my mind, Garry Wills has come closer than anyone else to a perceptive interpretation of the White House mood in the early years of the Nixon Presidency:

> The White House was under almost perpetual siege. People came in on tours and poured blood there, or carried insulting signs out front. The professors came, too, or praised the students for coming. No wonder those inside felt the aggression was all upon the other side, the outside.[2]

Observing that those who admired Nixon the most felt the greatest need to protect him, Wills continues:

> The protectors' strength grows from their charge's weakness, his demand for shelter, for quiet and surcease from insult; from the fact that he has been wronged so often and felt it so deeply. What was simply a crude manner in Mitchell became a principled ruthlessness in Haldeman, an insensitivity toward the outside fed from acute sensitivity to Nixon's wounds and exposed nerves. Thus power grew by feeling powerless; aggression always looked like self-defense. Only terrified men institute a Terror.[3]

Tom Charles Huston, the former Presidential aide who helped draw up an intelligence plan for the White House in 1970, remarked that "no one who had been in the White House could help but feel he was in a state of siege."[4] And only a President who felt himself besieged could have approved Huston's plan (later withdrawn because of J. Edgar Hoover's objections) for spying, surveillance, burglary, and a super-security agency.

The second of the contributory ingredients of Watergate —an amoral alacrity to do the President's bidding—was traceable less to flaws in his own character than to the political and cultural evolution of twentieth-century America. It was, in significant ways, a symptom of the times.

The heads-up, get-ahead, go-along organization men recruited for the White House staff were not uniquely evil. American politics, business, sports—in fact many, if not all, of the enterprises to which Americans turn their hands—are riddled with the same type of organization man. Theirs is a contemporary form of the compulsion to succeed observed by Alexis de Tocqueville in Americans of the early nineteenth century: "It is strange to see with what feverish ardor the Americans pursue their own welfare, and to watch the vague dread that constantly torments them lest they should not have chosen the shortest path which may lead to it."[5]

The will to win is an attribute highly esteemed by our society. In baseball Leo Durocher is venerated for the maxim "Nice guys finish last." Football coach George Allen is famous for telling us that it's not how you play the game, but whether you win or lose. The late Vince Lombardi topped them both with the aphorism "Winning isn't everything—it's the *only* thing."

In professional football, grabbing a face mask or hitting after the ball is dead is an infraction for the referee to catch and penalize—if he can. They're part of the game. The true organization man takes on the coloration and the value system of whatever organization—whatever game—with which he happens for the time being to be associated.

When the will to win is coupled with an uncritical belief in the rightness of one's own patriotic motives—dedication to clearcut causes like the advancement and protection of national security, the promotion of fiscal responsibility, the reduction of dependence on government—it is hardly surprising that a by-product should be the gut feeling that anyone who questions or obstructs the chosen path toward these enlightened aims is "the enemy." Political opponents are enemies. For people who had never worked in a government agency, on Capitol Hill, or with the media—the enemy may be the bureaucracy, the Congress, or the press.

"It was all but impossible not to get caught up in the 'enemies' mentality," wrote Jeb Stuart Magruder in *An American Life: One Man's Road to Watergate.*[6] And to beat an "enemy," convention allows you to do anything you have to do.

Any boss would need a firm sense of principle to restrain subordinates impelled by this combination of organizational zeal and patriotic fervor. In Richard Nixon, the White House staffers had a boss who, instead of restraining these attitudes, reinforced them. A staffer would need considerable fortitude to resist the pressures generated by such an atmosphere. Apart from peer pressures, the prestige of the Presidential office tends in itself to be awe-inspiring. "Within the White House precincts," wrote Richard E. Neustadt in *Presidential Power*, "lifted eyebrows may suffice to set an aide in motion."[7]

It takes balance and sophistication for a subordinate to realize that a President's whims are not necessarily cast in iron. When, finally, you make allowance for a limited sense of humor and assume a lack of imagination, the sum total goes a long way toward explaining, though it cannot excuse, the wrongs that were done.

ALL OF US would like to believe, of course, that our moral sensitivity is too acute—that the inner voice which tells us where to draw the line between right and wrong is too strong and compelling—to have permitted us to be guilty of such unconscionable acts as those associated with Watergate. But where our reaction does not smack of self-righteousness it should be tinged with self-doubt. Watergate was a tragedy not so much of immoral men as of amoral men—not so much of ruthless men as of *rootless* men. And there are thousands more back home where they came from—ready to root their identity in an organization, ready to "serve."

Even the combination of Presidential distrust and staff amorality might not have been enough to bring about Watergate but for the accumulated momentum of recent history. For two generations the "strength"—and hence the "greatness"—of Presidents had been expressed in terms of a zero-sum game with Congress and the Cabinet departments. These were also generations in which a sometimes obsessional concern with "national security" was the legacy of three hot wars and one cold one. Finally, it was a period in which the Congress had persisted in making the power of the central government more pervasive and ubiquitous.

As Neustadt put it, we measure a President "as 'weak' or 'strong' and call what we are measuring his 'leadership.' "[8] Nixon undoubtedly wanted to be perceived as a "strong President"—all the great Presidents were "strong." And what was the measure of a great President's strength? To quote Neustadt again, it was "his personal capacity to influence the conduct of the men who make up government."[9] For Nixon, maximizing this capacity demanded exploitation of every available means of influence, and these, by the time he became President, had been expanded far beyond anything within the reach of the great predecessors whose ranks he yearned to join. So also, in the previous decade, had been established the precedents for secrecy in the conduct of foreign policy, deception of the general public, invasion of personal privacy and manipulation of the legislative process.

In a thoughtful analysis of the trends which brought about what he has aptly called "the imperial Presidency," the historian Arthur M. Schlesinger, Jr., renders what to me seems a just verdict:

> Nixon's Presidency was not an aberration but a culmination. It carried to reckless extremes a compulsion towards presidential power rising out of deep-running changes in the foundations of society. In a time of the acceleration of history and the decay of traditional institutions and values, a strong Presidency was both a greater necessity than ever before and a greater risk—necessary to hold a spinning and distracted society together, necessary to make the separation of powers work, risky because of the awful tempta-

tion held out to override the separation of powers and burst the bonds of the Constitution.[10]

A President's siege mentality. An amoral alacrity to do his bidding. The aggrandizement and abuse of Presidential power. It is not likely that these ingredients will soon come together again, nor is it likely that institutional reforms can wholly eliminate the risk of its happening. Still, if reform can reduce the risk at all, we must pursue it. The wrongs of Watergate, in any case, were not all unique, and preventive measures will help not only to deter wrongdoing by White House occupants but to discourage commoner crimes as well.

As to some of these wrongs there is no action we can now take that might help to reduce the risk of their reoccurrence. The character of future Presidents, for one, is scarcely a subject suitable for legislative reform. The American people will have to rely in the future, as we have in the past, on our own good sense and alertness—and in two hundred years we have not done badly.

Nor is the character of the people around the President any more subject to anticipatory reform than that of the President himself. To the extent, of course, that we succeed in choosing good Presidents, we shall go a long way at the same time toward assuring that the people they select to advise them will reflect their own qualities. Large though the reservoir of organization men may be, there is also available an ample supply of able and high-principled men and women who stand ready to serve if called upon.

As practical means, then, of seeking to prevent the kinds of abuses that surfaced in Watergate, we are left with two promising areas of reform. The first embraces concrete actions to prevent specific abuses. The second involves more fundamental readustment of our governmental processes. The remainder of this chapter is concerned with the specific abuses; the next chapter will consider structural readjustments.

What, then, were the specific abuses brought to light by Watergate? What, more precisely, were those which require more adequate preventive measures? The pursuit of answers to these questions leads us into the present state of the law and the sorts of abuses that new laws can be designed to counteract. Having attempted to review the whole rancid Watergate scene, I see three types of abuses as falling under this heading: unfair campaign practices ("dirty money" and "dirty tricks"); invasions of privacy; and attempts to exert improper influence on government agencies. The rest of this chapter will consider each type of abuse, and safeguards against it, in turn.

WATERGATE WAS a windfall for the advocates of campaign-financing reform. Philip M. Stern, founder of the Center for Public Financing of Elections, had been working on behalf of such reform ever since 1962, and Common Cause had made the issue one of its major objectives from its founding in 1968. And although they and their allies had united behind the Federal Elections Act which went into effect six months before the 1972 election, they were far from satisfied to stop there. The new act did, it was true, represent the first major reform of campaign-finance laws in fifty years. Its key provisions—the requirement, for the first time in campaigns for federal office, of public accounting of all donations and expenditures, and the ban on covert shifts of money for the purpose of laundering donations through political committees—were useful as far as they went. To the reformers, however, it was plain that the 1972 act did not go far enough, and they seized upon the "dirty money" surfaced by the Watergate investigations as Exhibit A in the case for more far-reaching remedies.

What abuses, exactly, did the "dirty money" reveal? The most prevalent was the violation of shareholder trust and the concealment of corporate influence resulting from corporate campaign contributions channeled through individuals. But this was against the law even before 1972; indeed, all the illegal-contribution cases prosecuted by the Watergate Special Prosecution Force were brought under the old, and largely disregarded, Federal Corrupt Practices Act of 1925. These prosecutions not only illustrate what a difference it can make how rigorously an existing law is enforced but seem likely, in addition, to exert a long-term impact: their snowballing effect has already led to stockholder suits, company-sponsored audits, Internal Revenue Service hearings, and congressional investigations of corporate political contributions laundered through foreign bank accounts.

Dita Beard's heart attack, E. Howard Hunt, Jr.'s fright wig, and Bebe Rebozo's cache of Howard Hughes's bank notes made vivid the need for more effective means of enforcing the pre-existing prohibition against another common category of "dirty money"—unreported under-the-table cash. But the most disturb-ing aspect of the campaign-financing picture did not need to be exposed by the Watergate investigations and was not, indeed, in violation of any law. This was the danger of undue influence created by extremely large contributions. A special aura seemed to surround a really big contributor in the precincts of the Nixon White House; although I never did (or failed to do) anything I thought I should have done (or not done) because one of the President's "very good friends" was involved, it was impossible not to feel the need to tread warily in such a situation.

Under the impetus of Watergate and with the active support of the campaign-reform lobby, the Congress enacted a revision of the Federal Election Campaign Act which was signed into law by President Ford on October 14, 1974. The revision made the prohibition against unreported under-the-table money more diffi-cult to evade by banning cash contributions of over $100 and by requiring the designation of specific bank depositories. Exces-sively large contributions were henceforth made unlawful by limits for any individual of $1,000 for each election campaign and $25,000 annually for all federal candidates.* The act also closed the loophole which formerly permitted contributions to any number of campaign committees, all acting on behalf of a single candidate, and set sharp limitations on the total amounts that can legally be spent in any federal campaign.

The most far-reaching innovations contained in the 1974 law, however, went far beyond the steps necessary to prevent the influence of "dirty money." The provision for full public

* The top 21 contributors to the 1972 Nixon campaign gave a total of $8.2 million. The top 21 lenders and contributors to the McGovern campaign gave $2.9 million. Under the new law, it would take 11,100 contributors at the maximum level to yield what these 42 contributed.

Wingate College Library

funding of major-party Presidential general election campaigns, and public funding on a matching basis for Presidential primary campaigns, introduced a truly radical change into our traditional system of campaign financing. Although promoted as a Watergate remedy by Common Cause and other reform-minded groups and adopted by a Congress anxious to demonstrate its eagerness to legislate against Watergate, the subvention of Presidential campaigns is not a necessary means of correcting any campaign-financing abuse of the Watergate variety. These had been adequately covered by the other provisions of the 1974 revision.

Stripped of its Watergate rhetoric, the real aim of public funding can only be to broaden the base of campaign financing. I agree with the objective. But spreading the cost among taxpayers is not the only—or even the best—way of accomplishing this objective. The $1,000 limit on contributions imposed by the same legislation in itself goes a long way toward broadening the base. Moreover, as Senator Charles McC. Mathias, Jr., of Maryland demonstrated in his successful 1974 campaign, voluntary contributions can be sharply limited in individual amount and still be sufficient in the aggregate. Despite having imposed a contribution ceiling of only $100, Senator Mathias raised two-thirds of the funds the new law would allow him to spend. Thus, while raising money, he also retained a vital element in the political process: the sense of individual participation and involvement which comes from raising and giving many small contributions. The availability of a tax-return checkoff is bound to diminish such participation and involvement.

If we are eventually to go further toward making public financing an integral part of our political process, we shall have to resolve a number of thorny problems. We shall have to think through, for example, such questions as the desirable extent of public financing, its probable effect on the electorate, and the appropriate balance between private contributions and public financing. The question of how to divide public funds among primary candidates is particularly troublesome, but if the objective of public financing is to relieve candidates from the necessity of incurring obligations to contributors, primary campaigns should give the most concern to reformers. The contributions for which a candidate is most indebted are the earliest.

Campaign financing is an exceedingly difficult area in which to predict the effect of actions intended to be remedial. It is not even clear that the new limitations on contributions and expenditures are in fact beneficial. Having myself been a campaign underdog, I am concerned that such restrictions may unduly benefit incumbents and handicap their challengers. This concern is reinforced by a study of U.S. Senate general election expenditures in 1972 conducted for the Campaign Study Group of the John F. Kennedy Institute of Politics at Harvard. The Study Group reported:

> We concur . . . that the Congressional spending limits set in the 1974 Federal legislation are too low, and could lead to under-financing of such campaigns, and that the same could prove true of such spending limit legislation as the 1974 initiative in the State of California.
>
> We too believe such under-financed campaigns are likely to enhance the already great incumbent advantages over new and less well known challengers, and that less campaign activity can produce an even less well-informed and more apathetic electorate.[11]

As the Supreme Court decision invalidating personal spending limits made clear, the campaign-financing problem cannot be solved at a stroke.* More information and analysis will be needed. In addition to the questions I have already touched on, we should also give attention to such subjects as making disclosure and reporting requirements less burdensome for candidates; providing some "free" access to the media as an alternative to across-the-board campaign subsidies; and investigating ways in which the government can best encourage voter registration.

As to "dirty tricks," the federal penal code does not yet contain explicit prohibitions of things like obscene telephone calls falsely represented to be on behalf of a candidate, disruption of campaign gatherings by paid political operatives, or transmission of sensitive political information by paid political spies. Assistant

---

* *Buckley* v. *Valeo*, decided January 30, 1976.

Attorney General Henry E. Petersen called this gap in the law to my attention early in July 1973 when I asked him why Donald Segretti—whose shoddy, disruption-sowing 1972 campaign operation revealed just how dirty "dirty tricks" could be —had not immediately been indicted when his activities first came to light. Here, I thought at the time, was a golden opportunity for the President to take positive action toward restoring confidence in his administration: in this case, all he had to do was direct the drafting of legislation to close these gaps. It would be a small step, but one in the right direction both substantively and symbolically. And so I sent the President a memorandum urging him to propose a "Federal Code of Fair Campaign Practices" that would specifically prohibit a comprehensive list of below-the-belt political tactics. I also called the suggestion to the attention of General Alexander M. Haig, Haldeman's successor as the President's chief of staff, and later sent President Nixon a memorandum containing language for a press-conference announcement of this and other confidence-building measures. Nothing came of the idea. The President, it seemed, could not or would not take positive steps to restore confidence in his administration and himself. As time went on, it became clearer and clearer that his strategy would be defensive. Still giving him the benefit of the doubt, I charged this off to an error of judgment. I should, of course, have realized that Richard Nixon was more likely to be guilty than stupid.

Donald Segretti, as it turned out, pleaded guilty to three counts of distributing illegal campaign literature;* the other dirty tricks for which he admitted responsibility simply did not fall within any clear prohibition of existing law. I still think that the whole gamut of dirty tricks should be brought within a comprehensive ban along the lines of my proposed Code of Fair Campaign Practices.

THE SECOND specific area of Watergate-related abuses— intrusions on personal privacy—frighteningly exposed the addictive tendency of the abuse of power. It was their rationalization

* Segretti served a prison term of four and one-half months.

more than their extent that was frightening. Starting with the administration of Franklin D. Roosevelt in 1940, "electronic surveillance"—the polite, generic term for all forms of wiretapping, bugging, and eavesdropping—was used with Presidential approbation to monitor the activities of persons who seemed to represent a threat to the nation's security. A letter from Roosevelt to then Attorney General Robert H. Jackson, initiating the modern era of electronic surveillance for "national security," used the term "Fifth Column" to characterize the threat.

In the Kennedy administration, a certain newsman who published allegedly sensitive national security information; a noted foreign journalist, expert in Southeast Asian affairs; numerous American citizens, including an important congressional staff member who was involved in a legislative struggle over sugar quota legislation and a very high government official thought to be too friendly with diplomats of a communist nation—all fell within the ambit of "national security" electronic surveillance.

Under Nixon the most significant departures from previous practice were in "scale" and procedure: in 1969–1971 at least four newsmen and thirteen government officials were tapped in a program conducted through extraordinary channels.* White House staff members, including Dr. Kissinger's deputy, Colonel (now General) Alexander M. Haig, and later H. R. Haldeman, stating they were acting "on the highest authority," made direct requests to the FBI for these controversial wiretaps. Normally, national security electronic surveillance is recommended by the Director of the FBI to the Attorney General, who may approve or disapprove. In the case of the controversial Nixon wiretaps, the Attorney General was but a formal witness to a *fait accompli*. National security surveillances are routinely reviewed every three months by the FBI and the Attorney General; these taps were not reviewed.

Even in a situation where no clear guidelines were being applied to the unfettered exercise of a discretionary power which in itself rested on the implied authority of the President, the

* Two of the seventeen individuals were tapped twice, hence the references hereafter to nineteen wiretaps.

numbers in themselves should have flashed a warning signal to someone. Attorney General Mitchell must, it would seem, bear some of the onus for not making clear to the President that his administration was embarked on a dangerous and constitutionally dubious course. What is even more disturbing is that control over the taps was switched from the office of the President's top national security adviser, Henry A. Kissinger, where they had been handled by Colonel Haig, to the President's top political adviser, Bob Haldeman. A few taps were then kept in place long after they had any possible value in leading to the source of a national security leak, and after some of the targets of surveillance had gone to work for Democratic Presidential hopefuls. Worst of all, two of the taps never had any plausible national security justification in the first place.

The frightening thing is that invasions of privacy rationalized as these were rationalized could so *easily* have been extended further and so *easily* been made to appear consistent with what had been done before. From people suspected of leaking information regarded by the President as vital to the national security to people known to be opposing measures regarded by the President as vital to the national security, the step is obvious and logical, is it not? And from people who pass information to a communist regime to people who teach that communism is the wave of the future—that isn't much of a step either, is it?

When one realizes that rationalizations such as these can be invoked to justify the use of sophisticated electronic devices capable of listening through walls or overhearing conversations conducted in the middle of an open field, one would have to be a fool not to be alarmed about the danger to individual liberties inherent in the untrammeled exercise of executive authority to spy on American citizens. It was not for this that we fought for a Bill of Rights expressly prohibiting "unreasonable searches and seizures."

The ugly glimpse of an incipient police state revealed by the nineteen wiretaps was made all the more alarming by what we know about the infamous White House leak-stopping unit known as "the plumbers." No evidence, to be sure, has so far come to light (nor do I known of any) which confirms the widespread impression that Egil "Bud" Krogh, Jr., and his confederates engaged in breaking and entering, planting bugs, and tapping telephones on a scale exceeded only by "Mission Impossible." The alarm is justified, nevertheless, by two visible circumstances. One was the very *existence* of "the plumbers" as a secret appendage of the White House designed to operate outside the scope—and thus unconstrained by the statutory restrictions—of any official agency. The second was their *potential use* for any sort of dirty work under cover of whatever thin coating of "national security" Krogh's bosses, the President and John Ehrlichman, could get him (and themselves) to swallow.

When the President referred at Camp David to "the plumbers'" role in the break-in of the office of Ellsberg's psychiatrist, his references to the national security aspects of the situation were so portentous that I more than half believed him. (That in itself reveals how seductive these dangerous rationalizations can be.) This impression was reinforced in a talk with Krogh at lunch in my Defense Department office the following Tuesday, May 1.*

In a conversation with Bill Rogers the next day (the President's counsel Leonard Garment and I had gone to see him in his State Department office to get his advice, as a former Attorney General, on the problems raised by the break-in of Ellsberg's psychiatrist's office), I realized how improbable it was that the break-in had any national security connection whatever. Its real purpose, rather, must have been to get information that might somehow be used to discredit Ellsberg. The national security, in any case, could not have been a defense to a charge of conspiracy to violate Ellsberg's civil rights, as Judge Gerhard A. Gesell later ruled in the trial of Krogh's coconspirator John Ehrlichman.

* Krogh had come to seek my advice as to whether or not to confess his part in the affair. He seemed genuinely to believe that national security concerns were at stake. Having no knowledge of this but being aware that I might later have to prosecute him, I could only tell him that I thought we had reached a point where the public interest demanded as much openness as possible. Two days later Krogh phoned to inform me that the President had "released" him from any White House constraint on telling his story.

THESE, in their early, habit-forming stage, were the dangers. What should be the remedies—or the safeguards? Some people feel that electronic eavesdropping in any form is so utterly irreconcilable with the basic values of our society that it ought not under any circumstances be condoned. One may agree, however, with Brandeis that wiretapping is a "dirty business" without conceding that it can never be justified. Espionage too is a dirty business, and so is the systematic use of murder, mutilation, and planted explosives to enforce and protect the rule of organized crime. Having first attempted to launch a concerted counterattack against organized crime as early as 1959, when I became United States Attorney for the District of Massachusetts, I have long felt very strongly about this particular form of dirtiness. I do not, however, wish to be misunderstood. I am not arguing that government should be willing to stoop to the tactics of its domestic enemies. And even in the case of our foreign enemies I believe we should refrain from the first use of any provocative measure. In both cases, moreover, we should exercise scrupulous care in determining who our enemies—actual or potential— really are.

My position, I realize, has the disadvantage of requiring the drawing of lines in areas that are often shadowy and ill-defined. But then, I am one of those who believe that it is always possible to find a way of drawing a line where it is necessary to draw a line. In the case of intrusions on privacy, the line-drawing devices I would use are threefold: (1) clear, published guidelines; (2) a court-order requirement in all cases involving American citizens; and (3) where American citizens are not involved, a sharp distinction between domestic and foreign activities. Just these elements, in fact, were combined in the approach I was trying to develop during my five months at Justice, and I still believe that this is the right direction in which to seek more adequate safeguards of personal privacy.

To make clear why I come out where I do, I shall have to review a bit of history. In 1965, President Lyndon B. Johnson appointed a commission headed by Attorney General Nicholas deB. Katzenbach to make a study of the causes of the rising rates of crime and juvenile delinquency and submit recommendations for remedial and preventive action. The most important by-product of the study was the Omnibus Crime Control and Safe Streets Act of 1968. Only six months earlier the United States Supreme Court had rendered its decision in *Katz* v. *United States,* holding that electronic eavesdropping constituted a "search and seizure" under the Fourth Amendment, but also stating that the Court might be prepared to sustain the constitutionality of electronic surveillance conducted pursuant to carefully spelled out procedural requirements including warrants.[12]

Responding to this invitation, Title III of the proposed Safe Streets Act would allow federal law-enforcement agencies to apply for court orders permitting electronic surveillance of persons suspected to be involved in certain serious crimes. To obtain such a court order, a law-enforcement agency would be required to file an application with affidavits detailing the grounds for tapping a telephone or bugging a room. For example, the application would list the subject's contacts with known organized crime bosses, a summary of leads pointing to his involvement with loansharking, reference to tips from "usually reliable informants." The form of the application would be like that used in seeking a search warrant.

Title III was by far the most controversial part of the Safe Streets Act. Those who felt that no law-enforcement purpose could ever justify electronic intrusions on privacy opposed it bitterly; Attorney General Ramsey Clark spearheaded this group. Most law-enforcement officials, however, believed just as strongly that they could not reasonably be expected to do their jobs with all the advantages of modern technology on the other side. As Attorney General of Massachusetts at the time, I was convinced that there was no difference in principle between allowing the physical invasion of privacy pursuant to a search warrant and allowing an electronic invasion of privacy pursuant to a court-authorized wiretap, and I so testified in support of Title III at a hearing of the House Committee on the Judiciary. Amendments to strike Title III from the Safe Streets Act were decisively turned down in both branches of Congress. The Title has since proved to be a valuable weapon against organized crime, and to the best of my knowledge the indications of its abuse have been negligible.

The enactment of Title III, however, did not subject all electronic surveillance by the federal government to a court-order requirement. Four types of situations in which wiretaps and listening devices were then being used were left untouched. These were situations involving protection of the nation against hostile acts of any foreign power, obtaining foreign intelligence deemed essential to national security, protecting national security information against foreign intelligence activities, and protecting the United States government against unlawful overthrow. As to all four the executive branch claimed implied authority to carry out all necesssary measures, including electronic surveillance, and Title III specifically disclaimed any intention to affect whatever power the federal government might have to proceed without a court order. The Attorney General accordingly continued as before to act on specific requests by the FBI for permission to use taps or bugs for these purposes.

Then came the decision of the United States Supreme Court in *United States* v. *United States District Court*—the *Keith* case, so called because it involved a proceeding against Judge Damon J. Keith of the Eastern District of Michigan.[13] The Department of Justice was seeking to compel Judge Keith to set aside his order requiring the government to disclose its record of wire-tapped conversations in a prosecution for the dynamiting of a CIA office in Ann Arbor. Upholding Judge Keith, Supreme Court ruled that from then on court orders would have to be obtained for electronic surveillance against any domestic organization or United States citizen *except* in cases where substantial contact with a foreign power could be shown. As an immediate result of the ruling, taps on the Black Panthers and perhaps half a dozen other domestic organizations were ordered discontinued. Electronic surveillance for national security and foreign intelligence purposes continued without interruption.

This was how matters stood when I was sworn in as Attorney General in May of 1973. It was an unsatisfactory state of affairs, I thought, not because electronic surveillance was then being used for unjustifiable purposes but because the Congress and the public could have no clear idea of the fairness or consistency of the criteria for its use that were being applied by the executive branch. It was for this reason that during the hearings on my nomination as Attorney General, I promised to establish clear guidelines for all uses of electronic surveillance, including the areas still not covered by a court-order requirement.

Preliminary work on the guidelines was just getting under way when I had lunch in my "Martha Mitchell" dining room (its Williamsburg décor was her legacy to the Department of Justice) with Lloyd Cutler, a public-spirited Washington lawyer long recognized for his balanced and thoughtful approach to civil liberties issues. One of his clients was the nationally syndicated columnist Joseph Kraft, whose phone had been tapped and whose Paris hotel room had been searched in the name of some tenuous "national security" concern. We talked about the dangers to First Amendment rights inherent in eavesdropping on newsmen and the need for some external check on the electronic surveillance of American citizens even where foreign intelligence is involved. Mr. Cutler suggested that the court-order requirement be extended to all electronic surveillance of United States citizens, or at least of all journalists. I promised to give the suggestion very careful thought.

I was aware that it might sometimes be difficult to write a court-order application making clear the justification for overhearing the phone conversations of an American citizen in a situation involving foreign intelligence. Such a showing could be considerably more complicated than a showing of probable cause that a crime is being, has been, or is about to be committed. In some cases a lot of background information might be necessary to the explanation, and the consequences of its leaking could be seriously damaging.

Knowing that the FBI would be concerned about these difficulties, I asked Clarence M. Kelley, the new FBI Director, to develop a sample application for a hypothetical case. In mid-October Deputy Attorney General William D. Ruckelshaus, who had been Acting Director of the FBI and was working with the Bureau on a general review of its structure and functions, told me that the sample application had finally been completed but that the FBI still had strong objections to the whole idea. As things turned out, my resignation came before I saw the sample or heard the objections.

Six months later, having agreed to testify at a joint hearing on warrantless wiretaps to be held by two subcommittees of the Senate Judiciary Committee and a subcommittee of the Senate Government Operations Committee, I returned to the question raised with me by Lloyd Cutler. From the perspective of my cloistered office at the Woodrow Wilson International Center for Scholars, I came to the conclusion that there should always be some external check on the alleged need for the surveillance of American citizens. On April 3, 1974, I accordingly testified in favor of extending the court-order requirement.*

THE MOMENTUM for reform generated by the Watergate-related disclosures of invasions of privacy has so far been disappointing in its results. This is all the more remarkable given the relatively modest impact of the additional safeguards which seem both practical and worthwhile. The first two—clear published guidelines and the extension of court orders to all situations involving American citizens—both point to the need for the third: a sharp line of demarcation between domestic and foreign countersubversive, intelligence-gathering, and counterintelligence activities. No such line, of course, is clearly discernible merely by looking at the facts of the situation. The transgressions of the CIA detailed in the report of the Rockefeller Commission amply demonstrate that. The line has to be drawn administratively and policed administratively, and continuing congressional oversight is necessary to assure that it is observed. But these things are feasible; there is needed only the perception that they are important, and the will to carry them out.

* Joint Hearings Before the Subcommittee on Administrative Practice and Procedure and the Subcommittee on Constitutional Rights of the Committee of the Judiciary and the Subcommittee on Surveillance of the Committee on Foreign Relations, United States Senate, 93rd Congress, 2nd Sess., on Warrantless Wiretapping and Electronic Surveillance, p. 14. I still support the views there expressed.

The concern for the protection of privacy awakened by Watergate has, however, had at least one markedly positive impact. This was in stimulating action against abuses of the information being collected, stored, and used by organizations with computer-based record-keeping systems. Such computer systems have been multiplying like yeast colonies. Workers, students, patients, taxpayers, bank depositors, car owners and drivers, welfare recipients, parking violators—all of us are becoming the subjects of a network of records. Such records, accumulated and interconnected, create a significant risk of abuse. There is a corresponding need for safeguarding this stored information.

In July 1973, HEW Secretary Caspar W. Weinberger and I jointly unveiled a 350-page report on this problem. Entitled *Records, Computers, and the Rights of Citizens*, it was the work of a committee I had appointed in 1972. One of its recommendations was that the federal government should not maintain any personal data record-keeping systems whose very existence is secret. Another recommendation was that individuals who are the subject of a record should have the right to find out what information is in it and to prevent the record being used for a purpose other than that for which it was obtained. They also should be able to correct or amend it. These and other safeguards were designed as part of a Code of Fair Information Practices for all personal data systems.

Congressman Edward I. Koch of New York, a "liberal," and Congressman Barry Goldwater, Jr., of California, a "conservative," were among the first to endorse the report. They promptly introduced legislation incorporating the terms of the proposed Code, and a similar bill was dropped in the Senate hopper. The congressional machinery turned more quickly than usual, impelled in part by the steam generated by Watergate. In the summer of 1974, I supported the legislation in Senate testimony, suggesting changes which I was pleased to see become part of the bill signed by President Ford on December 31, 1974.*

---

* As of September 1975, 75 federal agencies had listed more than 8,000 record systems in the Federal Register! *The Washington Post*, September 16, 1975.

A THIRD AREA of opportunity to reduce the risk of abuse of
government power lies in the erection of barriers against attempts
to exert improper political influence on government agencies. It
is tempting in this connection to suppose that our government
would be pure and without reproach if only we could divorce
it from politics. Some people have seen in statements of my
own a disposition to embrace this illusion. And it is true that in
a speech to the American Bar Association in August 1973 I said,
"There is still a place for politics as usual—but not in the
Department of Justice." Though the remark drew quite a lot of
favorable comment at the time, I recognize its vulnerability to
my old boss Felix Frankfurter's dismissal of similar statements:
"One hears from time to time much shallow talk about the
elimination of politics as though politics—the free exchange of
opinion regarding the best policy for life of society—were not
the essence of a free and vigorous people."[14]

I was speaking, however, against the background of Watergate and the damage it had caused to public confidence in the
Department of Justice. Here is the statement in its context:

> In recent history, under both parties, the Attorney General
> has been more than a political appointee, he has frequently
> been—before and after he came to the Department of
> Justice—a political operative as well. Now, I have nothing
> against political operatives. I have been one myself. And
> there is still a place for politics as usual—but not in the
> Department of Justice. To the extent we are handicapped
> by the suspicion of political influence, we cannot afford to
> have at the head of the Department—or in any of its key
> positions—a person who is perceived to be an active
> political partisan. Past Attorneys General have, I know,
> been able to draw a line between their political and profes-
> sional responsibilities. But a citizen of the Watergate era
> who perceives an Attorney General wearing his political
> hat is scarcely to be blamed for doubting whether he ever
> really takes it off.
>
> I have decided, therefore, that one direct contribu-
> tion I can make to countering the suspicion of political
> influence in the Department of Justice is not only to

forswear politics for myself but to ask my principal colleagues to do the same. It is my earnest hope that those
who follow us will see fit to make the same promise.

Apart from public perceptions, it seems to me important
to underscore the difference between the proper role of the
political process in the shaping of legal *policies* and the perversion of the legal *process* by political pressure. White House
involvement in the ITT case illustrates both points. The President is certainly entitled to have something to say about whether,
as a matter of policy, the antitrust laws should be exerted against
conglomerates because of their aggregate market leverage,
whether or not they dominate any market. Conversely, the President cannot without undermining the integrity with which the
law is enforced tell the legal officers of the government what to
do or not do in handling a particular case. President Nixon's telephone call to Attorney General Kleindienst instructing him not
to appeal from a lower court decision dismissing the government's attempt to break up ITT was indefensible. This was true,
moreover, quite without regard to its possible connection with
ITT's reported offer to provide $400,000 toward the cost of
holding the Republican National Convention in San Diego.
Richard Kleindienst himself, though he later pleaded guilty to a
misdemeanor for failing to disclose this phone call in answer to a
question about whether he had ever been subjected to "White
House pressure" with regard to ITT, deserves credit for later
getting the President to agree that the appeal should go forward.
To protect the Department of Justice from that kind of
pressure, I issued an order as Attorney General requiring records
of contacts with Justice Department personnel by outsiders.
The order required employees to make a memorandum of each
oral communication from a "noninvolved party" about a matter
pending before the Department. The employee was directed to
keep one copy of the memorandum and place another in the case
file. A "noninvolved party" was defined as someone with whom
the employee would not normally have contact in the routine
handling of the matter. The definition embraced members of

Congress and their staffs, other government officials, including White House staff, and private persons not directly concerned in the matter. Only news media representatives were excluded.

This new reporting system, I believed, would result in at least two useful by-products. One would be a contemporary record of contacts with the Department that could be called upon should the need arise to rebut some accusation of improper influence. Beyond that, the system's very existence would be likely to discourage approaches to the Department by persons not confident of the purity of their motives. I have since urged —and still do—that a similar requirement be adopted by other agencies (regulatory commissions, for instance) having law-enforcement responsibilities.*

It is important, on the other hand, not to create the impression that there is something vaguely improper about political contacts with government agencies on behalf of constitutents. Elected officeholders come closer to performing the role of an ombudsman than anyone else in our system, and in so doing they help to mitigate the rigidities of bureaucratic processes that can otherwise all too easily become unresponsive to the special needs of particular individuals. Government administrators need to be reminded that their rules and regulations exist for the sake of people, not the other way around. In providing such reminders, the politician renders a service to the concerned government agency as well as to his constituent.

The true test of the propriety of a political contact is whether, on the one hand, it seeks simply to make certain that the unique circumstances of an individual situation are being considered fairly and sympathetically, or whether, on the other hand, it attempts to distort the merits in order to reward a friend, punish an enemy, or gain some unfair political advantage. Lines like this are, of course, much simpler to talk about than to apply.

* The idea is endorsed in "Removing Political Influence from Federal Law Enforcement Agencies," a Preliminary Report of the Special Committee to Study Federal Law Enforcement Agencies of the American Bar Association (1975), p. 43. The Special Committee also endorsed the idea of establishing an office of Inspector General in the Department of Justice, a proposal which I recommended in a letter to Acting Attorney General Robert Bork on November, 8, 1973. "Removing Political Influence," p. 37.

They have to be felt rather than seen. This is true, at least, if sense and sensitivity are to be part of the process of drawing them. Two kinds of attitude make the problem seem simple. Virtue is easy for the person of rigid scruple who avoids any action to which possible criticism or misunderstanding might attach. Conversely, scruples do not bother the politician whose motto is "To get along, go along."

The trouble with the first kind of attitude is that it leaves no room for the recognition that informal, unofficial, party political processes are a legitimate and necessary part of our system of democracy. The more we "purify" government by insulating it from the people who make the two-party system work and maintain its strength, the harder it becomes for any chief executive to accomplish the changes of policy which he was elected to carry out. The political parties, I believe, play a crucial role in providing a means for direct citizen participation in the democratic process. This is why I have always, in every public job I have ever held, taken pains to set up procedures for making sure that Republican party officials were consulted about or notified of actions, usually appointments of people, that concerned their areas. Such communication strengthens the political system without harming the governmental system. The officials with whom I have dealt, whether from Springfield, Massachusetts, Des Moines, Iowa, or Republican National Headquarters, have understood that I would not consider appointing an unqualified person or violating the merit system. But they have also known that I recognized the importance to preserving the two-party system of appointing a qualified Republican to a policy-making position in preference to a non-Republican whose qualifications were no better.*

When, after the election of 1952 (I had been working full time as a field organizer for the Massachusetts Republican State Committee), United States Senator Leverett Saltonstall asked me to join his staff in Washington, I thought about it for a few days and came back and said, "I'd like to join you, Senator, but on the legislative as opposed to the political side of your office's

* Compare the discussion of "affirmative action" in Chapter IX.

work." He laughed. Then, seeing the puzzled look on my face, he added, "It's *all* politics!"

After a few months of working on everything from compassionate leave cases to a speech about the St. Lawrence Seaway, I understood what he meant. The politician, by definition, serves a political function; he stands or falls on the basis of a political verdict. And everything he is or does or says enters into that verdict.

Leverett Saltonstall, wrote John Gunther in *Inside U.S.A.*, is "practically the nicest person anybody ever met."[15] And though no one (least of all himself) would regard him as the most articulate of politicians, none ever had a more unerring instinct for the precise location of the boundary between the obligations of integrity and the claims of political self-preservation. He could discern without having to spell it out where cooperation gave way to compliance and where compliance became capitulation to pressure. By cooperation I mean working affirmatively with the political system, as in helping to find ways of rewarding unsung party service. Compliance implies the willingness to let governmental processes be used to further a "political" interest where to do so does not distort the merits, as in taking advantage of the opportunity to announce an action favorable to one's own state or district.* Only capitulation entails a result unwarranted by the merits.

No one, of course, can be long exposed to major governmental responsibility without constantly being called upon to make these distinctions, consciously or unconsciously. The difficult area, obviously, is the one in the middle—compliance. During the 1972 Presidential campaign the White House instituted a "responsiveness" program under which federal departments and agencies were expected to be helpful where possible to the Nixon reelection campaign and to the interests of other Republican candidates. This was not a new idea. Other Presidents and their party organizations had taken it for granted that this was one of the advantages of incumbency. It was a political fact

---

* Here and in similar contexts below I have put the word "political" in quotes to indicate that I am using it, for lack of any equivalent, with reference to the electoral process.

of life. Nor did I personally take it amiss when, as Secretary of HEW, I was approached on this basis in the summer of 1972. The key issue, I knew, would be in determining what is "possible." Facilitating the opportunity for the announcement of grant and contract awards was legitimate, I thought. Expediting action on meritorious applications from friendly sources was also permissible. However, approving the funding of an application that could not meet consistent competitive standards was beyond the pale. The hardest problems, inevitably, involved situations in which the criteria of selection were unavoidably vague and the element of discretion was correspondingly large.

In the shadowland of "responsiveness," for which read "tilting the machine to produce a politically favorable result," Watergate has reduced the legitimacy of any "political" responsiveness whatsoever. In my previously quoted speech to the American Bar Association, for example, I announced that the Department of Justice would no longer give advance notice of grant awards to Senators and Congressmen. "While this is a time-honored practice—and there may be nothing inherently wrong with it," I said, "it does inevitably, if not intentionally, create the public impression that the Senator or Congressman had some sort of influence on the result when, in fact, he had nothing to do with it."

The interplay of "political" and meritorious factors in the handling of a particular situation is nowhere more subtle than in the perception of "pressure." The experienced politician may seem to be leaning hard on the executive branch decision-maker in order to impress his constituents with his zeal on their behalf and yet feel justified in taking it for granted that the decision-maker will nevertheless do the right thing. If the politician receives a weak but favorable response, he will be glad to take credit for the result, but he may have been equally ready to accept no for an answer. During my first three weeks as United States Attorney for the District of Massachusetts, for example, I received perhaps half a dozen phone calls from interested political "friends" about matters pending in my office. During the next three months I received another half-dozen calls. And during the remainder of my tour (another year and a bit more) I received about the same number; word had evidently gotten around that I was not inclined to be "responsive" to calls on pending cases.

When I received an instruction from the President via one of his assistants telling me to do something I did not think should be done, was I "under pressure" to do it? In one sense, perhaps yes, but to the extent that I believed I could convince the President that he was wrong (or induce him to back off simply because he knew I thought he was wrong), I did not worry much about the situation in the meanwhile. When, for instance, I got a call from Ehrlichman one day telling me to fire an HEW agency head who had made a public statement that angered President Nixon, I simply said that I would like to talk to the President about it at his convenience. By the time I saw Nixon, he wanted to forget the whole thing.

Another case in point: shortly after my nomination as Attorney General I paid a courtesy call on Senator James O. Eastland, the President Pro Tempore of the Senate and chairman of the Senate Committee on the Judiciary, the committee with which I would have most of my dealings as Attorney General. After a bit of preliminary small talk the Senator said, "I have two things I want to say." I braced myself. "The first is, I hope you can see your way to keeping on John Duffner as my source of information about nominees for judgeships." That was easy enough: I had inquired about John Duffner and was satisfied that he had been performing a valuable role as the Justice Department's liaison with the committee in such matters. I readily acquiesced. "The second thing I want," Senator Eastland continued, "is for you to know that I'll be calling you from time to time on something I want done." He paused. Here, I thought, comes a demand that I will have to reject. He went on: "I just want you to listen"—another pause—"and then do whatever you think is right."

These examples of the point that it is often easier to say no than it may at first seem lead to another point: the consequences of refusal to go along with something you are sincerely convinced is wrong are seldom as serious as you may anticipate. Having at one time or another been subject to most of these consequences, I can attest that they do not hurt very much. At the minimal end of the scale are signs of disfavor: communication of the word that the President is displeased, being dropped from White House dinner lists, and not having telephone calls returned. The in-between sanctions usually take the form of snags in the way of things you want to accomplish: unexplained difficulties plague the clearance of appointments that are of more interest to you than to the White House; legislative recommendations encounter inordinate delays; supplemental budget requests are nitpicked to death. At this stage, your principal concern is that your resistance may be more of a hindrance than a help to your department. Although the idea of quitting can then begin to be tempting, my own reaction was to try to wear down the opposition by persistent efforts to deal with each difficulty on its own terms without letting it appear that I doubted the good faith with which the difficulty had been raised. The most extreme sanction, of course, is being fired, and that has not been a truly fearful prospect ever since dungeons and chopping blocks ceased to accompany it.

Far better, however, than having to cope with disciplinary devices is the successful deployment of techniques of resistance. My first important lesson in such a technique came when I was Acting Secretary of Health, Education, and Welfare for several weeks in the spring of 1958 during the Eisenhower second term. The Food and Drug Administration was then in the market for the lease of a new laboratory building in Atlanta. The General Services Administration had invited bids, and the lowest bidder was the owner of a warehouse which he was offering for conversion into laboratory space. FDA officials were not happy with the building, mainly because false ceilings would have to be installed, and these, they insisted, could harbor rodents, thus making it impossible to be certain about the origin of the "filth" found in some laboratory specimen.

As luck would have it, the owner of the warehouse was also the Republican state chairman of Georgia. And he had friends. One was former Republican National Finance Chairman Sinclair Weeks of Massachusetts, then the Secretary of Commerce. Secretary Weeks telephoned me, spoke to me at a Cabinet meeting, and sent his assistant to see me. Several Republican Senators intervened on behalf of the Georgia state chairman, and one even came to my office to exhort me not to be pressured by Democratic bureaucrats into rejecting the low bid of a good Republican. On the other side, I had a visit from the Democratic Congressman from Atlanta, who happened to be the chairman of a powerful House committee with which we had important business. It was also apparent that the career civil servants in HEW were watching closely to see which way I moved—and why.

Under the circumstances, I decided, there was only one thing to be done: go into the entire situation with the utmost care and make certain the answer I reached was correct. This I did. The FDA, I concluded, was right. The building was unsuitable. The GSA should be asked to seek new bids. My reasons for this conclusion were fully spelled out in a detailed memorandum. Copies were sent to Secretary Weeks, the Senators, the Atlanta Congressman, and the state chairman himself. And I never heard another word from any of them.

It is not always possible, of course, simply to decide which of two answers is correct. The problem that has to be handled may present any of various possible courses of action, some clearly bad, some clearly preferable, some in between. Where in such situations I have encountered—or foreseen—pressure to acquiesce in a bad alternative but where it has seemed to me impossible to achieve the best, I have tried to define the least undesirable course I could accept and have then taken considerable trouble to win acceptance for this position.

That, essentially, is how I dealt with the issue of busing in 1972. The President was being strongly importuned by the Senators from Texas, Tennessee, and Michigan, as well as by a number of concerned mayors, to support an antibusing amendment of the Constitution. A number of such amendments had already been introduced in the Congress. Polls showed that these amendments had strong public support. I thought that tinkering with the Constitution was a bad idea. Given the fact that half of all American schoolchildren are routinely bused to school anyway, an amendment prohibiting busing for the purpose of desegregation would have been impossible to write, difficult to apply, and unsuitable to the dignity of the Constitution. A statutory measure, on the other hand, which sought to codify the limits on busing adumbrated by the Supreme Court itself in the Charlotte-Mecklenburg decision would not only be unobjectionable but, in the light of the widely variant lower-court rulings otherwise likely to be handed down, could be constructive. I dug in, therefore, along that line and, with the help of a number of people on my own staff, in the Office of Management and Budget, and in the White House itself, was able to hold it.

In the extreme case, resignation—or the threat of it—is the only ultimate means of maintaining a position from which no retreat is possible. As Edward Weisband and Thomas M. Franck have pointed out in their recent book *Resignation in Protest*, it is a course that has seldom been taken by Cabinet-level officials of the American government.[16] Its impact, when it does occur at any level, obviously depends both upon the visibility of the issue which precipitates the resignation and upon the perceived stature of the individual who resigns.

Firing and resignation. These are the ultimate weapons: the former as the President's most effective means of impressing his own will on the executive branch; the latter as a government official's only way of preserving his own integrity where all else fails. Either can have a part in preventing the abuse of power. Both were brought to bear on October 20, 1973, the Saturday which brought to an end my part in the drama of Watergate.

DURING the several days following the meeting with President Nixon at Camp David I gave a lot of thought to the question of appointing a Special Prosecutor. The more I thought about it, the clearer it seemed to me that I would have to do so. It was essential that the investigation of Watergate be independent not only in fact but in appearance. Public confidence in its integrity was essential. And though I believed I could meet the requirement of independence in fact, it was clear that I could not do so in appearance. I was serving in the fourth of four appointments by a President whose White House staff was under investigation and who might himself be implicated. I also knew myself to be a person in whom loyalty runs deep, and the struggle to preserve my independence would be painful. And so on Monday, May 7, 1973, seven days after the announcement of my nomination, I held a press conference at the Defense Department at which I announced my decision:

> I have decided that I will, if confirmed, appoint a Special Prosecutor and give him all the independence, authority, and staff support needed to carry out the tasks entrusted to him. Although he will be in the Department of Justice and report to me—and only to me—he will be aware that his ultimate accountability is to the American people.
>
> The person selected to fulfill this role will have to meet stringent standards of qualification. He must not only be an individual of the highest character and integrity but he must be widely so recognized. He must not have been associated with any of the persons alleged or suspected to have had a part in the matters under investigation. He must be judicious in temperament and independent in spirit. He must have a proven record of outstanding competence as a lawyer, preferably including trial experience.

The search for a Special Prosecutor began immediately and continued throughout the first two weeks of my nomination hearings. My assistants and I asked for names from many organizations and many individuals in all parts of the country. We assembled some 250. To narrow down the field we made hundreds of inquiries. Though Nixon had suggested names at Camp David, he and his staff kept hands off both the selection and the guidelines under which the new Special Prosecutor would work. Apparently it was as obvious to the President's staff as it was to me that there must be no basis for any later charge that the President had tried to influence an investigation that might implicate him.

My own confirmation as Attorney General went to the Senate Judiciary Committee for hearings. Though the committee had no "advise and consent" responsibility over the actual appointment of the Special Prosecutor, I offered to bring my nominee before it for questioning and to withdraw any name that the committee failed to approve. Archibald Cox, my final choice, had not been a prosecutor, but as Solicitor General of the United States he had for five years been responsible for all government litigation in the Supreme Court, including criminal cases. As a labor arbitrator and mediator of student protests he had shown, I thought, unfailing fairness and firmness. And because I knew him to be a man of unshakable integrity, I regarded the circumstances that he was identified as a Democrat and had been appointed Solicitor General by President Kennedy as unimportant except to the extent that they precluded the questions that might have been asked had I, a Republican, appointed another Republican.

The original terms of the Special Prosecutor's charter were my own; its final terms were worked out between Archibald Cox, members of the Senate Judiciary Committee, and myself. They provided that I, as Attorney General, would delegate to the Special Prosecutor "full authority" over the Watergate investigation, leaving to the Attorney General only his "statutory accountability for all matters falling within the jurisdiction of the Department of Justice." I had insisted on this clause because it seemed to me axiomatic that no one who delegates authority can thereby rid himself of all responsibility for its exercise. For this reason the charter also reserved to the Attorney General the power to remove the Special Prosecutor, but only for "extraordinary improprieties on his part."

All three of these key provisions—the full authority of the Special Prosecutor, the ultimate accountability of the Attorney General, and the terms of the removal clause—were to play a crucial part in the events of Saturday, October 20, 1973.

The immediate consequence of these provisions was to place me in a peculiar no-man's-land between the Special Prosecutor and the President. My pledge to respect Archibald Cox's independence barred me from the Attorney General's normal role as chief prosecutor for the government. Nor was it proper for me to serve as the President's legal adviser, a role also normal to the Attorney General. The man investigating the President's actions was exercising powers that I had delegated to him, and for me to advise the President on legal matters would put me in a conflicting position.

These inhibitions seemed to me to necessitate an arm's-length relationship with both sides. The issue arose at my first press conference as Attorney General. In answer to a question, I said that if a conflict developed between the Special Prosecutor and the White House, the President could not rely on the Attorney General for legal advice but would have to hire his own lawyer. From various sources word percolated back to me that the President was "deeply disturbed" by this statement—an indication to me that he had not clearly grasped the new relationships.

As time went on, I began, in limited ways, to try to act as "lawyer for the situation." Cox's efforts to gain access to White House documents kept encountering delays and roadblocks, and I tried to help remove them. General Alexander M. Haig, White House chief of staff, and J. Fred Buzhardt, White House counsel, constantly complained that Cox's investigations were exceeding his charter, and I found myself attempting to adjudicate jurisdictional boundaries. Nixon, meanwhile, was continually hearing from Republican loyalists and from his own staff that Cox was a "Kennedy stooge" out to "get the President."

It was a difficult situation, of course, but not more so than to be expected from such an unprecedented and abrasive set of relationships. At the close of a session in the Oval Office early in October, just after Vice-President Agnew resigned, the President remarked, "Now that we have disposed of that matter, we can go ahead and get rid of Cox." Whether this was an offhand remark or reflected a settled purpose I had no way of knowing at the time. It made no difference one way or another to what I had to do. I was well aware that the circumstances were precarious. All I could do, as "lawyer for the situation," was to try to cope as best I could with each problem as it arose.

The way I felt was reflected in a wartime experience I described to Al Haig on the way out of his office a few minutes after the President's remark about getting rid of Cox. "This reminds me," I told Haig, "of the first hard thing I had to do after my unit landed on the beach on D-Day. A soldier with his foot blown off by an antipersonnel mine was lying in a patch of barbed wire just back of the dune line. He was in agonizing pain. Somebody had to get him. I stepped carefully across the barbed wire, picked up the wounded soldier, and retraced my steps. All I could do was put down one foot after the other, hoping each time that nothing would go off."

Even after my resignation I continued to believe that the firing of Cox could be accounted for without attributing bad faith to the President, and I so testified early in November at Senate Judiciary Committee hearings.[17] The President, I thought, could genuinely have felt that he had made a reasonable effort to find a workable compromise between the principle of confidentiality and Cox's claim of access to the subpoenaed tapes. And it seemed at least understandable, if wrongheaded, for Nixon to demand that Cox be fired because he would not accept the compromise. (The first thing he said to me when I entered the Oval Office to resign was: "Brezhnev would never understand it if I let Cox defy my instructions.")

It was not until May 1974, when I tried to reconstruct the events of the week leading up to the "Saturday Night Massacre" for the benefit of counsel for the House Judiciary Committee, that I was finally forced to conclude that from the beginning of the week the name of the game had been: get rid of Cox. Get rid of him by resignation if possible. But get rid of him. The facts, as I look back on them, are not susceptible of any other interpretation. The game plan had to have—and did have—two chief components. One: induce Cox to quit or, failing that, put him enough in the wrong so that firing him would seem justified. Two: induce Richardson to go along.

THE SECOND WEEK of October was a tumultuous one. The Yom Kippur war had broken out in the Middle East on October 6. Four days later, Vice-President Spiro T. Agnew pleaded no contest to criminal income-tax charges and resigned. On October 12, the Court of Appeals for the District of Columbia upheld an order by Judge Sirica ordering the President to turn over nine tape recordings that had been made in his office. That same night Nixon announced that Gerald R. Ford would be nominated as the new Vice-President.

During this period I had taken the occasion at the close of several conversations with Al Haig to ask how things were going in the Middle East. One of my chief concerns as Under Secretary of State had been the effort to achieve a Middle East settlement, and I was deeply interested in the current situation. When I walked into Haig's office on the morning of Monday, October 15, in response to an urgent weekend call intimating that he wanted to discuss with me some important aspect of the Middle Eastern situation, I was ready for almost anything.

Haig began with an elaborate account of the dire state of relations between the United States and the USSR over the developing crisis. To hasten the point I said facetiously, "I'm ready to go, Al. Shall I go home and pack my bag?"

But the Middle East was not the real subject. It was only a curtain-raiser. The real topic was the proposition that the problems generated by Cox's investigation were causing an intolerable diversion of the President's time and energy from far more important matters. To bring things to a head, Haig said, the President was prepared to submit his own verified version of the subpoenaed tapes to Judge Sirica's court and—at the same time —fire Cox.

"If he does that," I said to Haig, "I will have to resign."

Haig called me early that afternoon with a new plan. It became known as the "Stennis proposal." The White House would prepare transcripts of the tapes, have the transcripts checked against the original tapes for accuracy by Senator John C. Stennis of Mississippi, and then submit the verified transcripts to the Special Prosecutor. If Cox went along with the plan, he would not be fired. Haig said he had sold the President on the Stennis proposal with the greatest of difficulty, that it had been "very bloody" for him, and that the President had angrily demanded that "this is *it*" for Cox, meaning that Cox would have no further access to Presidential tapes or documents.

As applied to the tapes and documents then under subpoena, the Stennis proposal seemed to me reasonable enough to be worth my trying to persuade Cox to accept it. I deliberately chose, however, to leave out of my negotiations with Cox and my subsequent discussions with the White House during the next several days any reference to a restriction on future access.

Despite my best efforts to get Cox to go along with the

Stennis proposal, he sent me a memorandum Thursday afternoon refusing to accept it. The memorandum spelled out his position in carefully reasoned terms.

That evening I went to Haig's White House office. In addition to Haig, the President's lawyers, Fred Buzhardt and Leonard Garment, were there. So also, for the first time at any Watergate discussion at which I had been present, was Charles Alan Wright, constitutional law authority and professor at the University of Texas Law School, who had argued the President's side of the tapes case before Judge Sirica and the Court of Appeals. I gave them copies of Cox's memorandum.

Wright had just been told about the Stennis proposal and seemed so thoroughly convinced of the generosity and wisdom of the President's willingness to cooperate with it that I urged him to try his own hand at selling it to Cox. The others agreed that if Wright did not succeed in convincing Cox to accept the proposal, Cox should be fired.

Believing that Wright was unlikely to succeed in persuading Archie Cox to change his mind, I went to my office at the Justice Department Friday morning prepared to resign. As soon as I learned that Wright had indeed failed, I called Haig and asked to see the President, knowing what I had to do. But that meeting with the President never took place. When I got to the White House, Haig had still another proposition, and it seemed that my need to resign had again evaporated: the tapes as verified by Senator Stennis would be submitted *to the court* and *the court* would be told that this was as far as the President would go, but Cox would *not* be fired.

The previous evening's cast of characters now reassembled in Haig's office. One of them handed me a copy of a letter from Archie Cox to Professor Wright. Cox's letter said that he could not accept the requirement that he "must categorically agree not to subpoena any other White House tape, paper, or document." I asked why Cox's letter addressed this issue, pointing out that in my negotiations with him, I had never attached any such restriction to the Stennis proposal. There must have been some misunderstanding. This muddied the record and put the President's position in unnecessarily bad light.

When I urged that a new letter be written to Cox setting the record straight, no one pointed out that there was no misunderstanding. No one said that Cox's letter correctly reflected the restriction put to him by Wright the night before. Cox, however, clearly recalls that Wright did in fact put it to him. And confirming Cox's recollection is the fact that Wright's follow-up letter *did not* withdraw the restriction and closed with the words: "The differences between us remain so great that no purpose will be served by further discussion. . . ."

When I left the White House that Friday morning, the idea of restricting Cox's right to pursue other tapes and documents was still alive, though whether and how it was to be carried out was quite unclear. I had said that I thought Cox would resign if it were put into effect. As to what I might do myself I said nothing further—not having expected to leave the White House as Attorney General, I had not yet had a chance to think through the implications of the new situation.

During the afternoon I called both Haig and Buzhardt to argue that the Stennis compromise should not be coupled with a restriction on Cox's future freedom of action and to indicate my changed view that Cox would not be induced to resign by this device. My position was noted and I was told that there would be further consultation before any decision was reached. I had no reason, at the time, to think again of resignation and even less to speak of it.

At seven P.M. the same day Haig read me over the telephone a Presidential letter which, he said, was already on its way to my office by messenger. The letter said: "I am instructing you to direct Special Prosecutor Archibald Cox . . . that he is to make no further attempts by judicial process to obtain tapes, notes, or memoranda of Presidential conversations. . . ."

I was angry and upset. But it was not until my meeting with counsel for the House Judiciary Committee that I fully understood the significance of this sequence of events. The President, I finally realized, thought he had found a formula for getting rid of Cox without precipitating my resignation. I was not to know until the last possible moment that the restriction on Cox was an integral part of the White House plan, and when I learned that the President had brushed aside my arguments against the restriction, his letter directing me to impose it was already on its way.

The plan confronted Cox with three possible choices. He would either have to acquiesce in the directive, which from the President's point of view would be fine; quit, which would also be fine; or refuse to obey the order, and that would create a justification for firing him.

The letter itself arrived about twenty minutes after Haig's call. I telephoned Cox and read it to him, stressing the point that I was merely informing him of it—not carrying out the instruction it contained. I telephoned him later that evening to let him know that I intended to release a brief statement making clear my objections to the President's instruction. (The statement was never released because I learned, after calling Cox, that the instruction had not yet been made public by the White House.)

After I returned home I discussed the situation with Anne. It was clear that I could not carry out the instruction. To convey the idea of going out in style, she referred to being buried in a "mahogany coffin." Later that night, jotting down thoughts about what to do next, I captioned them "The Mahogany Coffin."

I spent most of Saturday morning translating my notes of the evening before into a letter to the President. Cox, meanwhile, announced a press conference to be held at one P.M. My letter went to the White House moments earlier. I caught Cox on the way into his press conference and read him the key sentences:

> At many points throughout the nomination hearings, I reaffirmed my intention to assure the independence of the Special Prosecutor, and in my statement of his duties and responsibilities I specified that he would have "full authority" for "determining whether or not to contest the assertion of 'Executive Privilege' or any other testimonial privilege." And while the Special Prosecutor can be removed from office for "extraordinary improprieties," his charter specifically states that "The Attorney General will not countermand or interfere with the Special Prosecutor's decisions or actions."

Quite obviously, therefore, the instruction contained in your letter of October 19 gives me serious difficulty. As you know, I regarded as reasonable and constructive the proposal to rely on Senator Stennis to prepare a verified record of the so-called Watergate tapes and I did my best to persuade Mr. Cox of the desirability of this solution to that issue. I did not believe, however, that the price of access to the tapes in this manner should be the renunciation of any further attempt by him to resort to judicial process, and the proposal I submitted to him did not purport to deal with other tapes, notes, or memoranda of Presidential conversations.

With close associates and friends I watched Cox's press conference in my sitting room at the Department of Justice. He took the third choice: he could not, he said, accept the Stennis proposal and would go back to court for a decision on Nixon's apparent failure to comply with a court order. I did not have to wait long for Haig's call telling me that the President wanted me to fire Cox. I asked what time that afternoon it would be convenient for the President to see me.

MY MEETING with him was low-keyed but tense. Much was left unspoken. For me, by far the hardest part was having to refuse his urgent appeal to delay my resignation until the Middle Eastern crisis had abated.

"I'm sorry," the President said, "that you insist on putting your personal commitments ahead of the public interest." I could feel the rush of blood to my head.

"Mr. President," I said in as even a voice as I could muster, "I can only say that I believe my resignation *is* in the public interest." Nixon backed off, acknowledging that it was our *perception* of the public interest that differed.

Bill Ruckelshaus had also sent over a letter of resignation. The President refused to accept it and directed General Haig to fire him instead. Who, then, would be left to fire Archibald Cox? The Solicitor General, Robert H. Bork, was next in line. He believed that the President had the right to order Cox fired and had no personal compunctions about wielding the axe. He felt, however, that if he went through with it he should then resign himself. "I don't want to stay on and be perceived as an *apparatchik*," he said. Bill and I persuaded him that this should not in itself be a sufficient concern to justify the drastic loss of continuity at Justice that would result if he also resigned.

I then called Archibald Cox. Both of us had been law clerks for Judge Learned Hand. As we talked there came floating to the surface of my mind a passage from the *Iliad* inscribed by the Judge in Greek on the photograph of himself which he had given me after my year with him. He had taken a lot of trouble, he told me, in choosing a passage which struck him as suitable. I quoted the passage to Archie: "Now, though numberless fates of death beset us which no mortal can escape or avoid, let us go forward together, and either we shall give honor to one another, or another to us."*

It is difficult, in retrospect, to understand how Richard Nixon and his advisers could ever have supposed that I could be induced to fire Archie Cox on the ground that he had rejected a proposal for verification of the subpoenaed tapes that was tied to a restriction on his access to other Presidential tapes and documents. His position was not only defensible but right. By no stretch could I have construed it as amounting to an "extraordinary impropriety on his part."

The President, having vainly sought to make it appear that he had no choice but to get Cox fired, left me no choice but to resign. It was not a hard decision. My commitment to the inde-

* The passage is from Sarpedon's address to Glaukos. This rendering is as I quoted it to Cox and used it in a speech at the Appeal of Conscience Foundation dinner in New York on December 11, 1973. In a *New York Times Book Review* column on January 20, 1974, John Leonard, the editor, quoted an "anonymous letter" pointing out that my version of this passage departs from the accepted translations. "If," observed Leonard's correspondent, "Richardson had cared to be faithful to Homer he would have said, 'either we shall give honor to another, or another to us.' Changing 'another' to 'one another' makes Homer the author of the subtlest anti-Nixon comment of the season." Unfortunately, I cannot claim either the competence in Greek (though I did once study it) or the "scholastic temperament" by which he accounts for my "revisionism." I merely rendered the quotation as I remembered it.

pendence of the Special Prosecutor was a pledge to the Senate Judiciary Committee, to the Senate as a whole, and through the Senate to my fellow citizens. And although I could have foreseen that the firing and the two resignations would in combination produce a considerable public uproar, I could not have guessed that, all across the country, there were so many who would feel so strongly about the day's events. Three million messages descended on the Congress, the greatest outpouring of its kind that had ever taken place. In my travels since then, great numbers of people have told me that they spent hours attempting to send a telegram but simply could not get through to Western Union.

Part of this reaction came from outrage over the attempted frustration of an honest effort by the Special Prosecutor to dig out the truth. It was a protest against the breach of a commitment to his complete independence. There was also hunger for a demonstration of willingness to draw a line on an issue of principle. As Oliver Wendell Holmes, Jr., once remarked, "We live by symbols." That Saturday's events provided the symbolic focus for a declaration of conscience on the part of the American people themselves.

It is not often mentioned now, but there was an interval in the immediate aftermath of the departure from the Department of Justice of Archibald Cox, Bill Ruckelshaus, and me when Presidential power was asserted more blatantly than at any other stage in the whole sordid history of Watergate. This was when the FBI, on Richard Nixon's orders, occupied Bill Ruckelshaus's and my former offices at the main Justice building and barred access by members of the Watergate Special Prosecution Force to their own premises at 1425 K Street. The President ordered that Cox's entire staff be disbanded and that all Watergate investigative responsibility be turned back to the Criminal Division of the Justice Department. No new Special Prosecutor was to be appointed. And although Judge Sirica's order directing the President to comply with the pending subpoenas of tapes and documents had become final at midnight the previous Friday, the President instructed his lawyers to appear in court the following day and announce that he did not intend to comply with the order. He would instead submit to the court his own edited transcripts of the tapes. A government of laws was on the verge of becoming a government of one man.

It was then that the firestorm broke. The American people showed with unmistakable force that they would not tolerate a further abuse of power in the attempt to block investigation of the abuse of power. Acting Attorney General Robert Bork insisted that the Watergate Special Prosecution Force must retain responsibility for the investigation and that a new Special Prosecutor must be appointed. The overwhelming force of public opinion backed up the Acting Attorney General's firmness. The President capitulated. On the Tuesday which was to have been the day when only his own versions of the tapes were produced, his lawyers surrendered to Judge Sirica the tapes themselves.*

At his press conference on October 20, Archibald Cox had said: "Whether ours shall continue a government of laws and not of men is now for Congress to decide and, ultimately, the American people." Professor Cox was right, with this difference: it was the American people first, and only then the Congress, who decided that ours will continue a government of laws and not of men.

* More precisely, seven of the nine were turned over, and one of the seven had the notorious 18.5-minute gap.

II

Executive Encroachment:
Restoring the Balance

U NDER the American system there is a constant testing
of strength among the three branches. It is a form of
creative tension whose remarkable vitality over the years since
1787 would have delighted but not surprised the men who wrote
the Constitution. Starting with the aim of separating power in
order to prevent tyranny, the Founders set in motion a self-
adjusting mechanism under which one branch checks the excesses
of another or picks up initiatives avoided by another, with the
interaction of the whole generally resulting in a force for
moderation.

No governmental arrangement, of course, is perfect. Change
exerts a constant stress, and from time to time the pieces get out
of balance. Or perhaps the balance that worked well in another
day no longer works.

Growing out of the two most divisive events of modern
American history—the Vietnam war and the Watergate affair—
has come a general recognition of the need to redress the imbalance between the executive and legislative branches. The imbal-

ance had been developing for several decades; it is now clear that to correct it will require the Congress to make itself a more effective instrument. It is equally clear, at the same time, that the executive branch of government must be made more accountable both to the Congress and to the public.

And yet, despite the agitation over executive-legislative imbalance stimulated by the Vietnam war, the faults in our system demonstrated by the war were not primarily structural. Congress deliberately appropriated funds, approved resolutions, and took almost all of the other war moves urged upon it by a succession of Presidents. What went wrong was not so much the result of poor adjustment of the institutional relationships between the branches as it was of secretiveness and deception in the dealings of one branch with another. It was a product of the stealthy way in which two Presidents enmeshed the United States in that war and the almost equally stealthy way in which a third President got us out.

Congress, through the War Powers Act of 1973, has already taken steps to lock the barn door against the attempt by some future President to steal an identical horse. But while the Act spells out procedures that may prove valuable, it self-evidently cannot diminish powers conferred on the President by the Constitution itself. Our real protection must ultimately depend on the willingness of each branch to respect the responsibilities and prerogatives of the other—and that is a matter of spirit which does not lend itself to legislation.

Watergate, meanwhile, demonstrated an almost Byzantine secretiveness in the abuse of power. Some of these abuses took quite specific forms; remedies for these were discussed in the previous chapter. Others reflected the same habits of secrecy that cloaked the conduct of the Vietnam war. Hence, before proceeding to more general problems of accountability and balance, I shall first discuss the issue of secrecy in its two principal manifestations: executive privilege and the classification of government information.

Is THERE such a "thing" as "executive privilege"? Is "executive privilege" a "myth"? Much controversy has swirled around these questions. Contrary views are asserted with equal force and no less dogmatism on both sides. The antagonists marshal impressive arrays of authority in support of their respective views. Parliamentary precedents, Presidential utterances, congressional pronouncements, and the *obiter dicta* of jurists are combed and parsed. The important—the ultimate—issue, it is assumed, is how the Supreme Court of the United States will eventually define the scope of the President's power to withhold information from the Congress or the courts.

But the important question, in my view, is not how the Supreme Court may eventually decide individual cases. The more important question is how the coordinate branches of the federal government *should* deal with each other in matters involving access by one branch to information in the hands of another. This is a practical, not a legal, question. And while particular instances of disagreement between the branches may from time to time result in litigation which in turn evokes judicially declared rules, the vast number of such matters will continue to be handled, as they have been in the past, on the basis of commonsense considerations.

Even Raoul Berger, the leading scholarly exponent of the view that "executive privilege" is a "myth," concedes that practical considerations have a place. In testimony before the Senate Subcommittee on Intergovernmental Relations and Separation of Powers in April 1973, referring to communications between the President and his intimate advisers, he said, "On practical grounds it may be desirable to shield such conversations from Congressional inquiry, and Congress itself generally has not insisted on their disclosure." He then added, "But it does not follow that there is a constitutional basis for the withholding claim."[1] Granted. Lest, however, I appear to be conceding the opposite— that the constitutional claim has no basis—let me, before returning to the practical considerations, turn aside briefly for a summary review of the constitutional issues.

FIRST, then, as to what is undisputed. Heading this category is the proposition that the Congress has sweeping powers of investigation into and oversight over the activities of the other branches.* The Congress, in a phrase borrowed from parliamentary precedent, is the "Grand Inquest" of the nation. But are the inquisitorial powers of the Congress unlimited? To insist that they are, automatically sweeps the other pieces off the board: the constitutional game is over. And yet there is more to be said. Under the British parliamentary system there is no firm separation between the legislative and executive branches. In the absence of a written constitution, Parliament is supreme; it could at a stroke abolish or reconstitute every administrative as well as every judicial institution of the British government. Reason therefore requires examination of the question what difference, if any, it may make that we do have a written Constitution and that it does expressly separate the powers of government.

The Constitution certainly does not say anything about "executive privilege." Indeed, Berger tells us that the first use of the phrase goes back only to the Eisenhower administration. But may not a right to preserve the secrecy or confidentiality of some information in the hands of the executive branch be inferred from the very nature of the powers expressly conferred on the executive branch? The Constitution says nothing, either, about the power of the Supreme Court to protect the confidentiality of its deliberations on pending cases, but it is a power, surely, so intrinsic to the proper conduct of judicial business that to infer it seems both necessary and logical. It is no more difficult to infer a power to protect the confidentiality of the internal deliberations of the executive branch. In the words of the Supreme Court, "those who expect public dissemination of their remarks may well temper candor with a concern for appearances and for their own interests to the detriment of the decision-making process."[2]

Similarly, the President's express power to conduct foreign affairs must carry with it an implied power to protect the confidentiality of diplomatic exchanges with another country. But even if it is admitted that an express grant of power may carry

* I use the plural because I see no reason in principle for distinguishing between the branches: in practice (here, and already, we come back to practicalities) the proposition is commonly asserted only in application to the executive branch.

with it the implied grant of the other powers needed to carry it out, that does not, of course, tell us how such implied powers should be defined or delimited. Still less does it tell us whether their scope and limits are affected by the character of the proceeding in which the demand for information is asserted—whether a congressional investigation, a grand jury inquiry, the trial of a criminal case, or an impeachment proceeding. And even in the case of the Congress it may make a difference whether the demand comes from an individual Congressman, from a committee, or from an entire body.

These are the important analytical components of the constitutional issue. In *United States* v. *Nixon*, the Supreme Court demolished the contention that "executive privilege" is a myth. Pointing out that the evidence being sought did not involve military or diplomatic secrets, the Court held that "the generalized assertion of privilege must yield to the demonstrated, specific need for evidence in a pending criminal trial." But the Court's unanimous opinion also stated, "The privilege is fundamental to the operation of government and inextricably rooted in the separation of powers under the Constitution." The Court then added: "Nowhere in the Constitution . . . is there any explicit reference to a privilege of confidentiality, yet to the extent this interest relates to the effective discharge of a President's powers, it is constitutionally based."[3]

Significant constitutional issues, to be sure, remain undecided. *United States* v. *Nixon* involved a criminal proceeding, not a congressional inquiry; on the other hand, the evidence demanded did not concern national secrets. Considerations of comity and common sense, in any case, make it important still to rely, in executive-legislative relationships, upon practical considerations. What are these considerations? A sensible place to start is with two hierarchical lists: one ranking the purposes for which information is needed, from most urgent to least urgent; the second ranking the sensitivity of the information, from most to least seriously damaging if publicly disclosed. Other variables that may have a bearing include the comparative difficulty of preventing the leakage of information originally disclosed on a restrictive basis and, perhaps, the circumstance that a particular situation involves an inherent element of conflict as between the White House and the Congress. The separation of powers, after all, presupposes that the relationship among the branches of government will to a degree be adversarial.

Even separate powers should try to get along—and this is all the more true when their common responsibility is the general welfare of the same citizenry. In international relations the spirit of mutual accommodation is called "comity." In June 1973, "comity" was the theme that I kept hammering on during nearly four and one-half hours of Senate testimony on freedom of information, executive privilege, and secrecy in government. I was determined not to let myself get trapped in the kind of theoretical exercise which led Attorney General Richard G. Kleindienst, at a joint hearing of Senate Judiciary Committee subcommittees in April 1973, to assert that executive privilege was so broad that the President could withhold from the Congress all papers or information held by any of the 2.5 million employees of the executive branch. At one point, replying to Senator Edmund S. Muskie's statement that there had been 170 instances during the previous seven years in which House and Senate committees had encountered obstacles or delays in obtaining information, I said:

> I would just say, Mr. Chairman, that the fact that there have been 170 instances which did not get raised to the level of invoking executive privilege may be used to prove precisely the opposite point, that on the whole the situation does work fairly well.
>
> I have now been in four departments in this administration and I have dealt with almost all of the congressional committees by now, and in every single instance we have been able, I think, to work out on a reasonable basis an understanding with respect to the furnishing of information. In no case that I have ever been concerned with has executive privilege been invoked. There has been, it is fair to say, a number of situations involving negotiation over the scope of what would be made available, negotiation over the conditions under which it would be held, or disclosed, or nondisclosed by the committee.

But it seems to me that this is the kind of process that ought to take place recognizing that the branches are after all separate. . . .[4]

As it happened, this approach was put to the test only two months later. During the Senate Foreign Relations Committee hearings on the confirmation of Henry A. Kissinger as Secretary of State, questions arose as to his part in the nineteen security-leak wiretaps discussed in the previous chapter. The committee demanded that the Department of Justice furnish information as to who ordered the taps and for what purpose, who got the "take" from the taps, how long they were in place, and so on. This, clearly, was a situation in which there would have been precedent for invoking executive privilege. The FBI had never previously furnished information about national security wire-taps to any congressional committee and was anxious to avoid a precedent for access to its counterespionage files. I believed that it was also important to prevent additional embarrassment to individuals whose privacy had already been invaded. The com-mittee, on the other hand, had a legitimate need to know (and it could, if it chose to do so, hold up the confirmation indefinitely). The arrangement eventually worked out with the committee seems to me to have accommodated these competing considera-tions reasonably well: an FBI report summarizing the history of the nineteen wiretaps which had been prepared at the request of Acting Director William D. Ruckelshaus was made available to two senior members of the committee—Senator John Sparkman of Alabama and Senator Clifford Case of New Jersey—and these two Senators reported their findings to the other members. It was further agreed that no other Senate committee would demand the same information.

THE COMMON DENOMINATOR between executive privi-lege and the classification of information is the preservation of secrecy. Indeed, most of the instances in which, historically, executive privilege has been invoked have involved a primary concern with the leakage of sensitive foreign policy or defense information, rather than with protecting the confidentiality of the internal communications of the executive branch. For it has never been suggested, so far as I know, that the mere fact that information is classified justifies its being withheld from Congress. The effect of the classification is simply to impose constraints on the manner in which the information is safeguarded. It is by and large the public, therefore, rather than the Congress, whose access to information is impaired by the classification system.

The Task Force on Secrecy set up in the Pentagon in 1970 by the Defense Science Board was skeptical about the need for classifying information. It suggested that "more might be gained than lost if our nation were to adopt—unilaterally, if necessary —a policy of complete openness in all areas of information." The task force nevertheless reluctantly concluded that "in spite of the great advantages that might accrue from such a policy, it is not practical at the present time."[5]

On balance, it seems to me clear that the task force was right: we have no practical alternative to restricting access to some kinds of information. In the middle of hard bargaining over an arms control agreement, for instance, it would obviously prejudice the national interest to let our fallback positions become publicly known. It is equally plain that information about the capacity of our antisubmarine warfare technology, confidential communications with foreign heads of state, or military contingency plans must be closely held. In some instances, the mere possession of information, rather than its substance, requires its classification: the fact, for example, that it has been obtained by breaking a code.

Our point of departure should be the recognition that any restriction on access to information can only be justified by a specific public interest in secrecy which decisively outweighs the general public interest in the free flow of information. Overcautious classification impairs the public right to know without a corresponding benefit to a countervailing public interest. Where abuse of the classification system has the purpose of frustrating public accountability, a double detriment results: the right to know and the opportunity to correct mistakes have both been subverted. It is understandable in such a situation that a public-spirited holder of the improperly classified information should feel a strong incentive to turn it over to someone in a position to focus attention on the abuse. And yet in so doing the holder subjects himself, under existing law, to the risk of criminal prosecution.

What, then, can be done to help assure a fair balance among these competing interests? An obvious and important step is to create a systematic process for challenging the classification. It is astonishing in retrospect that nothing along these lines was done until March 1972, when President Nixon issued an executive order establishing such a process. The order reduced the number of agencies and officials with authority to classify information and established a schedule for the automatic declassification of documents within a specified period of time. It also provided for the review of the propriety of a classification at the request of any holder of the information and set up procedures by which a private individual can also seek declassification. An interagency Classification Review Committee was established to consider requests for declassification originally denied at the department level and to hear complaints about the administration of the order from people in or outside government. Repeated abuse of the classification process was made subject to administrative reprimand.

All this, so far as it went, was constructive. But what of the person who, unsatisfied by the review process, willfully discloses classified information? Should it be a defense to criminal prosecution that the disclosure did not in fact appreciably harm a significant national interest? Daniel Ellsberg's defense against prosecution for turning the Pentagon Papers over to *The New York Times* rested on an affirmative answer to this question, though the government's case against him was dismissed before the issue could be reached.* But this, as I said to Senator Muskie's subcommittee, amounts to allowing the leaker of classified information to take his chances that by the time of his trial, the danger

* Ironically, the reason for dismissal was in part that the government was unable to produce the results of the nineteen security-leak wiretaps quickly enough to satisfy the trial judge, although the government's case did not in fact rest on information obtained as a result of any of the taps.

of disclosure foreseen at the time of the classification has not materialized. An *ex post facto* defense seems to me just as wrong in principle as an *ex post facto* prosecution.

A solution fairer to the government—and fair enough to the individual also, I believe—would be to make it a defense that the person prosecuted for disclosing classified information had no adequate opportunity to challenge the classification or to seek external review of an agency's internal response to his challenge, but not to allow an opportunity for second-guessing the classification at a subsequent trial. The question is close. I see no practical way, however, of providing reasonably adequate protection for legitimate national secrets that does not run some risk of arbitrary official action. Here again, as in every other area of important public concern, we have no realistic choice but to allow room for the good sense and wise judgment of those to whom we have delegated responsibility. Nor does the fact that this trust has sometimes been abused make total distrust a workable alternative.

BUT NOT EVEN the soundest possible balance between the right to know and the need for secrecy can correct the more fundamental imbalance between the executive and legislative branches that began to develop long before Vietnam or Watergate. Much congressional oratory to the contrary notwithstanding, this imbalance did not come about because President after President has been grabbing fistfuls of power away from Congress. The Congress has thrust new functions into the hands of successive Presidents at least as fast as they have reached for them. Ever since the Great Depression made federal legislation the taken-for-granted response to every social and economic trouble, the Congress has been laboring to satisfy public demands for action on fronts ranging from minimum wages and farm prices to maximum hours and water-pollution tolerances. But for the Congress, the buildup of executive power could not have come about. As Senator Sam J. Ervin, Jr., of North Carolina put it, Congress itself has been "the chief aggrandizer of the executive."[6]

The resulting imbalance is usually described in terms of a

shift in the relative power of the executive and legislative branches. And it is true that the "new property" created by congressionally enacted benefits and programs has put into the hands of bureaucratic institutions an unprecedented degree of power to affect the lives of individuals. But this has been a shift of power from the individual to the state rather than from the Congress to the executive branch. The imbalance from which the Congress suffers most is a matter not of power but of capacity for coherent action—the ability to weigh competing claims, formulate a consistent strategy, and arrive at a sound consensus. A President, despite the inertia of the permanent government embodied in the bureaucracy, can at least speak for the executive branch as a whole. With a modest amount of skill and eloquence and a large amount of effort, he may even succeed in giving tone and direction to the entire federal establishment. As the only executive branch officeholder directly chosen by the people (Presidential candidates, not the people, choose Vice-Presidents), the President has a "bully pulpit" from which to educate and mobilize public opinion. And on top of these assets, he possesses the additional advantage, in choosing among conflicting policies and competing interests, of being able not only to call upon the highly developed analytical and integrative resources of the Office of Management and Budget but to tap the vast stores of talent and information distributed throughout the whole array of executive branch agencies.

The Congress, by contrast, has progressively been losing whatever capacity it once had to take coherent action. In the House, the caucus, not the Speaker, is now king, and once mighty committee chairmen have been toppled from their duchies. In the less numerous Senate, television may at any moment project any Senator onto the national stage, and the only Senators who do not think of themselves as potential Presidential candidates are those too old to dream. For the majority party particularly, party discipline is tenuous at best and at worst nonexistent. Under the circumstances, commonly agreed-upon legislative plans are difficult to formulate and almost impossible to carry out. Initiatives thus tend to be aborted before they can take coherent form.

UNTIL 1975 the Congress lacked any mechanism whatever for the rational setting of priorities. The process of congressional choice was impulsive, random, and fragmented. And although the budget requests of the executive departments were scrutinized closely by the House and Senate appropriations subcommittees, this was more a matter of counting the trees than surveying the forest. At no point in this congressional scrutiny was there an overview of the still larger forest—the budget as a whole. The Congress never looked at the claims embodied in one appropriations bill—such as for Labor and Health, Education, and Welfare —in relation to those embodied in the other appropriations bills —for Defense or for State, Justice, and Commerce.

Starting with the budget for the fiscal year 1976, the Congress began to work with a system designed to overcome some of these deficiencies. Under legislation enacted in 1974, each branch has established a Committee on the Budget to assist the Congress in focusing on overall budget totals, as well as on specific programs. These committees will receive reports on budget estimates from each Appropriations Committee of Congress, and a fiscal policy report from the congressional budget office. On this basis, the committees will formulate a concurrent budget resolution. How well the process will work remains to be seen. In principle, however, it provides the most important opportunity of the century for a readjustment of the balance of initiative in the direction of the Congress. Again, credit Watergate, which was cited again and again in the court of the debate as demonstrating the urgency of expanding the countervailing power of the Congress.

But even if the new Committees on the Budget perform well, formidable problems will have to be solved before a sound balance is restored. The committees will give the Congress a capacity to develop a budgetary overview comparable to that provided by the Office of Management and Budget for the President. They will not, however, have a role comparable to that performed by OMB in reviewing all legislative proposals originating in any executive branch agency and determining whether or not they are "in accord with the program of the President." The Committee on the Budget will not, in other words, have any jurisdiction or control over the committees which develop legislation creating the authority to spend money.

Operating autonomously, the legislative committees tend to view the passage of legislation both as the principal reason for their own existence and as an end in itself. No matter how high the pile of unfunded or partially funded existing laws, these "legislation mills" continue year after year to grind out new claims on the national revenue. The result is not only to expand the gap between promise and performance but to complicate the effort to develop a comprehensible strategy for the imposition of congressional priorities on government spending.* The same logic which led to creation of the Committees on the Budget points also to the need for some similar congressional mechanism for sorting out legislative priorities.

The effort, meanwhile, to keep the committee structure under control has been losing ground. Although the last major congressional reorganization (this was in 1946) reduced the number of legislative committees in both branches from eighty-one to thirty-four, it imposed no curb on the number of sub-committees any committee could have. On a single day in the spring of 1974, I counted fifty-two scheduled subcommittee hearings, and that record has probably been eclipsed by now. The Senate recently achieved the dubious goal of giving every majority-party (Democratic) Senator at least one subcommittee to chair. The situation with authorizing committees and sub-committees is even worse. In the case of HEW, for example, programs are authorized—and claims on scarce resources created —by forty different subcommittees with no coordination of any kind.

Back in the early years of the Eisenhower administration when Senator Leverett Saltonstall of Massachusetts was chairman of the Senate Committee on Armed Services and I was his legislative assistant, Senators seemed to me unbelievably busy. They weren't too busy, however, to become highly informed about committee matters. By 1973, when I was Secretary of

---

* The implications of the promise-performance gap are more fully discussed in Chapter III.

Defense, things had changed. How far the change had gone was brought home to me by T. Edward Braswell, Jr., chief counsel and staff director of the Armed Services Committee, during a break in a hearing declared so that the Senators could answer a roll call. Braswell, who had been hired by Senator Saltonstall at about the same time as I had been, told me that Armed Services Committee members were chairmen or ranking members of fourteen other committees and subcommittees. Each member of the committee served on an average of twelve other committees and subcommittees.

These impossible demands account for the fact that Senators are becoming increasingly uninformed about committee business and increasingly dependent on staff recommendations. And although most staffers restrict their freewheeling to situations in which their bosses cannot find the time to play a personal role, I remember one meeting with the senior Senator from a large state that is all too likely, if present trends continue, to become typical of such encounters. The Senator and I were trying to iron out differences between the administration and the Senate versions of an education bill. The Senator had just made a generous —and quite reasonable—concession. An aggressive staffer, to the Senator's face, told the Senator to withdraw the concession— and he did.

Given the burdens now placed on the Congress, it is not easy to find ways of improving congressional performance. Reducing overlap among committee jurisdictions, avoiding redundancy in committee hearings, strengthening the General Accounting Office and the Library of Congress—in some cases, even adding more staff—can all contribute to enabling the Congress to cope. The Institute for the Congress, a private nonprofit organization established early in 1975, will no doubt have additional suggestions. Measures of this kind, however, can never make more than a marginal difference. Until the present wave of self-assertiveness among the freshmen and sophomores gives way to the willingness to seek and accept effective leadership—and to the recognition that such leadership is not necessarily incompatible with allowing them to be heard—it is vain to hope that the Congress will achieve its full potential.

But not even the combination of better management and better leadership is a complete solution. The only real answer to Congress's problem of too much to do is not to attempt to do too much—not to try to be the nation's school board, sanitation department, reclamation district, policeman, housing authority, public works commission, and everything else all at once. Legislative attention should be focused, instead, on the major issues demanding national solutions, while leaving to others—state and local governments, profit-making and nonprofit private organizations, and individuals—matters that they are capable of handling more or less well on their own. To make this possible there must be a radical simplification of the functions of the central government. Simplification is also a necessary response to the need both for the increased accountability of the White House and for the intelligent exercise of citizenship. I shall have more to say about the former later on in this chapter; the latter is the principal theme of Chapter V.

WITH TIME and energy liberated by a clearer definition of priorities, a relaxation of the compulsion to legislate, and the simplification of federal functions, the Congress will be able to give more consistent and systematic attention to reviewing and evaluating the performance by the executive branch of the responsibilities conferred on it both by the Constitution and by the Congress itself.

The exercise of this oversight function, as it is usually called, offers the Congress an important and useful opportunity to enhance its own stature in relation to the executive branch. The Congress performs a vital role when it calls the executive branch to account for neglect of a serious problem, as in the hearings on conditions in nursing homes for the elderly held by Congressman (now Governor) David Pryor of Arkansas in 1971; when it exposes waste in the administration of federal funds, as in the hearings on cost overruns in the Department of Defense held by Senator William Proxmire in 1968–1969; or when it focuses on negligence as in Congressman Augustus Hawkins's hearings on the enforcement of affirmative action programs in federal agencies in 1975–1976.

One of the useful by-products of Watergate, I hope, will be to convince Congressional committees that there is as much— or more—political mileage to be gained through holding the executive branch to strict account for the exercise of its presently delegated functions as there is to be gained through devising new functions to be delegated. No area of government activity should be immune, either in theory or in practice, from regular, hard-eyed, hard-nosed congressional scrutiny. Some administrators resist such scrutiny because they fear that, pushed to petty extremes, it will become an obstructive nuisance. That is, of course, possible; but, then, too much of any good thing is always bad. As United States Attorney General I had several conversations with House Judiciary Committee Chairman Peter W. Rodino, Jr., soon to become celebrated for his firm and even-handed conduct of the Nixon impeachment inquiry, about cooperative arrangements for strengthening the oversight role of the various subcommittees of his committee over the activities of the Department of Justice. And while I balked at his request for permanent office space in the DOJ building for committee staff members, I nevertheless recognized the legitimacy of the committee's role and welcomed its interest.

The right balance, to be sure, is not easy to maintain. In recent decades the regular exercise of oversight responsibilities has more often tilted toward accommodation than toward aggressiveness.

Congressmen and agency heads have tended to develop cozy working relationships that have led to the dilution of the oversight function. House and Senate leaders have on occasion, at the request of chairmen who have grown close to the "overseen" agency, kept "troublemakers" from being put on oversight committees. And while such "troublemakers" are sometimes irresponsible, they may also have a nose for uncomfortable questions that ought to be asked.

The Joint Congressional Committee on Atomic Energy, which clashed repeatedly and sometimes bitterly with the Atomic Energy Commission in the late 1940s and the 1950s, required the AEC to keep it "fully and currently informed." So frequent was the contact generated by this requirement that, by the 1960s, it had created a close working relationship prone to sweep aside external criticism. The Central Intelligence Agency has always kept a "watchdog" subcommittee in each branch of Congress generally informed of its operations. Because intelligence work ordinarily has to be secret, this relationship has been extremely close. When illegal and questionable acts were uncovered, these "watchdogs" turned out to have been either unaware of the full range of CIA activities or to have accepted the agency's rationalizations. It took a number of internal and external reviews to uncover those questionable practices, though some, like the CIA-FBI mail surveillance program, continued for twenty years.

The Federal Bureau of Investigation under J. Edgar Hoover was even less subject to serious challenge than the AEC or the CIA. Except for a few polite questions at annual appropriations hearings, the FBI enjoyed virtually complete immunity from congressional scrutiny. In the course of preparing for the hearings on my nomination as Attorney General I quickly came to the conclusion that this was fundamentally wrong. As we have recently seen, even the FBI can benefit from being called to account from time to time. During the confirmation hearings I accordingly offered to cooperate with the Senate Judiciary Committee in working out procedures for the oversight of the Bureau. Later, with the concurrence of FBI Director Clarence M. Kelley, I wrote Chairman James O. Eastland a letter suggesting the establishment of a subcommittee for this purpose, and this was promptly done.

Given a clear sense of mission, congressional oversight committees can be useful to executive branch agencies without being soft on them. By staking out exclusive jurisdiction over an agency which in its day-to-day business handles sensitive information, such a committee can give the agency protection against overlapping inquiries by other committees. This not only minimizes the risk of leaks but assures that investigations and criticism are informed and balanced by an understanding of the agency's role and methods.

WHILE CONGRESS needs a clearer sense of direction, the executive branch needs a greater degree of accountability. In a curious sense, the cult of the "strong" Presidency has reduced the accountability of the executive branch. It has done so by letting it appear that the President was responsible for decisions that he could not possibly have known about. In all three of the administrations in which I have served, many important decisions were arrived at by a kind of collective process. This was accomplished, ordinarily, at a meeting in the White House of the senior people most directly concerned. In the normal course the issues for discussion had been identified in advance by Bureau of the Budget (later OMB) memoranda, by departmental critiques, or by White House staff papers. When Eisenhower's chief of staff Sherman Adams presided, the meeting would be held in the southwest corner office in the West Wing which has more recently been occupied by the other chiefs of staff I have known—H. R. Haldeman, Al Haig, and Don Rumsfeld. With Adams, former Governor of New Hampshire, no time was wasted in preliminary pleasantries.* If a consensus could be reached on a point not important enough to require Presidential attention, it would be regarded as decided. If not—or if it was of sufficient importance to be considered "Presidential"—it would be flagged for later submission to the President.

Although the press persisted in portraying Adams as a powerful decision-maker, he never attempted to be anything of the sort. No Cabinet officer in those days would have let him get away with it if he had. He did, however, perform an important role as an informal communicator of Eisenhower's views, and Cabinet members relied on him for this because they knew he was not prone to guess or to substitute his own opinions. I remember one occasion when, in reply to a question by my boss, HEW Secretary Marion B. Folsom, about some Presidential attitude, Adams snapped, "I don't know. You'll have to ask him."

"To ask him" was not so easy with President Nixon as it had been with President Eisenhower. In the days before Watergate, however, it was never my impression that this was primarily

---

* It could be unnerving to get a phone call from Adams. He had no use for flourishes like "Hello" or "How are you" or "This is Sherman Adams." He just began with whatever was on his mind, and you were in trouble if you did not recognize his voice.

because Nixon did not wish to be bothered, preferring instead to brood in lonely isolation. Nor, in my experience was it because Presidential watchdogs Haldeman and Ehrlichman impeded access. If I really needed to see the President, I was ordinarily able to do so reasonably soon.* It is a fact, nevertheless, that Nixon was harder for a Cabinet member to talk to informally than had been the case with Eisenhower. As I saw it, the principal reason for this difference was not so much that the two Presidents were so different in personal style (as they certainly were) as that the intervening years had brought about an enormous growth in the scope and complexity of Presidential responsibilities, many of them conferred on the White House by the Congress. Awareness of the enormity of these burdens had the effect of leading me, in common with most other Cabinet members, not to regard myself as "needing" to see the President except for a specific purpose, and only then if I could not find some other way of getting the result I wanted.

On each of the occasions when a new Washington assignment has brought me back to the national capital, I have seen that the demands placed on the federal government—and thus on the Presidency—had in the meanwhile been growing at an exponential rate. When I left HEW in 1959, the only people in the federal government worrying about water pollution were the career professionals at the Robert A. Taft Sanitary Engineering Center in Cincinnati. The only federal activity devoted to the treatment of heroin addicts was the Public Health Service Hospital in Lexington, Kentucky. Energy resources were presumed to be limitless—or at least the nation behaved as if they were. All of these problems—and many others—have since emerged as urgent federal concerns. The old problems, meanwhile, instead of disappearing, have become continually more complex.

Any increase in the number and scope of federal programs leads to a proportionally greater increase in the potential for conflict among them. As the range of federal concerns expands, program areas tend increasingly to converge and overlap. Fewer

* The one exception I can recall came in June 1972, when I cooled my heels for a week before I could see the President about welfare reform strategy. See Chapter V.

and fewer major problems still fall within the exclusive province of a single department or agency. Drug abuse is a good example. What, for instance, was to be done about heroin-addicted servicemen returning from South Vietnam? The Defense Department, the Veterans Administration, the old Bureau of Narcotics and Dangerous Drugs in the Justice Department, and the National Institute of Mental Health in HEW all had legitimate interests and responsibilities. They also had their own points of view, their own bureaucratic turf to protect, and their own solutions to propose. The White House is the one place where this kind of conflict can be resolved.

The number of demands on the Presidency has thus been growing both as a direct consequence of the increase in the responsibilities of the federal government and as an indirect consequence of the need to adjudicate conflicts among them. But not even this twofold increase fully reflects the growth in the burdens thrust on the White House during the past ten or fifteen years. A new factor has also been at work. This is the perception of structural interrelatedness. It is a perception that springs from the awareness that our society is a system of systems—that every segment is connected to every other, just as in the old spiritual "the thigh bone is connected to the knee bone, the knee bone is connected to the leg bone, the leg bone is connected to the ankle bone," and so on. Government cannot intervene anywhere without creating repercussions somewhere else.

In the Eisenhower administration we felt able to deal with health-care problems one by one—medical education and research, health insurance, hospital construction, preventive care, and the like. But by the time I found myself charged with developing health programs for the Nixon administration (this was in the fall and winter of 1970–1971), everyone concerned was acutely conscious of the interrelated factors which made it unrealistic to attempt to deal with any one aspect of health care in isolation from the rest. The "doctor shortage," for instance, was estimated at fifty thousand M.D.s. Should we prepare legislation to encourage medical schools to train more doctors? Or should we count on our other proposals—those aimed at keeping people well, reducing the incidence of illness and accidents, and making possible the more efficient use of physicians' time—to reduce the need for doctors? The relative success, or otherwise, of any of these proposals was bound to affect the need for the others. If we could have been sure, for example, that preventive health measures would be adopted and would actually work, the answer would have been clear. Given the limitations, however, both in our information and in our ability to analyze these interacting variables, I felt that we should not take the chance. The administration accordingly submitted legislation increasing the federal subsidy of medical education, with a bonus for schools expanding their enrollments, while at the same time going forward with recommendations aimed at reducing the demand for doctors. By 1985, as a result, we may well have a doctor surplus instead of a doctor shortage.*

In the case of the example just cited, our grasp of systemic interrelationships was sufficient to complicate the decision-making process, though not to affect the outcome. The point remains, however, that once the conscientious decision-maker becomes aware of such interrelationships, he cannot ignore them. To do so would be willfully to refuse to face consequences of his decision that he knows are important. And yet he can reckon with the implications of interrelatedness only at the cost of creating a requirement for coordination and integration where no such requirement was previously recognized. And since an individual department or agency is seldom in a position to be aware of all the interlocking elements of a complex problem, it becomes the responsibility of the White House staff and OMB to look for

---

* If a doctor surplus does materialize, it will not have been the first time that such a result was aided and abetted by government efforts to overcome a shortage. In the 1957–1958 period, the shortage that worried us most was that of school and college teachers. On October 4, 1957, the Soviet Union had launched the first earth satellite, and Americans began a race to catch up. The National Defense Education Act of 1958 contained provisions aimed at encouraging college students to go into elementary and secondary school teaching and at expanding graduate school enrollments. By the early 1970s, the nation was training more teachers and Ph.D.s than it could employ in teaching jobs. And while this was in part a consequence of such unanticipated factors as changing life-styles among the young and a draft which could be avoided by going to college and graduate school, the NDEA undoubtedly played a major role.

interrelationships unnoticed at earlier stages. The result, inevitably, is that progressively fewer decisions fall within the exclusive province of any one administrator; more and more have to be submitted to the President and—en route—get "massaged" by his staff.

No doubt the Nixon staff was eager for power. Reflecting the President's own attitude, it was also distrustful of the bureaucracy and prone to second-guess every recommendation originating outside the White House. As we now know, much of its time and energy was diverted into the attempt to punish "enemies" and to extract political advantage from the manipulation of government agencies. And yet, these tendencies aside, the Nixon White House could not avoid being a funnel into which an ever increasing volume of responsibility was poured. This phenomenon, in my view, had a decisive impact on shaping its operating style.*

The problem will not go away. Indeed, for President Gerald R. Ford the combined urgencies of inflation and recession have strongly increased its severity. Presidents may vary a little one way or another in physical energy or intellectual capacity, but none has more than twenty-four hours a day at his disposal. The more crowded the White House docket, the more frequently any President must call upon a staff capable of identifying opposing points of view, getting the parties together, promoting a consensus whenever possible, and narrowing down for the President's decision what only he can decide. The more numerous the issues that have to be handled in this way, the fewer the aspects of any particular issue that can receive the President's personal attention or be made the subject of a face-to-face meet-

---

* Curiously, in none of the discussions of the Presidency that I have come across has the exponential growth of the demands on the office received explicit recognition. Neustadt, Schlesinger, Hargrove, a panel of the National Academy of Public Administration (this was a panel chaired by Professor Frederick C. Mosher of the University of Virginia which prepared a report for the Ervin Subcommittee entitled "Watergate: Its Implications for Responsible Government")—all compare Presidents, administrations, and White House staff roles as if the requirements of the Presidency were immutable. This is to fall into the fallacy referred to later in this book as the "Mt. Washington fallacy." (Chapter VI.)

ing between himself and the principals. And the more difficult it is for the President to give much of his own time to every important matter or to discuss them all personally with the principals, the more crucial becomes the responsibility for formulating the issues for his decision and determining what—and whose—memoranda will accompany the issue paper.* It is by this process —this and the opportunity for easy access (and the last word)— that the White House staff acquires its power. And it is at this stage of the decision-making process, when people who are not ordinarily accessible to the press or available to congressional committees have their most potent impact, that the Presidency is least accountable to the people.

I KNOW of only three possible approaches to increasing the accountability of the Presidency. One is for the President to avoid deciding anything that he cannot personally discuss with the principals. The second is to cut down the number of matters that have to reach the White House at all. The third is to make the President's top assistants subject to Senatorial confirmation and define their functions by statute or—in the interest of greater flexibility—by executive order.

Given the present number of problems that cannot be resolved outside the White House, the first approach means that some are bound to be neglected or postponed until they become so aggravated that they force themselves on the President's attention. This approach amounts to making a practice of government by crisis. It is so obviously bad that I cannot imagine its being the deliberate choice of any President.

The second approach has two components, and each, in my view, is vital. One—and this is also my single most important prescription for the ailments of the Congress—is to simplify the functions of the federal government, thus reducing the number of decisions that have to be made at its top levels. The other

* In the departments I have headed, it was the responsibility of my immediate office to assure that all principals saw each other's staff papers on an issue submitted to me for decision. This meant that they could if they chose submit supplementary comments. Each knew, in any case, that as a matter of course—and due process—his own views would reach me.

is to increase the authority of federal decision-makers outside the White House who are both accessible to the press and available to congressional committees.

Given the conventional perception of the Nixon White House, I find it ironical that Richard Nixon's most far-reaching domestic initiatives would have had the effect of diminishing the flow of business into the White House and thus reducing the necessity for reliance on nameless and faceless staffers. These initiatives embraced both of the components referred to in the previous paragraph. The first—simplification of federal functions—was a major goal of Nixon's "New Federalism." Through its "special revenue-sharing" proposals, the New Federalism aimed at extensive consolidation of the number of federally administered programs of assistance to state and local governments. "General revenue-sharing," by distributing almost unrestricted federal funds to states and localities, was designed to help them carry out their own functions without having to call upon so much federal intervention. Other decentralization measures, including development of a nationwide network of Federal Regional Councils, had the same general objectives.

The second component—enhancement of the authority of federal decision-makers outside the White House—would have been one of the most important accomplishments of the reorganization of the executive branch proposed in Nixon's 1971 State of the Union message. Based on the recommendations of a commission headed by Roy Ash, then head of Litton Industries, this reorganization would have reduced the number of Cabinet departments from twelve to eight. State, Treasury, Defense, and Justice would have remained intact. All the other departments would have been consolidated into four: Human Resources, Community Development, Natural Resources, and Economic Development. Instead of being centered, like the existing departments, on the special interests most affected by government action, the four new departments would have been built around the major domestic functions of the federal government. The new departments inevitably would have had to be larger than the ones they replaced. The Department of Human Resources, for example, would have consisted of HEW in essentially its present form together with various bits and pieces (unemployment compensation, manpower development, food inspection, and college housing, among others) transferred from the Department of Labor, the Department of Agriculture, the Department of Housing and Urban Development, and the Office of Economic Opportunity. Similar transfers would have been made from the old interest-oriented departments to the other new functional departments.

All those whose habitual reaction to anything associated with Richard Nixon's name was "even if it was good I wouldn't like it" jumped immediately to the conclusion that a proposal to reduce the size of the Cabinet could only portend a new White House grab for power. Some of my own Cabinet colleagues, indeed, saw in the plan a move to downgrade the Cabinet. When Roy Ash finished outlining it to us at a meeting in the Green Room of the White House in March 1971, they jumped to their feet with questions zeroed in on this issue. At this point John Connally of Texas, who as a member of the Ash Commission had taken part in the plan's development, came to Roy Ash's rescue. It was the first time I had seen him in action, and I admired the skillful blend of humor, eloquence, and force with which he disposed of my colleagues' anxieties. Far from reducing the role of the Cabinet, the result of the reorganization would be to enhance it. This was so because each of the new Cabinet departments would bring under the direct control of a Cabinet officer issues that formerly had to be referred to the White House for resolution.

To me the argument was convincing if only because I had so often said much the same thing to people who advocated separating education and health from the rest of HEW and making them into separate Cabinet departments. HEW, I explained, was not a "conglomerate" but a "coalition." The interrelationships among HEW programs and activities are far more significant than their divergences. Their grouping in a single department was not haphazard or arbitrary. Nothing on a random list of the Department's most urgent concerns—poverty, drug abuse, alcoholism, juvenile delinquency, mental retardation, child development, the aging, rehabilitation of the handicapped—fell within the exclusive province of any one HEW operating agency. None was exclusively a "health" problem or an "education" problem or a "welfare" problem. All involved aspects of each. It was the job of the Secretary of HEW to promote cooperative solutions of such problems, to resolve jurisdictional disputes, and to coordinate the joint plan of attack. If health and education and the rest of HEW were split apart and made into three separate Cabinet departments each reporting to the President, this would not eliminate the need for some external authority to perform this integrative role. To be carried out at all, the task of integration would have to be assumed by the President's personal staff, either in OMB or under the Domestic Council. But OMB and the Domestic Council already have more than enough to do. Adding to their burdens would be bound to dilute accountability even more than it is already diluted.

The case for President Nixon's departmental reorganization plan presented the opposite face of the same argument. The functionally related activities scattered among several interest-oriented departments have to be coordinated somehow. Interdepartmental committees cannot do the job alone because their disagreements can all too easily end in deadlock. To prevent deadlocks some external authority is needed—and here is a role that invites reliance on the anonymous Presidential staff. Rather, therefore, than let this essential dispute-resolving function be performed invisibly and inaccessibly, accountability will be strengthened by resting it in a Presidential appointee who is visible to the public, available to the press, and accountable to the Congress.

But is there not a better way of increasing the accountability of the executive branch? Why not, instead of enlarging the role of a few Cabinet department heads in order to divest the White House of adjudicative and coordinating functions, make the Cabinet a genuinely deliberative body? A move in that direction, arguably, would make possible the sound resolution of issues cutting across departmental lines without the necessity either for reliance on anonymous and inaccessible White House staffers or for making still more unwieldy a handful of unmanageably bloated Cabinet departments. The British cabinet, after all, demonstrates that a cabinet can act by consensus, that its members can constructively participate in solving each other's problems. Why should not an American Cabinet, with the added advantage of a President who can make a final decision when a consensus is not achieved, do the same?

This thesis has, I must agree, a certain plausibility.* And the argument of history is certainly not dispositive. It is noteworthy, nevertheless, that seldom since President Andrew Jackson, whose administration gave us the first "kitchen cabinet," has the American Cabinet operated in the manner of its British counterpart. I can speak from firsthand observation only of the practice of two administrations—those of Dwight D. Eisenhower in his second term and of Richard Nixon in all but his last ten months of office. Commentators eager to sharpen the contrast between the Eisenhower and Nixon administrations have tried to create the impression that Cabinet meetings in the former were more "meaningful" than those in the latter. Not so—at least not in my experience. This, though limited in the Eisenhower era, did include attendance at several Cabinet meetings as Acting Secretary of HEW and at a number of others as Assistant Secretary. Among them all there was real debate at only one—although that is one debate more than I heard at the many Nixon Cabinet meetings I attended.†

Cabinet meetings in both administrations ordinarily focused on bland common denominators like the economic outlook, displays of budgetary breakdowns, or reviews of the status of administration legislative proposals. In the Nixon Cabinet, as a special treat, Vice-President Spiro T. Agnew would occasionally give us a travelogue.

Why was the discussion not more substantive and more spirited? Was there something about the personality or adminis-

* For purposes of the following discussion, I shall not press the point that only a few of the most critical interdepartmental issues could be dealt with in this way.

† The debate concerned the School Construction Assistance Act of 1959, which President Eisenhower agreed to submit to the Congress only after Richard Nixon, then Vice-President, had skillfully demolished each of the objections to it put forward by its Cabinet opponents.

trative style of Eisenhower and Nixon that inhibited genuine debate and the free exchange of ideas? This may have been part of the answer, but not, in my view, more than a small part. The explanation, moreover, must account not only for what I observed in those two administrations but for what I am told were equally unproductive Cabinet meetings in the Kennedy and Johnson administrations as well.

The President of the United States, in the first place, holds an elective office for a four-year term. The members of the Cabinet serve at his pleasure. And even though some Cabinet members may previously have served in elective office, their political base has seldom been truly national; no longer holding elective office, in any case, they no longer retain a real constituency.* In the British cabinet, by contrast, every member is an elected Member of Parliament, and all represent constituencies of roughly equal size. And while it is fashionable to typify the members of Nixon's Cabinet as, with a few exceptions, featureless nonentities unworthy of comparison with the giants who strode the earth in FDR's day,[7] this, even if it were true, would be irrelevant to the question of the usefulness of the Cabinet as such. I suspect, in any case, that the contrast is considerably exaggerated: for one thing, colorfulness is not the equivalent of effectiveness; for another, a Cabinet officer's actions and utterances now compete for attention with a far larger number of domestic and foreign events than used to come within the newsman's horizon in the New Deal era.

The contrast between the British and the American models also points up the second reason why our Cabinets do not have a more substantive role. The British Prime Minister, as his title implies, is first among equals; he can replace other ministers, but he has no independent authority to overrule them or tell them what to do. The President, on the other hand, not only has the power to remove and replace Cabinet officers but (in most

* In the Nixon first term, Romney, Volpe, Hickel, and Connally had all been Governors, Laird and Morton had been Congressmen, Finch had been a Lieutenant Governor, and I had been a Lieutenant Governor and an elected Attorney General.

instances, at least) the power personally to control the affairs of their departments. The Constitution itself, for example, makes him Commander in Chief of the armed forces and expressly charges him with responsibility for the conduct of foreign affairs. He alone of all the individuals seated around the Cabinet table has government-wide authority.

The last point leads to a third. Knowing that his fellow Cabinet officers have no real voice in the affairs of his own department, a Cabinet member is often reluctant to bring before a Cabinet meeting any still unresolved issue that he really cares about. The Secretary of Agriculture has no time to become familiar with health-insurance issues, but he may have firm views nevertheless. I may not know much about the relationship between free-market forces and agricultural price supports, but I may not know how little I know. Besides, we are all competitors for scarce funds. And in the rare case when a Cabinet member knows in advance that an issue will actually be decided at a Cabinet meeting, he is forced to take time in advance to lobby his fellow Cabinet members, with uncertain results.

The muted rivalry among Cabinet officers is mirrored in an almost adversarial relationship between the President and his department heads. For if each, to a degree, is the competitor of the others, all are competitors for the President's support. Cabinet members are forced by the very nature of their institutional responsibilities to be advocates of their departmental programs. This, essentially, was the point behind Vice-President Charles G. Dawes's famous remark that "the members of the Cabinet are a President's natural enemies."[8]

For all these reasons, I see no realistic prospect under our constitutional system that the accountability of the executive branch can be enhanced by remaking the Cabinet in the British image. I come back, therefore, to the view that the most practical approaches require the simplification of federal functions and a reduction of the interdepartmental role of anonymous nondepartmental people on the President's staff. Another step which, so far as it is feasible, would somewhat help was urged by Professor Erwin C. Hargrove of Brown University as one of the significant contributions to American government that could be made by the next President: "Indicating that he values independence in Cabinet members and department heads."[9] This is precisely the spirit in which Gerald R. Ford took office. Indeed, the aim of lowering the White House profile and enhancing that of the Cabinet departments led him for a time to delay the creation of a White House staff capable of playing a significant substantive role. Starting, however, with the appointment of Donald H. Rumsfeld as his chief of staff, it has become increasingly apparent that President Ford, like his predecessors, recognizes that no amount of confidence in his Cabinet officers does away with the necessity for coping with the problems of interrelatedness.

Where several Cabinet officers disagree on an issue involving each of their departments, a President cannot enhance the stature of one Cabinet officer except at the expense of the others. On the other hand, a President does not increase the stature of a Cabinet officer merely by backing him up in decisions that do not affect any other department or agency. That much is ordinarily easy—and routine. The real test of the President's interest in building up his department heads arises when he does not agree with a decision which (but for the President's disagreement) the department head would have full authority to make. Although minor issues lead to only minor tests and may seem insignificant, the manner in which these are handled can give a clear signal to all those around the President as to how much he values independent thought—and independent stature.

For a Cabinet officer, the crunch comes when his judgment on an important issue is not accepted. The President clearly has the right to expect a Cabinet member to support a final Presidential decision which has fairly taken into account the Secretary's view. If the issue is not worth resigning over, the Cabinet member ordinarily has no choice but to state accurately to the public the reasons why the President came to the decision he made and keep his personal views to himself. It would be a rare President, in such a situation, who encouraged the Cabinet officer to express his disagreement publicly, although that is certainly one way of demonstrating respect for the Cabinet officer while enhancing a climate of openness.*

There are times when it is necessary to be quiet even when you win. And silence may exact a political price. I took considerable criticism at the time—and it is still occasionally revived—for making no public protest when President Nixon announced that he had instructed the Department of Justice to "disavow" the HEW plan for desegregating schools in Austin, Texas. What actually happened was that the Federal District Court judge sitting on the case in Austin had rejected a plan developed by HEW experts at the Court's request and accepted instead a token plan proposed by the Austin School Board. It seemed to me mandatory that the government appeal this decision; otherwise, the credibility of our desegregation efforts throughout the South would be thrown into serious question. Attorney General John Mitchell agreed with me. Between us we persuaded the President to let the appeal go forward despite the anguished protests of his Texas friends.

Nixon's statement, announcing the appeal, that he had instructed Justice to "disavow" the HEW plan was meaningless except as a political gesture. In its appeal *from* the District Court's acceptance of the School Board plan, Justice would not in any case be appealing *for* the HEW plan: the only issue before the Court of Appeals would be whether or not the School Board plan could be found constitutionally sufficient. But I could not publicly make that clear without at the same time neutralizing the President's political gesture. And that would have been ungenerous—and, perhaps, a little *too* independent—since I had, after all, won on the issue that mattered.†

The situation is entirely altered, of course, if the President's decision is one that the Cabinet member cannot support in good

---

* In the British cabinet, the tradition of "collective responsibility" means that "all members of a government are expected to be unanimous in support of its policies on all public occasions. This is because divergencies among leading members of a government afford such wonderful openings to its opponents." John P. Mackintosh, *The British Cabinet* (New York, 1968), p. 445.

† Many public officials, caught in such a bind, solve the problem by having an aide supply the information to the press on a "background" basis. I did not do this for the same reasons that I did not speak out publicly.

conscience. No prescription can be written for where the line should be drawn. It varies with the situation and the individual. In my own experience as a Cabinet member, whenever I sensed that the evolution of some problem might reach a stage that I would find impossible to support, I tried to decide in advance where to draw the line. I then exerted all the ingenuity and resourcefulness I could muster to avoid being forced over that line. This approach worked well for me—until the end.

It has always amused me, incidentally, to note how firmly planted in the Washington scene is the assumption that those who hold important positions—Cabinet posts, for instance—must be driven by the love of power. Schemes to enlarge—or at least to protect—power are the stuff on which columnists batten and novelists fantasize—or vice versa. In my observation, however, anybody drawn to the idea of becoming a Cabinet member by the thought of a chance to wield power had better look elsewhere. If I ever exercised power, it was not an event that obtruded itself very forcibly on my attention.

I remember an interview with a candidate for the top administrative post at HEW. He was the executive vice-president of a major manufacturing company and had been thinking over whether he wanted to come to the department. Informing me of his conclusion, he said, "I've decided I'd like to help you with your decision-making."

I couldn't help laughing. "I'll be glad to have your help in my decision-making," I told him, "but I hope you don't think that's more than about one-seventh of what I do. The other six-sevenths of any Cabinet member's job consists of trying to get other people—his own associates, OMB, the White House, interest groups, the press, the Congress—to go along with what he wants to accomplish."

The third possible approach to increasing the accountability of the Presidency—making the top Presidential assistants subject to Senate confirmation and defining their functions—reflects form but not substance in searching for a solution of the problem. The National Academy of Public Administration panel referred to earlier carries formalism to the extreme. In its view, the White House staff would be limited to not more than fifteen top assistants and could not exceed fifty supporting professional employees. They would be prohibited by law from "issuing orders and interposing themselves between the President and the head of any department or agency." The President would be allowed to delegate to them only routine functions. Unless the proposed ceiling on the number of assistants is unduly low—and I have not tried to reach any independent judgment on that point—none of these recommendations would do any harm that I can see. But neither would they make any more than a marginal contribution to the strengthening of accountability. As I have tried to make clear, the delegation of responsibilities to assistants and their interposition between the President and department or agency heads are symptoms, not causes. The fundamental problems are the growth of Presidential tasks and the inescapable burdens of interrelatedness which lead inexorably to the enlargement of staff functions.

ALTHOUGH PUT FORWARD primarily as means of deterring and discovering future Watergates, two recent proposals for structural reform can also be regarded as indirectly aimed at strengthening executive branch accountability. One would make the Department of Justice "an independent establishment of the United States Government." The other would make permanent the Office of the Special Prosecutor.

If an "independent" Department of Justice means that the department should be wholly removed from the policy direction of executive departments that the President normally exercises, the idea makes very little sense to me. To make the department totally "independent" would be to put it under the total control of the Attorney General and thus render it unresponsive to the public will as that will is reflected by the President. Is this, in a democratic society, a good idea? I do not believe so. Ironically, some of the same people who advocate such independence for the Department of Justice were among those most disturbed by J. Edgar Hoover's assertion of *de facto* independence for the FBI. Their worry was that the FBI was "out of control."

The Department of Justice should, it is true, as I have previously urged, be insulated against interference with its conduct of pending cases. But this can be accomplished without divorcing it completely from the rest of the executive branch. Like other departments, Justice, as Solicitor General Robert H. Bork has pointed out, "implements those views of policy that win the continuing competition of ideas."[10] When, for example, a crucial and sensitive issue of civil rights arises, it may be necessary to take into account the views not only of Justice but also the concerns of the Civil Service Commission, the Equal Employment Opportunity Commission, the Department of Health, Education, and Welfare, and others. This is the kind of issue appropriate for Presidential leadership. Former Assistant Attorney General Burke Marshall, who headed the Civil Rights Division under the Kennedys and now teaches at the Yale Law School, put the matter well in Senate testimony:

> I do not believe that the abuse of power by the White House that has taken place justifies this grave an institutional change, that would permanently both insulate the Department of Justice from accountability to the policy direction and priorities of the administration, and at the same time insulate the President from political accountability for the conduct of the law enforcement functions of the Department.[11]

As to the idea of making the Special Prosecutor's office permanent, there arises the obvious question: what would it do? We have only twice needed to create such an office—once for Teapot Dome and again for Watergate. These neap tides of political morality came fifty years apart. If, as a people, having heeded the lessons of Watergate, we take seriously the responsibilities of citizenship, it may be another fifty years at least before another such crisis occurs. If we fail in these responsibilities, the recurrence will come much sooner, and no Special Prosecutor can prevent it.

MORE FAR-REACHING than specific reforms and more fundamental than structural realignment as the means of increasing executive accountability is amendment of the Constitution itself.

Does Watergate call for this? Serious-minded people have thought so. Some have argued that we should even move in the direction of a parliamentary system. Few, however, go so far as to advocate that we actually adopt such a system. Granted that parliamentary government has many admirable features, particularly as practiced by its parent country, I am convinced that the attempt to adapt it to the highly diverse political elements of this heterogeneous country would almost certainly lead to the creation of countless splinter parties. Such fragmentation would lead, in turn, to the necessity of government by coalition cabinet. The result, I think, would be likely to make the French Third Republic, by comparison, look like the Rock of Gibraltar.

More seriously put forward are procedural proposals for the removal of the President or Vice-President by means other than impeachment. One suggested amendment is for recall elections on the petition of a percentage of voters or by a majority or two-thirds vote of both Houses of Congress. Another would give Congress authority to call for a new Presidential election when it found that the President had lost public confidence so badly that he could no longer effectively perform his responsibilities. A variant of the latter proposal contemplates simultaneous dissolution of both Congress and the Presidency.

To my mind, the arguments against these proposals are convincing. Any new Presidential election under circumstances not justifying impeachment would inevitably be divisive. Moreover, in a case where some fundamental disagreement on a major issue lay behind the call for a new election, a congressional majority should not be able to put the President's job on the line while preserving its own tenure in office regardless of the outcome. Arthur M. Schlesinger, Jr., in *The Imperial Presidency*, quotes a Congressman as commenting on this proposal: It "would, in effect, take one-half of the parliamentary processes and not the entire parliamentary process," since Congress could dismiss the President but the President could not dissolve Congress. While there are some advantages in the simultaneous dissolution of both Congress and the Presidency, "one's instinct," Professor Schlesinger remarks, is "somehow against it." I share that feeling for essentially the reasons which he then goes on to point out:

The result might well be to alter the balance of the Constitution in unforeseeable and perilous ways. It might, in particular, strengthen the movement against the separation of powers and toward a plebiscitary Presidency. "The republican principle," said the 71st Federalist, "demands that the deliberate sense of the community should govern the conduct of those to whom they intrust the management of their affairs; but it does not require an unqualified complaisance to every sudden breeze of passion, or to every transient impulse which the people may receive from the arts of men, who flatter their prejudices to betray their interests."[12]

Two other proposals point in opposite directions from each other. One would repeal the two-term limitation established by the Twenty-second Amendment. The other would provide for a single six-year term. A President who has the possibility of running again is more likely, argue those who favor the first proposal, to follow policies capable of appealing to a majority of voters. As a strong believer in the democratic process, I find more congenial the argument for repealing the Twenty-second Amendment than the argument for a six-year term, although I think that the President's response to public opinion should as often be to try to educate and lead as to follow it. But there are sound democratic arguments for the Twenty-second Amendment —for example, that a skillful President could manipulate the advantages of incumbency to perpetuate himself in office despite having lost touch with the people—and I do not favor its repeal. Indeed, the Constitution has been working remarkably well just as it stands, and I have not seen a convincing case for any structural amendment.

It is characteristic of pessimists that they underestimate the capacity of decent people to respond to stress. It is characteristic of decent people, on the other hand—most of whom tend to be optimists—that they are slow to see evil or to react to a developing danger. But this impression of softness is often misleading. A coiled spring may yield easily to light pressure, but as the strain increases and the spring contracts, the counterforce also increases. The spring gives way so far as it must, and when the pressure upon it has been exhausted, it rebounds to its original form. And although its capacity to resist will have seemed barely sufficient, it may in fact have had much greater capacity for resilience than it was called upon to exert.

History is full of examples of this pattern of resistance. The reaction to the evil thrust of Hitler's totalitarianism illustrated it on a cataclysmic scale. Vietnam and Watergate illustrated it on a lesser scale, the former in response to manipulation and deceit, the latter in response to the abuse of power and the attempt to conceal it. In both instances the native resilience of American decency and good sense were immensely aided in reasserting themselves by the self-adjusting mechanisms of our constitutional system.

In the case of Watergate particularly, the capacity of the system to cope with stress was vividly demonstrated. Until I began looking back over those events, I had always thought of the phrase "checks and balances" in essentially static terms: dome, pediment, and pillars frozen forever in a symmetrical equilibrium like the front elevation of a Bulfinch building. I was, of course, aware that to be adaptable to changing circumstances, the Constitution requires flexibility in its interpretation; I had to this extent absorbed John Marshall's admonition, "We must never forget that it is *a constitution* we are expounding."[13] What I had not fully grasped is that the checks and balances were not designed simply to maintain equilibrium but when necessary to *restore* it.

At the time when the framers constructed the Constitution, the scientific discoveries of Sir Isaac Newton loomed large on the intellectual horizon. Newton's Third Law of Motion declares that to every action there is an equal and opposite reaction. Being keenly aware of the propensity of human nature for "vice," the framers took it for granted that greed, ambition, and the love of power would be powerful motivating forces. These forces had to be controlled in order to prevent any person or any part of government from gaining excessive advantage. What better way of accomplishing this than to use the thrust of one person's self-interest to generate an equal and opposite reaction from someone else's self-interest? The influence of this principle on the design of the checks and balances seems to me inescapable.* And if I correctly understand the principles of Newtonian mechanics, it followed that the resultant of these interacting forces, like the pressure of the wind against sail and water against hull, would be forward motion.

The United States government works best when the branches of government behave in accordance with the assumptions underlying the construction of these ingenious checks and balances. In the case of Watergate, the Congress and the Judiciary dealt with the excesses of the executive branch by asserting to the full the roles that the framers envisioned for them. The Senate subcommittee chaired by Senator Ervin went forward with public hearings on Watergate despite the concerns of the executive branch, as expressed by Special Prosecutor Archibald Cox. Judge John Sirica—Chief Judge of the District Court of the District of Columbia, one among almost four hundred federal District Court judges—ordered the President of the United States to comply with the subpoenas of a grand jury despite the President's strenuous insistence that to do so would subvert the separation of powers. The District of Columbia Court of Appeals and Supreme Court both sustained Judge Sirica's order. The House Committee on the Judiciary assumed the grave responsibility of weighing charges of high crimes and misdemeanors against the President and carried out that responsibility with dignity and fairness.

Nor was the function of containment and counterthrust limited to the branches of government. Although the framers did not visualize a two-party system as such, they certainly did envision a political struggle for power in which people would be organized in one way or another; and, as they would have predicted, the opposition party benefited from the embarrassment of

* Although I have not found any contemporary mention of the influence of Newton on the thinking of the framers, I did find a reference by Richard Hofstadter to the "ancient conception" of "balanced government" as having "won new sanction in the eighteenth century, which was dominated intellectually by the scientific work of Newton, and in which mechanical metaphors sprang as naturally to men's minds as did biological metaphors in the Darwinian atmosphere of the late nineteenth century." *The American Political Tradition* (New York, 1948), p. 8.

the party in control of the White House. The media also played
their ordained parts, and admirably so, not only in terms of the
full exercise of the rights conferred by the First Amendment, but
by the full exploitation of the opportunity to boost circulation,
enlarge the number of listeners, and—only incidentally, of
course—sell advertising. Citizens generally reacted out of a
variety of personal concerns: alarm about the growth of power;
anxiety about the vulnerability of their individual privacy and
individual rights; dismay over the perversion of governmental
processes and the dilution of their own votes.

It was just such a mixture of motives, some high-minded and
disinterested, some self-seeking, that the framers hoped would
combine to produce a result in the general interest. The great
strength of such a combination is that it does not depend for
its effectiveness on an extraordinary assemblage of talent or
experience at the apex of the system. It derives, rather, from the
ordinary qualities of ordinary people each performing their own
roles in their own ways under conditions of freedom. That the
process could work so well under such unprecedented stress
provides eloquent testimony to its resilience and durability.

Writing in 1783, Thomas Pownall observed that "there is in
these States, as in the animal economy, *a healing principle.*"[14]
Although similar in meaning to the Newtonian concept of checks
and balances, Pownall's metaphor has the advantage of connoting
a living process of regeneration and renewal. In the recovery of
this country from Vietnam and Watergate we have seen this
healing principle at work. And whatever may be the problems
of the future, Americans can now undertake them with the renewed assurance that comes from the awareness that ours is a
Constitution for all seasons.

III

The Corrosion of Cynicism:
Rebuilding Trust

AMERICANS have never been unquestioningly trustful of government. We have always treated our political system with regular doses of cynicism to keep it up to scratch. But a little cynicism goes a long way. Without basic trust between individual citizens and the officeholders to whom they have delegated responsibility for common concerns, no free, representative self-government is possible.

The decline in the percentage of adults recorded in opinion surveys as expressing trust in government began to be disturbing even before Vietnam; the "credibility gap" opened up by that prolonged and agonizing conflict accelerated the downward trend. The University of Michigan Survey Research Center found that the proportion of people trusting the government in Washington to do what is right "just about always" or "most of the time" declined from 81 percent in 1960 to 76 percent in 1965 and 61 percent in 1970. By 1974, the proportion had dropped to 38 percent.[1]

Since Watergate the erosion of trust has become alarming.

According to a poll conducted by Louis Harris and Associates for the Senate Committee on Government Operations late in 1973, the proportion of the adult public which agreed that "people running the country don't really care what happens to you" rose steadily year by year from 26 percent in 1966 to 63 percent in mid-1974. The proportion which agreed that "most people with power try to take advantage of people like yourself" was 33 percent in 1971, rose to 38 percent by mid-1972, then shot up to 60 percent by June 1974.

It is difficult, of course, to know how deeply rooted these cynical attitudes may be. My guess is that few of the people who endorse a proposition like "all politicians are crooks" have thought much about its implications. Most, I suspect, would agree that it is not true of the politicians they know personally, or would apply a loose definition of "crook" to a person they think is more interested in getting elected than in helping the people he represents. The Michigan Survey Research Center polls, on the other hand, have been conducted in the same way for twenty-three years. Regardless of the degree of cynicism reflected in the responses of the citizens polled, the downward trend in trust is deeply disturbing. No one knows how far cynicism can corrode confidence before democracy has been destroyed. Cynicism, in any case, need not be complete and total in order to be destructive. The same surveys which reflect an increase in cynicism and a corresponding decline in political trust also reveal a steady decline in the sense of political efficacy —the feeling that an individual can have an impact upon the political process. This decline leads to apathy. Apathy, in turn, narrows the base of political participation and enlarges the opportunity for political manipulation, thus making the cynic even more cynical. And so the downward spiral feeds on itself.

On the other hand, trends tend to generate their own countervailing forces—a fact that suggests caution in assuming that any trend can be extrapolated indefinitely. Watergate may yet prove to be illustrative of just such a tendency. Although for some people the impact of Watergate was to deepen their cynicism, for others it gave new urgency to the "new politics." Depending upon the staying power of the latter reaction, Watergate may yet prove to have been as significant for governmental and political reform as the Great Depression was for social and economic reform.

On the positive side, Watergate once again proved that it is seldom smart to be smart; that if you cut it too close, you're apt to cut yourself. I saw this demonstrated in the first campaign in which I worked. It was a campaign for a Housing Authority candidate in Brookline, Massachusetts, the town where I grew up. The other side had someone send a letter to voters pretending to support our candidate. The letter contained a racial slur on our opponent himself. The idea was that the apparent support of bigots would make our candidate appear to be bigoted. Actually, the letter boomeranged, hurting the opponent more than us, not because voters were influenced against him by the racial slur but because they suspected that he was responsible for the letter.

Massachusetts, by most accounts, is a state where professionalism in politics has reached a pretty advanced stage of sophistication. If there is such a thing as political "hard ball," Massachusetts might with some justification claim to have invented it. Having myself gone on from town elections to full-time participation in six statewide campaigns, I came into the 1972 Presidential campaign year thinking that I knew quite a lot about politics. When, therefore, finding myself in Miami Beach during July to testify on the Republican platform, I was asked to pinch-hit for Richard Kleindienst at a press briefing, my replies to questions about the Watergate break-in were sublimely confident. It was obvious, I said, that neither the White House nor the Committee to Reelect the President could have had anything to do with the burglary: quite apart from the fact that it was both immoral and illegal, it was blatantly "bush league."

The Committee to Reelect was, in fact, remarkably amateurish. At the time of the break-in, no one in a position of major responsibility had any real depth of political experience. John Mitchell began at the top as manager of the 1968 Nixon campaign. Hubert Humphrey's recovery from the disastrous Democratic Convention in Chicago having barely fallen short, Mitchell had automatically been cast in the role of a political mastermind. I never saw in him the "tough guy" he was reputed to be. In all my dealings with him when he was Attorney General he was unfailingly patient and reasonable. Puffing inscrutably on his pipe, he would reserve judgment until the last possible moment and then commit himself no more firmly than he had to. I feel sure that he thought Liddy and Hunt's espionage scheme sounded crazy but gave way in the end because he naïvely supposed that this must be the way the pros did it. His equally amateurish colleague, Jeb Stuart Magruder, certainly didn't know any better.

As we now know, the 1972 Nixon campaign was replete with lesser examples of the attempt to be "smart." Some, like Segretti's "dirty tricks," were both petty and repulsive. Others were just petty. An example of the latter sort that came directly to my attention at the time was both amateurish and adolescent. When in June 1972 the Congress enacted a Social Security benefit increase over the President's strong opposition, one young White House staffer had a bright idea: why not enclose with each of the 29 million newly enlarged checks a statement by the President taking credit for it? Better yet, print this leaflet in red, white, and blue with a picture of the President on it together with the Presidential seal! The staffer called HEW to "direct" the execution of his brilliant ploy.

Robert M. Ball, the extraordinarily able and experienced career public servant who then headed the Social Security Administration, was outraged. He told my assistant, who told me, that he would resign rather than permit any such flagrant politicizing of his agency. The Eisenhower and Johnson administrations, it was true, had used brief enclosures informing beneficiaries of an increase "enacted by the Congress" and "signed into law" by the President, but this was where Ball, with my strong support, drew the line. A "stuffer" conforming to these precedents was enclosed with the checks. Even this, as it turned out, drew pro forma protests from Democrats on the Hill; the original proposal, clearly, would have been an embarrassing liability to the administration.

Another lesson that should have been learned from Watergate is that there are few secrets anymore—at least, not for

long—particularly those secrets that involve official misconduct
or foolishness on the part of public officials. Such secrets are fair
game for investigative reporters, and the tangible rewards of
investigative reporting have never been so high. Bob Woodward
and Carl Bernstein, who gained visibility through their Pulitzer
Prize–winning coverage of Watergate for *The Washington
Post*, have, I hope, inspired a whole new generation of aggressive
young journalists. For there will always be amoral officeholders
who, lacking standards of their own, would do well to be mind-
ful of H. L. Mencken's observation that "conscience is the inner
voice that warns us somebody may be looking."

The public interest will no doubt also continue to benefit
from such unpleasant human attributes as vindictiveness, vanity,
and self-righteousness. These, in varying degrees, account for
most of the information leaks that embarrass administrators who
think they can get away with nudging some action in a partisan
direction or cutting some corner as a favor to a friend. On the
other hand, leaks often create the false impression that some
improper motive influenced a decision when this was not in fact
the case. Instead, the leaker may simply not have been informed
of the real reasons why some position he advocated did not prevail. He has simply leaped to a self-justifying conclusion. That
possibility, incidentally, is one of the reasons why I ordinarily
invite to any meeting at which a decision is to be made all
those who, no matter how junior, have been wrestling with the
problem.

There are some leakers, however, with whom I sympathize.
When there is no other way to get the truth out, when information is dammed up, its flow controlled in order to generate
power for the dam-builders, there may even be a duty to leak.
The question of when the leaker—or the whistle-blower—
should be immune from reprisal is analogous to the question of
when civil disobedience should not be subject to prosecution:
the leaker should be immune either when what he discloses is
unlawful or when the constraint on disclosure is unlawful, just
as there should be no prosecution for civil disobedience when
the law violated is invalid.

The Eagleton affair, the Agnew case, and the Rockefeller

hearing, though utterly different in other respects, have in common the unearthing of long buried information. For would-be politicians the moral is plain: don't have skeletons in your closets—or, if you do, take the initiative in exposing them. With the public eye more steadily fixed upon them than ever before, all politicians should be readier now to heed Will Rogers's advice: "Live your life so you won't be ashamed to sell your parrot to the town gossip."

As United States Attorney for the District of Massachusetts, I conducted an investigation in 1960 into the operations of the most powerful Democratic boss in Massachusetts, the late William F. Callahan. This investigation brought to light an extensive political empire presided over by Callahan and held together by payoffs and kickbacks to legislative floor leaders and political hatchetmen.* At the climactic stage I had Callahan himself under cross-examination for over a week of dodging and stonewalling. When, in the spring of 1961, I was replaced as United States Attorney, I was looking into the question whether or not the evidence which convinced me that Callahan was guilty of perjury would satisfy the "two-witness rule." (He was never indicted.)†

Callahan, meanwhile, was going over my entire previous life with a vacuum cleaner. As I later learned, he assembled information about every association and financial transaction I had ever had. The only pay dirt he struck, such as it was, was a series of automobile violations headed by a drunken-driving conviction in 1939 (I was then eighteen) and one for driving-

---

* The investigation was part of a strange proceeding presided over by Judge Charles E. Wyzanski, Jr., in which I was attempting to bring about the revocation of the suspended sentence imposed on a tax-evader named Thomas Worcester. The episode is described in an article entitled "Dirty Money in Boston" by Charles Whipple of *The Boston Globe* in the *Atlantic Monthly* for March 1961.

† Under the "two-witness rule" a defendant could be convicted of perjury only on the testimony of at least two credible witnesses; its purpose was to prevent submitting to a jury the question of who, as between the defendant and one prosecution witness, was telling the truth. The U.S. Penal Code was modified in 1970 to eliminate the two-witness rule for court or grand jury proceedings. If it were still in effect, few of the Watergate perjury indictments could have been brought.

to-endanger in 1951. In May of 1961, when *New York Times* reporter Anthony Lewis walked into Callahan's office to interview him for a series of articles on corruption in Massachusetts, Callahan's greeting to Lewis was "I know why you're here. You're here to help elect your drunken friend Richardson to the United States Senate."

In fact, I had no intention of running for the Senate, but in 1962 I did become a candidate for the Republican nomination for Attorney General of Massachusetts. Callahan's "whisperers" (drifters paid to move from bar to bar in order to plant a rumor against a political enemy) did an effective job. Although I have never in fact had a "drinking problem," the rumor they started in 1962 has continued to surface from time to time. In January 1969, Drew Pearson repeated it in a full column the day before my confirmation hearing for Under Secretary of State (I was then Attorney General of Massachusetts). Foreign Relations Committee confirmation proceedings are usually held in executive session, but I asked Chairman J. William Fulbright to open the hearing so that I could answer the Pearson column for the public record. This I did at considerable length. In five subsequent confirmation hearings for other positions, the committee chairmen, at my request, have put the Foreign Relations Committee testimony in the record.

The awareness that somebody may be looking—or investigating—or leaking—should go a long way toward "supplying the defect of better motives."* Similar prudential considerations, after all, commonly guide day-to-day dealings. Poor Richard was right: honesty *is* the best policy—and a good thing, too. If honesty had to depend only on its morality, there would be a lot less of it. In the case of our political system, not even the

---

* The phrase is from the famous passage of *The Federalist* No. 51 on the separation of powers under the Constitution: "The great security . . . consists in giving to those who administer each department, the necessary constitutional means, and personal motives, to resist encroachments of the others. . . . Ambition must be made to counteract ambition. The interest of the man must be connected with the constitutional rights of the place. . . . This policy of supplying by opposite and rival interests, the defect of better motives, might be traced through the whole system of human affairs, private as well as public." *The Federalist*, ed. Jacob E. Cooke (Middletown, Conn., 1961), p. 349.

public reaction to Watergate could supply overnight the entire
defect of integrity. For the short run, at least, our best hope of
arresting—and reversing—the downward spiral of cynicism and
apathy depends on the awareness that honest politics is the best
politics.

A s t o whether or not the lessons of Watergate are taking hold,
the verdict is still mixed. On the positive side is the evidence that
most candidates in 1974 felt obliged to emphasize their devotion
to the "new politics" of openness, candor, and responsiveness.
Though I have not made a systematic survey, I did play a small
part in the campaigns of over forty candidates in statewide, congressional, and local races and have collected information about
a number of others. Even candidates whose public records and
image made it unnecessary for them to do so went out of their
way to stress their deep-seated devotion to the principles of the
"new politics." Many candidates took the initiative in disclosing
their net worth and even their income tax returns—the first
election in which this has ever been done. A mere delay in releasing income tax returns became an issue in one congressional
district where the Republican challenger for whom I cam-
paigned made this his principal charge against the Democratic
incumbent. Taxes also played a part in the Democratic primary
for the United States Senate in Ohio, in which John Glenn defeated incumbent Senator Howard M. Metzenbaum, although
the situation involved only a legally disputed civil claim against
Senator Metzenbaum.
    The 1974 election also saw candidates voluntarily setting
ceilings on the size of the political contributions they would
accept—most often $100, but always far less than any amount
likely to create a sense of obligation and significantly lower than
the legally permissible maximum contribution.*

    * There are a number of examples of this phenomenon: Maryland Senator
Charles McC. Mathias, Jr.'s limit was $100—whether from an individual or a
group—as was the ceiling imposed by Congressmen Pierre S. du Pont of
Delaware and Stewart B. McKinney of Connecticut in their congressional
campaigns and by Congressman Robert H. Steele in his unsuccessful bid for
Governor of Connecticut. Former Attorney General Ramsey Clark, who
sought the seat held by New York Senator Jacob K. Javits, and Florida

Whenever voters were given the chance to express themselves directly on an issue involving standards of political conduct, they came down overwhelmingly on the side of stiffer
requirements. Examples were "Proposition 9" in California,
hailed by its supporters as the most sweeping reform of campaign financing, lobbying regulation, and conflict of interest in
the nation's history; and "Question 5" in Massachusetts, a campaign financing proposal for which equal claims were made.

What counts most, however, is the outcome of elections. If
the pattern of voter selectivity spells out a message, the candidates running in the next election will remember it even if no
one else does. Future candidates will not easily forget the message communicated by the manner in which voters picked and
chose among the members of the House Judiciary Committee
who sought reelection in 1974: All the Democrats voted for
impeachment; all were reelected. Six Republicans voted for impeachment; five were reelected. Nine Republicans voted against
impeachment; four of the nine lost.

If this were all the evidence there was, the verdict would
be clear. Confusing the picture, however, were a number of
campaigns in which candidates touched by charges of scandal or
conflict of interest were nevertheless reelected. In Pennsylvania,
a well-qualified Republican—Andrew Lewis—tried to capitalize
on the kickback indictments of several members of Governor
Milton Shapp's administration and on the circumstance that the
Governor, because of deductions, had not paid any federal or
state income taxes for several years. Governor Shapp was reelected. In Ohio, the incumbent Governor, John Gilligan, criticized his Republican opponent, former Governor James A.
Rhodes, for failing to answer the charge that he had diverted
campaign contributions for his own use. Governor Gilligan lost.

Governor Reubin Askew considered the primary and the election as "separate"
campaigns, accepting not more than $100 for each. Wisconsin Senator Gaylord
Nelson not only set a $500 limit, but when his campaign budget had been met,
returned proffered contributions. Congressman Paul N. McCloskey, Jr., of
California set his limit at $100 per individual and $500 for any group.
Pennsylvania Senator Richard S. Schweiker did not set a limit lower than that
established by statute, but reported all contributions including those which the
law would have allowed him to lump together as "miscellaneous."

In Nevada, Harry Reid, the Democratic Senate candidate, denounced Paul Laxalt, the Republican candidate, for refusing to disclose his financial holdings. The attack created sympathy for Laxalt, who narrowly won.

But neither these situations nor others somewhat resembling them in Vermont, Kentucky, and Michigan support generalizations about the "post-Watergate morality" any more than do the situations pointing in the opposite direction. Much more significant were the losses of five Republican governorships and forty-three Republican House seats, which brought Republican strength in each of these areas to its lowest level since the 1930s. While polls show that the melancholy state of the economy was a major reason for these losses, they also show that the reaction to Watergate and President Ford's pardon of President Nixon was also a significant factor.

On balance, I read the record of 1974 as pointing toward long-term improvement in the general level of political morality. Candidates and their handlers are aware that elections are decided by marginal shifts of voter sentiment, and notwithstanding the ambiguities just cited, they are far more likely to try to appeal to than to ignore voters who are sensitive to their standards of political conduct. The one really discouraging aspect of the 1974 elections was the low turnout of voters almost everywhere—nationally, only 38 percent of those eligible, the lowest since just after World War II. The explanation, apparently, is that many voters, in reaction to Watergate, must simply have decided to turn off and drop out. By this act, of course, they only succeeded in doing their share to guarantee perpetuation of the very conditions on which they turned their backs.

B U T I F the electorate's 1974 message was ambiguous, there is no reason why it cannot be made clearer in future elections. To restore trust, an increasingly large proportion of us must be willing to communicate with unmistakable force our rejection of narrow, divisive appeals to our selfish and separate interests. As it happens, I am a veteran, a lawyer, a New Englander, and a Harvard man, though not necessarily in that order. I would not, however, appreciate being asked for my vote on the basis that we (veterans) (lawyers) (New Englanders) (Harvard men) should stick together. Such an appeal would diminish either me or the candidate or both. And while it is true, as in the case of "ethnicity,"* that politicians are likely to be the last to ignore any individual attribute that contributes to a sense of personal identity, more and more Americans are demonstrating their impatience with the categories to which the political process used to be confident in assigning them. The breakdown of party affiliation is an indication of this, I believe, as is the tendency toward ticket-splitting. And while this independence in voter attitudes has been costly in terms of the weakening of the two-party system, it is also a mark of growing political maturity.

Is it possible to sustain this growth in maturity while preventing further erosion of the party organizations? The parties are still the indispensable means of selecting candidates, and as party affiliation declines, so also does grass-roots participation in the selection process. The parties are also—or should be—important vehicles for citizen participation in formulating positions on major issues. I have long been convinced that it is in the more vigorous exercise of this function that their hope for salvation lies. The people who volunteer for party service simply because they're "looking for something"—jobs, contracts, or favors—are too few in number to sustain the vigor of the party organizations. The number who become involved in political activity for no more reason than that they enjoy it is also small. Only by adding to these two groups people who really care about what the parties and their candidates stand for can the effectiveness of the two-party system be revived. And this requires a far higher priority for *ideas*, *imagination*, and *issues* than this country has seen for a long time. Without these, the other ingredients of party success—telegenic candidates, effective fund-raising, and good organization—can never be sufficient to check the decay of the party structure.

Politicians will treat us as we insist on being treated. We must show them, therefore, that a crucial element of our trust in

* See Chapter VIII.

them is the degree to which they demonstrate their adherence to the merits—the important facts, competing interests, and significant values—of the issues before them. This is a moral obligation which they undertake when they assume office. Obvious, you say? I thought so too until one day in the spring of 1974 when I tried to answer a professor of political science at a major Eastern university who flatly denied the relevance of morality to politics. "The politician," the professor argued, "is a broker among competing interests and conflicting points of view. The only relevant test of his performance is how well he performs his brokering function. He should not, therefore, in his political capacity, be subject to any moral judgment."

I could scarcely believe my ears. What do you say to that kind of heresy? I came back with some sort of answer, but I wasn't satisfied with it. This is what I now think I should have said:

Those who hold office in a representative democracy are more than brokers. They hold delegated powers. In the exercise of those delegated powers, they are responsible both for the honest exercise of their own independent judgments and for contributing to the possibility of intelligent choice by those they represent. It is this political responsibility which makes it essential that they adhere to the merits of the issues requiring choice. For them consciously to allow purely personal considerations to distort the merits of any issue is, therefore, morally wrong.

Is the desire for election—or reelection—a "purely personal consideration"? It is easy, of course, for a candidate to convince himself that suppressing, shading, or even misrepresenting a personal belief is justified by the greater good that can be accomplished by his holding office. There is something to be said, moreover, for the proposition that a constituency is entitled to have its predominant view reflected by its elected representative even though his personal opinion is to the contrary. The Michigan Congressmen, for example, who had been militant champions of forced busing for the South, but who in 1972 suddenly became vocal opponents of busing when it threatened their own cities, might plausibly have cited both rationalizations. Rationalizations they are, however, in my view. Representatives are more than delegates. As to how much more, Edmund Burke is to me the most persuasive authority: speaking to his constituents in Bristol, Burke emphasized that "your representative owes you, not his industry only, but his judgement; and he betrays, instead of serving you, if he sacrifices it to your opinion."[2] It goes without saying that it takes courage for an officeholder to express a view or take a position contrary to that of the electorate upon whose good will his political survival depends, and courage of that kind will always be rare. John F. Kennedy would not otherwise have been moved to write *Profiles in Courage*. Responsibility to the merits does not cease to be a moral obligation whenever it becomes hard to fulfill.

When decisions, votes, and policies are not based on the merits, when the positions taken by our elected representatives do not reflect their honest convictions, we as citizens cannot fulfill our own responsibilities to the democratic process. We may for a time attempt to penetrate the distortions and half-truths, correct for the angle, and detect the outright fraud, but the task is endless and discouraging. Small wonder in such circumstances that some of us resign ourselves to the assumption that "all politicians are crooks."

Just this was the attitude of all too many Massachusetts citizens in 1959, the year I returned to the state from my first tour at HEW. As the new United States Attorney for the District of Massachusetts, I soon learned why cynicism had become so pervasive. Corruption, that most primitive form of distortion of the merits, was so endemic that people had come to think of it as a normal feature of government business. A crime commission appointed by Governor John A. Volpe, a series of legislative investigations, and a federal grand jury convened by me turned up evidence leading to the prosecution of at least two dozen officials in half a dozen agencies. The most striking feature of the Massachusetts political scene, as I then saw it, was the subordination of programs and principles to personal relationships. Friendships and enmities, loyalties and feuds, courtesies and slights had an importance in determining political alignments that was exceeded only by the pocketbook. Amid the welter of personal conflict, the merits of issues were soon submerged.

As to the whys of this state of affairs, one could only speculate. One factor, certainly, was the indifference of the most comfortable, best-established groups in the community: turning their backs on the messy business of party politics, they satisfied their consciences by immersion in suburban town affairs and in the improvement of the Commonwealth's world-renowned hospitals, educational institutions, and cultural enterprises. Another factor, no doubt, was the spread of an attitude toward politics deriving from the days when an inhospitable Yankee community forced the newly arrived Irish and Italians to turn to political organization as the only available avenue toward security and advancement. In those early days, quite understandably, jobs, contracts, and miscellaneous favors became the lifeblood of Massachusetts politics. They still were, notwithstanding that the circumstances which made them so had long since largely disappeared. But the politician was still expected to go through the old motions, though they no longer served their old purpose. The result of this decline in function was a corresponding decline in status. No longer an esteemed benefactor and not yet a respected public servant, the politician, in the eyes of all too many citizens of Massachusetts, was a mere errand boy, remembered only when there was a ticket or a sidewalk to be fixed.

One of my most publicized cases involved the prosecution of an architect-engineer named Thomas Worcester who, in two and a half years, kicked back nearly $300,000, 10 percent of his gross fees from the Commonwealth of Massachusetts during that period. Some people asked, "What difference does it make? He's a qualified engineer, isn't he?" The answer is simple, and it illustrates what can happen when the merits are distorted. The public is entitled to expect that state agencies will select consulting engineers on the basis of their qualifications, not on the basis of their willingness to kick back a portion of their fees. Moreover, since Worcester's fees were based on a fixed percentage of the total cost of the jobs for which his firm did the engineering design, the money for the kickbacks had to come either out of his overhead or out of his profit—but not likely the latter. Cutting overhead meant cutting corners. Something had to give. One thing that did give was an overpass designed by Worcester's firm. It collapsed, barely missing a bus carrying a full load of passengers.

One afternoon in the summer of 1973, as I listened to George Beall, then United States Attorney for the District of Maryland, describe the rancid deals uncovered by his investigation into kickbacks by Maryland engineers, I recalled with revulsion one of the most powerful impressions of my earlier corruption-fighting days—the feeling that I had turned over a log and exposed to the light a scurrying colony of unpleasant creatures whose only reaction was one of annoyance that I had been so crass as to disturb their settled way of life. *A Heartbeat Away*, Richard M. Cohen and Jules Witcover's book about the investigation and resignation of Spiro T. Agnew, records the same reaction. The County Executive of Anne Arundel County, for example, a Republican named Joseph Alton, acknowledged in 1973 that he, too, was under investigation in the spreading kickback scandal.* "Alton insisted—" wrote Cohen and Witcover, "in an observation most revealing of the mind of a Maryland politician—that while he had probably done some indictable things in his time, he had never done anything wrong!"[3]

Alton might have been speaking for Spiro T. Agnew as well as himself. It was foreseeable in the summer of 1973 when I was negotiating with Agnew's counsel that this would be his attitude. It was also foreseeable that any disposition of the government's charges against him short of a jail sentence would lead many people to feel that the former Vice-President had benefited from a deal unattainable by any ordinary citizen. The Vice-President had a bargaining asset, however, that no ordinary person has: he was next in line to the Presidency. I saw no

---

* Alton later pleaded guilty to a charge of conspiracy to obstruct interstate commerce. On December 12, 1974, hundreds of his friends paid $10 a head to attend a "Thanks Joe" fund-raiser. Reported the Washington *Star-News* the next day: " 'This is one time the money that's been raised will be properly reported to you,' the 55-year-old Alton jokingly told the applauding crowd in the smoke-filled National Guard Armory."

chance that he would resign first, then take his chances on trial, conviction, and jail.

Richard Nixon was in deep trouble. And though I was not then aware of evidence personally implicating him in the Watergate cover-up, I had to reckon with the possibility that protection of the principle of confidentiality might not be the complete explanation of his refusal to surrender the subpoenaed tapes. Depending on what further investigation might disclose, it was possible that impeachment proceedings against the President might be taking place in the House at the same time as the charges against the Vice-President were being tried in the Senate. Alternatively, the Vice-President might be awaiting trial in a federal court, and the whole process, including the preliminary disposition of constitutional issues, the trial itself, and subsequent appeals, might take two years or more.* Agnew had the right in any case to put the government to its proof in one forum or the other. If, meanwhile, the Presidency should fall vacant, he would automatically succeed to it.

It seemed to me in the circumstances that Agnew's resignation must have first priority. But it was also essential to minimize the damage to public confidence in the law-enforcement system that would inevitably result from the short-circuiting of a full-scale trial. If Agnew was to be allowed to plead to one tax-evasion charge only and to receive a suspended sentence, it would have to be on the basis of a public record which disclosed all the pertinent facts. Agnew himself would acknowledge the validity of the government's case; a summary of our evidence, all of it under oath, would be filed with the court; and I would explain the considerations leading me to believe that a no-jail disposition was in the public interest. Negotiations with opposing counsel focused mainly on the Agnew statement, and on this score I agreed in the end to somewhat less than we wanted. This

* In our brief in opposition to the attempt by Agnew's lawyers to enjoin the Department of Justice from presenting evidence against him to a federal grand jury, we argued that a Vice-President could be tried and indicted by a federal court but conceded that he could also be impeached by the House and tried by the Senate. For this reason we stated that after indictment but before trial we intended to inform the House that our evidence would be made available to it if it chose to initiate impeachment proceedings.

concession was counterbalanced, however, by an even more complete summary of our evidence than I had originally hoped to get into the record.

Anthony Lewis of *The New York Times* has written that "the trouble with the Agnew deal, on reflection, is that in making it Elliot Richardson played God. He balanced all the interests as he saw them and made the final judgment himself, instead of trusting the institutions of law and politics to work."[4] The fact is, of course, that I could not escape responsibility for balancing all the interests as I saw them: had I come out the other way, it would have been because I gave greater weight to the importance of a full-scale trial than to the urgency of making room for a new Vice-President. The institutions of law also had their chance. The final judgment was not mine but that of a well-respected federal judge, Walter E. Hoffman, Chief Judge of the Eastern District of Virginia, the counterpart for that district of Chief Judge John Sirica of the District of Columbia. Courts that can command the obedience of a President can decline to accept the recommendation of an Attorney General.

EVEN MORE IMPORTANT to the restoration of trust than our rejection of divisive appeals and our insistence on adherence to the merits is the premium we attach to truthfulness in public transactions. Of course, truth is always important to a free society. It becomes uniquely important, however, when it is needed to neutralize the acid of cynicism. It takes far more consistent adherence to truth to restore confidence than simply to maintain it. Restoring it is like trying to brake a runaway freight car. Much more energy is required to slow the car down, stop it, then start it in the opposite direction, than is needed just to keep it moving.

The point is dramatized by the contrast between the current attitude toward government credibility and that which prevailed in 1958 when Gary Powers, an American pilot, was shot down over the USSR while flying a U-2 reconnaissance plane. The American government at first insisted that Powers was on a routine weather-research flight, but it soon emerged that the Soviets had in their possession Powers's aerial camera complete with exposed film. I was then a member of the Eisenhower administration and still remember the sense of humiliation felt by most Americans when the State Department had to swallow its cover story and admit that Powers had, indeed, been taking pictures over Soviet territory.

Describing this incident in his memoir, *Waging Peace*, President Eisenhower wrote, "In the diplomatic field it was routine practice to deny responsibility for an embarrassing occurrence when there is even a 1 percent chance of being believed, but when the world can entertain not the slightest doubt of the facts there is no point in trying to evade the issue."[5] If, in other words, we had had any chance whatever of being believed, we should have continued to lie. But this was at a time when the government was generally assumed to be truthful. It was long before Vietnam and Watergate had so badly damaged government's credibility. Now, as in reversing the runaway freight car, we must exert much more effort to restore credibility than was needed simply to maintain it. That is why it is essential for us to place a higher premium on candor and openness, honesty and truth than ever before.

But a premium on truth without access to truth is an unredeemed promise. The ways in which government acquires, controls, and uses information are crucial to all its relationships with the citizen. During my five months at the Department of Justice I had to deal with one problem after another involving some aspect of information management or information-gathering. In June came the testimony on freedom of information, executive privilege, and secrecy in government referred to in the previous chapter, and that month also saw the beginning of the effort to develop clear guidelines for electronic surveillance. In July, HEW Secretary Caspar W. Weinberger and I jointly announced the report of the Advisory Committee on Automated Personal Data Systems. Then followed in rapid succession the start of a government-wide study of the administration of the Freedom of Information Act, the order requiring the recording of outsiders' contacts with the Department,* and the

* See Chapter II.

issuance of instructions prohibiting the subpoena of any news-man except at the personal direction of the Attorney General. The chronic issue of prejudicial pretrial publicity was inflamed in August by Agnew's claim that the Department had leaked information about its investigation of him, and we had to launch an intensive inquiry into that charge. (So far as we could find out, the critical leaks had come from Agnew's own staff.)

While looking back over this experience, I came across James Madison's statement, "A popular Government, without popular information, or the means of acquiring it, is but the Prologue to a Farce or a Tragedy; or, perhaps both."[6] I was struck by its relevance to Watergate. Here, with a vengeance, was a government responsible to the people which had deprived them both of information and of the means of acquiring it. The consequence, which had at first seemed only the prologue to a farce, soon became the prologue to a tragedy and, for the Watergate actors, tragedy itself. But for the impetus it gave to the adoption of reforms and the restoration of openness, Watergate might have been a tragedy for popular government also.

In a sense, all the abuses of Watergate had been abuses of information: its theft, distortion, fabrication, misuse, misrepresentation, concealment, and suppression. Once you see it, the thread is plain. It runs from one Watergate abuse to the next and binds them all. For example:

> Theft of information: the bugging of Democratic National Headquarters; the break-in of Dr. Lewis Fielding's office to get Ellsberg's psychiatric records; the hiring of spies to steal information from the camps of political opponents.
>
> Distortion of information: this, for the electorate, was the net effect of illegal corporate campaign contributions; it also appeared in the slanted editing of Presidential tape recordings.
>
> Fabrication of information: this included the forgery during the New Hampshire primary of a letter purporting to be from Senator Muskie in which the word "Canuck" was used; the forged cable implicating the late President

Kennedy in the murder of Diem; the plan to use a national security "cover" for the Fielding break-in.

Misuse of information: under this heading came attempts to get the IRS to use income tax returns as the basis for investigating political enemies; efforts to exploit FBI files for "dirty tricks"; overtures to the CIA aimed at subverting its intelligence-gathering function.

Misrepresentation of information: a polite word for lies like President Nixon's bald assertion, "Far from trying to hide the facts, my effort throughout has been to discover the facts"; schemes to make the public believe that the Watergate break-in was being thoroughly investigated; the perjury that stretched from one case to another in a rancid sequence relieved only by the unintentional humor of the Presidential Press Secretary's announcement that all previous statements on Watergate were "inoperative."

Concealment of information: the payment of hush money; the omission of damaging portions of tapes; the shredding and destruction of documents; the attempts to exploit executive privilege as a means of shutting off the flow of information.

Suppression of information: the all-out effort to keep the lid on the investigation; the attempt to use "national security" as an excuse for covering up; the entire conspiracy to obstruct justice.

But if the wrongs of Watergate were sins against the sanctity of information, the events leading to redress of those wrongs were acts of redemption for the sanctity of information—investigating it, extracting it, leaking it, confessing it, revealing it, publishing it. The unfolding drama of Watergate centered on this interweaving of abuse and investigation, concealment and disclosure. Both the turning point and the dénouement hinged on revelations, the former (the almost casual disclosure by Presidential assistant Alexander P. Butterfield that all conversations with Nixon were recorded) leading inexorably to the latter (the damning conversation of June 23, 1972, in which President Nixon ordered a halt to the investigation of the Watergate break-in).

Like the Watergate wrongs and the manner of their redress, the reforms to which they have given impetus also concern information. In the case, for example, of the theft of information, little can be done to strengthen the laws against burglary, but much can be done to provide better protection of personal information. And just such legislation, as we know from Chapter I, has been spurred by Watergate: tightening of the court-order requirements for electronic surveillance, a code of fair information practices for automated personal data systems, and tighter restrictions on the availability of criminal histories. The second type of abuse—distortion of information—has been the target of campaign-reform legislation. Lest there be any doubt on the point, it is worth emphasizing that the purpose of this kind of legislation is to prevent distortion. After all, dirty money creates obligations which, because they are undisclosed, the voter cannot take into account; dirty tricks create false impressions of the opposing candidate and his organization. As to fabrication, there is still a need to stiffen the penalties against "dirty tricks" through legislation along the lines of the Code of Fair Campaign Practices mentioned in Chapter I. In the case of the other abuses of information listed above, the obvious reason why reform proposals have not surfaced is that changes in existing law—the penalties for perjury, for instance—would not appreciably narrow the range or reduce the risk of future abuses.

IN THE SAME PASSAGE in which Madison referred to popular government without popular information as the prologue to a farce or a tragedy, he went on to say, "Knowledge will forever govern ignorance: And a people who mean to be their own Governors, must arm themselves with the power which knowledge gives."[7] Whether regarded as the prologue to a farce or a tragedy, Watergate dramatized the tension between government's affirmative responsibility for the disclosure of information and government's responsibility to protect information against disclosure. As between the two responsibilities, it seems to me clear that the people's right to "arm themselves with the power which knowledge gives" must have precedence. It cannot be an absolute priority, of course; its effect, rather, should be to place a heavy burden on the justification of nondisclosure.

On their face, the exemptions from disclosure specified in the Freedom of Information Act sustain that burden—they cover, for instance, things like instructions to the negotiators of government contracts, FBI procedures for protecting the lives of kidnapping victims and dealing with aircraft hijackers, confidential information furnished to regulatory agencies, and, of course, genuine national security information. These exemptions, however, are not self-executing. Much depends on the spirit in which they are administered. As Attorney General, I attempted to encourage more sympathetic and consistent administration of the Act: for example, by persuading the Civil Service Commission to include instruction on the subject in its training programs, convening an interagency symposium on its administration, and launching a government-wide study of how the executive branch could better organize itself to administer the Act. Finally, just before leaving the Justice Department I ordered the Civil Division not to defend any government agency against a freedom of information lawsuit unless the agency had consulted the Department's Freedom of Information Committee before finally denying any request for information.*

By the time I left Justice, I had become convinced that these steps were too limited. For one thing, they were not adequate to assure consistency in resolving conflicts between the right to know and the legitimate qualifications of that right. Nor was a department, responsible for defending other agencies against demands for disclosing information, in the best possible position to tell them how to balance those interests. At the time of my resignation I was planning to convene a broadly representative group charged both with following through on the report of the HEW Advisory Committee on Automated Personal Data Systems and with responsibility for the work just getting under

* On October 17, 1974, President Ford vetoed a series of amendments to the 1974 Freedom of Information Act; Congress overrode the veto in February 1975. From the standpoint of the executive branch, the most objectionable amendment called for judicial review of classified information to determine whether or not it could be withheld.

way on administration of the Freedom of Information Act.* Although I failed to persuade my successor, William B. Saxbe, to go forward with this project, I still think that it would be useful to approach informational issues from a perspective embracing the entire range from situations in which the government has a duty to disclose information to situations in which the government has a duty to protect information from disclosure. I constantly hear well-meaning civil libertarians shift back and forth, sometimes in the same sentence, between criticism of one government agency for the failure to protect information from disclosure and criticism of another agency for refusing to disclose information.†

In addition to access to information and, where justified, the protection of information, another essential element of trust in government is reliability of information. Not only government actions but countless private decisions depend on the accuracy and objectivity of the data collected by government information-gathering agencies. There must be no room for doubt about the honesty and accuracy of agencies like the Census Bureau, the Bureau of Economic Analysis of the Commerce Department, the National Center for Health Statistics in HEW, or the Statistical Reporting Service of the Department of Agriculture. This consideration requires that they be headed by experienced career professionals enjoying the civil service protection which enables them to resist the pressure of political officeholders who do not like what they report. It also requires alertness on the part of the consumers of statistics—who include the general public—in resisting any threat to the independence of their agencies. When, in 1971, the White House attempted to

---

* The staff director for this combined project would have been David B. H. Martin, who, as executive director of the Advisory Committee, had been both the innovative and the driving force behind its recommendations.

† At a Senate hearing on legislation to implement the recommendations of the Automated Personal Data Systems report, I suggested the creation of a statutory commission charged with developing government policies for this whole spectrum of issues. Joint Hearings before the Ad Hoc Subcommittee on Privacy and Information Systems of the Committee on Government Operations and the Subcommittee on Constitutional Rights of the Committee on the Judiciary, 93d Congress, 2d Session (1974), pp. 44–45, 50–51.

assert political control over the Department of Labor's Bureau of Labor Statistics in order to be able to slant its employment data in a direction favorable to the Nixon administration, the resulting public outcry was amply justified. Given professional responsibility and public vigilance, no additional statutory or administrative safeguard is needed. Without this combination, no such safeguard will suffice.

ADEQUATE ACCESS to reliable information will not only contribute to restoring trust in the democratic process but help to assure the quality of the process. Having met thousands of people from all sorts of backgrounds in all parts of America, I know that this country does not lack thoughtful, conscientious citizens. Not everyone, of course, can have an informed opinion about everything. Most individual Americans, nevertheless, are fully capable of making sensible judgments about important issues. More of us are better educated than ever before, but education is not the *sine qua non* of responsible citizenship. A lack of education is not to be confused with a lack of intelligence.

As important, in any case, as the ability to make independent judgments about complicated issues is the ability to decide on whom to rely for such judgments. Ordinarily intelligent but poorly educated individuals commonly make astute assessments of the degree to which they can safely trust a better-educated person. Some of the men in my medical basic training platoon at Camp Pickett, Virginia, in the summer of 1942 were college graduates; others had never gone beyond grammar school. Most of our officer instructors were M.D.s. The men whose formal education had been cut short were at least as well able as the college graduates to spot the fakers among our instructors. The explanation, I think, is that the intelligent individual who is conscious of having to depend upon the advice, judgment, or leadership of better-educated hierarchical superiors cultivates an instinctive ability to identify those whom he can safely trust. It is a compensatory talent developed in somewhat the same way that a blind person learns to rely on a sharpened sense of hearing. If I am right, this goes a long way toward explaining why our democracy has worked as well as it has for as long as it has.

But if democracy is not endangered by a decline in the supply of thoughtful, conscientious citizens armed with accessible and reliable information, it is threatened by an explosive growth in the volume of competing claims for our attention. Our capacity to reach reasonably informed judgments about anything is on the verge of being overwhelmed. As the result, perhaps, of my own involvement in four efforts during three years to compete for the attention of my fellow citizens (two statewide political campaigns, one Greater Boston United Fund campaign, and a campaign for the enactment of a state sales tax), I first began to be seriously disturbed about this problem in 1965. The intervening years have not reassured me. Nor did Russell Baker, writing in October 1974:

> We consume our history so fast to get on to the next tidbit that there is no time to digest it, and so become a people without memory.
>
> Whatever happened to George McGovern? Who was Elliott [sic] Richardson? Where is little Tania's Leningrad diary?[8]

The situation would be bad enough if we had only complexity to cope with. As it is, trivia multiply at least as fast as complexities. And as the serious demands on our attention grow greater, so also do the influences tending to distract it. *The problem, I suspect, has no real solution.* It can only be minimized. For this purpose a combination of responses is necessary. Several— improvement in the capacity for synthesis, the simplification of governmental choices, and a heightened awareness of the responsibilities of citizenship—will be discussed in other chapters of this book. That leaves the question of whether the media can or should be more helpful to the citizen as he tries to pick his way through the clutter.

On the face of it, the answer to this question turns both on what the media are willing to sell and on what the citizen is willing to buy. As some astute commentator on the fourth estate every once in a while discovers, the media are in business for profit. Indeed, it is difficult to imagine any basis on which they could otherwise be at once popularly accessible, rich in variety, and free of government control. The very characteristics of the media that are least helpful from the standpoint of the conscientious citizen struggling to be informed—stress on the dramatic, the colorful, and the topical at the expense of the significant, the sober, and the enduring—may be necessary to attract the attention of a wider audience to important subjects.

Even so, it is fairly arguable that the media tend both to underestimate the maturity of their audiences and to overindulge the impulse to cultivate their least responsible customers. Granted that a clash between personalities is ordinarily of more interest to most people than the objective exposition of a serious issue (and that many people will never be aware of the serious issue unless they are exposed to it through the personality clash), the tendency of political journalists to exploit the "let's you and him fight" gambit is often overenthusiastic. It is one thing to report a conflict between personalities, but quite another to foment one. Mark Harris, in "The Last Article," a *New York Times Magazine* essay subtitled "Freedom *From* the Press," remarks:

> To the brain damaged by media, whenever two objects exist they must be placed in competition—cops and robbers, success and failure, Democrats and Republicans, win and lose, guilty and innocent, happy and sad, yes and no. A conflict must always be established, a face, a contest; and, whenever possible, someone must be drawn into the trap of saying something provocative about someone else.[9]

Although I repeatedly noted this tendency during my years as an elected officeholder in Massachusetts, I supposed that it was more characteristic of the provinces than of Washington. Not so: virtually every press contact I had at the State Department sought to inflate or create some "rift" between Secretary of State William P. Rogers and me or Presidential assistant Henry A. Kissinger and me or among the three of us. My very first press conference at HEW featured the same kind of attempt as between my predecessor, Robert H. Finch, and me and Presidential assistant John D. Ehrlichman and me. One has to be careful in responding to such attempts or one may create a strain where none existed before.

The aim of creating news also lies behind efforts to elicit an answer that would be newsworthy only if it was ill-advised. I have held scores of press conferences in which it was obvious that there was no way in which I could expect anything I said to receive more than local coverage (if that) unless I put my foot in my mouth. At lunch with editors and reporters of *The Washington Post* a few days after an HEW press conference, I complained that what I had said—although some of it seemed to me important—did not receive a single line of national coverage. "But you didn't give a direct answer to my question about what you think of Senator Long's handling of welfare reform," said a reporter who had been present.

"Of course not," I replied. "I'm all for candor but I'm not stupid."

In *The Center*, a perceptive book about the nation's capital, the late Stewart Alsop compared the Washington press corps to a pack of beagles:

> There is even a physical resemblance: not all reporters have stumpy legs and prominent tails (though some do), but almost all develop in time the anxious, preoccupied, self-important air of beagles. The resemblance, however, is more spiritual than physical.
>
> The beagle is a highly competitive dog, but he is always ready to follow uncritically any other beagle who claims to have smelled a rabbit. When one beagle gives tongue, all the others instantly join in, and off the whole pack scurries, each beagle yelping like mad in order to convince the onlookers that he was really the first to pick up the scent. Sometimes the scent is actually that of a rabbit, but quite often the beagles, as they chase each other around in circles, giving tongue lustily, are simply smelling each other.[10]

The tendency of the Washington press to travel in a pack, Alsop pointed out, "helps to create one of the most striking phenomena of Washington journalism: the fashions in news."[11] One subject will suddenly become journalistically fashionable, then just as suddenly go out of fashion. No less than in the garment indus-try, this characteristic derives its justification from the pressures of competition: no newspaper or network can afford to let the others get ahead, and the best protection against that danger is to stay with them.

For the general public, the price of fashion in news is high in terms of the neglect of other important developments. Nor can this cost be excused on the basis that this is what the audi-ence wants: on the contrary, the public is likely to be bored long before the fashion changes. For government officials vogues in the news can be sheer exasperation. During the six months from midsummer 1971 to midwinter 1972, I well remember that no matter what I had to say about welfare reform or national health insurance or juvenile delinquency prevention, I scarcely ever got a question from the press about anything but busing. The questions were never new, and neither were my answers. Had I known that the subject would be fashionable for so long, I should have made a recording of all the usual questions and answers, handed it out at the start of every press conference, and saved time all around.

The kinds of excesses I have been describing have at least the excuse of competitive zeal. The chronic use of labels, stereo-types, and clichés to characterize people and events has no such excuse. It can be accounted for only by laziness. In Douglass Cater's novel *Dana*, a former top-level government administra-tor complains:

> They assign you an adjective early in your career. "Smart," "Tricky," "Ruthless," "Wheeler-dealer." It's a matter of chance which adjective you get. But once you've got it, all the powers of heaven and hell can't change it. They put it in their clip files and every time they do a story on you, out it comes. Washington is a city of one-adjective men, branded for life by the press.[12]

As one who has often felt diminished by labels ("Boston Brahmin," for instance), I applaud the crusade against them conducted by Richard Harwood who, when he was *The Wash-ington Post*'s "ombudsman," wrote: "The label is not the animal and we in the news business ought to know that by now and know, too, that the labels and stereotypes we deal in—wittingly or not—are often more disturbing and confusing to the audience out there than the people and conditions we hang them on."[13]

"The publishing business," observed Supreme Court Justice Potter Stewart in a sesquicentennial speech at the Yale Law School in 1974, "is . . . the only organized private business that is given explicit Constitutional protection."[14] The First Amendment forbids any "prior restraint" on the freedom of the press— it forbids, for example, injunctions against the publication of material allegedly damaging to the national security or against the publication of a concededly libelous attack. Even after publication, a libelous attack on a public figure is actionable only if he can show that the publisher maliciously disseminated a damaging untruth. Nor can newspapers be required to grant a "right of reply" to political candidates they have criticized. Unlike the British, we have no Official Secrets Act and have virtually abolished contempt proceedings for pretrial publicity.

It follows, as Justice Stewart pointed out, that government cannot "regulate the press so as to make it a genuinely fair and open 'market place for ideas.'" Nor would I, even if I could, reinterpret the First Amendment so as to make this possible. Deeply as I believe that "a genuinely fair and open 'market place for ideas'" is vital to the proper role of the citizen as I conceive it, I cannot imagine any way in which government could be given the power to supervise the fairness of the press or other media that would not risk more than it accomplished. If Watergate taught us nothing else, it showed us how dependent we are on the media's exercise of *their* freedom for the preservation of *ours*. The question of how the media can become more useful to the citizen is addressed, therefore, not to government, but to the media themselves. What standards of self-restraint—and affirmative responsibility—should accompany their unique and extraordinary power?

Some media managers, to be sure, resist the imputation of power. Newspaper publishers point to the powerful competition of the electronic media in their circulation zones. And yet only 215 cities in the United States now have more than one newspaper, and in all but 60 of these the papers have a single owner. The progressive decline of newspaper competition coupled with the growth of television network news has increased the relative power of both. As to the latter, no greater power to influence public opinion has ever existed than to select and edit the items making up network news programs. The early evening programs reach an estimated 42 million people simultaneously. And yet network executives, when I have confronted them with the enormity of their responsibility, have uniformly exhibited a "who, me?" reaction. They prefer to believe that they are merely transmitters of "the news," as if "the news" were a tangible object which anyone could readily recognize when he saw it.

In fact, television news coverage is even more prone than the print media to let the immediate drive out the important, the sensational supersede the significant. I vividly recall a Senate committee hearing which had begun with TV lights blazing and cameras grinding while four Senators, one after another, delivered blatantly oversimplified—even demagogic—statements attacking the position which they knew that I, as lead-off witness, would be advocating. There was no way I could compress a reply into thirty or forty seconds—the outside limit of TV news time that I might hope for. I could only preface my prepared statement by telling the Senators that it would answer them in due course. At this point bells rang to announce a roll call. During the recess I complained to CBS correspondent Daniel Schorr that the situation seemed to me unfairly rigged. "I sympathize," he told me, "but there's nothing you can do about it. Television news programs can't communicate truth. They can only project shadows of the truth—like Plato's shadows in the cave. We can't use your kind of careful, deliberate statement—we just don't have the time."

Only one other institution in this country possesses concentrated and unreviewable power to an extent comparable to the media. That is the Supreme Court itself. And as in the case of the Supreme Court, the institution's own self-restraint is our only protection against the abuse of power. Although the Court has not always exercised the degree of restraint which my revered teachers Felix Frankfurter and Learned Hand thought appropriate for an appointive body with unlimited tenure, it does to some extent, as Mr. Dooley put it, "follow th'iliction returns." President Franklin D. Roosevelt's Court-packing plan aroused widespread criticism, but it was in fact followed by a shift in the Court's attitude toward New Deal legislation.

The media, too, are conscious that in the long run they cannot afford to arouse serious distrust and antagonism. For them, the analogy to the Court-packing plan was the Agnew antimedia campaign of 1969–1971. Agnew's strictures against the media also aroused criticism, and in many of the same quarters. His complaints sounded a note, however, that awoke sympathetic vibrations in people who had no use for Agnew personally and who would hate to have to credit him with helping to stimulate the kind of self-criticism so admirably epitomized by the *Washington Post* study referred to above.

For all I know, of course, the Agnew offensive may have had no causal connection whatever with the *Post*'s introspection. Neither does the sequence of events prove that the Court-packing plan caused the Supreme Court's shift. But the date when the *Post* appointed its first ombudsman—November 1970 —is suggestive. Even more so is Philip L. Geyelin's introduction to the *Post* study. Mr. Geyelin, the editor of the *Post* editorial page, quotes Walter Lippmann's 1920 warning that, if publishers do not attempt to deal with "an increasingly angry disillusionment about the press, . . . some day Congress, in a fit of temper, egged on by an outraged public opinion, will operate on the press with an ax." Mr. Geyelin comments: "If that counsel was appropriate to the 1920s, the evidence of our senses commends it more than ever in the 1970s."[15]

Mr. Geyelin is right, with this qualification—Supreme Court decisions since 1920 have radically diminished the size of any axe the Congress could now get its hands on without amending the Constitution first. The important point, however, is not what the threat of reprisal makes prudent, but what responsibility requires. It would be no more fair to the media than to the Supreme Court to leave it that their exercise of restraint is only a reaction to external pressures. Notwithstanding the profit motive, most of the people who run the media recognize—and act upon—a higher sense of obligation.* I feel sure they would agree with a statement by Walter Lippmann written forty years after the warning quoted above: "Responsible journalism is journalism responsible in the last analysis to the editor's own conviction of what, whether interesting or only important, is in the public interest."[16]

But what should the media do to establish a broader and firmer base for the high standards maintained by their most responsible members? Achievement of this objective would at the same time afford a means of adjudicating legitimate complaints and provide a vehicle for creating public confidence in the media. The media's leading spokesmen, however, have strongly resisted proposals for a national monitoring body acting under an established code of standards to hear and adjudicate complaints. They fear that such a body would threaten to encroach upon First Amendment territory. Codes alone, without adjudicating machinery, have also been resisted, allegedly because they serve only as pious admonitions useful mainly for their public relations value—which, it is said, is all that is accomplished by codes of ethics like that of the American Bar Association. Underlying this criticism, I suspect, is the fear that the existence of a code would lead to the creation of some kind of enforcement process. It seems difficult to account, otherwise, for the ferocity of the media attacks on the recommendations of the Reardon Commission for standards of fairness in the reporting of judicial proceedings notwithstanding the fact that the Commission's recommendations were directed to counsel and not to the press.†

Given these attitudes, it is not surprising that the National News Council, which was established in 1973 in accordance with a recommendation of the Twentieth Century Fund, has

* The American Society of Newspaper Editors is, as of this writing, drafting a new code of ethics which will be the first revision of the Canons of Journalism since they were established in 1923.

† The regulations have since been incorporated into the American Bar Association's Code of Professional Responsibility and adopted as a court rule in the federal courts.

so far had only a limited impact. A private and independent institution, the Council has the function of examining and reporting on complaints concerning the accuracy and fairness of news reporting. Its jurisdiction is limited to the principal national suppliers of news, which include the major wire services, weekly news magazines, newspapers, and television and radio networks. The Council has no regulatory power and does not operate under any published code of standards. Its influence depends solely on publication of its findings.*

Among the National News Council's sharpest critics are James Reston, Max Frankel, and Tom Wicker of *The New York Times*. Regarding the Council as a combined judge and jury, they have refused to cooperate with it in any way. Other press people are less critical but doubt the Council's potential effectiveness; *Washington Post* publisher Katharine Graham commented that it "may be peripheral if not merely cosmetic." Of some 250 complaints received in its first year, the Council adjudicated 44 and, of that number, upheld only 4. While this record may reassure those who feared that news organizations would be bombarded by Council criticism, it gives credence to the impression that the Council is ineffective or not sufficiently discriminating in judgment. In any case, the greatest obstacle to the Council's development to date is public ignorance of its existence or its function; to survive and gain greater effectiveness it has to become more widely known.

Resisting the jurisdiction of an external body but recognizing a responsibility for self-policing through internal means, several newspapers have in-house ombudsmen charged with relaying reader complaints to the appropriate staff members and providing critiques of daily news coverage in memos to the editors. *The Washington Post* is the leading representative of this group; the independence of its present ombudsman is reinforced by a contract under which the temptation to pull his punches is eliminated by a provision barring him from any sub-

---

* Local variants of the News Council approach are being tried through the journalism reviews that are now published in fourteen major cities, or through statewide press councils which operate in three states—Minnesota, Hawaii, and California.

sequent editorial position with the paper. Other newspapers rely on prominently featured letters-to-the-editor columns or "op ed" pieces as outlets for critical or opposing views.

From a strictly legal standpoint, there is no basis for the concern that a nongovernmental external body having some measure of responsibility for discipline or regulation of the media might encroach on First Amendment territory. The First Amendment prohibition against abridgment of the freedom of the press has no application to a private agency which can act only in situations where its jurisdiction has been voluntarily accepted. I can understand what worries the media, however, to the extent that the voluntary acceptance of such jurisdiction could create pressures toward compliance with external controls which might conflict with the commands of conscience.

Out of this debate, I hope, will come in due course a broader base for responsible self-government by the media. We can be grateful, meanwhile, for the indications that leading representatives of the media are more actively seeking to meet the need for a steady, long-range look at the urgent issues of the foreseeable future. *The New York Times*, for example, at intervals throughout 1974, published a thoroughly researched, highly informative series on the world food crisis. I also found impressive the essay by Philip Foisie, assistant managing editor of *The Washington Post*, which was included among the papers published in the previously mentioned self-study. Mr. Foisie noted that the paper had not "developed the knack of identifying and writing regularly about problems before they become crises, especially when those problems first appear at a distance, are hard to tell and hard to explain to the reader, and generally fail to conform to our definition of 'news.' "[17] He went on to identify some of the trends—among them the limit of resources, limits on growth, the limits of power, and the spread of terror—that he thought would govern news developments through the 1970s.

By way of encouragement to the news media while they continue to work at the task of strengthening their own standards of responsibility, I cannot improve the substance (though I have slightly amended the transcript) of what I said at the close of a speech to the American Society of Newspaper Editors in Atlanta in the spring of 1974:

> One thing, in any event, is clear: there cannot be, there should not be any external authority capable of reviewing the degree of responsibility with which you exercise your own obligations to the truth.
>
> And because of the higher premium on the truth that should now exist, you have a harder job than you have ever had before. I can only urge that you search your consciences, that you pray, worry, and work at the task, but keep your sense of humor—and make sure that you take enough time off and have enough fun so that you don't get all uptight about your awesome role.

In the end, our ability as citizens to assure that we are well served by our purveyors of information is as good as, if no better than, our ability to assure that we are well served by our politicians. For the amoral officeholder, we, the people, are the "someone" who may be watching. For the high-minded public servant, we are the source of his recognition and reward. And if there is to be a premium on truth, it must be the premium we place on it. So it is with the media also. The Supreme Court *may* follow the election returns. The media *certainly* follow their circulation figures and their Nielsen ratings.

But then, the survival of our system has always depended on us, the people. This was the most radical—and the most innovative—of the ideas that emerged from Philadelphia in 1787: the idea that all the institutions of government are representative of the people and continually accountable to us, thus giving us a permanent stake in the exercise of power and in the protection of our individual interests.

The ultimate corruption—the ultimate cynicism—is a loss of trust and confidence in ourselves.

IV

Excessive Expectations:
The Necessity for Choice

M ANY OF US who joined President Eisenhower's administration at the beginning of his second term came to
Washington in high hopes of helping to build a new political
consensus. As we visualized it, this consensus would rest on a
strong belief in the individual tempered by the awareness that in
a modern industrial society government must assume ultimate
responsibility for protecting the individual against the harshest
consequences of freely operating economic forces. We were
embarking, we thought, on an important joint venture whose
goal was nothing less than the creation of an exciting new blend
of conservatism and compassion.* Our philosophy began and,
some people thought, ended with an utterance by Abraham Lincoln which we quoted at every opportunity: "The purpose of
government is to do for people what they cannot do at all or do
so well for themselves."

* This belief had received an encouraging boost from *A Republican Looks
at His Party* (New York, 1956), Assistant Secretary of Labor Arthur Larsen's
then recent book on "modern Republicanism."

President Eisenhower himself had given a lift to our enthusiasm in his victory speech to the nation on election night:

> ... And now let me say something that looks to the future. I think that modern republicanism has now proved itself. And America has approved of modern republicanism.
>
> And so, as we look ahead—as we look ahead to the problems in front, let us remember that a political party deserves the approbation of America only as it represents the ideals, the aspirations and the hopes of Americans. If it is anything less, it is merely a conspiracy to seize power and the Republican party is not that!
>
> Modern republicanism looks to the future. . . .[1]

The budget sent to the Congress by President Eisenhower on January 16, 1957, seemed to reflect this sense of commitment to the future. The requested appropriations for resource development and welfare programs called for substantial increases, and funds for a new program of federal aid to school construction were also requested. The total budget was $72 billion, $3 billion more than the previous year and $12 billion higher than the objective proclaimed in the first Eisenhower campaign four years earlier. (A decade later, "modern Republicans" would have more than enough reason to be skeptical of "throwing money at problems." But for the moment dollars were our—and the public's—main measure of commitment to social problem-solving.)

As things turned out, the high hopes of "modern Republicans" were swamped by the backwash of another statement made later on the same day the President submitted his budget. Responding to a press conference question, George M. Humphrey, Eisenhower's self-assured and opinionated Secretary of the Treasury, warned that federal spending must be cut or, he asserted, "I will predict that you will have a depression that will curl your hair . . . there are a lot of places in this budget that can be cut."[2]

Then brand-new to the job of Assistant Secretary of Health, Education, and Welfare for Legislation, I confidently assured my staff that this was nothing to worry about. The budget was the President's document, not the Secretary of the Treasury's. It had, moreover, been in preparation for months, and most departments and agencies had already been subjected to reductions substantially below their requests. I was wrong. In a press conference three days later President Eisenhower said:

> Well, in my own instructions to the Cabinet and heads of all offices, I have told them that every place that there is a chance to save a dollar out of the money that we have budgeted ... everybody that is examining the many details ... ought to find someplace where they might save another dollar.[3]

Later that week I attended a meeting in the Cabinet Room at which Presidential assistant Bryce Harlow passed on instructions to the same general effect. "So far as HEW is concerned," I said with a degree of brashness that it surprises me to remember, "we aren't going to admit that the President didn't know what he was doing when he submitted our budget."

The Humphrey attack aroused misgivings in President Eisenhower which he never wholly shook off. From 1957 on, the thrust of a confident new philosophy gave way to a halfhearted, halfway approach to domestic issues. Neither the "conservatives" nor the "moderates" of the President's own party were satisfied. And instead of taking part in an exciting joint effort to build a new majority, I found myself spending large parts of the next three years doing battle on behalf of HEW programs against the chronic negativism of White House and Budget Bureau staff. That was the era which inspired *Washington Post* cartoonist Herblock to invent the label "Department of Not-Too-Much HEW," and he wasn't far from the mark.

The principal victim of the deflation of "modern Republicanism" was the heir-apparent to Republican leadership, Richard M. Nixon himself. He, better than anyone else, knew what was happening to him. I remember seeing him leave Cabinet or congressional leadership meetings literally trembling with pent-up frustration after some "modern Republican" proposal had been shot down. He was, after all, only the Vice-President, seldom free even to speak up at such meetings, much less to take direct issue with the President. And yet the record being made was the one on which he would have to run. Nor would there be much he could do later to separate himself from that record: maintaining the goodwill of the popular President was far too important.

Nixon's premonitions proved valid. A little more "modern Republicanism" could easily have spelled the difference between defeat and victory in 1960 in an election determined by less than one vote per precinct. Wider and longer-lasting consequences than the loss of a single election resulted from the failure to use the four years of the Eisenhower second term to show that individualism could be both compassionate and creative. Nixon's defeat cleared the field for a less progressive brand of individualism, and it was easily foreseeable that it would both dominate the 1964 Republican Convention and drag down the 1964 Republican ticket.

John F. Kennedy's victory gave a new lease on life to the simplistic assumption that more money and more government are the infallible cures for whatever ails us. President Kennedy himself had been slow to act on this assumption, partly, no doubt, because his election had been so close and partly because he could not bring himself to swallow it. Lyndon B. Johnson, however, entered his full four-year term uninhibited by either constraint. The margin of his victory, for one thing, had been overwhelming. For another, President Johnson, despite his reputation as a crafty manipulator, was a true disciple of the New Deal. And what, after all, was the Great Society but a Texas-style version of the New Deal turned loose, not on a depression or on long overdue reforms, but on the conquest of poverty, deprivation, and suffering in all their still-lingering forms?

The Great Society was programs, scores of them. I was Lieutenant Governor of Massachusetts when the legislative mill began to roll, and despite the fact that I had been out of HEW for only three years, I still could not keep abreast of its prodigious output.

The Great Society was also promises, and every program generated its own array. Out of the promises grew expectations which flourished uncontrollably. My associate Richard G. Darman has suggested an interesting analogy between boom-bust cycles in the economy and boom-bust cycles in public expectations. The Eisenhower second term included the recession of 1958 and the downside phase in public expectations. President Kennedy's New Frontier was a turnaround period for the economy as well as for public expectations. The Great Society coincided with the rising phase of both. Even in the most favorable circumstances it would have been impossible to satisfy the compounded expectations resulting from the rising phase of the expectations cycle and the inflationary push exerted by the Great Society promises. As it was, public expectations reached their most superheated stage during the mid-1960s at just the moment when they collided with the growing demands of an unpopular war. This combustible mixture burst into flames of anger and resentment—and cities burned.

By the time the Nixon administration took office, the expectations and economic cycles both required cooling off. The second requirement was more apparent than the first, but even the first was observable. The British journalists Lewis Chester, Godfrey Hodgson, and Bruce Page, reporting on the 1968 Presidential election in their book *An American Melodrama*,[4] concluded that a principal defect of this country was its inability to distinguish between the rhetoric of its greatness and the reality of its limitations. Struggling as I soon was with the attempt to meet real and pressing human needs, I became painfully conscious of this disparity. What HEW could do to help people was limited by constraints on available funds, by shortages of trained personnel, and by gaps in knowledge. Political and economic realities placed sharp restrictions on the possibility of relaxing these constraints. The problems we faced would have been difficult even if public expectations had been realistic. Exaggerated expectations compounded the difficulty. Speaking to my HEW colleagues late in 1971, I said:

> In our own time, great though the growth in our resources, the growth in our expectations has been even greater. Today these expectations are like a giant helium-filled balloon cast loose from its moorings, sailing beyond sight. We must somehow bring our expectations back to earth:

We must level with each other. For either we shall understand the reality of what can and cannot be done over
time, or we shall condemn ourselves to failure, and failure
again and again.*

The problem, as I saw it, was more than a cyclical phenomenon. It was also caused by basic trends in our social and political evolution. One was the steady, long-term growth in our
national affluence. Although inflation and recession have recently
suspended its normal rate of increase, real disposable income
doubled between 1935 and 1952 and doubled again between 1953
and 1970. The proportion of those living in poverty, meanwhile,
decreased much less rapidly.† During those affluent days we
experienced increasing pangs of conscience: with so many of us
living so well, we ought surely to be able to overcome the
deprivation suffered by the rest.

A related and reinforcing factor is that we now know how
to neutralize or overcome causes of human suffering which earlier
generations could only accept and endure. If we can conquer
polio, why not cancer? And if we can eliminate some of the
causes of mental retardation, why not most of the causes of
crime? The nearer we come to acquiring the means of combating the age-old scourges of mankind, the more impatient and
frustrated we grow with our failures to conquer those that still

---

* The quotation is from a paper which I called my "Castro speech"
because it contained all the things I would have liked to say to my 110,000
fellow workers if only I could have rounded them up in some great plaza and
harangued them, like Fidel Castro, for three or four hours. The closest approximation to this that I could manage was to deliver an abbreviated version
orally to three groups of several hundred HEW employees and then to get
the Department to publish the entire message. The printed version was entitled
Responsiveness and Responsibility.

† The "poverty line" is described by a threshold dollar amount which will
purchase the minimum essentials covered by an economy-food plan. Established
for the first time in 1959, the figure is revised annually according to the
Consumer Price Index. In 1959, the poverty line was set at $2,973 for a
nonfarm family of four; 22.4 percent of Americans were living on that amount
or less. In 1965 the figure was $3,223; 17.3 percent were then living in
poverty. Five years later 12.6 percent were living under the $3,968 amount.
The 1975 poverty line was $5,038, while those living in poverty still totaled
more than 11 percent.

remain. What we suffer silently or even cheerfully when we see no chance of improvement becomes intolerable as soon as we learn that a cure is possible. And then we must have the cure immediately.

Our impatience toward delays in curing social ills reinforces the "don't just stand there, do something" impulse. It is a natural, often compassionate, reaction. In simpler times indulging it could not do any great harm. Not to do so, indeed, would often have been callous. When George Washington came down with a fever and sent for a doctor, the doctor rode over with leeches in his saddlebags and dutifully applied them to the General's armpits. At that crude and unscientific stage in the art of medicine, its practitioners were ignorant of any real treatment for fevers. It would have taken an uncommon doctor to say, "General, I have no confidence in the medical value of bleeding, but I don't know what else to do." It would have been equally remarkable if Washington had asked, "Doctor, what makes you think these leeches will do me any good?" Both, more likely, would have taken it for granted that the doctor should "do something" even though completely unable to demonstrate the medical value of that "something."

In our own day the "don't just stand there, do something" syndrome can only inflate already exaggerated expectations. Though we cannot afford it anymore, we are just as prone to it as ever. It encourages, for example, the illusion that we know how to cure alcoholism, treat heroin addiction, and rehabilitate criminal offenders. In fact, we do not. The state of the art in these areas is about where the treatment of fevers was in George Washington's day. In the case of alcoholism, the very success of Alcoholics Anonymous—which is still, by and large, the most effective approach to the problem—depends on the premise that no alcoholic is ever "cured." During its thirty-nine years of existence the Public Health Service hospital for heroin addicts at Lexington, Kentucky, never had a success rate higher than 33 percent, and even now we have no better answer than to substitute another addictive drug—methadone. As for criminal offenders, Professor David J. Rothman of Columbia, in a book review I happened to come across shortly before I became Attorney

General of the United States, set an admirable standard of bleak honesty:

> Today's reformers, having inherited past failures, correctional facilities that do not correct and release procedures that only embitter inmates, can only bemoan the Atticas, point to the community, and state that efforts at amelioration will not make things worse. They have no grand solutions. Nothing works to reduce recidivism—not vocational training, not intensive probation supervision, not frequent therapy sessions. Indeed, they suspect the concept of rehabilitation, recognizing that it has often done more mischief than good.[5]

The beginning of wisdom—and a long step toward the restoration of confidence as well—is to admit that we don't know what we don't know. It is also important to know what we do know. When I arrived at the Department of Justice, one of the first things I did was to ask my staff to search the "literature" on corrections to see whether they could find any lead at all to the reduction of recidivism. They turned up a few scraps of data supporting one real possibility: the consistent provision of genuine opportunities for satisfying work.* This was encouraging! The Bureau of Prisons could be used to test the hypothesis. The help of business leaders could be enlisted. Community organizations could be aroused. I was looking forward to making the project one of my top priorities. Watergate and the Agnew case were distractions, but they would soon pass, and I could then get on with more important tasks. . . .

THE "DON'T just stand there, do something" impulse has fed —and been fed by—the political process. Politicians in every

---

* Several months later, after I had left the Justice Department, I attended a conference in New York on the Vera Institute of Justice's "Wildcat Program." Over the past two and a half years, this program has provided 2,730 former prison inmates with "supported work"—subsidized jobs with special supervision and assistance. Forty percent of the workers in the program have graduated to regular jobs in the economy. Another 17 percent are still in the program, and 18 percent have left for reasons of health or relocation in other cities. Only 25 percent have dropped out or been fired.

age, I suppose, have been guilty of exaggerated promises. In our own time nothing has so much inflated the currency of political promises as the simplistic assumption that every conceivable problem must have some legislative solution. The readiest answer to the constituent's question "What have you done for me lately?" is "I sponsored a bill."

The fallacy that enacting legislation will solve any given problem is hard to kill. There are, to be sure, many problems which cannot be solved without new legislation. But all too often, new legislation merely publicizes a need without creating either the means or the resources for meeting it. The result is Capitol Hill's oldest continuous floating shell game—a now-you-see-it, now-you-don't system under which the same money is moved around from program title to program title: when one looks under the title for the money, it typically is not there.

In an extreme version of the shell game, we see a flourish of self-congratulatory press releases hailing the passage of legislation which creates no new authority whatsoever. Each such law woos a particular constituency, addresses a specific problem, and sets up a new bureaucracy. More often than not, the enactment of such legislation misleads the public into believing that nothing has been done before and that something is about to happen. In the two and a half years I served as Secretary of HEW, Congress enacted into law ten pieces of legislation authorizing us to do what we were already doing. One example was the purportedly new authority to make grants for communicable-disease control. It so happened that this activity was among the oldest at HEW—dating back, in fact, to 1878.

More commonly, however, the game begins with the sensational discovery of a need that can plausibly be labeled as "unmet." Take, for instance, the care and treatment of aching feet. Have you ever stopped to think about the consequences of our shameful failure to guarantee adequate access to skilled foot care? Imagine the following scene: Father comes home from a long day on the factory floor. His feet are killing him. He eases himself into his armchair, turns on the television set, and turns off the rest of the world. Children's appeals for attention or help with homework get short shrift. Mother cannot penetrate the shell of self-absorption. Family quarrels follow. Father escapes into alcohol. He loses time from work. He's fired. The family splits up. Mother and children go on welfare. One child drops out of school, another is put on probation for car theft. The social costs mount.

The solution? Obvious: new categorical legislation (1) promising $900 million a year in formula grants to support podiatric services and (2) creating a new Institute of Foot Diseases in the National Institutes of Health.

A farfetched example? I wish it were. The fact is that just this kind of rationale has been used over and over again. If the resulting legislation is implemented at all, it is at the cost of spreading resources still more thinly over existing programs. The legislative committees which create new claims on limited resources do not have to specify where the money is coming from. Any committee member can choose as his target for reduction any program that is not important to his own district. The big-city Congressman can propose taking the money out of farm subsidies. The rural Congressman can propose taking it out of urban renewal. Both can attack waste in defense spending. For all legislative committee members the political payoff is in the gratitude they receive for showing that they "care about solving problems." The bigger the price tag, the deeper the gratitude.

The appropriations committees have no such freedom— and get no such payoff. They cannot appropriate money for a new program except at the expense either of existing programs or of a higher deficit. This explains why, time after time, the spending ceilings authorized by the legislative committees are not only higher than anything the executive branch can in good conscience request but higher than anything the appropriations committees are willing to provide. The hopes raised by the authorizing hoopla are dashed by the less flamboyant hand of the appropriating process. In fiscal 1973, for instance, new health manpower legislation authorized $1.1 billion for training grants, scholarships, fellowships, and student loans for doctors, nurses, and other health personnel. Less than half that sum was appropriated—an outcome hard to explain to thousands of disappointed men and women in medicine, many of whom put the entire blame on the executive branch. More and more of the same kind of shortfall has steadily widened the gap between authorizations and expenditures. For HEW alone, the outstanding face-amount of these unredeemed promissory notes grew from $200 million when I left HEW in 1959 to $13 billion when I left in 1973. Is it any wonder that confidence in government began to erode long before Watergate?

It would be wrong, however, to leave the impression that legislative committees are never concerned with the cost of their programs. On the contrary, the awareness of cost constraints accounts for other variants of the shell game. One consists in holding the legislative price tag to an amount substantially lower than the full cost of delivering the advertised service. An example is the program for nutrition of the elderly sponsored by Senator Edward M. Kennedy in 1972. The concept was humane: far too many old people suffer both from inadequate diets and from social isolation. One hot meal a day served at a community center would not only supplement their diets but bring them together in a congenial social setting. President Nixon let it be known that he did not oppose the bill. It rolled through both branches of Congress virtually without opposition. The President signed it into law and promptly requested a supplemental appropriation for the full authorized amount—$100 million. Congress appropriated the money, and HEW went to work on putting the program into effect. By the time our spending hit the maximum authorized annual rate, we would be reaching, we estimated, just under 5 percent of the eligible elderly. An honest program would have required at least $1.9 billion more per year.

The below-cost price tag variant was exploited on an even grander scale in the day-care legislation vetoed by President Nixon in 1971. Because its purpose seemed to me worthy, I had devoted considerable effort in meetings with the sponsoring Senators—Walter F. Mondale, Jacob K. Javits, and Gaylord Nelson—to persuading them to agree to reduce as far as reasonably possible the minimum family-income level at which the care would be free and the minimum family-income level at which the family would pay full cost—$4,500 in the former case, $12,000 in the latter. I was convinced at the time that the result was defensible, and I certainly did not agree with the President's veto message that the bill was objectionable on the ground that it committed "the vast moral authority of the National Government to the side of a communal approach to child rearing."* But the better I understood the scope of the implied promise contained in the bill, the more uneasy it made me. The maximum authorized annual appropriation was $2 billion. The full cost for all eligible families would have been $11 billion—$9 billion more per year.

Another variant of the cost-constraint version of the legislative shell game takes the form of an attempt to avoid an apparent commitment to the entire eligible population. The most convenient way to do this is to disguise the program as one designed to finance only "pilot" or "demonstration" projects even though so many similar projects have already been carried out that nothing of importance remains to be learned from more of the same. The real intent of such programs is to serve, not to demonstrate. As of fiscal 1973, HEW was spending about $9 billion per year for services to limited numbers of people who, for one reason or another, had the good luck to be chosen as beneficiaries of this kind of phony "demonstration" project. It is remarkable, when you come to think of it, that the federal government has not yet been faced with a lawsuit demanding equal treatment for all those just as needy but not so lucky.†

To expose the costs concealed by the legislative shell game, I asked my staff late in 1971 to estimate how much it would cost in fiscal 1972 to extend all of HEW's service delivery programs to every eligible person. For the nutrition of the elderly I knew that it would be an additional $1.9 billion. I also knew that Head Start was reaching only 15 percent of the entitled children. The Community Mental Health Program was serving about 20 per-

* I tried hard to get this particular phrase out of the message and later concluded that President Nixon's insistence on retaining it was probably explained by his desire to placate the right-wing critics of his China policy. The language echoed their attacks on the day-care bill, and the veto message was dated December 9, 1971, just six weeks after the ouster of the Republic of China from the U.N.

† The legal implications of analogous claims for equality are discussed in Chapter IX.

cent of its intended beneficiaries. And the shortfalls in some of HEW's other programs were even wider.

When I got the estimate early in 1972, it exceeded my wildest surmise. It turned out that the additional cost for fiscal 1972 alone would be $250 billion—enough to double that year's *entire* federal budget! The expanded programs, moreover, would require the recruitment and training of at least 20 million more professionals, paraprofessionals, and volunteers.

Nor were these dismaying projections based on extravagant cost estimates. Cost and quality are not equivalents, of course, although there is a close correlation in the case of most services. We deliberately chose, however, not to use figures obtained from the most exemplary providers in each category of service. Had we done so, our aggregate estimate would have been far more than $250 billion.*

THERE ARE no easy ways of closing the gap between expectations and resources. To cut defense spending and transfer the money saved to social programs may look at first glance like a possible approach, but it does not withstand close examination. The amounts transferred would not, in the first place, begin to close the gap. Besides, we have already gone a long way toward "reordering our priorities." Defense spending was 42.5 percent of total federal spending in 1968, the last year before the Nixon administration took office.† In 1976 it was 26 percent—the lowest proportion since 1950. As a percent of total public spending (federal, state, and local), defense spending was 29.2 percent in 1968 and only 17 percent in 1976—even lower than in 1950. HEW's share of the total federal budget, meanwhile, increased from 7.5 percent in 1954, when the Department was first established, to 34 percent in 1976.

* In arriving at the estimate, we first sought for each service category data showing the entire existing cost range. To allow for some qualitative improvement above the existing median, we selected the cost figure at the 67th percentile within this range. In the case of Head Start, for example, the annual cost per child in fiscal 1972 varied from $1,048 in Arkansas to $1,970 in New York. To estimate the cost of serving all eligible children we used a figure two-thirds of the way between Arkansas and New York.

† All the references in this and the following paragraph are to fiscal years.

In 1957, my first year at HEW, the Department's budget was $2.5 billion. In 1976 the Department will expend about $120 billion. The nation's defense establishment, by contrast, is smaller than at any time since before the Korean war. Military and civilian manpower has been reduced by 1.6 million since 1968. Purchases from industry are down to their lowest level, in real terms, since 1951; in dollars of constant buying power, they are down by $22.3 billion from 1968. Defense-related employment in industry was 2.3 million in 1964, 3.2 million in 1968, and declined to 1.6 million in 1976—50 percent below 1968 and 30 percent below 1964. As a former Secretary of Defense—and in spite of being a former Secretary of HEW—I would be strongly opposed to any substantial further reductions in these numbers without the reciprocal restraints on the USSR that are the objective of the continuing strategic-arms-limitation and balanced-force-reduction negotiations.

What about higher taxes then? To be of real help in closing the gap, a tax increase would have to be huge. Its effect would be a massive additional transfer of resources from the taxpaying majority to the disadvantaged minority, and it is awe-inspiring to contemplate the powers of persuasion that would have to be invoked in order to win the majority's support for any such result. A huge tax increase, in any case, might weaken the incentives needed to sustain economic growth. In that event higher tax rates would produce lower tax yields. Instead, therefore, of reducing the expectations gap, the tax increase could have the consequence of making it even wider.

Since our resources cannot be expanded enough to satisfy all our expectations, the only alternative is to scale down the expectations. This demands choice. Choice is the basic reality. It is made all the more difficult and saddening by the fact that the things we have to give up are not bad or trivial, but only somewhat less important than the things we select.

For most Americans, the worst recession since the Great Depression brought a cold awakening to the necessity for choice. We are beginning to understand that we cannot have everything at once. But to recognize that choices have to be made and to possess the means of intelligent choice are not the same thing.

Realism in facing the necessity for choice must be matched by improvement in our methods of exercising it.

WHERE GOVERNMENT programs are concerned, our ability to compare the advantages and disadvantages of one alternative with those of another is crude and inexact. Take, for instance, the comparison of the costs and benefits of one program with those of another. Nothing could be more fundamental to the possibility of intelligent choice. At the present stage of cost-benefit analysis, however, such a comparison can rarely be reduced to dollar figures without a result so artificial that we lose confidence in it. Yet just such a comparison is implicit in every budgetary decision: the budget forces a choice between a dollar spent on one program and a dollar spent on others.

For example, we often speak of a single human life as infinitely precious. But when it comes to matching sentiment with money, it is obvious that we constantly place limits on what we are willing to spend to save a life. Each year we tolerate thousands of deaths which could be prevented. The highway-accident and lung-cancer numbers are all too familiar—each is about 60,000 annually. Half the highway deaths are associated with drinking; most of the cancer deaths with cigarette smoking. Many of these deaths are preventable, but only at a price. Not preventing them also costs money—for treatment before death, for training a replacement for the deceased, for family dependency benefits, and so on. We can thus derive the outside limit of the dollar value we put on a single life by taking the total net cost of preventing 5,000 deaths by the most economical means and dividing this total by 5,000. The result is the value per life that we are not willing to pay.

In the case of highway deaths, one of the most economical means of saving lives would be to expand the system of accident treatment centers set up by Richard B. Ogilvie when he was Governor of Illinois. At the dedication in 1972 of the new regional center in Peoria I was told that the system had already brought about a sharp drop in the Illinois highway death rate. Through the consistent application of military medical techniques perfected in Vietnam, deaths from accident-related injuries in the period January to June 1975 were 29 percent lower than the period January to June 1971, despite a 17 percent increase during the same interval in the number of highway accidents. Only the three neighboring states of Missouri, Iowa, and Indiana have so far established accident treatment centers based on the Illinois model. On the basis of the Illinois figures, extending the system nationwide would save 8,800 lives annually. Why don't we do it?*

In May 1972, Mary Lasker, the nation's most effective chamion of health research, and Mike Gorman, head of the National Committee Against Mental Illness, brought to my attention an even more dramatically economical opportunity for saving lives: the expanded treatment of high blood pressure. Twenty-three million Americans have high blood pressure, but only half of them are aware of it, and less than one-eighth are receiving adequate treatment. It is the major causative factor in 250,000 deaths annually. The estimated annual loss in productivity and income is $10 billion. Treatment is relatively simple, and inexpensive. A successful detection and treatment program could save 80 percent of the lives lost from hypertensive complications each year.

I was deeply impressed and immediately got Dr. Theodore Cooper, then head of the National Heart and Lung Institute, to organize a national high blood pressure education program. Since then, a private, nonprofit, educational organization called Citizens for the Treatment of High Blood Pressure has been calling attention to the magnitude both of the problem and of the opportunity to combat it. By comparison, however, with our investment in all manner of marginal life-saving ventures, the scale of this effort remains ludicrously small.

Part of the cost-benefit problem is obscured, of course, by talking about what "we" are willing (or not willing) to pay: depending on what is done (or not done), the cost falls on different people. In the case, for example, of deaths caused by air pollution, the Coordinating Committee on Air Quality Studies of

---

* *The* most economical means of reducing highway deaths, of course, is to reduce highway speeds. During the eights months after the "energy crisis" of 1973–1974, when there was wide observance of a 55 mph speed limit, highway deaths dropped by 7,000, or an annual rate of 18 percent.

the National Academy of Sciences and the National Academy of Engineering estimated in September 1974 that automobile emissions may account for as many as 4,000 deaths and 4 million illness-restricted days per year. The closest the committee could come to measuring the dollar cost of these effects on health was to place them somewhere between $0.5 and $3 billion per year. The dollar value of the annual benefits from improving air quality would be between $2.5 and $10 billion, and the annual costs of controlling automotive emissions would be between $5 and $10 billion. Depending, then, on which end of the range of the committee's cost-benefit estimates you take, improving air quality would pay half its cost or yield a return double its cost. In either case, the people who pay the costs in higher automobile prices do not receive the benefit in the same proportion.*

IMPORTANT though cost-benefit analysis is to the possibility of intelligent choice, it has suffered up to now from a nearly fatal deficiency: a dearth of data on which to base comparisons. This may account for the brevity of its fling during the heyday of program planning and budgeting in the last years of the Johnson administration. I know of only one way to supply this lack. That is through rigorous evaluation; we cannot otherwise find out how well—or how poorly—a particular effort is succeeding. And only if we know this—and know also the effectiveness of an alternative approach to the same objective—can we compare the two. Only thus, moreover, can we judge the value of pursuing the objective at all versus that of devoting the same resources to some wholly different purpose.

For several years now it has been common for congressional legislation to contain a specific directive to set aside for evaluation some fixed proportion of the funds provided for carrying it out. In fiscal 1974, the most recent year for which complete figures are available, $90 million was being spent on evaluation, mostly through contracts with outside organizations. These funds have spawned a host of consulting firms and foundations, many

---

* In order to count the cost of the deaths in which automotive emissions were a causative factor, the committee placed a value of $200,000 on a single human life.

of them in the category denounced in 1969 by Congresswoman Edith Green, then chairman of the Special Subcommittee on Education of the House Committee on Education and Labor, as the "educational-industrial" complex.

As Secretary of Health, Education, and Welfare, I sympathized with Mrs. Green's feeling that too large a share of the money spent on evaluation—like that spent on research—goes to contractors whose only visible qualification is a staff of ex-employees of the contracting agency. I also believed that a more basic weakness of the process was the contracting agency's own inability to define with precision exactly what it wanted to have evaluated and then to monitor the contractor's performance of the defined task. I recall, for example, one contract undertaken by HEW in 1972 in order to evaluate the State Equal Opportunity Grant Program. The study was poorly conducted and yielded useless results. The futility of asking grant recipients such questions as "Are you glad you received a loan?" can only be matched by the agency's surprise that no more than 89 percent responded affirmatively.

Another source of weakness in the evaluation process is the mistaken assumption that the normal object of evaluation is a "program" in the sense of the whole range of activities called for by a particular piece of categorical legislation. These activities are ordinarily of very different kinds—typically, formula grants to state and local governments, project grants to nonprofit organizations, and support of training programs. Attempts at evaluation addressed to this kind of bureaucratic laundry list are seldom useful. A "program" to combat juvenile delinquency, for example, may be rated as successful because the formula grants are being promptly distributed to the designated state agencies and spent on the specified purposes, because research projects are being funded at competent institutions, and because stipends are being awarded to suitable trainees—all without a dime's worth of evidence that the program is having any demonstrable effect in cutting down juvenile crime.

A much more useful type of evaluation focuses on *output* measures, not just input measures, and the full range of possible contributors to that output. It examines a way of doing something—a method of teaching reading, for example, or an approach to the treatment of alcoholism. It attempts to determine whether or not the method works—and if so, how well. It seeks to find out what it would cost to get some improvement. It looks for better and cheaper ways of achieving the same results—and here we get back to the link between evaluation and cost-benefit analysis."* It considers, finally, both the possibility that an improvement in the evaluated program might impair the system of which it is a part and the value of other benefits that have to be given up in order to attain the program objective.[6]

It is, to be sure, difficult to develop adequate means of measuring program effectiveness. I have long been convinced, however, that one reason why the methodology of evaluation is still so primitive is that we have not really wanted to face the answers that good evaluation would produce. Having indulged the "don't just stand there, do something" impulse in response to to a problem we suspected we could not solve, we preferred to be lulled by the illusion that we were doing something about it rather than to discover that we were only going through the motions. This subconscious preference for the bliss of ignorance is now giving way to awareness of the harsh necessity for the wise application of scarce resources and the dangers of inflated expectations. Auditing agencies only a few years ago confined their inquiries to the legality of government expenditures. Now, under the leadership of Comptroller General Elmer B. Staats, who serves as Congress's watchdog over federal spending, they are making it a routine practice also to look into the efficacy of the expenditures. As Mr. Staats remarked, in a recent address, "From where we sit, it appears that both the executive and legislative branches of our Government have been more concerned with starting new programs that with making certain that those

* The distinguished psychologist Donald T. Campbell has suggested calling upon program beneficiaries as experts on their effectiveness. (*Psychology Today*, September 1975, p. 51.) In HEW in 1970 and 1971 we tried a somewhat similar approach using students with "community" backgrounds as evaluators. Called PEBSI (for "Program Evaluation by Summer Interns"), the experiment indicated that useful data about a community's needs can be obtained by using intelligent and articulate residents.

we already have are working satisfactorily or could be improved."[7]

For choice to be really intelligent another element is needed. This is the ability to take into account components of "cost" to the quality of life not ordinarily reflected by dollars in the budget and not easy to quantify. A fully adequate system of accounting would reflect the air pollution costs consequent upon the federal highway program. We would charge ourselves for the loss of recreation, fishing, wildlife, and aesthetic values resulting from the development of our rivers and harbors. We would be able to reckon with the possibility that federal dollars collected from some sources may have more adverse effects on economic and social activity than those collected from other sources.

When in 1972 I first visited Tokyo, a pall of eye-smarting smog hung low over the city. Traffic crawled. The "Bullet Train" I took that afternoon ran through endless miles of ugly urban sprawl. It was palpably apparent that Japan's leaping rate of economic growth had been accomplished at fearful cost to the quality of life. I recalled a case I studied in law school in which the directors of a corporation had been found liable for declaring a dividend out of a surplus that would not have existed if the company's accounting system had properly reflected the costs of depreciation. Japan's national accounting system, I thought, suffers from the same inadequacy. So, for that matter, does that of every other industrial country, including our own.

Appropriately, the Japanese have been among the first to recognize the need for better social accounting. In 1973 a subcommittee of the Economic Council of Japan published a report entitled *Measuring Net National Welfare of Japan* which, though recognizing the inherent difficulty of the task, attempted to express in monetary terms the benefits of leisure time, the work of women in the home, and the cost of environmental pollution and urbanization. The next year the United States took an official but much less ambitious step toward the measurement of national welfare when the Office of Management and Budget published its first series of *Social Indicators*, a statistical compendium covering such items as life expectancy, higher education, and leisure time.

The inherent difficulty of converting social indicators into a comprehensive system of social accounting is pointed up by the situation of women. In both Japan and the United States, the increase in the proportion of women who are gainfully employed outside the home has added many more hours of employment than the shortening of the work week has subtracted. This has increased per capita income, as that is conventionally measured. But what has it done to the "net national welfare"? As my former Woodrow Wilson Center colleague Professor Mancur Olson has pointed out, if you assume that new kitchen gadgets and other modern appliances are so efficient that women are still producing just as much in the home as before despite their jobs and that they still have just as much leisure also, then the extra market output is pure gain. If, on the other hand, you assume that working wives have to cut a few corners and frequently feel harried as well, then the net national welfare ought to be diminished by an allowance for the home production and relaxation that have been sacrificed in favor of the extra market output. Which of these assumptions you choose makes an enormous quantitative difference—a difference so great as to dwarf any reasonable estimate of the dollar cost attributable to environmental pollution or crowded living conditions.*

Quantitative measures of satisfaction and dissatisfaction will always be hard to come by. One could imagine an index of cultural opportunity or an index of "uglification." We might even find a way of recording annual trends affecting such elusive values as peace and freedom. It seems unlikely, however, that we will ever find a way of expressing these values in some neat index, reduce them to a cost-benefit analysis, or put a dollar sign on them. As the late Edward R. Murrow once observed, no cash register rings when a man changes his mind for freedom.

Whatever the difficulty of improving our social accounting —and however approximate it may remain—it seems to me ex-

---

* According to a Social Security Administration study, the housework done by the average American housewife in 1975 was worth $4,400. Wendyce Brody, "The Economic Value of a Housewife," Social Security Administration, Office of Research and Statistics, 1975.

tremely important to pursue the effort. Until we learn how to assess social and environmental, as well as economic, performance, our processes of choice will continue to produce unintended and distorted results.

I remember well a depressing day in a devastated city. Not since coming through Nuremberg on the way home after V-E Day had I seen anything like it. Here again were heaps of rubble. Here also were the gaunt skeletons of gutted and windowless buildings. But here the least damaged structures sheltered squatters. Garbage festered in the vacant lots. This was not the devastation of war. It was the slow accumulation of neglect and decay: resentful tenants, defaulting landlords, marauding vandals, fires that had escaped the control of shivering drunks and addicts.

This was New York City in 1971—the Bathgate area of the Bronx. My guides were Dr. Martin Cherkassky, the head of the Montefiore Hospital, and Dr. William B. Lloyd, the director of the Martin Luther King, Jr., Health Center, an affiliate of the hospital. We stopped near a corner. "See that drain?" Dr. Cherkassky said. "It kept overflowing for a long time before we could get the city to do anything about it. Because of it seventy-one children from all over the city died of meningitis." He looked at me with fierce eyes. "We *must not* forget that *housing* is health and *food* is health and *sanitation* is health. What we do—and fail to do—about these things is more important to the health of poor people than *anything* we doctors can do for them."

CHOICE, no matter how intelligent, is a bleak exercise. We cannot be blamed for wanting to have our cake and eat it too. And although it is essential, in order to reduce the resentment and frustration arising from disappointment of excessive expectations, to confront the necessity for choice, it is also important to make sure that the resources we can afford to bring to bear are stretched as far as they will go. One way of gaining the maximum possible return on the investment of these resources is to develop better and more efficient methods of coping with our serious social problems. A promising place to look is toward the potential of new technology; since we cannot escape paying its indirect social costs, we would be well advised to make the most of its direct social benefits.

The potential return from the application of new technologies to human-service delivery should, on its face, be dramatic. For to a very considerable extent, the human-service sector of our economy—which has grown up in response to the pressures of industrialization—has, ironically, itself escaped industrialization. In health, in education, in social service delivery, the pattern is essentially one of cottage industries. The technology remains highly labor intensive; in this respect, it is more remarkable for its similarity across the ages than for its more commonly noted changes. In view of this lag, the human-service sector is arguably ripe both for the introduction of labor-saving technologies and for the substitution of new capital-based technologies.

New telecommunications technologies seem especially promising. "Sesame Street," the children's educational television program, reaches 7 million preschoolers for one hour a day at a cost of $1.23 per student per year. Head Start, by comparison, a "comprehensive child development service program," costs more than $1,000 per child per year for educational results not yet shown to be better than those of "Sesame Street." Cable television, meanwhile, is adaptable to a tremendous variety of uses. It could, for example, provide adult education and university extension courses tailored to individual needs, deliver medical and public health information to people in their homes, and inform the public about where to go for various community services.[8]

New technology can also help to improve the efficiency of health-care services while at the same time increasing their responsiveness to individual patients. Computer networks—with proper safeguards for personal privacy—can, for example, be used to ensure that personal medical histories are made promptly available for the treatment of patients who happen to be away from their home-area doctor. New technology also offers the promise of widespread application of such procedures as telephonic transmission and interpretation of electrocardiographic data; low-cost ultrasonic X-ray imaging; and the use of two-way cable-television transmission to simplify the logistics of consultation and referral. Such advances bring within the reach of remote communities scientific resources that could not otherwise be widely dispersed except at prohibitive cost. There could be no better illustration of the ways in which technology can be harnessed to humane concerns.

But even dramatic advances in technology will not—and should not—displace the need for concerned and capable people. As the estimates I cited earlier make clear, the numbers of professionals, paraprofessionals, and volunteers required to fulfill the implied commitments even of our existing programs are so enormous that no conceivable applications of new technology could eliminate more than a fraction of the total manpower shortfall. We could, however, go a long way toward overcoming this shortfall by combining new technology with the more efficient use of trained manpower. Scarce professionals would be replaced by paraprofessionals and paraprofessionals by volunteers.

To accomplish this reallocation of human resources we shall have to overcome a series of irrational barriers. One is fear—the fear of a loss of status or employment on the part of those who now belong to the so-called helping professions, and a fear on the part of the consumer of a service that its provider is not adequately qualified. The first of these concerns is already being dispelled by a growing awareness that the existing backlog of unmet needs is so vast that there is far more than enough for every professional to do. Indeed, the status of the "helping professions" can only be enhanced by placing more paraprofessionals and volunteers under their supervision.

To the second concern the best answer is to demonstrate that the paraprofessionals and volunteers who carry out some part of a service function can in fact do that part well. This in turn requires that we carry out a systematic analysis of the service tasks to be performed so as to identify the minimum amount of training necessary to enable a person to carry out a part of the whole task with reasonable competence. It also requires that we learn how to measure the ability to perform. While I was at HEW, the Office of Child Development, recognizing that the growing demand for day-care services could never be met simply by increasing the supply of child-care specialists with college or graduate-school training, undertook to develop a way of measuring the ability to perform of a new kind of paraprofessional called a "child development associate." The importance of this effort, I thought, far transcended its applicability to the need for expanded day-care services. If we could learn how to measure the ability to perform of a "child-care associate," we could do away with the need for reliance on rigid credentialing requirements in many other occupations also. The ability to pass an examination, after all, does not prove that a person who passes it will be good at doing the job for which it is a requirement; neither does failing the examination prove that he or she cannot do the job.

The associate program was undertaken in 1972 under the direction of Edward Zigler, then director of the Office of Child Development. In July 1975 the first group of child development associates were awarded their credentials on the basis of their daily work with children. There are 5,000 CDA's in the process of earning credentials, and it is estimated that there could be as many as 100,000 associates within a decade. Dr. Zigler estimates that by hiring apprentice-trained personnel rather than college graduates for positions in day care, Head Start, nursery school, and other preschool programs, the nation would have sufficient funds to staff preschool facilities for twice as many children as are presently enrolled.

Among the roles appropriate for the "indigenous nonprofessionals" who should play an important part in all community services, I have long believed that the most needed is that of "neighborhood counselor." As matters now stand, people in all the established "helping professions"—public health nurses, public welfare caseworkers, psychiatric social workers, rehabilitation counselors, and the like—have to devote a large part of their time in their day-to-day work to lending a sympathetic ear, giving commonsense advice, and making referrals to some source of help. This essential service draws more heavily on their basic human understanding and their general knowledge of community resources than on any specific professional training they may once have had. Rather than use these expensively trained specialists for a job that could be done as well or better by community people, we should instead develop short, intensive programs designed from the outset to prepare people for counseling and referral. These "neighborhood counselors" would be the most numerous and widely dispersed of our service providers, and they would become as intimately familiar with the urban neighborhoods in which they serve as an agricultural agent with his own rural area.

THE GREATEST POTENTIAL of all for reducing the expectations gap lies neither in new technology nor in the more efficient use of trained manpower. It lies, rather, in the expanded use of volunteers. De Tocqueville, when he visited this country in 1831, was amazed by the readiness with which people voluntarily got together to help their neighbors. This, happily, is still a characteristic of the American people.

The number and variety of agencies using volunteers has risen dramatically in the last decade. Opportunities for service are no longer confined to such traditional users of volunteers as hospitals, institutions for the handicapped, and family service agencies; agencies like mental health clinics, correctional facilities, and welfare departments have also discerned their value. A potential volunteer looking for the right slot is presented a bewildering variety of opportunities. In her thoughtful and informative book *Breaking Into Prison: A Citizen's Guide to Voluntary Action*, Marie Buckley describes the contributions, from individual tutoring of illiterate prisoners to teaching art or music, that volunteers can make. "Since the prisons can't come to the community," she points out, "the community—the volunteers—must go to the prison."[9]

The National Center for Voluntary Action is dedicated to "stimulating and strengthening volunteer services and voluntary organizations in their unique contribution toward the prevention and alleviation of social problems." In a recruitment brochure entitled "Everyone can help someone," the NCVA lists ninety-eight possible volunteer jobs in a dozen categories from civic affairs, civil rights, community programs, consumer services, and ecology, to education, employment, health, and housing. According to a 1974 Census Bureau survey, one out of four Americans over the age of thirteen does volunteer. Nearly 37 million Americans, or 24 percent of the adult population, volunteered an average nine hours per week in 1974. This represents a healthy jump over the 18 percent who volunteered in 1965, and the NCVA reports recruitment trends indicative of a steadily increasing rate for the future.

Among the many positive developments in the use and deployment of volunteers, perhaps the most promising is the widening concept of *who* can be a volunteer. Not long ago, it was assumed that only the reasonably affluent and leisured could afford to give of their time. The typical volunteer was a white, middle-aged, middle-class housewife. Now we have learned that the young, the elderly, the poor, the handicapped, even the incarcerated have a contribution to make. Not only can everyone contribute, but everyone can benefit. To know that we are needed is often the beginning of self-realization. A prisoner who teaches a fellow inmate to read, or helps to renovate a crumbling tenement for use as a day-care center, is a real prospect for rehabilitation. A welfare recipient who volunteers to ease an overworked social worker's load by being a caseworker aide has a better chance of breaking out of the poverty-dependency cycle than one who takes an occasional unskilled job.

Stimulated by Office of Economic Opportunity experiments patterned on the Peace Corps, a whole new category of "para-volunteers" has emerged—people paid a small amount, usually not more than the minimum wage, to do needed work which an agency could not afford to have done by a full-salaried person. Though purists deplore this alloy of charitable impulse and pecuniary reward, it creates opportunities for people who could not afford to give their time for nothing. These paravolunteers occupy a place partway between the professional and the pure volunteers comparable to that filled by the paraprofessional, and at their best they do it with sympathy and skill. And as the organizations representing the "helping professions" come increasingly to recognize that there is far more than enough work to go around, hostility should give way to appreciation.

Under a reorganization plan adopted in 1971 the experimental paid-volunteer programs were brought together with the Peace Corps under a new umbrella agency called ACTION. Among them were VISTA (Volunteers in Service to America), RSVP (Retired Senior Volunteer Program), the Senior Companion Program, the National Student Volunteer Program, the University Year for ACTION, and the Foster Grandparents Program. I had a chance to observe the last of these several years ago at a shelter for homeless children in New York City. The foster grandparents had time for closer continuing contact with the children than any of the professional staff, and it was obvious that the children were fond of them. It was also apparent that the old people got tremendous satisfaction from their role. I could imagine how they felt. During my last two years in college and first year of law school a friend and I spent almost every Wednesday afternoon at a Boston South End settlement house with a group of elderly pensioners. Calling themselves simply the Old Men's Club, they came together once a week from lonely and isolated rooms for a few hours of companionship and conviviality. They taught us whist and cribbage, and we loved to hear them reminisce about their early lives. Although we felt we gave them very little, they were touchingly grateful for the mere fact that we were there.

Indeed, it must be the fact that people feel good about being volunteers that explains why their numbers have increased as leisure has increased. This feeling makes volunteers their own best recruiters of new volunteers. Here, I believe, lies our single best hope of reducing the expectations gap. And to the extent that it is through volunteer action that we do succeed in closing it, we shall also succeed in preserving one of the most enduring and valuable attributes of American life.*

---

* It is on this account, primarily, that I find myself (somewhat to my own surprise) taking a more libertarian position than William F. Buckley. In *Four Reforms* (New York, 1973), Buckley proposes that all college applicants be required to spend a year between high school and college performing some kind of public service. By way of example, he suggests jobs as attendants in nursing homes, where young people could provide inexpensive unskilled labor as well as companionship for the patients. And yet to make this kind of

CHOICE, as I acknowledged a few pages back, is a bleak exercise. It is time also to acknowledge that there are limitations on the extent to which choice can be a rational process. No matter how good we become at cost-benefit analysis and evaluation and social accounting, the hard choices will, in the end, have to turn on some combination of values, feelings, and instincts. The contribution of rational processes is to narrow the range within which we have to rely on values, feelings, and instincts. These processes can help us to build a bridge partway out over the gulf between where we are and where we want to be. The more numerous the choices to be made, the more clamorous the competition among them; and the more apparent the impossibility of satisfying them all, the more need we have of just such bridging structures.

To reach the final, most difficult decisions—those in which the ultimate elements of choice cannot be reduced to measurable quantities but which involve genuine clashes of competing interests—is the task of the political process.* Here we come back to the need for trust in those who exercise political leadership and to the essentiality of their dealing with us openly and honestly. Because the ultimate grounds of choice cannot be made subject to quantitative measures, it is all the more important to be as forthright and explicit as possible in spelling out how the choice was made. It is not enough that the process of choice should in fact be fair and compassionate. It must also be accessible to the full view of those who are most affected by it and offer them the greatest possible opportunity to take part in it. In the long

---

contribution obligatory would, to my mind, destroy much of its value. Although we do not now have enough volunteers for such services, I would hate to be in charge of providing useful opportunities for two million new "public service" entrants a year, most of whom would rather be doing something else.

* James B. Rule, in "The Problem with Social Problems," has pointed out that "a close and critical look at the array of 'social problems' in America today shows that few of them represent authentic 'problems' in the sense of conditions equally undesirable from all political and social standpoints. Quite the opposite: conditions like pollution, racism, poverty, and the like are basically oppositions of interest—not social problems but social conflicts, overt or concealed." *Politics and Society*, February 1971, p. 51.

run, the preservation of confidence in our political system depends on such accessibility and such participation. For only if the factors of choice that outrun the capacity of objective analysis are made understandable to those whose expectations have to be deferred or overruled can they fairly be asked to accept the legitimacy of those choices. And only thus can we hope to restore confidence in the fairness and integrity of our governmental system.

The Complexity Explosion: Simplification and Synthesis

THE PRECEDING CHAPTER dealt with the importance of confronting the necessity for choice. It also discussed ways of acquiring a better grasp of the potential consequences of choice. These are necessary conditions to the preservation of free self-government, but they are not in themselves sufficient. It is also essential to keep the choices that have to be made within the range of ordinary understanding.

For the last twenty-four years, the University of Michigan's Survey Research Center has been asking people if they agreed or disagreed with the following statement: "Sometimes politics and government seem so complicated that a person like me can't really understand what's going on." Fifteen years ago, in 1960, 40 percent of those responding disagreed with this statement. Eight years later, 28 percent disagreed. In 1974, only 26 percent did not think that government was getting too complicated for the average citizen to understand.

This reaction to complexity has a profound effect both on

our trust in government and on our ability to make intelligent choices about the actions of government. For a free society, the ultimate challenge of the foreseeable future will consist not simply in managing complexity but in keeping it within the bounds of understanding by the society's citizens and their representatives in government. Unless we in America can succeed in this, we shall lose their power to make intelligent—or at least deliberate —choices. We shall no longer be self-governing. We shall instead be forced to surrender more and more of our constitutional birthright—the office of citizenship—to an expert elite. We may hope it is a benevolent elite. But even if it is not, we shall be dependent on it anyway. Rather than participating in the process of choice, we shall be accepting the choices made for us.

SOME RATES of change are linear—for instance, the annual increase in per capita consumption of energy. Others are compounded like the interest on a savings account—for instance, population growth. The most dramatic rates of change are the product of several rates of change multiplied by each other. In the case, for example, of environmental deterioration, Professor Paul R. Ehrlich of Stanford has made the point that "population size acts as a multiplier of the activities, consumption, and attendant environmental damages associated with each individual in the population."[1] In other words, population $\times$ affluence $\times$ technology = pollution, a compound of compounds.

Complexity is a rapidly growing product of similar multipliers. Complexity = population growth $\times$ the rate of concentration of population in urban areas $\times$ the urban population's increasing per capita consumption $\times$ the real annual increase in disposable income.

As an urban area gets bigger and richer, its transportation and distribution systems must diversify and expand. The flow of office workers in and out of the central city every day compels the construction of ever more tangled loops of highway and then, in desperation, of mass transit systems. As real income grows and less of it goes into necessities, it creates demand for a continually wider range of consumer choice. This demand can only be satisfied by the increasing specialization of the systems providing goods and services. These systems, too, become more diversified in their own consumption and manpower requirements and thus more complex to manage. Environmental deterioration, itself a product of other multipliers, also multiplies complexity because the means of combating it have to expand in scale, variety, and sophistication. And aggregate complexity is multiplied again by the complex linkages among urban areas.

We have no standard measure of the growth of complexity, of course, any more than we have of net national welfare. It seems to me plausible, nevertheless, that certain measurable rates of growth, all increasing faster than the GNP, may serve as rough indicators. One is office space: the more complex the system to be managed, the more planners, coordinators, and communicators are required to manage it and the more room they need. Although there is no central repository of office-space statistics, the figures for individual cities are revealing. In Boston, for example, office space construction during the last seven years increased 600 percent over the previous decade, while the population actually decreased. For the same period, the GNP barely doubled.

Not surprisingly, congressional demand for office space has grown even faster than metropolitan-area demand. The first Senate office building, built in 1908, served for fifty years. In 1958 the second building more than doubled Senate office space. A third is now on the drawing boards. The House started out in 1908 also with only slightly more space than the Senate but doubled it twenty-five years sooner, doubled it again in 1965, and is now trying to poach on the new Library of Congress Annex.

In the past twenty years, congressional staff employment has increased by 300 percent while state and local government employment has risen by 250 percent and federal executive branch employment by only 33 percent. Part of the explanation, as the previous chapter suggests, may be that the Congress is not simply a reactor to complexity but a generator of it.

Other probable indices of complexity are miles of telephone wire, court caseloads, and computer capacity. All have grown faster than the GNP—the slowest (miles of telephone wire) 23 percent faster, the fastest (computer capacity) 391 percent faster.*

On the face of it, the developments which best reflect the growth in complexity are also those which have enabled us to cope with it. This is most obviously true of computers. It is hard to imagine how, without them, we could handle the dense air traffic at LaGuardia or O'Hare, the booming use of credit cards, or the enormous volume of Social Security contributions and payments. The Social Security system employs 15 large-scale computers, 30 small-scale computers, and 9 special purpose systems to keep track of the wage records of 83 million workers. These computers also handle 35 million monthly benefit payments and process 95 million Medicare claims a year. Altogether, nationwide, some 170,000 general-purpose computers are now in use,† compared with about 5,400 in 1960.

The expansion of computer capacity and sophistication has been at least as dramatic as their increase in numbers. Computers have long since outgrown such relatively simple tasks as the handling of payrolls, billing, and accounting. Interconnected computers now being developed will quickly and automatically exchange the data needed for management decisions among all the applicable information banks. And yet more computers and better computer technology may not for much longer be able to keep up with the proliferation of complexity. According to Frederic G. Withington, an A. D. Little consultant who has been making annual studies of the data-processing industry, it is foreseeable that by the early 1980s "the treadmill of information systems development should stop, or at least shift to some new

	1960	1970	Percentage Increase
* TELEPHONE:			
Miles of wire	316 million	628 million	98
U.S. COURT OF APPEALS			
CASELOADS			
Cases commenced	3,899	11,662	198
COMPUTERS	(1966)	(1974)	
	31,000	171,000	466
GNP (1958 dollars)	$487.7 billion	$722.5 billion	75

† These are the figures for 1974.

dimension and new ultimate objective."[2] This suggests that most of the major applications of computer technology to management and administrative tasks may already have been achieved—that these applications, indeed, may have masked the true rate of increase in complexity—and that benefits from future adaptations will tend to be increasingly marginal. If this prognosis is true for other devices like duplicating machines, telecommunications equipment and high-speed transportation systems, the bursting thrust of complexity may break through our mechanical efforts to contain it and cascade over into the kind of catastrophic "overshoot" forecast in *The Limits to Growth*.*

It is quite conceivable, of course, that to predict the exhaustion of technological capacity to cope with complexity would be just as wrong as to accept the *Limits to Growth* prediction of technology's inability to cope with population growth, material shortages, and environmental pollution. The technologists have done so many unbelievable things in the years since I was an unbelieving reader of the comic strip "Buck Rogers in the Twenty-first Century" that I am reluctant to regard anything as beyond their reach. Still, there are two things the technologists seem unlikely to achieve any time soon. One is an increase in the number of hours in the day. The other is a speedup in the rate of oral communication. And so long as the technologists remain unable to accomplish these feats, the burgeoning complexity of modern society will continue to press down upon us. As it does, it will increasingly endanger the survival of individual dignity and the possibility of free self-government.

FAR FROM pursuing policies designed to enhance public understanding and counteract complexity, the actual if not the intended result of many government actions over the past several decades has been to compound confusion on both counts. Government's response to the proliferation of economic and social problems has been to foster an even wilder profusion of governmental activities. As of 1976, the federal government had some one thousand categorical aid programs financing 19 percent

* See Chapter IX, p. 327.

of state and local government expenditures. Promoted by the legislative shell game described in the previous chapter, this almost random procreative process has spawned a bewildering multitude of bureaucracies, regulations, and guidelines. Typically, a neighborhood health center in North Carolina found in 1970 that its most serious operational mistake was to seek funds from a number of federal agencies. Grant application expenses exceeded $51,000. Expert staff time diverted from productive work was irreparably lost. Federal agency guidelines were inconsistent, application procedures varied widely, and review levels were multilayered and complex. In exasperation, the project director wrote to HEW:

> I see now that I made a gross mistake to encourage my staff to make approaches to a broad spectrum of Federal agencies to fund different aspects of our program. None of the agencies seem to understand that we do not run categorical programs at the Health Center, but that we conduct integrated, family-oriented team delivery of service, and the task of educating all our reviewers to this is really too much.

At the time I was sworn in as Secretary of HEW, in June of 1970, people were saying that the department was a sprawling, unwieldy conglomerate, impossible to manage. For a while I thought they might be right. When someone asked me what it was like to come back to my old department after nearly twelve years in other jobs, I said it was like seeing an old friend who, since we last met, had grown very fat. During those dozen years the number of different departmental programs had tripled and was rapidly approaching 300. Fifty-four of these overlapped each other; 36 overlapped programs of other federal departments. Almost $19 billion was being spent through some 40,000 institutions and agencies. Including Social Security and Medicare, HEW was responsible for about a third of the entire federal budget. I soon learned, however, that the problem was not that HEW was "unmanageable." Having served there before and having also spent two years dealing with health, education, and welfare problems in Massachusetts, I did not find it impossibly difficult to get on top of the day-to-day administration of the Department. But tending machinery was one thing; defining what we were trying to do and why we were doing it, and developing ways to measure how well the job was done—this was something else again.

By the end of 1970 I saw my primary task as that of trying to make the whole of HEW greater than the sum of its parts. As matters stood, the whole was actually less than the sum of the parts—the minus being a consequence of overlap, duplication, slippage, turf protection, and miscellaneous bureaucratic infighting. In an effort to eliminate this waste of effectiveness I wrote and circulated to my principal advisers a memorandum called "Performance Priorities." Stressing the importance of making the most of the limited resources available for meeting urgent human needs, it set forth in broad terms the critical interrelationships between management of research, improved evaluation, grant consolidation (reduction in the number of categorical programs), and services integration (reduction of fragmentation at the point of delivery). Months later I discovered that I had not succeeded in getting across much of what I had been trying to say. It was this discovery, primarily, which induced me to try to spell it all out in my "Castro speech."*

By this time we were heading into 1971. I had been fortunate in persuading Laurence E. Lynn, Jr., whose analytical capacity had greatly impressed me when he was a senior member of the National Security Council staff, to leave the Stanford Business School and return to government as Assistant Secretary of HEW for Planning and Evaluation. He was beginning to spend part of every week in Washington, and I was looking forward to his being on board full time by the middle of June. My confidence in him quickly proved justified. After only a month on the job he came to me with recommendations calling for a quantum jump in HEW's planning capability. Instead of a piecemeal process which, for various legitimate reasons, had become dominated by new program development, Larry Lynn proposed that goals, priorities, and resource-allocation decisions be made subject

* See Chapter IV, pp. 126–27.

to a coherent, comprehensive stratgey. For HEW this was a radical idea, but I agreed with it in principle. Under Larry's direction work on alternative strategies got under way.

Among the alternatives developed in that first year I chose a strategy—institutional reform and the prevention of dependency on public support—that would not bring about major short-run disruptions but would serve as a vehicle for gearing up the planning process. Although HEW had for some years been making five-year projections of program costs, we began for the first time to take a more systematic look at the implications of these cumulative claims. This analysis, reinforcing my preexisting concerns about excessive expectations, program proliferation, and better analysis of the trade-offs among competing claims, convinced me that HEW's problem was both simpler and more fundamental than "unmanageability." The plain fact was that the "system"—of which HEW itself was but a part—was out of control.

Nearly half the entire federal budget—about $150 billion—was devoted to the protection and development of human resources. More than two-thirds of this amo....t was spent by HEW, and two-thirds of that, in turn, went to meet requirements like Social Security benefits and federal matching of state welfare expenditures—requirements which, because they are governed by the Social Security Act, are only nominally subject to the appropriations process. Dividing up the remaining one-third required the adjudication of countless competing claims, and as we saw in the previous chapter, the resources available were nowhere near sufficient to meet them all. The structure was so complex, accountability so much subdivided, and the number of separate funding decisions so vast that only the specialist could hope to be adequately informed about the ways in which the money was parceled out. Not even the most conscientious, concerned citizen could be expected to have intelligent opinions about how to divide limited resources among more than three hundred HEW "programs." For the conscientious, concerned citizen to be excluded from this process, on the other hand, was profoundly inconsistent with the concept of a democratic, self-governing society.

In comparison with the magnitude of the issues at stake—decisions affecting the lives of almost all Americans—the number of individuals who played a direct part in resolving them was ludicrously small. From initial preparation to final passage, the HEW budget for fiscal 1975 was looked at as a whole by only 51 people. Twenty of these were in the executive branch: 9 in HEW, 4 in the Office of Management and Budget, 6 on the President's staff, and the President himself. The other 31 were members of the two congressional appropriations subcommittees and their staffs: 11 Senators and 3 staff members, 14 Congressmen and 3 staff members. (This tally assumes—somewhat generously—that all members of the appropriations subcommittees at some point scrutinized all the HEW appropriations requests.)

The more I saw of this narrowly based system, the more clearly I came to realize that a democratic society had unwittingly created a monster—a benevolent one, to be sure, but a monster nevertheless. The unwieldy creature had its own self-serving purposes, its own organic processes, its own insatiable appetites. Surrounded by a dense categorical jungle, protected by layers of bureaucratic barbed wire, and tended devotedly by interest-group representatives, it had become all but inaccessible to broadly based public opinion. My most important task as Secretary of HEW, I concluded, must be an attempt to bring the monster under democratic direction and control.

To me this was a matter of more profound concern than any programmatic issue, however important. Even if I believed (which I do not) that specialists and experts would make wiser choices among competing claims than would be made under a system which involves concerned citizens, shutting the citizen out of the process of choice is too high a price to pay for better management. It is the *opportunity* to be heard and to exert an impact—and more particularly the *awareness* of this opportunity—that is critical. The burgeoning complexity of HEW was destroying the opportunity of the citizen to be heard and to exert an impact on the department's choices. I would have been outraged if some benevolent despot had been strangling democratic processes. I was no less outraged because complexity was the villain.

The only solution that I could see was the direct and obvious one: to *simplify*—to streamline the structure within which choices are made, to cut down the number of matters that require choice, and to open up the process to broader participation. These conclusions on my part merged with Larry Lynn's continuing work on a follow-up strategic plan. By the early fall of 1972, he and his colleagues had completed a 200-page paper outlining a complete, top-to-bottom overhaul of HEW programs. Officially captioned "Comprehensive HEW Simplification and Reform," it had somehow come to be known as the "Mega Proposal." Although I offered a magnum of champagne as the prize for a less pretentious name, I got only tongue-in-cheek suggestions. "Mega Proposal" stuck. By whatever name, I still regard it as the most soundly conceived, well-thought-out, and far-reaching policy initiative for which I have ever been responsible.

As its first step toward simplifying HEW functions and making them more accessible to public understanding, the Mega Proposal divided most HEW activities into three broadly defined groups: the provision of financial assistance to individuals; the provision of financial assistance to state and local governments ("special revenue-sharing"); and federal assistance in building the capacity of human-services institutions to meet human needs.* Financial assistance to individuals embraced three major programs: income assistance for poor families, health insurance, and student assistance. I shall return to these both because of their intrinsic importance and because they so well illustrate the evolution of our thinking. But first I want to say something about special revenue-sharing and capacity-building.

The simplification and clarification accomplished by the latter two components of the Mega Proposal would have been dramatic. Not only would the total number of HEW programs have been drastically reduced—from over three hundred to

---

* The Mega Proposal also identified two other groupings of HEW activities—the direct or indirect provision of services, and regulation and standard-setting—for which no internal restructuring was contemplated. The origins and aims of the Mega Proposal are described by Larry Lynn and his former deputy, John M. Seidl, in a paper entitled "Policy Planning at HEW: Thinking the Unthinkable in a Domestic Agency" which occupies, together with the full text of the Mega Proposal itself, the entire Spring 1975 issue of the quarterly journal *Policy Analysis*.

about ninety—but those which remained would have been grouped in easily intelligible combinations centered on the Department's principal functional responsibilities—health and education and welfare. Capacity-building was a useful synthesizing concept simply as such: by bringing together under three headings the project-grant authorities concerned with developing and testing new ideas, improving state and local services, and overcoming critical shortages of trained personnel, it would have done much to make these authorities more comprehensible and manageable.*

I was aware, of course, that no combination of initiatives as far-reaching as the Mega Proposal would be easy to sell. Experience with welfare reform and earlier, more limited administration proposals for special revenue-sharing had already demonstrated that.† Welfare reform had run into heavy attack from both standpatters and radicals. Special revenue-sharing had encountered reflexive hostility from interest groups dedicated to protecting their direct access to federal funds. It was characteristic of such groups that they refused to be mollified even by assurances that the total pool of federal funds available to them would not be reduced and might even be increased. From their standpoint it was enough to condemn the whole concept that the funds would no longer be earmarked for their particular benefit: to get their share they would have to go, not just to the appro-

* Under the first heading—research and development—22 authorities would have been telescoped into 6 broader ones. Under the second—services development—47 authorities would have been reduced to 5. Under the third—manpower development—dozens of programs aggregating $1 billion in authorized annual spending would have been consolidated into authorities for health, education, and social services, with total spending authority cut in half because noncategorical student aid would have been expanded separately.

† General revenue-sharing and "special revenue-sharing" both involve the transfer of federal revenues to the states and localities. The principal difference between the two is that the former relies on what in the Eisenhower administration we used to call the "put it on the stump and run" approach, while the latter restricts use of the money to some broadly defined purpose in which there is a substantial national interest. The Advisory Commission on Intergovernmental Relations distinguishes special revenue-sharing from block grants, both of which allocate money to state and local government for broad purposes, on the basis that the former does so without application or matching requirements.

priations subcommittees of the Congress but to the far more numerous appropriating bodies of state and local governments. Nor was there, in the light of the reaction to the earlier, more limited special revenue-sharing proposals, any reason to suppose that simplifying project-grant authorities would have easier going. The result of such simplification, after all, would inevitably be to merge or close off a substantial number of federal funding pipelines.

I refused to believe, nevertheless, that these approaches to simplification were an impossible dream. As Attorney General of Massachusetts I had taken part in the battle for block-grant funding under the Omnibus Crime Control and Safe Streets Act proposed by President Johnson in 1967. United States Attorney General Ramsey Clark insisted that the Department of Justice itself should hand out the money on a project-by-project basis. The National Association of Attorneys General supported a House of Representatives amendment allotting the funds among the states on a block-grant basis for projects approved by the states' own criminal justice planning commissions.* As a member of the NAAG Executive Committee, I took it upon myself to round up support for this amendment from governors, lieutenant governors, and my brother attorneys general. The House adopted it by a nearly two-to-one vote, and it prevailed in conference with the Senate. This was the first substantial departure from the established categorical-grant pattern.

The field of elementary and secondary education offered more recent and more relevant encouragement. In this field the block-grant approach was first proposed in 1971 not, as in the case of the Omnibus Crime Control Act, for application to a brand-new program but for the consolidation of thirty-three existing categorical-grant programs. The proposal had been put forward, moreover, with the full support of the United States Office of Education (part of HEW) and with considerable support from members of the National Association of Chief State School Officers. This breakthrough came about because

* The amendment was proposed by Congressman (later Governor) William T. Cahill of New Jersey.

Terrel H. Bell, who was Acting Commissioner of Education when I came to the Department in 1970, turned out to share with me a sense of urgency toward doing something about the chaotic jumble of categorical programs with which each of us had earlier attempted to cope in state and local capacities. With my encouragement, he and his colleagues in the Office of Education developed a grant consolidation plan combining the thirty-three categorical programs into a single grant providing funds for five defined purposes—compensatory education of disadvantaged children, education of the handicapped, vocational education, aid to areas where federal employees lived or worked on tax-exempt property ("federally impacted areas"), and educational support services. This became the first of the administration's so-called special revenue-sharing programs. Submitted to the Congress in the spring of 1971, it met with little enthusiasm at first. Gradually, however, thanks in large measure to the persuasiveness of Congressman Albert H. Quie of Minnesota, the ranking Republican on the House Committee on Education and Labor, the climate improved. By late 1972, when the Mega Proposal took shape, the prospects of the education special revenue-sharing proposal looked promising enough to offer a real hope that other grant consolidation packages would eventually prevail.*

But these were only encouraging signs that a major effort might succeed, not a substitute for it. It would be essential to appeal over the heads of the interest groups to broader-based organizations and to the general public. Our natural allies would be the representatives of the general-purpose governments most burdened by federal paperwork and most plagued by categorical fragmentation—the governors, the county executives, the mayors, and the city managers. Less easy to enlist, but of tremendous potential value, would be broadly based groups like the League

* The Education Amendments of 1974, though far short of HEW's 1971 proposal, contain the first modest steps ever taken toward consolidating educational funding authorities: three existing authorities have been consolidated into a larger program of library and learning resources; three others have been merged into a support and innovative program; a third creates a single state grant program for adult education.

of Women Voters, the General Federation of Women's Clubs, the Committee for Economic Development, the United States Chamber of Commerce, the American Jewish Committee, and Common Cause. The Mega Proposal, I thought, had a real chance of arousing their interest and enlisting their help because it was coherent, comprehensive, and *big*. The same would be true—and more so—of the press and the general public. Audacity! That, or nothing, would carry the day.

We now return to the provision of assistance to families and individuals, starting with income assistance and then proceeding to health insurance and student assistance. The Mega Proposal's approach to income benefits for the poor would have made a major contribution to the objectives of simplification and intelligibility, and it would also have created a far more equitable income-maintenance system than the unfair, inefficient, and fraud-prone nonsystem we call "public welfare." To make clear how the Mega Proposal approach would have met these objectives—and to provide some insight into the difficulties of reconciling them—I shall say something about how we got into our present mess and quite a lot more about the Nixon administration's attempts to get out of it.

The people who designed our existing public welfare programs seem not to have understood that the main difference between the poor and the rich, as Ernest Hemingway pointed out to Scott Fitzgerald, is money. In the traditional welfare view, poor people are poor because they are foolish or untrustworthy, or both. If simply given money, they will spend it unwisely—something the affluent never do, of course. Acting on this traditional assumption, the framers of our welfare laws charged social workers with working out "budgets" for poor families—so much for food, so much for rent, so much for laundry, and so on.* If

---

* A *New Yorker* "Profile," entitled "A Welfare Mother," described a situation all too common among welfare families: "Hardly any two consecutive checks the Santanas received were alike, because the Department of Welfare attempted to take every new development in the family's situation into account. When Gabriel was hospitalized for dehydration for a couple of months, shortly after his birth, his semi-monthly food allowance of nine dollars and ninety-five cents and his fifty-nine-cent diaper-laundering allowance were

there was a man in the house, the family could get no benefits, and by enforcing this restriction a supposedly responsible government may well have split up as many families as drink ever did. With a foresight that only a rhinoceros could envy, the welfare system prescribed that for each dollar earned, the poor would lose a dollar of benefits.* A more effective disincentive to work would be hard to imagine. Both restrictions—the man-in-the-house rule and the confiscatory "tax rate" on earnings—illustrated the tendency of inadequate planning to generate unanticipated side effects.

Compounding complexity, benefit levels varied widely among the states: in 1974 the average monthly benefit for a recipient of Aid to Families with Dependent Children was $98.40 in New York and $14.35 in Mississippi. On top of this, the system divided needy people into several different benefit categories: in addition to families with dependent children, there were the elderly, the permanently and totally disabled, and the blind. Most of the members of these groups—and many other low-income individuals as well—benefited from eligibility for food stamps. A small proportion in any or all categories also received housing allowances. And as if these depressing sources of complexity were not enough, variations and errors were invited by the fact that the system depended for its administration on the subjective decisions of caseworkers.

In an attempt to clean up this mess, the Family Assistance Plan proposed by President Nixon in August 1969 would have

deducted from the family's expenses for the duration of his hospital stay. When each of the children reached the approximate age of two, his or her laundry allowance was eliminated. When the Santanas occupied a particularly dark apartment, or one in which the heating system didn't function and they had to turn up the gas stove and move their mattresses to the kitchen to keep warm, they received an extra allowance for electricity or gas." *The New Yorker*, September 29, 1975, p. 49.

* Since 1967 the Aid to Families with Dependent Children program has permitted coverage of families in which an unemployed father was in the home, but as of February 1974 only 4.2 percent of all AFDC recipients belonged to such families. As a work incentive, an employed family head is allowed to keep $30 plus one-third of monthly earnings and an allowance for work-related expenses (day care, transportation costs, uniforms). Each state determines what work-related expenses it will recognize.

established a uniform national income floor for all those truly unable to work. Its most far-reaching innovation would have extended coverage to the working poor, thereby achieving "horizontal equity" as between families with a full-time working head and families in which no one was working or in which the family head worked only part time. To encourage employable people to work, the "tax rate" on earnings would be 50 percent: that is, for each dollar earned, benefits would be reduced by fifty cents. The slogan of the day was "workfare not welfare": all employable people, including the mothers of school-age children, would have had to register for work. If a mother got a job, free day care would be provided for her children. If she refused one, the family's benefits would be reduced.

In *The Politics of a Guaranteed Income*, Daniel Patrick Moynihan, who had a major role in persuading President Nixon to propose the plan, remarks, "The central political fact about the negative income tax is that Democrats did not dare be first to propose it and Republicans did." He continues:

> It is perhaps the ultimate irony that the Nixon proposal for a negative income tax was drafted by Democratic advocates who not months earlier had had the same proposal rejected by the Johnson Administration. (This in turn forced many liberal Democrats to reject the proposal, which, had it been put forth by one of their own, would surely have been hailed as the largest social achievement of the second half of the century. . . .)[3]

Pat Moynihan's use of the labels notwithstanding, the Family Assistance Plan was not really a negative income tax nor did it guarantee an annual income: only families could receive benefits, and the work requirement was integral to it. Some liberals hailed the Family Assistance Plan nevertheless. One was former HEW Secretary John W. Gardner. In a chance meeting with him just after I succeeded Robert H. Finch as Secretary of HEW, he told me that he would love to have been able to launch something like it but knew that he could never get it through the Johnson White House. John Gardner's Common Cause was a staunch member of the coalition which for nearly three years fought to get FAP through the Congress.*

With the help of this coalition and resourceful backup from HEW Under Secretary John G. Veneman, Ways and Means Committee Chairman Wilbur Mills—then at the peak of his considerable influence—steered FAP through the House in April 1970 by a comfortable margin. Hearings in the Senate Committee on Finance were scheduled for a month later. The chairman, Russell Long of Louisiana, is that rare hybrid, a conservative populist. A few of the members were sympathetic to FAP, though most viewed with suspicion any federally administered program costing a lot of money. The ranking Republican, Senator John Williams of Delaware, might well have opposed FAP anyway, but he had never been consulted while the proposal was being developed and had not even been invited to a White House meeting held to discuss plans for the Senate hearing. Having already announced his retirement, he was determined that the climactic achievement of his Senatorial service would be FAP's destruction.

On that fateful June morning when Bob Finch finally came before the Finance Committee, Senator Williams was ready and he was merciless. The Senator's weapon was one no one had paid much attention to before: the "notch problem."† Was the Secretary aware that in Chicago, under the Family Assistance Plan, earning one more dollar could cost a family of four $1,783? In Phoenix, $1,000? In New York City, $1,715? No matter that this was a consequence, not of FAP itself, but of the fact that when combined FAP benefits and earnings crossed a certain threshold the family would lose its eligibility for Medicaid, food stamps, and a public housing allowance. HEW did not understand its own program. HEW had not done its homework. HEW prom-

---

* Among the others were the AFL-CIO, the National Association of Counties, the League of Women Voters, the American Jewish Committee, the ADA, the NAACP, the National Council of Churches, the National Urban League, the UAW, the United States Governors' Conference, and the United States Mayors' Conference.

† On a chart showing family income as the combination of cash and benefits in kind, there is a sharp drop at that point. That is the "notch."

ised to go back and see what could be done to overcome these fatal defects.

On June 24, 1970, I succeeded Bob Finch as Secretary of HEW, and my turn came in July. (I had pointedly declined to accept Senator Williams's suggestion that I seek a postponement on the ground that I needed more time to prepare.) HEW was ready with proposals for sliding-scale reductions in Medicaid and food stamps geared to the increase of family income. HUD was going to submit a housing bill amendment that would eliminate the housing-allowance "notch." But now we had a new problem. By reducing Medicaid, food stamps, and housing allowances, as well as cash benefits, in proportion to the increase in family income, we had increased the "tax rate" on earnings from 50 percent to as much as 80 percent. This would reduce the incentive to work. But to eliminate the notch problem *and* reduce the tax rate would enormously increase the cost of the program. This was partly because lowering the tax rate increased the amount a family could earn without losing all its FAP benefits. It was also because the number of families eligible for some benefits increased rapidly as the benefit cutoff level went up.

While Senator Williams was stirring up the right wing, the late Dr. George Wiley, head of the National Welfare Rights Organization, was mobilizing the left. An organization primarily of welfare mothers, the NWRO wanted minimum benefits of $5,500 for a family of four; this, according to HEW's estimate, would have cost at least $50 billion more in its first full year (then assumed to be fiscal 1975) than the existing welfare system. The NWRO was also outraged by the requirement that mothers of school-age children would have to register for work. At one point during Bob Finch's tenure NWRO members barricaded themselves in his office for a whole day.

My own most memorable encounter with the NWRO came in 1972 at a convocation of the Albert Einstein College of Medicine. I had just stood up to listen to the glowing citation which accompanied the award of an honorary degree. At that moment Dr. Wiley, surrounded by a group of his welfare mothers (and a few fathers), came from the back of the hall, climbed up on the stage, and began to read a citation in quite a different vein. This citation was written in blurred ink on a roll of toilet paper; it conferred on me the degree of "Doctor of Inhumanity." To the pained embarrassment of the deans and other dignitaries, fearful that an attempt to turn off Dr. Wiley might provoke violence, such mouth-filling phrases as "monster of inhumanity," "callous and unfeeling functionary," and "oppressor of motherhood" rolled off the roll. I stood there woodenly, feeling that the words I was hearing had scarcely less application to me than other more flattering citations. When Dr. Wiley, having concluded his reading of the inscribed tissue, attempted to thrust it upon me, I preserved my wooden posture.

Caught in a crossfire between right and left, the 1970 version of FAP died with the expiration of the Ninety-first Congress. Its 1971 version, introduced as H.R.1, contained changes designed to strengthen the work requirement and provide better protection against fraud. It went through the House again in June. John Williams had retired and Wallace Bennett of Utah was now the ranking Republican on the Senate Finance Committee. Chairman Long kept promising action but finding new reasons for delay. Though Under Secretary Veneman and I offered him and Senator Bennett HEW's cooperation in adapting their ideas to our approach (or vice versa), they never took us up on it. In April 1972, instead, they put forward their own plan. Under this plan no one in a family with an employable member would get any benefits at all unless the employable member did some kind of work, even if only, to use Senator Long's favorite example, picking up dead dogs along the highway. The government would in effect be the employer of last resort. Secretary of Labor James D. Hodgson and I denounced the plan as "a $9 billion step backward . . . into the leaf-raking schemes of the 1930s." I had meanwhile negotiated with Senator Abraham Ribicoff of Connecticut, himself a former HEW Secretary, a compromise version of H.R. 1 somewhat more generous than the one which passed the House.

By June 1972, when the Finance Committee reported out the Long-Bennett bill, four possibilities existed: no bill, H.R. 1 in its House-passed form, the Ribicoff compromise, or a more "liberal" (i.e., more expensive) substitute proposed by Senator Edward

M. Kennedy and other Senators responsive to the NWRO. Public hostility to "welfare" had increased since 1969. Senator George McGovern, the front-running candidate for the Democratic Presidential nomination, was already in trouble with his National Income Insurance Plan. The Democratic National Convention was about to be held in Miami.

We in HEW had done a lot of nose-counting. We thought that the Ribicoff compromise, with a strong push by President Nixon, could muster a majority. His own legislative staff was not convinced, particularly as Russell Long had announced he would lead a filibuster against the compromise if it seemed to have a chance of success. I knew that with the increase in public hostility to welfare, President Nixon's enthusiasm for his own reform plan had cooled. Given his opponent's visible embarrassment on the welfare issue, it would have been hard to persuade him to go beyond the House-passed bill even if the chances of the Ribicoff compromise had been less doubtful. We in HEW had invested so much in the cause, however, that I had to make the attempt. At a meeting in the Oval Office I argued our case with all the eloquence at my command, but the President decided that the administration should stand on H.R. 1 The Supplemental Security Income program for the aged, blind, and disabled—a far-reaching reform in itself—was adopted, but welfare reform for families failed to pass the Senate and was dropped in conference.

We had to try again, of course. Of that I had no doubt. We also had to learn from our mistakes. Looking back, I could see that we had pursued simplicity and equity without fully understanding all the complexities of the system we were attempting to reform. Whatever his motives, John Williams had rendered a service by focusing attention on the "notch problem." There was much to be said for the Long-Bennett view that those who could work should work. And the NWRO had been right in insisting that making a home and caring for children *is* work.

We should also have pursued with greater consistency the aim of taking unnecessary decision-making out of the hands of government and placing it in the hands of individuals. The Ribicoff compromise had, it is true, contemplated eliminating the food stamp program and adding its expenditures to basic family income benefits. (Hard to administer and riddled with fraud, the food stamp program was the channel of distribution for $2.9 billion worth of food to 13.5 million Americans in fiscal 1974.) The same considerations would also have called for converting other benefits in kind into cash benefits. Among the programs which might be "cashed out" in this way were the public housing allowance and nutrition for the elderly. Total expenditures for these programs in fiscal 1974 were $540 million. This amount added to the cost of food stamps would have produced a total of nearly $3.5 billion that could be used to make the basic income benefits more adequate.

The income-assistance plan put forward in the Mega Proposal was designed to take advantage of everything we had learned. It proposed that the amount of a family's benefits be determined by the number of family members not available for work. Any family member who could reasonably be expected to work (every able-bodied person over sixteen years of age and not in school) could increase the family's income only by working. There would be a marginal tax rate of 50 percent on earned income and 100 percent on unearned income. All employable individuals would be assured training, a regular job, or—if necessary—a public service job, with incentives to find work through the regular market. Rather than require mothers of school-age children to work, then pay someone else to look after their children, only mothers having no children under fifteen would be considered available for work; this assumed that children fifteen and over would not need formal arrangements for after-school care. And benefits in kind would be cashed out.

Something like the Mega Proposal income-assistance plan will in due course be adopted. In 1974 HEW Secretary Caspar W. Weinberger recommended a program very like it to President Ford—and Weinberger, as those who knew him as director of the Office of Management and Budget would readily attest, is no softheaded "liberal." Professor Milton Friedman, the principal architect of the "Chicago School" of economic thinking, has won many "conservatives" to the concept of a guaranteed income. The present system, in any case, is so inequitable, so inefficient, and so susceptible to fraud that it must eventually provoke its own replacement. And that will be a victory for intelligent self-government as well as for humane concern for the unfortunate.

THIS COUNTRY'S odd assortment of devices for meeting health-care costs boasts many of the same bizarre characteristics as its welfare system. Equally the product of historic evolution, shortsightedness, and sheer accident, our health-financing devices are comparably complex, unintelligible, and unfair. Their principal components are Medicaid, Medicare, and private health insurance. In 1974, private health insurance covered about 26 percent of the nation's total personal health-care bill; Medicaid covered 11 percent; Medicare covered 13 percent; the rest was paid out of pocket. Each has its own defects, and the combination is impenetrably complicated.

Medicaid suffers from aggravated inequity. In a handful of states, it pays for all forms of health care needed by the poor: outpatient, dental, maternal and pediatric, psychiatric, surgical, long-term. In these states the maximum income level for eligibility is relatively high (as of September, 1975, $5,000 in New York, $5,100 in California, and $5,300 in Massachusetts). The federal government is required by law to reimburse a percentage of state Medicaid expenditures varying with state per capita income. The three above-mentioned states have been claiming 36 percent of all federal matching funds for Medicaid although they have only 21 percent of the nation's population. The remaining states have correspondingly inadequate programs. The poorest (Mississippi, Arkansas, and Alabama), despite the more favorable federal matching share, have been receiving only 4 percent of total federal Medicaid matching funds.

Medicare, by contrast, has the merit of providing uniform and reasonably adequate health-insurance coverage for everyone over sixty-five who is covered by the Social Security system. Medicare costs, however, have become staggering. Medicare expenditures have increased from $3.4 billion in 1967 to $15 billion in 1975. This financing squeeze threatens both to contract Medicare benefits and to force old people to pay a higher share of the costs out of their own pockets. And as costs have increased, so has the bureaucratic burden imposed by Medicare on the health-care system. Since the working people who are taxed to pay for Medicare have a right to be satisfied that their money is being spent wisely, Medicare cost and quality-control requirements have become constantly more demanding and detailed.

Private health insurance, although its coverage in some form now reaches 76 percent of the population, is inadequate in its protection of low-income families not eligible for Medicaid and not belonging to some employee group plan.

All the plausible approaches to simplifying and reforming this jerry-built structure point toward the desirability of a national health-insurance system providing an adequate level of benefits for all or most of the population. The question of how best to do this has produced a welter of competing and contradictory approaches. Among the objectives that have to be brought into some kind of balance are relating premium cost to ability to pay, minimizing bureaucratic interference with the health-care system, improving cost and quality controls, preserving a role for the private health-insurance industry, permitting responsiveness to local requirements, and discouraging over-utilization.

It is, of course, impossible to give equal weight to all these objectives. The point is illustrated by the two leading national health-insurance proposals being debated at the time when the Mega Proposal was under development. One was a bill sponsored by Senator Kennedy and Congressman Mills. Comprehensive in coverage, adequate in benefits, and capable of massive leverage on the delivery system, it would also have been highly centralized in its administration and oppressively top-heavy in its bureaucratic structure. The cost in its first full year (as of fiscal 1973) would have been over $100 billion, half of which would come from general revenue, the other half from a payroll tax. It would totally have eliminated private health insurance. The other approach was the "National Health Insurance Partnership Act," which was submitted to the Congress by the administration in February 1971. The Partnership Act combined a federally financed substitute for Medicaid with a requirement that all employers provide a specified minimum level of health benefits with the premiums divided between the employer and the employee. This approach would have avoided excessive centralization by preserving a major role for the health-insurance industry, but it was complex in structure, unsatisfactory in its coverage of single individuals and small employee groups, and (except for welfare families) took no account of ability to pay.

The Mega Proposal attempted to combine the comprehensiveness and structural simplicity of Kennedy-Mills with a residual role for private insurance and highly progressive financing. Called Maximum Liability Health Insurance (MLHI) and financed by a progressively scaled income-tax surcharge, it would have paid for all health expenses exceeding a specified proportion of individual or family income. Like the Kennedy-Mills bill, it would have supplanted Medicare and Medicaid (except for long-term care) and eliminated both the Medicare payroll tax and income-tax deductions for health expenses. With government-financed protection against catastrophic costs, a family could then, if it chose, buy private health insurance for expenses below the income-related level at which MLHI took over. But MLHI also had the defects of its qualities. Its reliance on federal tax support, for example, would tend to create some of the same bureaucratic top-heaviness which is such a glaring defect of Kennedy-Mills. Being limited, moreover, to the coverage of catastrophic costs, it would have been likely to divert health-care dollars into high-cost procedures.

As THE THIRD component of its effort to simplify government assistance to families and individuals, the Mega Proposal undertook to rationalize the federal role in higher education. From the time in 1958 when the National Defense Education Act was enacted until adoption of the Higher Education Amendments of 1972, the number of narrowly targeted higher-education programs grew from fifteen to over one hundred—about the same rate of proliferation as in other human-resources areas. Meanwhile, the proportion of students attending independent institutions was cut in half, dropping from 50 percent to 25 percent of the total, while enrollment in tax-supported institutions rose correspondingly.

By 1970, the Washington representatives of the higher-education organizations, known collectively as "Dupont Circle" after the address of their headquarters, were agreed on a federal remedy for the fiscal crunch just then beginning to be felt. The remedy was an institutional aid formula under which every college and university, public and private alike, would receive so many federal dollars per enrolled student. It had their unanimous backing primarily because it was the only thing on which they could agree. I could not convince them that it made no sense to spread federal money in an even layer across the entire higher-educational landscape. Why should endowed institutions and tax-supported institutions, high-cost institutions and low-cost institutions, efficient, economically run institutions and wasteful, extravagant institutions, major universities and two-year colleges, all get the same amount per student? This approach, I argued, evaded the real issues of federal policy toward higher education.

Congresswoman Edith Green, chairman of the Higher Education Subcommittee of the House Committee on Education and Labor, was the sponsor of a bill embodying the Dupont Circle formula, and when higher-education legislation began to gather momentum in 1972, Mrs. Green was stubbornly committed to the all-out support of the formula. With our urging and the help of the Carnegie Commission on Higher Education,* the Senate subcommittee chaired by Senator Claiborne Pell of Rhode Island adopted a substitute formula tying federal institutional aid to numbers of federally assisted students. The Senate concurred, and after a bitter wrangle in conference, this formula became part of the Higher Education Amendments of 1972 which, at the time, I hailed as "landmark legislation." The institutional aid provisions, however, have never been funded, and I now think they were a mistake: a formula is a formula, and although this one was geared to an identifiable federal interest, its application bore no

* The Carnegie Commission on Higher Education, located in Berkeley, California, was established in 1967. Under the direction of Chairman Clark Kerr, the Commission conducts policy studies in higher education.

relation to the relative financial need of the recipient institution and did not appreciably help independent as against tax-supported institutions.

It does not follow, on the other hand, that alternative forms of institutional aid are more attractive. To the contrary, the bureaucratic complexities of any attempt to measure the particular financial needs of individual institutions and to tailor federal assistance accordingly are horrible to contemplate. The attempt, moreover, would virtually compel excessive federal intrusion into institutional affairs. Far better, then, to concentrate federal support for postsecondary education on student assistance, with adequate recognition of tuition costs. Giving individuals the power of choice in the educational marketplace can help preserve diversity and pluralism while at the same time relieving pressure on the finances of those institutions which, because of their high tuition costs, have had to devote a large share of their own resources to student aid. This was the Mega Proposal approach, and I still regard it as sound.

THE MEGA PROPOSAL was respectfully received when I presented it to President Nixon's top domestic advisers at a meeting in the Roosevelt Room of the White House on December 12, 1972. When I left HEW a month later to become Secretary of Defense, the pangs I felt were sharpened by the awareness that I was endangering the survival of the Mega Proposal not simply by my own departure but because Larry Lynn and his principal deputy, John M. Seidl, had also decided to leave. I was hopeful, nevertheless, that even without our continuing involvement the Mega Proposal's inherent logic would in due course prevail.

As matters turned out, the Nixon administration never did adopt the Mega Proposal as an integrated policy initiative. Among the explanations, I think, were Watergate, interdepartmental disagreements, and—perhaps—a lack of commitment to the essentiality of simplification. The proposal has had a continuing impact, nevertheless, on HEW planning and thinking. The administration's 1973 health-insurance proposal grew directly out of it, as did the income supplementation plan presented to President Ford by HEW Secretary Caspar W. Weinberger in the fall of 1974. This new plan embodied all the essential elements of the Mega Proposal income-maintenance plan: a strong work incentive; a penalty for refusal to work; and the cash-out of benefits in kind (food stamps and housing allowances primarily).*

The Mega Proposal was also the basis of a social-services special revenue-sharing bill sent to the Hill early in 1974. Combining six major formula grant programs (child welfare, vocational rehabilitation, developmental disabilities, services to families, services to the aging, and the nonexperimental parts of Head Start), it would bring together spending authorities totaling $3.2 billion, 90 percent of which would be earmarked for services to the poor. As this consolidation moves forward, the consolidation of health programs should follow.†

I remain hopeful that these and other elements of the Mega Proposal will eventually be adopted. More than twenty years ago I served as the secretary of a committee to study the organization and structure of the government of Brookline, Massachusetts, a town of about fifty thousand people. We worked hard for two years and made a number of carefully considered recommendations. To our huge disappointment, the recommendations were all rejected by a lopsided town meeting vote. As it turned out, however, thoughtful citizens of the town continued to discuss them. Ten years later, similar recommendations by a simi-

* The work incentive contemplated that the cash income supplement would equal one-half of the difference between a family's actual income level and its "break-even" income level. The able-bodied unemployed with no child-care or other home responsibilities would be referred to state employment services for help in obtaining a job or training opportunity. And as the penalty for the refusal to work, eligibility for income supplementation would cease and the amount of the family's benefit would be reduced accordingly.

† President Nixon's 1971 State of the Union message proposed six special revenue-sharing programs—in addition to education, they were urban development, transportation, law enforcement, manpower training, and rural development. The manpower training proposal, which covered programs under three separate acts with total expenditures of $863 million in fiscal 1974, went through at the end of 1973. A community development revenue-sharing program has also been enacted which consolidated all of HUD's existing community development programs. These include Urban Renewal, Model Cities, Neighborhood Facilities, Open Spare Land, and Basic Water and Sewer Facilities.

lar committee (my wife was the secretary of this one) were approved by an almost equally lopsided vote.

Thoughtful citizens, I feel sure, will continue to discuss the Mega Proposal and consider the applicability of its ideas to areas outside HEW where the functions of the federal government have been allowed to become excessively complex. And in due course the time of these ideas will also come.

To ACHIEVE intelligibility and strengthen democratic processes it is not enough to reduce complexity and fragmentation only at the top. Such efforts are also needed at the community level. The average middle-sized city has between four and five hundred service-providing agencies. Eligibility for their help is normally based on residence, but the applicable residential areas are not consistent. One agency accepts only the residents of a city, a second accepts only the residents of a district within the city, and a third accepts only the residents of a neighborhood within the district. A father is helped by one program at one location, his daughter by another elsewhere, and his elderly parents by still another program at still another location.

The welfare mother struggling to free herself from dependency must deal with entirely separate agencies, many of which maintain only the loosest of ties with each other. Her needs may include counseling or rehabilitative services for emotional or physical problems, help in learning a new job skill that would make her employable, homemaker services, and day care for her children so that she can get into a training program. With such a list of service needs—and it would not be unusual—she is certain to face an endless round of visits to different agencies. She will be shuttled from one office to another, given incomplete information, and—almost surely—emerge believing that "the system" has not only failed her but abused her.

In July 1974, testifying before the House Committee on Education and Labor, HEW Under Secretary Frank Carlucci* told the committee that multiproblem clients are more nearly the

* As this is written, U.S. Ambassador to Portugal.

rule than a rarity. He cited the examples of Contra Costa, California, where it was estimated that 75 percent of clients required services from more than one agency; Jonesboro, Arkansas, where the proportion of multiproblem clients was 68 percent; Nyssa, Oregon, where it was 42 percent; and Devil's Lake, North Dakota, where it was 40 percent. But even these figures, Mr. Carlucci said, were probably understated. A study of a Roxbury, Massachusetts, agency found that only 25 percent of the agency's clients at first mentioned more than one problem, but agency staff later discovered that 71 percent actually had multiple-service needs.

As Lieutenant Governor of Massachusetts in 1965–1966, I became increasingly disturbed by the tendency to lose sight of the whole person—to subdivide a person's problems and parcel them out to a host of different agencies. Not only are the agencies devoted to helping people too numerous, too limited in function, and too isolated from each other, but they can be fiercely jealous in protecting their own turf. The so-called helping professions are fully as guild-minded as any craft union. No wonder that government is so often perceived as impersonal and indifferent. As a creative matter, the system is stifling. As an intellectual matter, it is almost incomprehensible. And as a human matter, it can be downright cruel.

The opportunity to make these discoveries did not come with the job of Lieutenant Governor. It came about because, having lost the Republican nomination for Attorney General in Massachusetts to Edward W. Brooke in 1962, I had no plans to run for anything in 1964. Former Governor John A. Volpe did have plans. Having been narrowly upset in 1962 by Endicott "Chub" Peabody, a Yankee Democrat, he saw in me a ticket-balancing asset for their return match. Just a few weeks before the 1964 Republican State Convention he put to me the idea of my running for Lieutenant Governor. I wasn't greatly interested. The Lieutenant Governor of Massachusetts has very few duties, and I had no wish to spend two years with nothing better to do than to try to improve my chances for some higher office. But then it occurred to me that I might be able to make use of my experience in HEW during the Eisenhower administration. "I'll run, John," I eventually told the former Governor, "but only if you'll agree that if we're both elected you will delegate to me responsibility for coordinating all the state's health, education, and welfare programs." He did agree, and in the teeth of Senator Goldwater's defeat in Massachusetts (he got barely more than a fifth of the state's vote) we both squeaked by. On the day of our inauguration I had ready for Governor Volpe's signature a letter carrying out the promised delegation.

Coordination, as it turned out, wasn't all I had hoped it would be. I met regularly with the heads of all the human-resources agencies (public welfare, public health, mental health, vocational rehabilitation, education, corrections, and youth services). We identified problems of overlap, duplication, omission, and inconsistency, but we seldom solved them. From time to time, as a by-product of better communication, we were able to iron out particular difficulties or mount a combined attack on some budgetary or administrative issue. It became increasingly clear, however, that to overcome fragmentation in human services there must be added to coordination at least two other ingredients: first, joint planning among service providers and, second, the power to see to it that the joint plan is carried out.

How could this be done? One way to find out was to experiment. Just then I happened to talk with William A. Bronstein, a Brockton, Massachusetts, banker who headed the local community services planning agency. It turned out that he was already seeking a way of improving the coordination between the voluntary agencies and the public agencies serving the Brockton area. With the help of a small HEW grant obtained through the good offices of that extraordinary public servant, the late Mary E. Switzer, then administrator of the Social and Rehabilitation Service, planning for the project got under way in 1965. It was the first, so far as I knew, embracing both public and voluntary agencies.

Another way to encourage effective joint planning was by legislation. One day, in the middle of a flight to Washington with my legislative assistant, Martin A. Linsky, it suddenly struck me that the federal government, instead of promoting fragmentation, should be holding out affirmative inducements to service providers to communicate with each other, to engage in joint planning, and to establish comprehensive systems for meeting the needs of people. When we got back to Boston, Marty and I immediately began to draft a piece of federal legislation designed to carry out these objectives. Calling the bill the Community Services Act of 1966, I took it to Washington to get it introduced by the chairmen and ranking members of the House and Senate HEW appropriations subcommittees—Senators Lister Hill of Alabama and Jacob K. Javits of New York, Congressmen John Fogarty of Rhode Island and Melvin R. Laird of Wisconsin. They would be appropriate sponsors, I thought, because they were better able than anyone else in the Congress to see how impossibly fragmented the delivery of human services had become. It was not hard to get them to introduce the bill. I then sent copies, together with an explanatory statement, to the human-service agency heads in every state. Many wrote back offering to testify in its support. Then came my election as Attorney General of Massachusetts. My successor as Lieutenant Governor did not inherit my health, education, and welfare role, and no one else in the Statehouse was in a position to push the bill.

When I became Secretary of HEW in 1970, I quickly found that the problem of human-services fragmentation was even worse than I had remembered it. The basic concept of the 1966 bill was more needed than ever. A task force headed by departmental counselor Jonathan Moore, whose resourcefulness, tenacity, and astute judgment were my mainstay at HEW as they had been at State and were later to be at Defense and Justice, took this concept as a starting point and hammered it into a new and substantially improved approach to the integration of human services. Called the Allied Services Act of 1972, the new bill was modest in cost and voluntary in application but broad in scope. One of its titles would help the participating states pay for plans dividing their territories into human-services areas, designating the services to be combined in community-based systems within those areas, and describing means of integrating such common-denominator activities as outreach, intake, referral, and so on. A second title would provide funds to states and local service areas to meet the initial cost of consolidating services, support activities, and management functions. The third title would loosen certain categorical constraints—for example, by allowing the transfer of up to 30 percent of categorical-grant funds from one program to another and the waiver of federal restrictions interfering with a state's ability to implement its plan.*

Although the national organizations representing general-purpose governments strongly support the bill, its interest-group opponents have to date succeeded in keeping it locked up in committee. They fear, they say, that the integration of human services "will dilute the unique expertise and capabilities that each separate categorical program brings to bear." They also claim to be worried that the authority to transfer funds from one program to another would make possible wholesale shifts of funds, thus leaving some needy group without services. These concerns seem to me implausible. The purpose of the act is to combine expertise, not dilute it. The fund transfer authority would simply permit localities to use categorical funds where they are most needed. One is forced to conclude that the real reason for interest-group opposition is the familiar reason—preservation of their own control over a federal funding source.

Meanwhile, states and localities have been moving forward on their own—partly, I would like to think, as a result of awareness of the Allied Services Act. The Council of State Governments reports that twenty-six states now have comprehensive human-resource agencies.† Human services-oriented agencies are also being formed in many cities—and a few counties—throughout the country. Seattle, San Diego, Chattanooga, and Minneapolis, for example, have created departments of human resources or human services. In other cities the chief executive has created offices with human services coordinating responsibility. The

* The most recent version of the bill was reintroduced in the House on October 2, 1975, by Congressmen Quie, Perkins, Brademas, and Bell and referred to the Committee on Education and Labor.

† These include public welfare and social services and at least three of seven other major areas—health, mental health, mental retardation, corrections, youth services, vocational rehabilitation, and employment security.

Chattanooga program interconnects over one hundred human-services agencies throughout the metropolitan area via a computerized intake and referral system. Any person, no matter what his problem, can walk into any agency and be sure of access to the entire network of agencies. A centralized transportation system and central purchasing, data-processing, and other support services have resulted in substantial economies.

The Brockton Multi-Service Center is still one of the most comprehensive projects. Testifying on behalf of the Allied Services Act in July 1974, Under Secretary Carlucci, who had recently visited the project, described a multiproblem case identified by the project director as typical: A woman with mental health problems was assigned a case manager as the single point of contact for her and her family. Soon after her first visit, she was committed for a thirty-day period to a state mental hospital. Her husband, who had lost his job, was assisted in getting on welfare. Temporary foster care was provided for their children. The case manager then arranged for community-based mental health services for both husband and wife so that the family could be reunited, persuaded the parents to enter adult education classes, found a new job for the husband, helped the family qualify for food stamps, and procured new clothing and Head Start enrollment for the children.

AT THE HEART both of the Mega Proposal and the Allied Services Act were simple synthesizing principles. In the case of the former, these included reliance on cash as the primary medium of income support for the individual, the functional organization of federal support for state and local services, and the capacity-building concept. In the case of the latter, the synthesizing principle was respect for the whole person. A similar effort to discover and apply a better synthesis—to discern unifying elements in what looks at first like a confused jumble—must be the starting point of every effort to cope with complexity.

My own impression, reinforced by an informal and unscientific poll of my middle-aged contemporaries, is that our children's generation has considerably greater capacity to handle the present order of complexity than we have. Perhaps it is because they have not lived so long and thus have not been required to adjust to as much change as their parents have had to absorb. But I think it may also be due to the much wider exposure to the world that television has been giving them from infancy onward. They take for granted patterns and relationships—conceptual structures—that are harder for us to see because we superimpose on our perceptions an overlay of earlier experience.

Any level of complexity, in theory, can be embraced within some more comprehensive synthesis, and we can always keep on creating new syntheses until we achieve intelligibility—the ability to grasp and cope with reality. "If somebody can't say it simply," the economist Wassily Leontief has said, "it's because he doesn't understand it himself."* The double helix of a DNA molecule is a complex structure serving as a link in a highly complex process, but it explains so much—the reproduction of the species and the replication of individual attributes—that its discovery has been, in a sense, vastly simplifying. What is required, essentially, is the ability to discover order in spite of confusion. A Monet landscape communicates reality, though it does not show every leaf.

These examples, to be sure, are the products of extraordinary talent. We cannot achieve more adequate syntheses simply by wishing for them. And yet nothing in our time has so seriously frustrated the enhancement of intelligibility as lazy acquiescence in the notion that the "two cultures" C. P. Snow wrote about are forever two and divisible.[4] The disciple of the "liberal arts" is happy to embrace Aristotle's *Physics* within his field of learning without pausing to note that Aristotle himself would have been likely to regard his labors as more closely linked to those of Einstein or Heisenberg than to those of Unamuno or Sartre. Great philosophers, indeed, like Spinoza and Whitehead, have always seen their task as that of inventing hypotheses that can help to account for the whole reality we perceive, not just a narrow slice of it. The rewards of science, on the other hand, have usually gone to the opposite extreme—to the discovery of new knowledge on a narrow front, rather than to synthesis on a

* Professor Leontief made this remark during an "evening dialogue" at the Woodrow Wilson International Center for Scholars in the summer of 1974.

broad front. Our need now is for people whose conceptual creativity can help us to comprehend the world of science.

IN ADDITION to better synthesis, the effort to cope with complexity demands better planning. For a long time in this country "planning" was a dirty word. Its bad reputation was partly, no doubt, a well-deserved consequence of its association with the all-embracing determinism of the Soviet "five-year plans." Since planning implies intervention in the natural course of events, letting government plan goes against the grain of a country which has good reason to be proud of its free institutions. And yet plan we must, as we are rapidly learning. Population pressures on the land, shortages of key commodities, and growing demands for the more equal sharing of our total resources all create demands for government intervention that must be met by some kind of response. One cannot reach a rational decision about what to do in these cases without an adequate understanding of the potentially wide repercussions of a given course of action (or inaction).

Understanding of widely ramifying interactions is obviously not easy to achieve. It must rest on a solid foundation of reliable information and a high level of analytical capability. It must also be broad in its scope and middle to long-range in its focus. Analysis of the possible effects of government intervention into a given situation is commonly thought of as part of the planning process, but it seems to me important to distinguish this kind of analysis from planning. It is different because it governs neither the selection nor the execution of a particular course of action. A plan, on the other hand, should embrace goals and objectives, lay out steps toward reaching them, and provide for the periodic assessment of progress toward its fulfillment. To keep the distinction clear, I shall refer to the former process as "strategic analysis" and reserve the term "planning" for the latter.

Since planning, as I have defined it, necessarily implies intervention, and since the need for planning will increase, free societies will have increasing need to expand their capacity for strategic analysis. Their citizens will otherwise find government intruding itself ever more pervasively into their lives, for only through sound strategic analysis is it possible to minimize the tendency of government intervention to beget further government intervention.

It is a tendency that I have often observed. When, for example, the Supreme Court of the United States struck down the "separate but equal" doctrine in 1954, it may at first have seemed that all that would be necessary to get rid of a dual school system would be to send half the white children to formerly all-black schools and half the black children to formerly all-white schools. But suppose the white children and the black children were still segregated in separate classrooms? To make sure that this did not happen, federal authorities had to look inside the school buildings. Suppose they found an all-black third-grade said to be justified by achievement tests showing the black children to be in need of compensatory help? To be satisfied that this justification was genuine, the federal authorities then had to ask to see the test scores. What about the athletic teams, the cafeteria, the senior prom, extracurricular activities? When I got to HEW in 1970, detailed guidelines covering just such matters had long been promised. For a time I was imprudent enough to lend my own support to the fulfillment of this promise. In due course, however, I became convinced that too much is too much, and we made it clear that we expected such problems to be worked out by local biracial committees.

To avoid the quicksand, it is essential to start with a clear perception of the probable effects of intervention. It is the defining characteristic of a system that if you put a strain on it anywhere, this strain will be transmitted throughout the structure; if you poke it in one place, it will bulge somewhere else. When you don't know just what will happen when you pull or poke, you're likely to have to find a remedy for an unintended effect. The remedy makes something else go wrong, and this necessitates further correction, and so on. The result can be like trying to even up the legs of a chair so that it will sit firmly on the floor: you take a little off one leg and then a little off another and another until you end up with a legless chair.

To understand the consequences of our possible actions without having to pay the price of error, we must, as the technocrats say, "build models." This is an artistic process not unlike drawing a cartoon. As a cartoonist for the *Harvard Lampoon* (drawing for it was my principal extracurricular activity in college), I learned that to draw a recognizable caricature you have to study a face from every angle and in all of its expressions. The result must convey, but not spell out, the telling details. Similarly, a planning model must be abstracted from underlying data which have been sensitively selected; the abstraction itself must not misrepresent their weight and proportion. Once the model has been constructed it can, of course, be tested against reality just as a cartoon can be tested against its subject.

The first step, for any given planning purpose, is to find out what data are relevant and what is their weight and proportion to each other and to the whole. Planned experiments can help produce the needed input. As Alice Rivlin, director of the new Congressional Budget Office, has pointed out, "Experiments may be expensive compared with traditional forms of social research, but even the costs of major experiments are small compared with the costs of social policies that do not work or that might have been significantly more effective if experimental results had been available."[5] As an alternative to deliberate experimentation, we should be focusing more attention on learning how to apply consistent yardsticks to the vast number of different approaches to common problems that are constantly being tried out all over the country by state and local governments and voluntary agencies. We could then take better advantage of the spontaneous experiments which occur in what Justice Oliver Wendell Holmes, Jr., called the "insulated laboratories" of our federal system.

THE MOST clear-cut recent example of the need to plan is the energy crisis. As Attorney General I attended meetings of the Cabinet Committee on Energy where, months before the Arab embargo, the need for comprehensive planning machinery—and the incredible lack of it—were both inescapably apparent. We had no comprehensive data, no planning machinery—not even any authority strong enough to end the jurisdictional infighting that seemed to grow in bitterness as the problem grew more serious.

Such was the state of affairs when, in August 1974 during a trip to the Soviet Union, I met with Vladimir Kirillin, Chairman of the Soviet Council of Ministers' Committee on Science and Technology. He grilled me persistently on the status of American planning to meet the energy crisis. I did my best to answer his questions, but my replies did not seem adequate even to me. It is inconceivable that they could have been convincing to him.

But if I was unable to convince Mr. Kirillin that this country could devise and execute a plan for a limited segment of its economy while preserving a major role for free market forces, I was equally unpersuaded by his and other Soviet planners' attempts to convince me that the Soviet central planning ("Gosplan") machinery will be adequate to the task of meeting substantially increased consumer demand. They were already aware, they assured me, that the complexity of the production and distribution system would inevitably have to grow at a rate much faster than the growth in individual consumption; Brezhnev, in fact, had pointed this out in a speech to the Central Committee of the Communist party the previous May.

The current five-year plan contemplated an 85 percent increase in production of consumer goods; the next five-year plan would project an increase at least as great. When I pressed the Soviet officials to explain how they proposed to refine the planning system to meet the new order of complexity created by these increases in productivity, their invariable answer was that it would be through the adaptation of American management methods! Having headed the two biggest departments in the American government, one (HEW) as measured by expenditures and the other (Defense) as measured by manpower, I thought I knew something about the strengths and limitations of American management methods. "If that's your best hope," I told them, "you can't get there from here."

What I was trying to say to the Soviet planners is illustrated by the example of the Department of Defense. The Department has by far the most sophisticated planning capacity anywhere in the United States government today—it must have, or it could not operate at all. But good as it is, the Pentagon's planning does not yet really embrace the national defense system as a whole; at best, it assembles bits and pieces of systematic analysis into a façade of comprehensive planning. To be truly comprehensive, the national defense planning system would have to start with the responsibilities of the United States for maintaining a stable structure of international peace, translate these responsibilities into potential demands on our military capability, and on that basis define service missions, determine force levels and training requirements, and procure weapons systems. All these steps, moreover, would have to be consistent with realistic projections of available resources in the light of present and foreseeable technologies.

As Secretary of Defense my greatest hope—and firmest resolve—was to create a collaborative process that would fully engage the uniformed services in thinking through these interrelated issues. The intended result was to be an intelligible set of priorities and requirements that could form the basis for a new national consensus about the perennial claim of the military establishment for a major share of our national resources. This would have been a formidable—perhaps impossible—task even for the Pentagon, which is a relatively self-contained and highly disciplined universe. The same approach, even though stretched to its utmost limits, could not conceivably be made adequate to deal with the economic activities and service functions of the society as a whole. This country's array of competitive forces, innovative impulses, spontaneous initiatives, and creative adaptations is far too multifarious to be brought within the compass of a centralized planning system. Our largest manufacturing corporation, General Motors, is responsible for only 2.5 percent of our GNP, but its operating divisions have more autonomy than entire segments of Soviet industry. This is why I doubt the ability of the Soviet planners to handle the demands that will be thrust upon them when the Soviet economy has become as complex as ours already is. When I think about the problems facing them, my reaction is to thank God for our (relatively) free markets.

But even if there could be conjured up some future generation of computer models capable of simulating the entire economy, I cannot imagine their being able to come close to matching the flexibility and resilience of our existing pluralistic system. I am convinced that the displacement by some central authority of the autonomous decision-making now carried out by state and local governments, private organizations, and individuals would exact an excessive price in the form of gross inefficiencies and stultifying rigidity. And even though I were shown to be wrong in this conviction, I would never willingly see us forced to accept the loss of responsiveness to individual people and the dilution of their participation in the political process which are such palpable costs of the Soviet system even at its present, still relatively simple, stage of economic development.

In this country, the number of critical, long-term national needs that cannot be met without some degree of government intervention and control is bound to increase. The Soviet Union, on the other hand, must either learn how to let go of much of the decision-making now being done at the center and allow it to be done by individual industries, components of those industries, and subnational units of government or else be forced to accept the increasing inefficiency consequent upon its incapacity to cope with the increase of complexity. For both countries, a basic necessity will be to assemble the data indispensable to understanding each component of the system of systems constituting the society as a whole.

Paradoxically, our capacity to understand the dynamic interrelationships of our own society—and, as a corollary, our planning ability—needs to be more highly developed than the Soviet Union's. In the USSR, total intervention is the automatic consequence of total planning, and the price in loss of freedom has already been paid. If a Gosplan blueprint for one part of the economy turns out to have unforeseen and undesirable consequences for another part, whatever corrective action may be called for does not necessitate any new government authority or any new sacrifice of autonomy. If, on the other hand, we attempt some form of limited intervention but do not clearly understand what we are doing, we may then have to intervene more

deeply. A likely consequence is that we end up sacrificing more
flexibility and freedom for the sake of the public purpose which
prompted the initial intervention than we would have been willing to sacrifice had the whole cost been known at the outset. The
example of Vietnam is analogous; that of wage and price controls
is precisely in point. Because we cannot possibly foresee all the
side effects of the attempt to regulate wages and prices, we cannot keep the controls in place for long without being forced
either to abandon them altogether or to dig ourselves even more
deeply into a totally planned economy. This, as I read it, was the
lesson taught by Phases I, II, III, and IV of the "New Economic
Policy" so grandiloquently announced in the summer of 1971.*

The conclusion I come to, then, is that planning capacity,
like military capacity, should be adequate to any contingency
but called upon only when and as actually needed. The existence
of the tool must not become the excuse of using it. Thus we must
do the necessary strategic analysis, but avoid the temptation to
leap from analysis to intervention and from initial intervention
to deeper intervention. But first we shall have to make it the
responsibility of some government agency to assemble the
required data base and shape the needed analytical tools. As matters stand, a lack of governmental capability results in an excess
of governmental intrusion. We need a new government agency
in order to prevent the creation of unneeded government agencies. The new agency should be located in the executive branch,
but its work should be common property accessible alike to other
agencies, the Congress, and the public. This consideration, I
believe, points to the desirability of placing the function of
strategic analysis in an independent agency; OMB, where it
would otherwise be logical to lodge it, is too closely tied to the
President. Wherever located, the analytical process should be
called upon first—and most frequently—for the information on
which independent, private decisions can be based. In the situations where private decisions are fettered by noncompetitive
restraints, vigorous antitrust law enforcement should seek to
make the market more free. In the situations where free market

* See Chapter IX, p. 341.

processes fail adequately to serve compelling public interests, analysis can help illuminate the choice of indirect means—tax policies, loan guarantees, and other financial incentives—that can influence the market without preempting its functions. Given competent strategic analysis, adequate precision in planning, and reasonable skill in the administration of indirect devices, large-scale government intervention and control should then be necessary only in such dire—and hopefully temporary—circumstances as war or severe national crisis. And because precise planning depends upon a grasp of the underlying data as firm as a cartoonist's perception of his subject, the achievement of this capacity will immensely enhance the opportunity for public understanding of critical choices.

Simplification, synthesis, strategic analysis, and planning—can these measures, even in combination, make a significant impact on the inexorable onslaught of complexity? I think they can, but only if they are pursued with determination, resourcefulness, and an urgent sense of their critical importance. It is not the probability of success, in any case, that should spur the effort, but the possibility of failure. For to fail is not only to make inevitable the forfeiture of everything accomplished by the strengthening of accountability, the restoration of trust, and the illumination of choice but progressively to diminish the viability of free self-government.

VI

Government Gone Wrong:
Returning Power
to the People

THE PREVIOUS CHAPTER argues that simplification is necessary to preserve the possibility of intelligent choice. Where simplification concerns federal functions, it also contributes to the decentralization and dispersal of power. This is because simplification eliminates excessive and overlapping federal constraints on the performance of tasks already being carried out elsewhere in the system. The result reduces the number of decisions made by people at the top layer of government without increasing the number that have to be made by others. But all federal restrictions and requirements are assertions of federal authority. Their elimination thus has the effect both of contracting federal authority and expanding state, local, or private authority. Simplification, therefore, does shift power from the center to the periphery, and the outcome is, in a real sense, decentralization.

As ordinarily used, however, decentralization refers to the actual shift of a task from a central authority to a peripheral one. The case for decentralization as thus defined must therefore rest on a footing much broader than simplification. To me, the arguments in favor of decentralization are powerfully persuasive, but perhaps that is only because they speak to my experience and echo my prejudices. Be that as it may, a bare summary should be sufficient to make clear the premise on which this chapter is based.

The United States already has a high degree of decentralization—or, more accurately, of noncentralization. Under the Constitution, our states and localities have always retained the powers which they did not choose to delegate to the central government. In this country, therefore, the only real debate centers on whether we should encourage a reversal of the long-term trend which for decades has steadily increased the relative power of the central government within the federal system. Parts of this trend, of course, have been legitimate and necessary: the federal government is the necessary instrument for protecting the citizen against abuses of concentrated economic power, downturns in the business cycle, fluctuations in agricultural prices, pollution of the continental air mass, and a host of other consequences of the interdependence of our social and economic system. The inward flow of power, however, has also contributed to the ills and excesses that are the concern of much that I have said in previous chapters. Starting from the point we have now reached, selective decentralization will help to cure the ills and correct the excesses. It will make government more responsive, more accessible, and more manageable. By dispersing power, decentralization will diminish our vulnerability to its abuse. And because the dispersal of power reduces the size and increases the proximity of the units which possess power, the individual thereby gains greater opportunity to exert an impact on the way it is exercised. Individual liberties and the individual's control over his own destiny will both be strengthened.

To overcome the gravitational pull which for decades has been attracting power toward the center, we have to distinguish among its components. One that deserves to be neutralized is the "don't just stand there, do something" impulse: "End poverty!" "Stop drug abuse!" "Prevent crime!" For those moved by these categorical imperatives it is irksome to have to deal with scores of state governments, thousands of local governments, and hundreds of thousands of voluntary organizations. The ready answer—the direct route—is to exert pressure at a single point, call upon federal funds, enact a new law, set up a new agency. And, paradoxically, at the head of the march on Washington we often find state and local officials. The paradox is explained when we recognize that their primary allegiance is not to relationships within their own level of government, but to the groups at every level that are centered around the aims and needs of their own profession or service.

The programmatic ties binding professional colleagues at different levels of government are commonly stronger than the horizontal affiliations connecting the administrators of unrelated programs at the same level.

When I came to HEW late in 1956, the first thing Secretary Marion B. Folsom asked me to do was to analyze the role of the Children's Bureau, one of the Department's oldest components. Should its functions be split up among other departmental agencies? My eventual answer was no. The Children's Bureau, I found, was not really an autonomous entity but the core of a bundle of personal relationships among people who shared a common concern about maternal and child health programs and services to crippled children. This core extended vertically down through all layers of government into the voluntary agencies having similar concerns. To break up the bureau would destroy those relationships. Such links explain why state and local officials are so often found aiding and abetting an exercise of federal power which appears to override their own agency's authority but which actually serves a cherished program objective that has encountered some state or local obstacle.

However, the effort to avoid a local inconvenience often ends up creating a federal roadblock. What seemed to be an easy route to a quick solution becomes wearisome and time-consuming. One year, I remember, all the reformers in Massachusetts joined in applauding Ellen Winston, then head of the

Welfare Administration, for her firmness in threatening the Commonwealth with a cutoff of federal matching funds unless it amended its civil service law to require a bachelor's degree for social workers. Two years later the Poverty Program was touting the employment of "community people" in social service roles, and many of the same reformers were looking for ways of avoiding just such rigid restrictions.*

　　After prolonged and repeated exposure to people convinced that Washington must have the secret of a quick cure for any serious social ailment, I eventually realized that they simply do not understand the limitations on the federal capacity to meet human needs. With a few exceptions like Social Security, housing allowances, and health services for Indians, Eskimos, and merchant seamen, federal agencies do nothing directly to help anybody. The teachers, the healers, the social workers, and all those others who try to cope with people's problems are employed by state and local governments and private agencies, not Washington. The federal government can contribute by helping identify needs to be met, disseminating knowledge of better methods of providing services, supporting personnel training, and supplying financial assistance. In trying to do more, Washington can only get in the way. And while a secondary and supporting role for the federal government in meeting human needs is partly a consequence of the way our federal system was built, a sensitive awareness of people's problems and a sensible understanding of how best to respond to them would have brought us out at the same place. To adapt Voltaire, if we did not already have a federal system, we would have had to invent one.

ANOTHER COMPONENT of the push toward Washington has been distrust of the capacity of state and local government. Addressing the concern that "the federal edifice is buckling under the weight of a top-heavy steeple," Max Frankel of *The New York Times* has said that "the rest of the American struc-

---

* In both instances, I was among the reformers. For my present views, see the discussion of credentialism, Chapter III.

ture of government is in no condition to support anything."[1] His view of local government accords with that of the well-known sociologist Amitai Etzioni: "On the local level, power elites can gain their way more readily, nepotism and unvarnished corruption are more rampant, civil service standards are lower, the cost per unit of achievement is higher, and disregard for minorities is greater."[2]

There is still some evidence for that view, certainly, but state and local governments are gaining in competence almost everywhere. Although still handicapped by inadequate salaries and professional standards, shortsighted restrictions on staffing, and political corruption, the trend is sharply upward. The court-decreed demise of legislative malapportionment has helped. Better-trained people are coming into the state and local career services. Fiscal, structural, and ethical reforms are gathering momentum. And this momentum is likely to grow as responsibility is more clearly fixed on state and local governments and their enhanced power offers greater promise of a worthwhile return on the reformers' investment of effort.

In 1973, 30 states took some action on property tax relief; every state now grants it in some form. The same year, 10 states did something about equalizing school financing between school districts, even though the Supreme Court had just decided in the *Rodriguez* case that the Constitution does not compel equalization.* In the 1970–1972 biennium, 43 states improved the salaries and staffing of their legislatures.[3] As of June 1974, 24 states had adopted energy conservation plans and 17 had granted their governments emergency powers to deal with the energy crisis. All the states had offices of consumer affairs, 10 of which were operating before the creation of any federal consumer office. Virtually every state had some land-use planning authority and all 50 states had established air pollution control regulations before the federal Clean Air Act was passed in 1970.

The states have shown comparable initiative in responding to public demands for higher standards of political morality. Common Cause reported in 1973: "Are most state legislatures

---

* The *Rodriguez* case is discussed in Chapter IX.

unresponsive and recalcitrant? That's a common belief, but Common Cause has found exciting changes going on in the legislatures. . . . There was enough state progress in 1973 to put Congress to shame."[4] In that year half the states passed major legislation on campaign finance or government ethics and accountability. Nine states improved their laws assuring public and press access to government information and meetings. Five states passed laws establishing codes of ethics for state executive and legislative employees, bringing to 33 the total which then had some conflict-of-interest legislation.

At the city and county level the picture is, of course, uneven. With Newark, New Jersey, at one extreme and Beverly Hills, California, at the other, it is obviously impossible to develop a statistical composite that is not reminiscent of the classic definition of a statistician: a man with one foot in a bucket of ice and the other on a bed of hot coals remarking, "On the average, I'm fine." Like other governments, the cities and counties are torn between the demands placed on them and the resources available to them; as in the case of other governments, their best means of easing the strain is to improve their performance.*

Despite this strain, what I have seen in my recent travels has been reassuring. Teamwork between alert, aggressive mayors and county executives, professional administrators, and concerned citizens is delivering better government in places as different and distant from each other as San Diego, the Twin Cities, Indianapolis, Kansas City, and Atlanta. John Fischer, long-time editor of *Harper's* magazine, recently made a survey of American localities from which he drew the conclusion that the successful "experiments in social reconstruction nearly all have three things in common":

> (1) They have simplified, strengthened, and pulled together a multitude of local government units that were outmoded and impotent. . . .
> (2) The new regional authorities deal only with

* For a useful exposition of ways in which local government can be made more effective, see Brian W. Rapp and Frank M. Patitucci's forthcoming book, *Improving the Performance of City Government.*

regional problems; they interfere as little as possible with cherished and time-hallowed local institutions.

(3) They grew out of the initiative of private citizens . . . just ordinary people willing to labor for years for no reward except to make their communities better places to live in.[5]

As to state and local corruption, more of it has probably been uncovered during the five years from 1969 to 1974 than during any previous half-decade. Not counting the results in any of the 91 other federal judicial districts, just three of my former Justice Department colleagues—United States Attorneys Herbert J. Stern of New Jersey (now a federal judge), James R. Thompson of the Northern District of Illinois, and George Beall of Maryland—brought indictments during that period against 144 corrupt state or local officials. The combined five-year total of federal and state prosecutions for corruption was sickeningly large. It may be, however, that what appears to be an uncontrollable epidemic of corruption is actually the result of unprecedentedly effective efforts to uncover it. Courageous and aggressive prosecutors like Stern, Thompson, and Beall have developed a high degree of skill in using a powerful new tool: the ability to obtain for a small-fry criminal conspirator a grant of immunity from the use of his testimony against himself in return for its use against a bigger fish.

As Attorney General of Massachusetts I tried to get immunity legislation through the state legislature. The closest I came was when an immunity bill went through the Massachusetts House, only to be defeated in the Senate by a handful of votes in the closing hours of the session. This happened as the direct result of lobbying by Bristol County District Attorney Edmund Dinis, who thereby prevented my organized crime unit from immunizing witnesses who might have testified to his possible connections with the Cosa Nostra "family" centered in Providence, Rhode Island.

We are also witnessing a clash of cultures. Contemporary prosecutors tend to represent traditional middle-class values— efficiency, honesty in financial dealings, the precedence of issues over political loyalties—that are alien to the old-style political organization which survived on jobs, contracts, and miscellaneous favors and regarded graft as a necessary means of lubricating the machine. In New York City a recent investigation of corruption in the construction industry implicating 170 city employees and 63 business executives exposed what Mayor Abraham D. Beame called a "way of life of doing business with the city" which "may have existed for decades." The other places where similar ways of life have been exposed—Jersey City, Chicago, Baltimore—are cities in which the old machines had their strongest hold.

Where old-fashioned graft is effectively prosecuted, there is reason to hope that this will produce long-term improvement in the overall level of political morality. Such improvement certainly seems to have occurred in Massachusetts, where the work of the Massachusetts Crime Commission, the resulting prosecutions by Attorney General (now Senator) Edward W. Brooke, and my own investigations as United States Attorney reached a crescendo in the early 1960s. A concerted attack can generate a wave of public outrage which at its climax lifts the standards of political conduct to a level at which they tend to remain even after the outrage has subsided. Intermittent exposure of chronic corruption, on the other hand, may merely confirm the cynical assumption that all politicians are crooks.

I HAVE TOUCHED on two major components of the trend toward top-heavy central government—the impatient demand for a quick cure of social ailments and disdain for the capacities of subnational governments. Since World War II, the only other important component has been the growth of demand for government services. Fed by the postwar surge of marriages, births, home ownership, and urbanization, the demand for services burst upon state and local governments already hobbled by the inadequacies and inequities of their tax bases. To be required to respond to this demand by reliance solely on their own taxing capacity was bound to mean either that the response would be highly uneven or that the poorest states and localities would be badly hurt in their ability to compete for industry and jobs.

The obvious solution was to seek help from a taxing authority which could ignore disparities among state and local tax bases and which had no concern with interstate or intermunicipal competition. The nation has only one such authority—the federal government. And so, as the multiplier effects of the postwar surge began to compound themselves in the late 1950s and early 1960s, the governors and mayors and county executives hopped the planes to Washington, met with the President, set up Washington offices, and beat on the doors of their Senators and Congressmen.

Washington responded, but in Washington's way. Executive branch agencies saw the chance to promote their own programmatic objectives by directing the use of the money. The Congress, being charged with raising the necessary revenues and making the necessary appropriations, saw the chance to make sure that congressional purposes were also served. These impulses were reinforced by the notion that the federal government has a duty to see to the wise use of federally collected revenues and the belief—in which both branches joined—that the states and localities could not be trusted to do so on their own. The result was a new spurt of narrowly drawn legislation and a new outpouring of bureaucracy's usual product: regulations, guidelines, and reporting requirements.

It was, of course, understandable that both the executive branch and the Congress should see fit to take advantage for their own programmatic purposes of the straitened circumstances of state and local governments. The same could not be said for the assumption that the resulting subordination of state and local autonomy was warranted by a presumed obligation to exact state and local accountability for the use of federal funds. An even less convincing justification was the alleged superiority of narrowly drawn programs as vehicles for advancing national interests. As I shall attempt to explain, neither rationalization is valid.

First as to the presumption of accountability: the fact that the Internal Revenue Service collects money which the Congress then appropriates says nothing whatever about how much federal control should be exercised over its expenditure. No logic that I can see requires the level of government which spends tax revenue to be any more accountable to the level of government which raises it than is required by the terms of the gift. And if the Congress chooses to give away federal funds without strings rather than tie the money to some specific purpose, the recipient's accountability for those funds is the same as its accountability for any other expenditures.

It follows, then, that the distribution of federal funds among the states and localities does not have to be justified by its direction into some restricted use. It can be enough that the latter need the money and cannot raise it themselves without adding to the strains created by their unequal situations. And since the purpose of the distribution is to overcome inequalities among state and local tax bases, it also follows that the revenue should be shared on a basis favoring the poorest states and communities. To let the amount of income taxes collected in a particular state be the only measure of the share of federal revenue allocable to that state would be to make the rich richer and force the poor to remain so.

These, of course, are the very considerations which led to the enactment of general revenue-sharing in 1972. They make irrelevant the question whether the shared revenue is used to fund new programs, absorb the cost increase of old ones, or make possible a reduction of local property taxes. The essential objective is fairness among localities.

These same arguments were the ones I used back in 1965 to promote support for a sales tax whose proceeds would be distributed among all the Massachusetts cities and towns on a basis that would give the most help to the poorest communities. When, a few months after I became Lieutenant Governor, Governor Volpe asked me to take on this promotional task, the first thing I did was to organize a representative statewide group called "Citizens for Fair Taxes" with local chapters in most of the state's larger communities. Again and again at "Citizens" meetings all across the state, I hammered on the contrast between the stricken city of Fall River, impoverished by the abandonment of its textile mills, and the fortunate town of Somerset just across the river, where two big power stations paid most of the taxes. I pointed also to the plight of the crowded little city of Chelsea, which could afford to spend on public education only one-fourth as much per pupil as the Cape Cod towns, although the latter, because their tax bases were enriched by summer homes whose owners sent their children to school elsewhere, had tax rates of only one-tenth the Chelsea rate. Thanks to public recognition of the inherent unfairness of such situations, the sales tax went through the Democratic-controlled legislature over the opposition of its own leadership.

Second, as to the notion that the endless accumulation of narrowly drawn categorical-grant legislation would actually advance the targeted national interests: both the Congress and the executive branch were slow to perceive that program proliferation is ultimately self-defeating. One well-designed categorical grant-in-aid program can be genuinely effective in promoting a specific national interest. Each of several such programs may elicit the desired response. As the number grows, however, a point is reached at which the leverage exerted by any given program has been almost completely dissipated: state and local administrators, having a large bunch of federal carrots held out to them, are free to select only those which feed the activities they would have undertaken without any special inducement. The upshot is that excessive grant proliferation results in *less* benefit to any given national interest than it would receive from its proportionate share of a block grant. Why less benefit? Because the value of the categorical grants has been diminished by ballooning overhead, prolonged delays, and endless aggravation.

Despite these demonstrable facts, the proponents of federal action still cling to the belief that without some combination of federal carrot and stick, states and localities will neglect "critical" problems. What is sufficiently "critical" to justify federal intervention is seldom self-evident, of course. The assumption, in any case, that a given problem is in fact being neglected by other levels of government is often dead wrong—more often now, in fact, than ever before. As I have again and again discovered during constant travels around the United States, state, local, and voluntary agencies are the originators of the most exciting and innovative social programs being developed in this country today.

State, local, and voluntary responses to a particular problem may, to be sure, be quite uneven and slow to get under way, but that is likely to be the case despite the inducement of a federal grant. This is conspicuously true of programs in which matching grants are allocated among the states on a basis proportional to the amount each state is willing to put up. Take Medicaid, for instance: in fiscal 1975, 37 percent of federal matching funds went to only 3 states, and 63 percent to 47 states.* And in the case of project grants, which are awarded only to applicants able to satisfy all the standards of eligibility, the impact is bound to be spotty. This is not to say, of course, that the total response to a given problem is not greater than it would be if there were no federal program—only that the enactment of a federal program is no guarantee against either unevenness or delay.

Even in situations where a need for federal leadership can be demonstrated, it does not follow that pulling strings attached to federal funds—or, more often, trying to push them—is the best way of meeting that need. A better way is through providing what, for lack of a better term, is commonly referred to as "technical assistance." I have long urged the creation of a corps of federal agency representatives who, working out of their regional offices (there are now ten coextensive regions for most of the major domestic federal departments and agencies), would provide information about federal fund sources, transmit knowledge about what other states and localities are doing, pass on what has been learned from recent experimental projects, and call attention to significant research findings.† They would also explain alternative approaches to meeting a local need or solving a local problem and in so doing help to identify matters about which the community ought to have more information before making a decision.

The attempt in 1972 to adapt this approach to federal edu-

* See Chapter V, p. 173.
† The value of "technical assistance" is directly dependent, of course, on all the steps toward better evaluation, research management, and the like, that are discussed in Chapter IV.

cation programs led to my worst failure to anticipate a hostile congressional reaction in all my years at HEW in two administrations. Believing that local school boards and administrators should regard these programs as an array of resources to be called upon to meet their needs as they saw them, I encouraged the Office of Education to experiment with a series of "education renewal centers" through which federal funds could be funneled into local school systems. HEW would help pay the centers' staffs, and the Office of Education would create a nationwide cadre of education extension agents working directly with local school people just as agricultural agents work directly with farmers—to inform them about and help them test new ideas, products, and processes.

A useful plan, I thought—certainly not one to which anybody would be likely to have strong objections. When Sidney P. Marland, the Commissioner of Education, began to get rumblings of criticism from Capitol Hill, I discounted them. Even after hostility began to spread, I was confident that a careful explanation of what was being proposed would make clear that, contrary to our critics' concerns, funneling funds through regional centers would neither disregard categorical requirements nor diminish accountability to the Congress. But when Senator Alan Cranston of California introduced an amendment to the pending higher-education bill specifically prohibiting education renewal centers, the best I could do was to get him to agree to a compromise permitting a few renewal centers on a pilot basis. In the House-Senate conference, even this compromise was eliminated, and the centers were dead. The episode was a sharp reminder of how jealously the legislative committees guard the categorical concept—to the point, even, of regarding themselves as school boards for the nation.

The demise of the education renewal centers will prove, I hope, to have been only a temporary setback for the underlying concept. One of the most constructive results of simplifying the categorical-grant structure can be to free thousands of federal employees from the necessity of tending grant-in-aid machinery—issuing regulations, formulating guidelines, processing applications, disbursing funds, accumulating reports, and monitoring the observance of restrictions. Such simplification will let them devote their time instead to helping the people who help others.

In no area is technical assistance more needed than in the improvement of state and local planning. As I pointed out in the previous chapter, the key to social-services integration is joint planning. Better planning is also essential to better and less costly health care. The "state plans" now required by most grant-in-aid programs, however, are not really plans at all. They remind me of the real estate appraisals I used to look at as United States Attorney for Massachusetts when I was investigating land-taking frauds in the federal highway program; the typical appraisal contained 95 percent boilerplate, 5 percent substance. Often hundreds of pages long, "state plans" tell you all about the history, demography, resources, and government of the state, but precious little else.

A "real plan," as distinguished from a "state plan," is a document which sets forth goals, priorities, and timetables and specifies the means of meeting them. A "real plan" should be constructed from the bottom up with the genuine participation of the most affected communities and groups, not imposed from the top down. Whenever feasible, it should also contain output measures that can tell the planning agency what has been accomplished: measures like the number of heroin addicts still employed six months after treatment, the degree of improvement in reading test scores, or how much has been saved by an improvement in efficiency.

The opportunities for these forms of national leadership will be furthered not only by simplifying the grant-in-aid structure but by continued progress toward the regionalization of federal functions—itself a form of decentralization. Regionalization came a long way under the Nixon administration. When that administration came in, most of the domestic departments of government did not have regional offices with defined territories, few of the regional headquarters were in the same cities, and regional boundaries were seldom consistent. These anomalies made it hard for the regional directors of one department to communicate or cooperate with the regional directors of the other departments. Although the problem had long been recognized, the vested interests of the departments, the headquarters cities, and the latter's political patrons, made it extraordinarily troublesome to solve. I remember attending meetings on the subject at the Bureau of the Budget during the Eisenhower administration, and attempts to work it out go back at least to 1937. The problem was finally solved in 1969 for most of the grant-making agencies and departments, and since then Regional Councils have been set up in each of the ten regions.*

But it is one thing to reconcile regional boundaries and create Regional Councils; it is quite another to transfer decision-making authority to the regional directors and the regional representatives of federal agencies. Robert H. Finch, my predecessor at HEW, worked at this; I gave the effort consistent support; my successor, Caspar W. Weinberger, carried it on. All of us found the going slow. Agency heads often feel nervous about turning authority over to "the field," and members of Congress frequently resist a process which makes the decision-makers more easily accessible to state and local officials than to themselves. In a backhanded compliment to Cap Weinberger for his contributions to regionalization, the Congress has recently inserted language into several bills specifically prohibiting regionalization.† This, in my view, is a step in precisely the *wrong* direction. We should instead be seeking ways of strengthening the Regional Councils and bringing them closer to state and local authorities. Indeed, I think we ought to consider enlarging them to include state, county, and municipal representation.

* The Departments of Health, Education, and Welfare, Housing and Urban Development, Labor, the Office of Economic Opportunity, and the Small Business Administration were the original members of the Federal Regional Councils in 1969.

† An amendment to the General Education Provisions Act, which sets forth requirements as to privacy rights of parents and students, established a review board whose activities, except for the conduct of hearings, may not be carried out in any of HEW's regional offices. Similarly, the Health Manpower Act of 1974 prohibits regional offices from awarding grants or contracts and from reviewing and commenting on grant applications to be presented to the National Advisory Council on Health Professions.

TENDENCIES SIMILAR to those which expanded federal functions have also placed authority in the hands of larger units of state and local government than is justified by any real advantage of size. In government, scarcely less than in business, the notion that bigger is better too often commands uncritical assent. An example is the common assumption that larger government units are more economical and efficient than small ones —that the fragmentation of metropolitan areas makes municipal services costly and inefficient. In 1956, during one of my interludes of law practice, I was associated with three other young lawyers in founding an organization dedicated to just this assumption. Called the Greater Boston Area Council and composed of representatives of all the area's cities and towns, its purpose was to identify government functions that could more efficiently be administered on a basis transcending municipal lines and to recommend means of consolidating them. Governor Christian A. Herter addressed a crowded kickoff meeting of the Council at Boston's handsome old Symphony Hall. The members approved an agenda. Committees were appointed. We were in business—but not for long. By the end of the year three of the four founders had moved on to other occupations, and the venture collapsed. Its only enduring legacy was a piece of legislation which gave birth to a regional planning body for the metropolitan Boston area.

Although I have often cited this episode to illustrate the generally valid point that a few people can make the difference in any undertaking, it is less clear to me now than it was then that our departures precipitated the Council's collapse. If our premise had been right, the Council might well have sustained its initial momentum with or without our help. We supposed, for example, that the consolidation of suburban police departments would reduce the cost of police protection and improve its quality. To the contrary, a 1973 study by Elinor Ostrom and Roger Parks (both of the University of Indiana) of the police departments in 104 American cities indicates that size does not appreciably affect the per capita costs of police services; furthermore, the quality of police performance, as measured by citizen evaluations,* is higher for departments that serve suburban areas of 20,000 people or less (or center-city areas of 100,000 people or less) than for departments serving larger areas. Other studies point to similar conclusions with respect to a number of other functions—for example, urban renewal, education, and fire protection, which can be just as economical for populations as small as 25,000 as for units up to 250,000.

To the extent, of course, that technological innovations take over a larger share of these functions, it is likely that economies of scale will favor larger units but not necessarily larger units of governance. Many services which could best be performed with populations of, say, 250,000 or more could nonetheless be perfectly well performed by the private sector—with various communities of much smaller scale individually purchasing these services, and together providing the necessary population base to achieve the desired economy.

In place of the presumption that bigger is better I would put the presumption that smaller is better. Just as openness in government has a constant value which should prevail over all but the most compelling reasons for nondisclosure of information, so responsiveness and accessibility have constant values which should prevail over all but the most compelling reasons for centralized administration. Nor would I—if I were the judge— let this steady downward and outward pressure be overcome by a merely marginal showing of economy or efficiency: responsiveness and accessibility are worth more than any such marginal gain. I am ready to acknowledge, however, that some government functions could be decentralized only at vastly excessive cost. An obvious example is Social Security. Because the amount of the monthly benefit payment to a retired or disabled worker and his family varies with the duration of his employment and the amount of his earnings over a working lifetime, and because the benefit checks should follow him wherever he

---

* Evaluation ratings were based on the likelihood of a citizen's having been a victim, having reported a victimization, and/or having received police assistance in some form. See Elinor Ostrom and Roger Parks, "Suburban Police Departments: Too Many and Too Small?" *Urban Affairs Annual Review*, Spring 1973.

may choose to live, it would be utterly impractical to turn the Social Security system's record-keeping over to the states.

Other situations which resist decentralization—or justify centralization—involve "spillover" effects. The drainage of a river basin typically has no relation to lines of political jurisdiction, and air movement is oblivious of them. These geographical facts justify regional or national regulatory authorities. Other forms of "spillover" occur when the benefit of a service is shared more widely than its cost or when a cost is shifted to people who get no benefit. An excellent public library will attract and benefit citizens other than the taxpayers who support it; an upstream community can dump untreated sewage into a river and force downstream users to pay for water treatment. In such cases it is frequently argued that "jurisdictional size" should be large enough to "internalize" the spillover costs. The costs, to be sure, should be distributed over the broader base, but this can be done without enlarging or merging administrative jurisdictions. As I have previously pointed out, the geographical area within which taxes are levied need not—and should not by itself—determine the level or unit of government charged with administrative accountability.

There are some situations in which—despite my bias in favor of smaller units of government—I am persuaded that a responsibility should be moved to a higher level of government than that which now has it. A fair system of minimum income benefits for families, for example, can be managed so much more efficiently by a single entity than by a large number of state or county agencies that I have become a convert to the belief that it should be administered nationally.* In the case, however, of social services to welfare families, the situation seems to me quite otherwise. Here there are no overriding practical considerations pointing toward national administration, and a local agency can in any case respond more sensitively and flexibly

---

* While centralizing eligibility determination and payments administration, the welfare reforms discussed in Chapter V would cash out various benefits in kind and eliminate budgeting for individual families by social workers. These steps would *decentralize* decision-making by transferring it all the way from government to the individual and the family.

than a national agency to the particular needs of an individual family.*

In my view, another deserving candidate for a higher place in the hierarchy is land use—or some aspects of it. In this case the move would be from the local to the regional or the state level, and the justification is simply that problems like green-area protection and access to low-income housing which are of vital concern to a whole state or metropolitan area cannot be handled on an exclusively local basis. To solve such problems demands planning—and that means planning with teeth. But this, on the face of it, can be done in broad strokes for the area as a whole while leaving the intermediate details to specially constituted regional bodies and the ultimate details to the municipalities, with appropriate provision for citizen participation at each level.

Given a steady preference for decentralization, the same factors which in a given case may be sufficient to overcome this preference—major economies of scale, administrative practicability, geographic realities, the necessity for coherent planning—are also chief among those which should influence the choice of the level appropriate for a government function. If, in other words, significant economies of scale are achieved as the population served approaches 150,000, and if these economies rise only slowly from 150,000 to 250,000 and flatten out above that, then the appropriate size of unit for that function is between 150,000 and 250,000. Similarly, the considerations which point to a need for physical planning in a metropolitan area also define the area over which the planning agency should have jurisdiction.

There remains the question whether to rely on a unit of general-purpose government or create a special-purpose entity. Richard P. Nathan, who as Assistant Director of the Office of

* It is possible, of course, to think in terms of the factors justifying decentralization rather than, as I approach the subject, in terms of the factors justifying centralization. David O. Porter and Eugene A. Olsen, for example, in an article entitled "Some Critical Issues in Government Centralization and Decentralization," speak of "mutual coordination among workers," as in the delivery of social services or classroom teaching, as an administrative factor justifying decentralization. The difference is in the placement of the burden of proof. *Public Administration Review*, January-February 1976.

Management and Budget in the early days of the Nixon administration was one of the principal architects of the New Federalism, has identified as one of its elements a preference for general-purpose governments over special districts and particular functional agencies. I share that preference because it seems to me important to work within the framework of general-purpose governments rather than go further in the direction of fragmentation.* Some programs, however, must serve a widely dispersed group—the blind, the mentally ill, or the retarded, for example—making up only a small percentage of the population. In such a situation the program may have to take in an area embracing several local governments, thus making it impractical to put it under the jurisdiction of any one of them. Conversely, neighborhood-level organizations can be valuable in affording opportunities for citizen participation even though their functions are necessarily restricted. Where the number of such organizations leads to problems of fragmentation, a more comprehensive neighborhood-government body can serve the purpose of bringing the small organizations together much as the joint-planning entities brought into being by the Allied Services Act would offset fragmentation among social-services agencies.† Indeed, my Woodrow Wilson Center colleague John Mudd, who headed Mayor John Lindsay's neighborhood government program in New York City, has told me that just such an integrative role was a primary objective of that project.

The value of decentralization down to small-scale neighborhood units is strongly confirmed by a massive study undertaken for the National Science Foundation by Robert K. Yin and Douglas Yates of the Rand Corporation. Entitled *Street-*

---

* In my view, the Community Action Agencies ran into unnecessary difficulties by being established outside both service-providing agencies and municipal governments. While there was a need to try to respond to the problems of poor people on a basis transcending the narrow and often rigid limitations of the former, this could have been done within the framework of the latter. In *Regulating the Poor* (New York, 1971), Richard A. Cloward and Frances Fox Piven suggest that the reason for bypassing city halls was that President Lyndon B. Johnson had a political interest in end-running the established units of government so as to solidify the Democratic party's hold on its urban-poor constituency.

† See Chapter V.

Level Governments: Assessing Decentralization and Urban Services and published in 1974, the study reaches four important conclusions. First, "One of the most significant implications of decentralization is that it brings the analysis of service problems down to the street-level." Second, an "important effect of decentralization lies in the improved understanding of neighborhood institutions and citizen participation." And, in words I rejoiced to find, the study adds:

> An improved understanding [of neighborhoods] is essential and may ultimately lead to more effective plans for neighborhood institution building. And neighborhood institutions are extremely important because they provide a persistent opportunity and point of entry for citizen participation. To move beyond erratic protest efforts, citizens need ongoing institutional structures through which they can channel their energies and in which they can find a ready vehicle for expressing their views.

Third, urban decentralization "may sustain a strong, human-service orientation in urban policy" by emphasizing "the street-level relationship between the servers and the served." Fourth:

> . . . the decentralization experience has probably counteracted the previous trend in which servers and service bureaucracies were becoming increasingly accountable to themselves alone. And what may have become institutionalized is the notion that clients have a right to significant influence over service delivery as well as the ever present threat that client power can be called upon to act as a curb whenever service bureaucracies become unresponsive.[6]

From my perspective, the authors' most important conclusion was that, given a choice between a federally initiated policy or a locally initiated policy, they would "opt for locally based policies reflecting the diversity of neighborhood characteristics and service characteristics." They based this conclusion on the finding that "federal support was not a major condition of success on the one hand, and, on the other hand, that the complexity of the neighborhood service setting calls for a hand-tailoring of an innovation to its environment." As between comprehensive and service-specific strategies, they concluded that "decentralization strategies must be tailored to fit particular services. Decentralization should not be thought of as a single policy instrument but as an array of instruments, some of which are better suited than others to particular services."[7]

BY MAKING GOVERNMENT more responsive and accessible, decentralization expands the opportunities for citizens to participate. As power is pushed outward from the center and subdivided among a greater number of smaller units, more people can play a larger role in the decisions that affect the quality of their lives.*

But why, after all, should participation be important? Don't most people prefer to leave government decisions—even those of nearby local governments—in the hands of those whose job it is to make them? That way they have more time for their own pursuits. But this only begs the question: what *are* their own pursuits? What is the difference, really, between taking an interest in having a nice lawn and taking an interest in having a safe community? What is the difference between having well-fed children and having well-educated children? There is at least this difference: if you don't cut your own grass or hire someone to do it, it won't get cut. If you don't feed your own children, either they starve or someone takes them out of your hands. But your taxes pay policemen to keep your community safe; they also pay teachers to educate your children. For these tasks, they, not you, are directly responsible. They are the experts. Yes, but whose job is it to make sure they get needed support and do a good job? The police commissioner's and the

---

* De Tocqueville believed that men acquired a "taste and habit" for serving their fellow citizens by working for their good. To this end it was necessary "to give each part of the land its own political life so that there should be an infinite number of occasions for the citizens to act together and so that every day they should feel that they depended on one another." Quoted in Martin Diamond, "The Ends of Federalism," *Publius: The Journal of Federalism*, Vol. 3 (Fall 1973), pp. 129, 146.

school board's? Whose job, then, is it to make sure that the police commissioner and the school board are conscientious and qualified? Would you let George do it? Does that mean that all of us should be willing to give George the last word? What kind of government is that?

In thinking about citizen participation, I have always found it difficult to separate desire from duty—the "want to" from the "ought to." My own belief in citizen participation is philosophical—even religious. Philosophies are endlessly arguable. Religions are not arguable at all. And yet I cannot escape the conviction that the need to exercise choice, to exert an impact on the events which affect our lives, to influence the flow of things around us rather than merely be influenced by them—the need for a sense of autonomy, in short—is basic to the psychology of all human beings.

During my years in government I visited Puerto Ricans in New York, talked with Mexican-Americans in San Antonio, heard the complaints of American Indians in Cleveland, sat down with students in San Diego and North Carolina, met with black and white educators in Louisiana and coal miners in West Virginia. I heard the same themes constantly reiterated. Recognition. Respect. Equality. Opportunity. Participation—the chance to be heard, to make a difference. I remember particularly well a "listening trip" to Cleveland in 1971 during which I met with a group of welfare mothers at the end of a long day. I braced myself for a barrage of heartrendingly familiar complaints about the inadequacy of benefits, the inequities of the pending reform proposals, and the arbitrariness of welfare regulations. But no— the only thing the mothers really wanted to talk about was my recently announced promise to give parents a voice in the way their local school systems used Elementary and Secondary Education Act funds to help overcome the educational handicaps of disadvantaged children. How soon would the new requirements take effect? What did we mean by giving parents a "voice"? How much real influence would parents have?

If I am right in the conviction that people *want* a sense of autonomy, it would be natural for the frustration of this desire to be expressed in anger, anxiety, alienation, or anomie. Believing that these are in fact prevalent reactions to a sense of political powerlessness, early in my tenure as Secretary of HEW I asked the Office of the General Counsel to undertake an analysis of opportunities for citizen participation in HEW programs. On the basis of this analysis I concluded that our goals for citizen participation should be to devolve power to citizens, to reduce alienation, and to improve program effectiveness. To pursue these goals we needed more knowledge of the actual results of experiments in citizen participation conducted during the previous decade. In the spring of 1972 I therefore commissioned a study by the Rand Corporation of prior experience with various forms of citizen participation in order to assist HEW in expanding citizen participation in its own programs.[8]

Unlike the Rand study of street-level governments which so delighted me, this study was a serious disappointment: it failed to confirm my preconceptions. Its analysis of fifty-one case studies turned up no convincing evidence that citizen participation in local activities reduces a general sense of powerlessness. At best, it found that participation contributes to a sense of personal efficacy only with regard to the specific program or activity in which the individual participates. The evidence, however, was so scanty and ambiguous that, reviewing the Rand report, I kept thinking of the old answer to the question, how is your wife—compared to what? For instance, one study cited in the report asked a total of 630 neighborhood leaders whether people like themselves had any say about what the government does; 46 percent said they had not. But this could mean any number of things: that there were no institutional means of making their voice heard, that there were institutional means but nobody listened, that the authorities listened but simply did not agree, and so on. Why not, moreover, look at the glass as half full—slightly more than that, in fact? After all, 54 percent of the leaders interviewed said they *did* have a say about what the government does.

As to whether people feel a vicarious sense of efficacy when others like themselves are involved in some form of participation, the only answer I can reach on the basis of the evidence at hand is—it depends. In the case of one school, PTA members knowledgeable about PTA affairs felt a higher sense of efficacy toward that school than did parents who were not aware of or involved in the PTA. In the case of a second school, parents who knew about the activities of an aggressive citizens' advisory committee felt a lower sense of effectiveness toward their school's affairs than was felt by parents unfamiliar with the committee's work.

Looking at how people feel about participation, I see an intermediate stage between personal participation and vicarious participation: this is a stage at which the citizen has an opportunity to participate but is under no particular pressure to do so. Neglect of this kind of opportunity—for example, the failure to vote in an election—is frequently cited as evidence of apathy. But the mere fact, standing by itself, that a citizen does not choose to participate tells us very little. On the face of it, much depends on the form and availability of the participation as well as on the citizen's perception of its impact. If participation involves going to meetings, the convenience of their times and places will make a difference. The organization may be so large, or give its participants so minor a role, that their sense of participation is diluted to the point of meaninglessness. The opportunity to be heard may be adequate, but that isn't worth much if nobody listens. The authorities may listen, promise to do something, but consistently fail to follow through. They may listen but decline—for good reasons or bad—to accept the citizens' views. Any of these things—or a combination of them—would be bound to deter participation.

Paradoxically, the ease and adequacy of the opportunity to participate, together with a feeling of confidence in the government body which invites participation, may seem to deter participation. One of my associates at the Department of Justice had been the chairman of the school board in a Milwaukee suburb with a population of about twenty thousand. Before he became chairman, the board had a long history of acrimonious meetings. Hundreds of people came. The old board, insisting that matters such as the appointment of key personnel were within its sole province to decide, refused to listen to citizens' views on these subjects. Meetings were held within strict time limits no matter how many people still wanted to be heard.

The new board decided to allow anyone to speak up on any matter pending before it. It let it be known that it was prepared to sit as long as necessary so that everyone who wished to express his or her views would have an opportunity to do so. At the first meeting of the new board some 350 people were present. After that, attendance fell off steadily. By the time the new board had been in office six months, attendance had settled to an average of 70 or 80 people, and there it remained. Was this indicative of decreased citizen interest? Hardly. It could only have been indicative of increased citizen trust.

Notwithstanding the ambiguity of the evidence, I hold fast to the intuitive belief that there is a correlation between participation and political efficacy, on the one hand, and between powerlessness and alienation, on the other. It would take more rigorous scientific inquiry than the fragmentary studies reviewed by the Rand Corporation to persuade me to abandon this commonsense proposition. But the case for citizen participation would still stand even if it could not be shown that participation contributes to a person's sense of being somebody or that it serves as an antidote to the feeling of powerlessness. The case for participation can also be supported on either—or both—of two additional grounds that have no need of psychological proof. One is that of duty: the very possibility of representative democracy requires that a substantial number of its citizens accept some degree of responsibility toward the successful working of the democratic process. Those who hold powers delegated by their fellow citizens are accountable to those same citizens for what they do. The citizens who delegate power retain a duty to hold their surrogates to account. Accountability can be exacted only through participation. One may or may not fulfill this responsibility, but he can shed it only by renouncing citizenship itself.

As I view it, participation is a moral imperative inseparable from a belief in the significance and dignity of the individual.

The second nonpsychological pillar of participation is the

instrumental value of participation—its usefulness as a means of bringing about needed social change. Whether because they lack more fundamental data or feel no need for it, most advocates of citizen participation speak of it in these terms. They argue, for instance, that including consumers in health-care planning and decision-making will assist the providers of health care to identify the needs of the population served. Services will be made more accountable and responsive to consumers. The participation of consumers in the planning and delivery of services will also help to inform them about what services are available.

The Rand study, although noting that "citizen participation does not promise to change the general level of political alienation in our society," confirms its instrumental value. "Citizen participation on boards and committees," the study says, "effectively meets the HEW goals of devolving power and enhancing program effectiveness." Citizen governing boards are more effective than citizen advisory committees, but both help to increase community support for local agencies, to bring in outside resources, and to improve services. The three most important ingredients of successful citizen participation, the study found, are meaningful influence over the budget, a substantial role in investigating complaints, and a staff responsible to the citizen participant organization.

NOT EVEN citizen participation, of course, is immune from the consequences of excess. Criticisms of citizen participation, however, usually turn out to be criticisms of its aberrations. Irving Kristol, for example, has argued that "to make all the people legislators is willy-nilly to abolish the category of private citizen altogether."[9] But this would be true only if everybody had the right to vote on all the choices we normally depend on legislators to make. The real question is, under what circumstances should what sorts of groups or constituencies be given the chance to have a voice in what kinds of things—not necessarily to vote, but at least to be consulted or heard, to become a part of a consensus, to be recognized as part of a community.

Another form of excess is what Daniel Patrick Moynihan has called "government by a process of private nullification."

The example he cites involved the proposed construction of a Columbia University gymnasium in Morningside Park. The elected representatives of the community—all black—voted for it several times; the black students, asserting that the elected representatives did not speak for the community but that they did, blocked the proposal. But this was an episode in an extreme situation: the bloody and tumultuous Columbia riot which, following the "Free Speech" movement at the University of California at Berkeley, touched off a wave of student activism.[10]

Radical advocates of citizen participation—which they prefer to call "participatory democracy"—have their own formula for excess. Insisting that "participatory democracy" can flourish only outside the regular political system, they view "parallel institutions" as necessary either, in Staughton Lynd's words, "to transform their Establishment counterparts" or to "grow into an anti-Establishment network, a new society."[11] Similarly, Tom Hayden has argued that "community unions, freedom schools, experimental universities, community-formed police review boards, people's own anti-poverty organizations fighting for federal money, independent union locals—all can be practical pressure points from which to launch reform in the conventional institutions while at the same time maintaining a separate base and pointing towards a new system."[12] The tendency of parallel institutions, however, is to "reinforce the ghetto" and to entrench "leaders who are most strongly pro-ghetto, economics oriented, and separatist."[13]

But none of these observations applies to citizen participation in general. To attempt so to apply them would be to fall into the fallacy of supposing that if something is true of one member of a class, it must also be true of all other members of the class. I call this the "Mt. Washington fallacy." In each of my Massachusetts political campaigns, my field organization director made a special effort to enlist a "coordinator" in every one of the Commonwealth's 351 cities and towns, including Mt. Washington, the smallest, which had only 38 registered voters. Seventeen other towns had fewer than 300 registered voters, but each had its own "coordinator." I was grateful for the field director's conscientiousness, of course, but I could not resist

222 THE CREATIVE BALANCE

asking him whether he also intended to recruit a "coordinator" for every apartment house and neighborhood with 300 or more voters. He had no such intention. Why not? Because a field organization is based on towns, not on groups of voters, and a town is a town is a town.*

Thus "government by private nullification" is not a characteristic of citizen participation. It is what happens when a self-appointed group constitutes itself as speaking for a community in defiance of its duly elected representatives. Nor is "to make all citizens legislators" incidental to citizen participation. It could only mean one of two things: either pure democracy or an absurdly confused, overlapping, and redundant participatory structure. As to the former, the practical limitations are obvious. New England towns, for instance, elect neighborhood representatives to their town meetings once the number of people who want to attend becomes unmanageable—usually when they begin to overflow the capacity of the town hall. The other possibility—that every government service is administered by an elected board whose frequent meetings every concerned citizen is somehow expected to attend—is no more compelled by the aim of citizen participation than the design of a Rube Goldberg contraption is compelled by its function.

The contentions that citizen participation leads to inefficiency, the diffusion of decision-making, and excessive demands on the citizen's time are subject to the same comments. But it is also worth pointing out how aptly these contentions illustrate the Mt. Washington fallacy. What looks like the diffusion of

* Should a more dignified name be called for, I propose—in emulation of Alfred North Whitehead—"the fallacy of unitary equivalence." It is an analogue of what Whitehead called "the fallacy of misplaced concreteness," which is the fallacy of supposing that every abstract concept must have a counterpart in the "real" world—for example, the academic tendency to talk about "economics" or "political science" as if they were not merely labels but things. It might also be called the "Gertrude Stein fallacy." As exemplified in the proposition "a sovereign state is a sovereign state is a sovereign state," the fallacy has had mischievous consequences, for instance in the General Assembly of the United Nations. Another example is the failure after the establishment of the state of Israel to find a means of dealing with the Palestinians: being stateless, they were treated not as a people aggrieved but as "the refugee problem."

decision-making from the perspective of the New York City Hall looks like massive centralization from the perspective of a Massachusetts town. The "neighborhood government" project headed by John Mudd subdivided the city into 50 areas with about 150,000 people in each area. In Massachusetts, only Boston has a population larger than 175,000; the median size of the towns is 5,400. To subdivide New York into neighborhoods of this average size—or into the 654 neighborhoods identified by the City Planning Department—would not only be to diffuse decision-making but to create impossible span-of-control problems. All of which simply goes to show the artificiality of assuming that a neighborhood is a neighborhood is a neighborhood.*

Parallel institutions are not a requisite for significant citizen participation. As a long-term arrangement, they make no sense. But then, their advocates do not intend that they should make long-term sense. The parallel institutions would serve temporarily to speak for the "effectively disenfranchised," meanwhile either transforming their establishment counterparts or being transformed into the institutions of a new society. In either case, they would cease to be "parallel." And if neither happened, well, they would still have served the purposes of radicals like Saul Alinsky who urged the poor to create their own organizations in order to induce conflict, thus "rubbing raw the sores of resentment."

But there is nothing in the concept of citizen participation which dictates that participatory institutions have to be parallel to and outside of some preexisting set of institutions. When—

* The British economist E. F. Schumacher believes that "the upper limit of what is desirable for the size of a city is probably something of the order of half a million inhabitants. In places like London, or Tokyo, or New York, the millions do not add to the city's real value but merely create *enormous* problems and produce human degradation." (*Small Is Beautiful: Economics as if People Mattered* [New York, 1975], p. 67.) And certainly there are good reasons for trying to hold down the growth of metropolitan areas. See Chapter VIII. But the initial factor, I believe, is *neighborhood* size—optimally somewhere between 5,000 and 10,000. See Claude Lévi-Strauss, "Social Structure," in *Anthropology Today* (Chicago, 1953), pp. 523-524. An important reason why London, despite its size, has remained so livable is that it has preserved its local neighborhoods.

and to the extent that—some existing institution does not adequately afford the opportunity to participate, it can be reformed or supplemented. That reform in a given case is alleged to be impossible because the institution is in the hands of a self-perpetuating group may be important in deciding how to correct the situation, but it has no broader significance.

THE SERIOUS DESIGNER of opportunities for citizen participation must approach his task essentially the way the framers approached the drafting of our federal Constitution. The first task of the constitution-builder is to sort out the criteria by which to identify opportunities for such participation. It is impractical, obviously, to give a community of people responsibility for the command of troops. The opposite is true of the scraping of lead-based paint from dilapidated dwellings. Among the factors which can make a given function more or less suitable for citizen participation are such variables as the directness of its impact on the individual, his family, or his community; the scope of the geographical area within which, as a matter of practical necessity, the function must be exercised; the importance, again as a practical matter, of uniformity of administration within this area; and the necessity for reliance on professional expertise. It is crucial, moreover, not only to find a way of involving the right citizen participants, especially the recipients of services, but to give them a role that will make their participation real and not fictitious.

In addition to defining the functions appropriate for participation, the constituency entitled to participate, and the role of the participants, the constitution-builder must also choose among possible vehicles for participation. He must consider, for example, whether to provide for citizen participation through their own voluntary organizations or through representation on some official body. He should also bear in mind that there are limits on how much representative democracy and participatory mechanisms can satisfactorily cope with, on how much people will in fact want to participate, and on the likely response to the call of duty. In recognition of these limits, as much room as possible should be left for individual autonomy. Such autonomy finds a high degree of expression in the private marketplace. Indeed, as a purchaser and consumer the individual engages in an important form of participation: the marketplace makes prompt allocative decisions on the basis of a whole set of individual "votes."

Before they get very far, the constitution-builders for any group, however small, must have the answers to questions like these—questions which, though they may seem obvious, do not always get asked. And yet the failure to ask them—and to find answers—is bound to make it impossible for any organization either to govern itself or to manage its external relations with other organizations. The point was unintentionally made one day in 1971 by a group from Newark, New Jersey, which took over a conference room in the HEW North Building and demanded to see the Secretary. They refused to say why but insisted that it was extremely important and that no one else would do. Meanwhile they would stay put if necessary for the rest of the week. When I heard about the situation, I decided that rather than aggravate it I'd better interrupt whatever I was doing and see them. They turned out to be a group of about fifteen people, mostly black, who felt aggrieved by the management of a Newark health center largely funded by HEW. The center's board, they complained, had not only excluded them from representation but had fired the only administrator in whom they had confidence.

"What do you want me to do?" I asked. "Do you really want somebody in Washington telling people in Newark how their health center board should be organized?"

"You can tell the board it should be representative of the community," they said.

"Fine," I said, "but what community? Who should be represented? Everybody who lives within some defined geographical area? What area? Or everybody, no matter where he lives, who is served by the health center? And would that mean everybody who has ever been served or only those who come regularly?"

They did not have the answers. Neither do countless other community organizations. The failure to recognize such questions, get them thought through in advance by those most directly concerned, and build the answers into the organization's charter and by-laws all too often, as in the Newark case, makes inevitable a struggle between "professionals" and "community people" which tears both the "community" and the "program" to pieces. Of course, not even a conscientious effort to anticipate such questions can resolve every issue any more than adoption of the Constitution of the United States could foreclose all future clashes of interpretation. A constitution does, however, answer the most fundamental questions and confine the remaining issues.

The Massachusetts mental health and mental retardation legislation enacted in 1966 illustrates both the value of careful constitution-building and the impossibility of preventing all future problems. As chairman of the drafting group, I spent more time on the provisions for citizen participation than on any other parts of the legislation. Some of the threshold questions were answered for us by the federal Community Mental Health Act of 1963. That act provided for federal support of comprehensive community mental health centers serving areas embracing somewhere between 75,000 and 200,000 people.* These would be areas larger than most of our Massachusetts cities and all of our towns, but smaller than several of our counties and larger than the rest. This meant that administration of the community mental health centers could not be added to the functions of any existing government entity but would have to be made part of a new special-purpose structure with its own territorial boundaries. And since to provide local financial support of the centers would have required a complex mechanism and would also have added to an already overloaded property-tax base, it followed that most of their funds would have to come from the state mental health agency.

---

* If the population served is greater than 250,000, the center begins to become large and impersonal; fewer centers serving larger areas would also be less accessible. On the other hand, a population of 75,000 is the smallest that can make efficient use of the minimum necessary professional staff—a psychiatrist, a clinical psychologist, and psychiatric nurses. Whether the population served should be at the upper or lower end of the permissible range may depend, of course, on its geographical distribution.

With these matters resolved, we then had to consider how to give the people in the area served by each community mental health center as much of a voice as possible in its management. The only practical way of doing this that we could think of was to make the administration of each center subject to the policy direction of a broadly representative citizen board. But how were the board members to be chosen? Just as it would have been too troublesome to create a special funding mechanism, so it would have been impractical, for this one government function alone, to provide for the direct popular election of the board members. We had no choice but to make the boards appointive. And since, for the whole state, there would be a great many of them, we decided that it should be the Commissioner of Mental Health rather than the Governor who made the appointments.

The last and most difficult question was, what powers should the boards have? Since the centers were part of a state-wide system largely funded by the state, we could not give each board final authority over its own center's budget. Equally clearly, we could not permit the boards to override the judgments of the center staffs on professional matters. The best we could do, then, was to give each board the power to approve the selection of the director, to participate in the development of the area budget, to approve contracts and other fee-for-service arrangements with voluntary agencies, and to exercise certain other enumerated powers and responsibilities.

Some of these provisions, it was clear, would have to depend for their more specific content on the manner in which they were carried out. This was most obviously true of the clause giving the boards the right to "participate in" the development of the budget. What, exactly, did this phrase mean? It was apparent that the spirit of its application would be crucial. And so, in fact, it has been. Instead, however, of a generous interpretation, it has had a grudging one. The result bears out the Rand study finding that influence on the budget is the most important factor in the effectiveness of a citizen board. Because the Massachusetts mental health center boards have not had a significant influence on the centers' budgets, they have not been really effective. Only now, ten years after their creation, is Dr.

William Goldman, the state's new Commissioner of Mental Health, trying to give the boards genuine stature by giving the budget-development clause of their charter the full effect originally envisioned.

AS IN THE CASE of the Massachusetts community mental health center system, every effort to create the opportunity for citizen participation confronts the constitution-builder with its own particular set of constraints. In that case the constraints stemmed principally from the geographical pattern of Massachusetts' general-purpose governments. The effort to broaden the base of participation in such governments must take into account a very different set of constraints. The officials at the top layer—in the city hall, for example—must be able to exercise some degree of supervisory responsibility for the subdivisions of the city government, including those in which citizens participate, and to bring about some coordination among city functions. And if citizen participation is to mean anything, the representatives of citizen "constituencies" must be able to get a hearing from city hall.

How many participatory units are feasible depends partly on the degree of autonomy accorded to the city's geographical and functional subdivisions. If, for example, New York City's five boroughs were made autonomous, each—in theory—could have fifty neighborhood governments of its own instead of a fraction of the fifty now allotted to the whole city. But constraints of history and sentiment and political inertia are also real. It scarcely seems likely, therefore, that New York will ever be subdivided into a large enough number of units for each unit's neighborhood government to match the median size of Massachusetts towns. And while I feel sure that New Yorkers must regret the impossibility of their achieving this ideal, I can only assume that they acquiesce in it as part of the price of living in what, alas, it is no longer fun to call "Fun City."

For a large city, in any case, the creation of opportunities for citizen participation is not the only function of a neighborhood government. Where there is a large number of street-level participatory organizations, the official neighborhood government structure, as pointed out above, should serve an integrating and coordinating role analogous to that of the joint planning bodies called for by the Allied Services Act.* In both cases, the comprehensive entity (neighborhood government or planning body) can have an umbrella board made up of representatives of the street-level organizations or, as the case may be, the local service providers. Going back to the example of the Massachusetts community mental health system, I had hoped at the time we were designing it that the state would adopt a similar approach to public welfare, public health, and vocational rehabilitation. Each of these services could be administered in areas geographically coextensive both with each other and with the mental health areas. And for each such area there could be a citizen board whose membership was largely—if not completely —drawn from the membership of the mental health, public welfare, public health, and vocational rehabilitation citizen boards.

ONCE A MANAGEABLE STRUCTURE of general- and special-purpose participatory units has been designed, the next task of the constitution-builder should be to formulate the appropriate procedures for its governance. Harlan Cleveland (in an article entitled "How Do You Get Everybody in on the Act and Still Get Some Action?") wisely cautions against eliminating from "the process of getting things done the very ambiguities which leave room for discretion, improvisation, imagination, and plain common sense." He cites the example of the Pacific island villagers who do not have ready access to Robert's Rules of Order and "do not share our Western enthusiasm for dividing a meeting in two by voting":

> To plan an important operation, the villagers gather in a circle and the village elder solicits what we moderns would call input from all concerned. Gradually, those who are not much interested in the particular decision will edge their way to the perimeter, while those whose oxen might be gored press toward the center to make themselves felt.

* See Chapter V.

When the talk and the participants are thoroughly exhausted, the leader suggests a consensus; if he guesses wrong, the talk resumes until those really concerned decide to compromise or silently acquiesce. At this point, in the participatory West, we would destroy the consensus by insisting the meeting end with a recorded vote—giving an equal voice to those who care less, dividing a many-sided complexity into a two-sided simplification, freezing in its intransigence the losing minority, molding the future by political arithmetic rather than the reasoning consciences of the human beings concerned.[14]

And yet formal procedures have their uses, at least in societies like our own where "the reasoning consciences of human beings" are not displayed by all of the people all of the time. No organization has been more bitterly criticized for its undemocratic, manipulative conduct of meetings than Students for a Democratic Society. Why so? Because, according to Terrence E. Cook and Patrick M. Morgan, in the thoughtful introductory essay to their book *Participatory Democracy*, "Explicit written rules on membership, elections, and parliamentary procedure are usually not in evidence. The idea is that unstructured discussions, resolutions, and voting will generate the truest expression of the people's will."[15] The result was the dictatorship of a student elite in the guise of "participatory democracy."[16]

CONSTITUTION-BUILDING for America's third century is a task which demands our best intellectual effort and most understanding insight. The first essential is the conviction that it is *necessary*. This, certainly, in the light of the failures and frustrations of the Articles of Confederation, was the attitude of the framers toward the creation of a national government. A second essential is the conviction that the effort is *important*. And while the constitutions now needing construction are for regions, neighborhoods, and special-purpose groups rather than for a nation-state, this does not make the task unworthy of the wisest judgment that we can bring to it: Athens—the largest of the Greek city-states—had no more than forty thousand adult male citizens at the time of Pericles. If we are really as concerned as

I think we should be about the submergence of the individual, we must be prepared to accept some sacrifice of the premium we have habitually placed on speed and efficiency and put in its place an ungrudging preference for citizen participation in collective decisions.

VII

Worker Discontent:
Enhancing
Job Satisfaction

A SOCIETY DEDICATED to the maximum practicable degree of self-fulfillment for all its members must be concerned with how they are occupied in that half of their lives spent at work. What we do during eight hours a day, five days a week, more or less, for most of our lives is bound to have a profound impact on our sense of identity and self-esteem. The quality of our lives in large part depends on the quality of our work.

Mark Twain once remarked that "Work consists of that which a body is obliged to do and Play consists of that which a body is not obliged to do." This makes the definition of work turn not on what a person does and not on whether he gets paid for it but on how he feels about it. Was Mark Twain himself, when he wrote or lectured, working or playing? By this definition half the members of a professional football team might be classified as "working," the other half as "playing."

Being paid, on the other hand, is not a definitive test either. What about the housewife? It makes no sense to say that a woman who cares for her own children is not working, but if she takes a job looking after the children of others, she is working. *Work in America*, the report of a special task force which I appointed when I was Secretary of Health, Education, and Welfare, suggests defining work as "an activity that produces something of value for other people."* This takes in the housewife, and it also includes the unpaid but socially useful tasks performed by volunteers. All that's left out is activity which, though intended to produce something of value, is not in fact valued by others—for instance, writings that no one will publish.[1]

The economic purposes of work are obvious: by means of work we furnish the goods and services demanded by society; by means of wages we are enabled to partake of them ourselves. Unfortunately, a large part of the labor force obtains only the economic rewards of work. For most people, jobs are endured, not enjoyed. Perhaps this is why the Calvinists made a virtue of work—as they did of wearing a hair shirt. I think of the need for endurance every time I remember a summer job welding steel spools and socket wrenches from seven P.M. to seven A.M. five nights a week. For me, the experience had so many new and sometimes startling dimensions (a foreman, for instance, who amused himself by burning the hair off rats with a blowtorch) that I had little occasion to invoke the "work ethic." But I knew that the job would end with the beginning of law school. Often since, in visiting factories, I have been impressed by the relative

* HEW task force, *Work in America* (Cambridge, Mass., 1973), p. 3. In my foreword to *Work in America*, I wrote, "In the breadth of its perspective and its freshness of outlook, this report literally takes on everyone, not excluding some of the thinkers in the present Administration. Manpower policies, medical care strategies, educational and welfare concepts, and more, are intelligently scrutinized by the writers. I cannot recall any other governmental report which is more doughty, controversial, and yet responsible than this one" (p. viii).

equanimity with which so many people seem able to endure monotonous, uncomfortable, repetitive jobs.

There are, to be sure, advantages in work that requires attention but not much thought. One can think about other things —bowling, union business, family problems, the meaning of life. One can also leave the work behind at the end of the day: no briefcase to take home, no midnight calls to answer, no speech to write (or deliver). Every situation has its own combination of pluses and minuses, and more often than not they pretty well balance out—often enough, anyway, so that the adaptive capacity which is one of the human creature's most distinctive attributes can make up the difference.

Of course, work serves a number of social purposes other than the economic function of providing the goods and services needed and desired by ourselves and our society. For one thing, the workplace helps to meet the need for companionship. When I first began to visit factory gates in the early morning during political campaigns, I took it for granted that workers due to start a shift at 6:00 A.M. would tend to arrive in a bunch during the last few minutes before the beginning of the shift. Not so. They come to work in a steady trickle starting as much as forty-five minutes before shift time; the number arriving in the last five minutes is no greater than the number arriving in any five-minute interval during the preceding half-hour. Some join in a sociable cup of coffee at the factory canteen. Others take their time setting up the day's work, meanwhile analyzing sports results, swapping jokes, ribbing each other. I've seen this happen at many different kinds of factories—textile, toothbrush, paper products, shoe machinery, machine tool, electronics; the explanation, obviously, is that people find an important source of personal satisfaction in the associations of the workplace.

Work is also the most important ingredient of status. It is not hard to imagine some sort of equation which expresses the status of Americans in terms of numbers supervised, years of graduate education, pressure of responsibility, and/or difficulty in mastering a particular skill. By and large, compensation is commensurate with status, although there are some occupations —teaching, the ministry, the judiciary, and elective office—

which carry a degree of automatic status (and psychic satisfaction) such that the salary levels are correspondingly discounted.

The recognition that status is a form of compensation in itself led me when I was young to think that any well-constructed Utopia ought to reserve its highest material rewards for those who do its most unpleasant work. Such a Utopia would educate everyone up to the full limit of his potential, thus producing a surplus of people equipped for demanding assignments. Alternatively it might keep a duty roster and assign undesirable jobs the way KP used to be assigned in the Army. A job like head of a big company or university president (this was before students, faculties, and alumni had each independently concluded that running the university was its own prerogative) would go to the highest bidder from among a pool of applicants all so highly qualified that a choice between them on the basis of merit alone would be impossible.*

Not only status but self-esteem is bound up in the kind of work we do. Work contributes to self-esteem in two ways. The first is through creating a sense of competence; a person thus acquires a sense of mastery over both himself and his environment. The second comes from engaging in an activity that produces something valued by other people. The first component of self-esteem—a sense of mastery—is internal and depends on the challenge of the job. The second—the value attached to one's work by others—is external. A person with high self-esteem is someone who has a high estimate of his own value and finds that others agree.

Although one of the ways in which work contributes to self-esteem, the achievement of a sense of mastery, is more than a means to an end. In my scheme of things, it comes as close to an end in itself as a human being can have. Self-fulfillment implies the development and exercise of individual capacities. And the word "exercise" is the right word. Capacities that are stretched and applied develop like muscles. Unused capacities atrophy, also like muscles. We enjoy what we are good at, and

---

* There were, to be sure, practical difficulties with this simple scheme. How, for example, would the winner have acquired the resources necessary to outbid his competitors?

we get better at what we are good at by doing it. In this, I think, we resemble the snakes observed by Emerson during a walk in the woods: "After much wandering and seeing many things, four snakes gliding up and down a hollow for no purpose that I could see—not to eat, not for love, but only gliding." And why not, after all? It must be a great satisfaction to be able to glide the way a snake—and only a snake—can.

Learned Hand saw in "the joy of craftsmanship" the human equivalent of gliding:

> Values are ultimate, they admit of no reduction below themselves; you may prefer Dante to Shakespeare, or claret to champagne; but that ends it. Nevertheless, I believe you will agree to put among the most precious and dependable of our satisfactions the joy of craftsmanship. In that I include all effort to impose upon the outside world an invention of our own: to embody an idea in what I shall ask your leave to call an artifact. It is not important what form that may take; it may be in clay, in bronze, in paint or pencil, in a musical score or in words; it may even be in a sport; it may be in the mastery or exercise of a profession; it may be in a well-balanced nature, like Aristotle's "Great-Souled" man; or it may be in redeeming the world. It is enough that we set out to mold the motley stuff of life into some form of our own choosing; when we do, the performance is itself the wage. "The play's the thing."[2]

"The play's the thing." Could Judge Hand have intended a play on Mark Twain's distinction between "work" and "play"? Society affords no greater satisfaction, certainly, than the performance of a task which challenges but does not overtax a person's most highly developed talents and skills. It is a satisfaction that no one else can give and no one else can take away. All others—sex, listening to music, skiing, even dry-fly fishing—can suffer from satiety. As William Faulkner remarked, "You can't eat for eight hours a day nor drink for eight hours a day nor make love for eight hours a day—all you can do for eight hours is work." But Faulkner then adds the sardonic observation:

"which is the reason why man makes himself and everybody else so miserable and unhappy."[3]

As to those lucky enough to experience the joy of craftsmanship, Faulkner is wrong. In *Working*, Studs Terkel's marvelous book of recorded interviews with over a hundred individuals of as many different occupations, craftsmen surface in every trade, no matter how menial. Even jobs which on their face might seem monotonous and unrewarding can be approached in a spirit which leaves room for what Thorstein Veblen called "the instinct of workmanship."

Terkel encounters the elevator operator, for instance, who remembers his passengers by name, welcomes them back after vacations, and stays abreast of office rotations in order to provide reliable directory assistance. "One-Swing Al," a parking lot attendant, prides himself on never having hit a car in his thirty years of "car-hiking":

> After twenty-five, thirty years I could drive any car like a baby, like a woman change her baby's diaper. I could handle that car with one hand. I had a lot of customers would say, "How you do this? The way you go around this way?" I'd say, "Just the way you bake a cake, miss, I can handle this car." A lotta ladies come to you and a lot of gentlemen come to you, say, "Wow. You can drive." I say, "Thank you, ma'am." They say, "How long you been doin' it?" I say, "Thirty years. I started when I'm sixteen and I'm still doin' it."[4]

A gravedigger describes his work with humble respect. Gravedigging is like a trade, he explains to Terkel, and while it doesn't require academic education, it does require expertise. "Not anybody can be a gravedigger. You can dig a hole any way they come. A gravedigger, you have to make a neat job. . . . A human body is goin' into this grave. That's why you need skill."[5]

One way of expressing the satisfaction that flows from "doing it right" is in terms of integrity: both the completion of the job and the fulfillment of a personal standard of workmanship convey the idea of wholeness. Terkel's interviews also underscore the importance of integrity on the part of the employer. The unhappiest people Terkel encounters are those who work for a firm that condones or encourages deceitfulness. This can be psychologically upsetting to the point of causing physical distress. A middle-aged installment dealer, for example, tells Terkel how his ulcer came from working in a furniture business which routinely used "bait and switch" tactics. ("Advertise something at a ridiculously low rate and then expect the salesman to switch the customer to something else.")[6] There is also the telephone solicitor for a newspaper who was instructed to base her sales talk on the pretense that new subscriptions were to benefit a local charity. "At first I liked the idea of talking to people," she reflected. "But pretty soon, knowing the area I was calling—they couldn't afford to eat, let alone buy a newspaper—my job was getting me down." One prospect responded that although he would like to help, he wasn't interested in receiving the paper. He was blind. The solicitor was overcome: "Here I was sitting here telling him a bunch of lies and he was poor and blind and willing to help . . . I got sick in the stomach."[7]

There are indications, however, that the instinct of workmanship has long been losing ground. Attempts to assess the degree of worker dissatisfaction were spearheaded in the 1940s and 1950s by two pioneers in work psychology, A. H. Maslow and Frederick Herzberg. Their research on the variety of workers' needs requiring fulfillment on the job stimulated much of the attention focused on job dissatisfaction in the 1960s. Efforts to determine the number of workers suffering from "blue-collar blues" during those years soon yielded the realization that white-collar ranks were not immune to the malady either.

Careful scrutiny of the available data yields scanty proof of widespread worker alienation. The Gallup Poll, for instance, has conducted a worker satisfaction study eleven times since 1949, using a sample group of 1,500 people who have been asked, "On the whole, would you say you were satisfied or dissatisfied with the work you do?" The number answering "dissatisfied" has been steadily rising since 1969; in 1973 it was 11 percent. Some commentators have seized on this as confirming the trend toward worker alienation. The 1973 figure, however, is less than the 13 percent recorded as dissatisfied in 1965, and just over half the 20 percent so recorded in 1949. Furthermore, Gallup's sample has always included students, retired people, housewives, and the unemployed. If the data are narrowed down to exclude those who do not work for pay, the increase in job dissatisfaction over the past several years becomes progressively smaller.

The most comprehensive information on job satisfaction assembled to date comes from interviews with 1,533 workers conducted in 1969–1970 by the Michigan Survey Research Center for the United States Department of Labor. Based on many more questions than the Gallup Poll, the Survey Research Center findings were reduced to five significant facets of job satisfaction: comfort (physical conditions at work, job speed, transportation to work); challenge (variety, opportunity to learn, skill required); pay (including job security); resources (machinery, supplies, assistance from the boss); and co-worker relations. Worker attitudes were recorded on a 1–5 scale, with 5.0 indicating very high satisfaction and 1.0 very low satisfaction. The results ranged between a low of 3.06 (financial rewards) and a high of 3.45 (resources). The survey was repeated in 1973, with no significant changes of result, and slight drops in only two measures (comfort and co-worker relations). Three-plus on a scale of 1 to 5 may not indicate wild enthusiasm, but it is firmly on the side of job satisfaction rather than dissatisfaction. No more than the Gallup results do the Survey Research Center findings support the belief in widespread worker alienation.

If there has been a significant increase in job dissatisfaction, one would expect it to show up in increasing industrial unrest and lower productivity. Some studies claim to have found just such an interaction occurring over the last decade or so. And it is true that between the late 1950s and the early 1970s there was some increase in strike activity and job turnover and a small decline in productivity. These trends are explainable, however, without reference to a change in worker attitudes. A report to the Ford Foundation by three highly qualified economists attributes the slowdown in productivity to the increasing proportion of women and young people in the labor force and to the growing proportion of the gross national product represented by services and governmental expenditures. "Women and younger people," they say, "are less productive than older males, at least during their first years in the labor force, and productivity in the service and government section has been growing less rapidly (if at all) than productivity in the manufacturing section."[8]

Despite the statistical analyses which downgrade the seriousness of worker alienation, indications of malaise have prompted numerous comprehensive studies of worker dissatisfaction. Work dissatisfaction was the theme of the 43rd American Assembly in November 1973, which was attended by eighty leading American industrialists, academicians, union leaders, administrators, and journalists specializing in the field of work. Among them was Jerome Rosow, former Assistant Secretary of Labor, who concluded:

> The notion that people work only for money and seek their real satisfactions away from work is not valid. People have real needs at the workplace and the more these are satisfied, the greater their personal involvement and motivation to participate at their highest levels of achievement.[9]

The malaise which eludes statistical surveys surfaces clearly in anecdotal material. Nora Watson, a twenty-eight-year-old staff writer of health-care literature interviewed by Terkel, goes straight to the source of much worker dissatisfaction. "I think most of us are looking for a calling, not a job. Most of us, like the assembly line worker, have jobs that are too small for our spirit. Jobs are not big enough for people." She contrasts her own attitude with that of her father, a preacher in a small mountain town in western Pennsylvania: "For all that was bad about my father's vocation, he showed me it was possible to fuse your life to your work. His home was also his work. . . . There's nothing I would enjoy more than a job that was so meaningful to me that I brought it home."[10]

Other Terkel interviewees expand on feelings that have to be compressed into one-word answers in job satisfaction surveys. Their comments focus on such grievances as the stultifying monotony that leaves humans feeling like robots, excessive supervision, and lack of status. A receptionist who tells Terkel, "[I'm] just a little machine. A monkey could do what I do," reflects a common dread of weekdays:

> One minute to five is the moment of triumph. You physically turn off the machine that has dictated to you all day long. You put it in a drawer and that's it. You're your own man for a few hours. Then it calls to you every morning that you have to come back. . . . Until recently I'd cry in the morning. I didn't want to get up. I'd dread Fridays because Monday was always looming over me. Another five days. . . .[11]

Her feelings are shared by the steelworker who says, "Let's face it, a machine can do the work of a man; otherwise they wouldn't have space probes. Why can we send a rocket ship that's unmanned and yet send a man in a steel mill to do a mule's work?"[12]

Those employed in menial service jobs suffer from society's prejudices against low-status work. A washroom attendant in a hotel tells people only that he "works at the Palmer House," hoping they will assume he's a waiter. A janitor explains that his jacket reads "Building Engineer," because engineer is "just a word that people more or less respect." The problem is summed up by a manual laborer as "non-recognition by other people." And not all those who feel a lack of recognition are as irrepressible as the waitress who tells Terkel, "When somebody says to me, 'You're great, how come you're *just* a waitress?' *Just* a waitress. I'd say 'Why, don't you think you deserve to be served by me?'"[13]

These workers represent a wide range of skill levels, aspirations, and achievements. It is striking, however, that none complains primarily of the purely material aspects of his job—wages, hours, or vacations. An apparent explanation is to be found in Frederick Herzberg's distinction between the "extrinsic" and "intrinsic" aspects of work.[14] The former include things like pay, grievance procedures, and working conditions. The latter include achievement, responsibility, and challenge. Job dissatisfaction is a product of bad extrinsic conditions of work. But good extrinsic conditions cannot produce satisfaction: this can only come from a positive combination of intrinsic factors. According to *Work in America*, increases in productivity have been found to correlate in certain industries and occupations with increases in satisfaction, but not with decreases in dissatisfaction.

A GLANCE BACKWARD tells us why intrinsic satisfaction levels have declined. Management has traditionally proceeded on the assumption that workers are motivated by money alone. This "money-instrumental" view of the worker's relationship to his job dates from production techniques born of the Industrial Revolution. As family manufacturing units gave way to specialized, large-scale forms of enterprise, it was discovered that maximum efficiency was attained when each worker handled a single phase of a mechanical process. The resulting increases in output were tremendous: Adam Smith described an eighteenth-century pin factory which produced 240 times more pins after dividing the assembly process into 18 distinct operations.[15]

Smith believed that the only driving force in a capitalist system was money. "It is not from the benevolence of the butcher, the brewer, or the baker that we expect our dinner, but from their regard to their own interest." Applying the same principle to workers, Smith viewed high wages as the only significant work incentive. "Where wages are high . . . we shall always find the workmen more active, diligent, and expeditious than where they are low."[16]

By and large, Adam Smith's assumption that management would pursue maximum productivity and labor would pursue maximum wages stood up remarkably well. When in 1913 Henry Ford began to experiment with the first continuous production line in a Highland Park, Michigan, garage, he was setting in motion a revolution that made possible both cheaper automobiles and higher wages. The same workers who made

Model Ts that sold for $400 also made history by being the first to be paid $5 a day—Ford explained that this high wage reflected the principles of profit-sharing and efficiency engineering. And, of course, better-paid workers could buy more Model Ts.

What Ford's common sense and initiative began, Frederick Winslow Taylor elevated into the doctrine of "scientific management." Realizing that the speed of assembly-line production depended on the speed with which the slowest task could be performed, Taylor devised formulas by which each worker's maximum output would be realized. After studying laborers engaged in shoveling at a Bethlehem Steel Plant, for example, Taylor designed special shovels and shoveling techniques. Adoption of the "science of shoveling" paid off: 3½ years after his visit to the steel plant, 140 men were doing the work formerly done by 600, and those still employed had received a 60 percent increase in wages.[17]

The principles of scientific management were soon being introduced by Taylor's disciples in factories across the country. Armed with stopwatches, "time-study men" broke down every step of a manufacturing process into its smallest components, timed each component, and compiled precise instructions on how to handle each one. Efficiency was seen as an end in itself. The worker, to be sure, was being asked to perform a monotonous task, but what of that? He was, after all, being paid for it at a rate sufficient to compensate for the monotony. And nobody ever told him that work was supposed to be fun.

The combination of efficiency, productivity, and high wages has brought American workers unprecedented affluence. By 1973, the median income of American families was more than $12,000. Until "stagflation" began to set in in 1974, real income rose considerably faster than the rate of inflation. During the five years ending in 1973, minimum salary scales for police patrolmen increased an average 7.3 percent each year; production workers in private industry received an average 6.6 percent increase annually. Over the same period, the consumer price index increased at an annual rate of 4.6 percent. At the end of the period, over 80 percent of all American workers were receiving more than four weeks' paid vacation, together with eight paid holidays.

These trends gave rise to the assumption that wages would continue to go up forever. The recent wave of wage constraints and unemployment represents the first serious setback to this assumption for more than one whole generation of workers. For young workers in particular, the expectation of work offering steadily higher wages has made their attachment to a specific job tenuous. They see quitting, striking, or absenteeism as economically feasible alternatives to boring jobs. Unemployment benefits make it possible for laid-off workers to be selective in choosing new jobs; in spite of the high unemployment in early 1975, employment agencies in New York and Chicago reported great difficulty in filling openings for elevator operators, watchmen, and cab drivers. People weren't "jumping at the $2.50-an-hour job just to get a job," noted one state official.[18]

The evolution of the American economy has now reached a point at which it is possible seriously to question the sufficiency of the "money-instrumental" view. We are beginning to see situations in which additional wages are not an economically feasible means of compensating for unsatisfying work. And while it is still no doubt true that if money could do it, money would do it, two competing factors are at work: one is the industrial manager's need to find a way of recruiting and retaining workers on some basis that does not require a wage level that would eliminate the profit margin. The other is the wage earner's resistance to the job even for more money. Management would also do well to look to the factors affecting job satisfaction when well-paid workers phone in sick or merely fail to show up on a Friday or Monday because their boats or their hunting or their gardening take priority over a day's pay.[19]

Sweden exhibits an advanced stage of this development. Absentee rates of 18 percent are not uncommon there; in the United States 4 percent is considered high. Many Swedish workers spend weekends in their country homes, and if they choose to stretch the weekend by a day or two, they simply call in sick; no doctor's certificate is required. Should a Swedish worker become dissatisfied with his job, the labor market is so tight that he can easily find another one; unemployment is only about 1 percent. Turnover runs as high as 30 percent. In these circumstances, it is hardly surprising that Sweden is the bellwether in the effort to increase the intrinsic satisfactions of industrial work.

THE PROFILE of today's labor force suggests some of the reasons why signs of worker malaise are now so prevalent. Statistically speaking, the typical worker is much better educated, more affluent, more apt to be female or young, and less unquestioningly committed to the "work ethic" than his counterpart of an earlier generation. In 1950, the average worker had completed only 9 years of school; today, he has completed 12.5 years of school. Most of this 3.5-year gain has accrued to male blue-collar workers. The implications are mixed. On the one hand we have workers who are more informed, aware, and ready to be participatory members of society. On the other, these same qualities can lead to a sense of frustration and discontent if they cannot be brought to bear on the job.

Over a third of the 1,533 workers questioned in the University of Michigan Survey Research Center survey felt that their educational backgrounds were excessive in relation to the requirements of their jobs. Dissatisfaction was especially strong among workers with "some college," well over half of whom reported that their work could be handled by someone with a high school diploma or less. The Ford Foundation report found that workers who regarded themselves as educationally *under*-qualified were more satisfied than those whose training closely matched job requirements. The latter group, on the other hand, was substantially more satisfied than workers who considered themselves overqualified.

During the same 25-year period in which the average schooling of male blue-collar workers has increased from 9 years to 12.5 years, the median level of schooling for professional and technical workers has remained slightly over 16 years. The proportion of young people, however, who have completed 16 or more years has gone up sharply. In 1974, the nation's universities enrolled 1,190,000 candidates for advanced degrees, more than four times the 237,000 enrolled in 1950. The number of doctoral degrees awarded annually leaped meanwhile from 7,000 to 33,700.

Major shifts in the composition of the labor force have also influenced recent attitudinal changes. Disproportionately swelling the clerical and service ranks, the number of employed women has doubled in the past 25 years, growing from 17.5 million in 1950 to over 36 million in 1975. Over 45 percent of all adult women were employed in 1975—more than a third of the total work force.

"Women's lib" notwithstanding, single-minded devotion to a career is still a trait more common among men than among women. Professor Eli Ginzberg of Columbia University has found that most working women who balance job goals with caring for home and family are willing to give up increased job responsibility and additional income for the sake of homemaking —especially when the household includes a working husband. The opportunity for advancing long-range career goals is not, therefore, the primary standard by which most women choose jobs. While younger women in larger numbers have started to enter the ranks of professional and technical workers, over two-thirds of working women are still concentrated in three of the lower-status occupational categories: clerical, service, and operative. Since these jobs are seldom challenging, it is not surprising that both the Gallup and Michigan Survey Research Center polls recorded more women than men as expressing negative attitudes about their work.

Both the population bulge in the eighteen-to-twenty-four age bracket and the trend toward early retirement have resulted in a younger work force. As previously noted, young workers are prone to register discontent; in one recent survey, workers under the age of twenty-nine accounted for half of all those found to be dissatisfied with their jobs.

In addition to producing job dissatisfaction among young people obliged to take jobs for which they feel overqualified, the current education explosion is fast propelling us toward a "credentials society" in which a college degree may be required for a position as sales clerk. According to the United States Office of Education, only one-fifth of the estimated 50,000 Ph.D.s receiving their degrees in 1980 will find university employment. The situation is scarcely better for the 30,700 lawyers admitted to the bar in 1974; according to the Department of Labor, they competed for a total of 16,500 legal jobs. As these qualified job applicants fill openings further down the economic scale, the result will be to compound the overeducation problem and create still more worker dissatisfaction.

Fortunately, two developments seem likely to ease this pressure in the coming years. The first will affect the demand for highly educated workers. The 1973 Manpower Report of the President predicts greater increases in occupations requiring an advanced education than in those involving less education. For the years 1972–1985, the report estimates an annual 3.1 percent increase in the number of new professional and technical positions. This compares with a 1.6 percent increase in service workers and a 0.4 percent increase in nonfarm laborers over the same period. The second development will affect the supply of highly educated workers: with the last cohort of the postwar baby boom now in college, the college-age population has dropped and the birthrate is declining. It is possible, therefore, that the proportion of the work force which is young and over-educated will also decline.

The attitudes of young workers are affected not only by educational achievement levels but by the character of their educational experience. Young workers who, as students, were expected to budget their time and take responsibility for the completion and quality of a finished piece of work are prone to react adversely to close scrutiny by their supervisors and to resent being given a small part of a large task with no sense of its relationship to the whole. This complaint is voiced by members of paper-pushing assembly lines as well as of automotive ones. Judson Gooding, the author of several articles on worker alienation, tells of one young former executive who quit his job with a major corporation because he "felt like a small cog. . . . The decisions were made in those rooms with closed doors. . . .

The serious error they made with me was not giving me a glimpse of the big picture from time to time, so I could go back to my little detail, understanding how it related to the whole."[20]

Having participated as decision-makers in the administrative and curricular problems of universities, young people do not share their older colleagues' unquestioned respect for hierarchical authority. In a 1971 poll of college students, sociologist Daniel Yankelovich discovered that only 36 percent of the students did not mind the future prospect of being "bossed around" on the job, a substantial drop from the 56 percent who held this view in 1968. This attitude helps to explain the Michigan Survey Research Center's finding that young workers tend to feel little attachment to a given job. It comes through plainly in a conversation between Terkel and a twenty-three-year-old college graduate employed as a proofreader:

> I'm not afraid of the boss. I think he's sort of afraid of me, really. He's afraid of the younger people who work there because they're not committed to the job. The older person, who's got his whole life wrapped in the organization, has a sword hanging over his head. The boss can keep him from getting a promotion, getting a raise. If he screws up, he can be fired. His career is hanging in balance. If I make a little mistake, I'll say, "That's too bad, I'm sorry it happened." This guy'll freak out because his career is dangling there. Consequently, the boss doesn't have that power over us, really. The tables are sort of reversed. We have power over him, because he doesn't know how to persuade us. We do the job and we do it fine. But he doesn't know why. He knows why the older guys work— because they want to get ahead. He doesn't know why we work.[21]

A reduced commitment to work seems to stem partly from the diminished acceptance by young people of the theory that "hard work will always pay off." Yankelovich found that although 69 percent of college students agreed with this statement in 1969, only 39 percent agreed in 1971. Seeking to account for this shift in opinion, *Work in America* highlights the gap between the high expectations of college graduates and the lack of challenge offered by static job-market positions. The report cites the case of a young woman who has recently graduated from college: having just received a plaque certifying her mastery of a Xerox machine, she complains, "After you've been in the academic world, after you've had your own class (as a student teacher) and made your own plans, and someone tries to teach you to push a button—you get pretty mad."[22]

Yankelovich notes that young people anticipate a great deal of intrinsic reward from their jobs; in listing job objectives, they rank both challenge and the opportunity to "make a contribution" high above job security or promotion. When actual fulfillment falls short of desired levels, their reactions appear in the negative columns of worker satisfaction surveys in disproportionately large numbers.

PROPOSED SOLUTIONS for the worker dissatisfaction problem are as varied as the assessments of it. Since we cannot—and would not if we could—reduce the level of worker affluence, cut back on educational attainment, or alter significantly the profile of the work force, we have no choice but to emphasize reforms that can be directed either at extrinsic factors, like hours or working conditions, or at intrinsic factors affecting job content. The potential for any such reform depends in the first instance on management's willingness and ability to undertake it. Generally speaking, considerations of acceptability and cost make it easier for management to deal with extrinsic than with intrinsic factors. Operating within a cost-benefit framework, management will not ordinarily authorize an expenditure for improvements in the workplace unless it seems likely to yield a corresponding increase in productivity. If, for example, installing air conditioning cuts the aggregate number of trips to the water cooler, the cost of installation can be justified by the additional minutes workers spend on production. From this standpoint, any corresponding improvement in worker morale is viewed as a bonus. Projects of this kind obviously do not address the troublesome problem of job content, but they do succeed in packaging the job more pleasantly.

Among the remedies that focus on extrinsic factors, "flex-time" is one of the most publicized and the most promising. More than five hundred companies in the United States are now experimenting with do-it-yourself scheduling of the work day which frees workers from the traditional nine-to-five strait-jacket. An employer sets a "band-width" work day during which the office or plant will remain open, 7 A.M. to 7 P.M. for instance. Within that period, he establishes "core" hours, generally 10 A.M. to 3 P.M., when all employees must be present. Employees fill in the increment of an eight-hour day at their own discretion; they may opt to arrive at work early and leave at 3 P.M. for shopping, children's carpools, or personal recreation. Late-night entertainers or early-morning tennis addicts can reverse the pattern and work from 10 A.M. until 7 P.M. Some firms allow employees to put in six hours one day and ten the next as long as they work a fixed total number of hours per week.

A broad range of companies have instituted flextime, including The First National Bank of Boston and the Social Security Administration in Baltimore. Over six hundred workers participate in the bank's program; one of its assistant vice-presidents notes that absenteeism and turnover have dropped markedly since the establishment of flextime, while productivity and morale have risen. In the Social Security Administration, the popularity of flexible hours has prompted Commissioner James B. Cardwell to plan its introduction where practical to all the agency's seventy thousand employees within the next two years.

Flextime can be of distinct benefit to several groups of workers, especially mothers and students. For example, it permits mothers to plan their work days around the hours their children are in school, leaving free time in the afternoon during which to arrange extracurricular lessons, attend to medical appointments, or simply to spend time with their offspring. This last consideration appeals to sociologists who are concerned about the impact on the family of the increasingly large number of working women. In 1974, one out of three mothers with children under six years of age worked outside the home, a statistic which in itself attests to the desirability of enabling working mothers to maintain contact with their children.*

Flexible working hours are also a boon to students who work and adults who wish to continue their education. More than half of the ten million Americans enrolled in institutions of higher education have jobs. This number includes both full-time students who work only a few hours a week and full-time workers who take one or two night courses; hence the proportion of time spent on the job varies widely. Flextime makes it possible for many workers and students to manage their double load by minimizing the number of conflicts in hours. The benefit is twofold: workers who had to postpone their educations in favor of wage-earning can schedule their jobs around classes at local schools. Students, conversely, are aided in earning tuition or expenses when a weekly quota of hours, not nine to five, defines their work week.

The institution of flextime also serves as a palliative for that chronic metropolitan malady, rush hour; the dissolution of 5:30 traffic jams could save a substantial number of wasted hours, frazzled nerve ends, and gallons of gasoline consumed by cars standing fogbound by emission fumes. Workers can also plan their schedules around seasonal daylight factors, making safety-after-dark problems less of a risk.

While this new approach to the work week obviously cannot solve all the problems of worker dissatisfaction, evaluation studies have proved its effectiveness in improving worker attitudes. A recent survey of the Social Security Administration

---

* Cornell psychologist Urie Bronfenbrenner has argued that there is a direct association between family disorders and the rising number of working mothers. There are few substitute parent figures, like grandparents or nurses, in contemporary American homes. Professor Bronfenbrenner believes that a mother's extensive absence during the time her young children are at home can be the beginning of unintentional neglect that results in truancy, juvenile crime, and worse. A recent *Wall Street Journal* editorial used Bronfenbrenner's findings as a basis for encouraging firms to match their time schedules with family needs where possible. (September 24, 1974, p. 24.) A successful case in point is the Honeywell, Inc., division that operates a mothers' shift; mothers come to work when their children go to school and leave when school ends. These women are replaced by college students during the summer.

workers on flextime found that 70 percent were happier with their jobs than they had been previously, 78 percent spent more time with their families, and 82 percent were better able to cope with child-care problems. Individual workers' comments registered positive satisfaction with self-scheduled work: some expressed delight as commuters in finding empty seats on the subway, others mentioned the sense of heightened on-the-job responsibility, and one cited the benefit of no longer having to compete for one bathroom when preparing to leave for work in the morning.

Opposition to flextime has been minimal; workers who favor the old hours can adhere to them. Obviously, flextime does not lend itself to some assembly-line processes that involve continuous operation of machines, although certain Control Data Corporation plants have found it possible to offer their production workers changeable hours. In organizations where its introduction is practical, the working environment stands to benefit from the sense of increased responsibility and shared commitment on which the concept is based.

IF THE INTRINSIC FACTOR of job content is to be effectively altered, one must move from extrinsic reforms like flextime to more complicated efforts to enrich the work experience by redesigning jobs. Most recent experiments along these lines fall roughly into two categories: changes in the methods by which work is assigned, and greater diffusion of responsibility and control.

The first approach involves modifying the assignment of duties, with the objective of providing greater variety within a given job area. Alternatives to assembly-line production, the most publicized of which are the experiments at Sweden's Volvo and Saab plants, are based on this principle. Both Volvo and Saab have abandoned the conventional conveyor-belt system. Volvo employees now work in teams of about fifteen members on car bodies carried by battery-powered dollylike vehicles. The dollies are rubber-wheeled to cut noise levels, and their speed can be regulated by the workers themselves. The plant is subdivided into small work areas to create a workshop environment. Volvo management has also instituted work rotation; pay levels are commensurate with the number of different skills that workers have mastered. Saab has switched to similar small production groups and has established development committees to facilitate communication between worker representatives and production planners.

Although absenteeism and turnover have declined, these Swedish experiments have not yet been able to demonstrate an increase in productivity. Nor is the verdict in terms of job satisfaction yet decisive. A group of six American auto workers who spent four weeks working in the Saab-Scania plant at Soedertadje near Stockholm found that group assembly, while offering somewhat more variety than the assembly line, was as tedious as the Detroit system once the novelty had worn off.[23] A five-year veteran of the Volvo plant concurred, remarking that "there is a certain amount of monotony. It can't be avoided."[24]

American companies, meanwhile, are experimenting with a number of other approaches to job redesign. Some have replaced small, highly fractionated jobs with piecework assignments, or given workers the responsibility for a complete assembling and testing sequence. Both the Corning Glass Company and Motorola, Inc., have gone one step further: employees initial the units they assemble, thereby becoming individually accountable for the product's quality.

In other plants, tasks of a custodial or service nature have been integrated into more challenging assignments so that no employee does only "housekeeping" chores. Certain factories lend themselves to an approach under which workers learn several skills and then rotate among a number of different assignments. Even slight variations of assignment afford the wage earner a more stimulating daily routine and an enlarged sense of the overall production process.

Another approach calls for the introduction of greater worker autonomy. If a worker feels that he is in charge of his job, he is likely to identify his own successful progress with that of the firm. Feeling a sense of personal responsibility, he will make a more effective contribution to overall output. Many firms have given employees the task of setting production standards and quotas for themselves. Supervisors become team leaders and production decisions are made by a group vote based on information provided by the management. Progressive development of this method culminates in the formation of autonomous work groups that make production decisions independently of higher-level management, but in conjunction with the firm's needs.[25]

A highly successful example is the program introduced by General Foods in its Pet Food plant in Topeka, Kansas. Having first analyzed the serious worker alienation problems plaguing an existing plant, management incorporated into the new Topeka facility features designed to provide a high quality of working life and ultimately promote high productivity. The plan called for autonomous work groups, self-government for the plant community, decision-making power at the operator's level, and pay increases proportionate to the number of jobs that a worker could master. The economic benefits deriving from this exemplary operation have been twofold: first, although it was originally estimated that 110 workers would be needed to run the plant, institution of the team concept in lieu of individual assignees proved that fewer than 70 workers could handle production. Even greater dollar-saving factors have been the improved yield, minimized waste, and avoidance of shutdowns.

While group assembly methods focus on the factory floor, some companies are trying to ease alienation problems by inviting workers into the conference room. Such experiments have heightened interest in the European experience with worker participation in decision-making. First developed more than twenty-five years ago, the West German model is composed of two distinct boards—a supervisory board sets policy and appoints a management board that carries it out. In the coal and steel industries, the supervisory board includes equal numbers of shareholders' and workers' representatives with one "neutral" member chosen jointly by the two sides. In other industries, there is one workers' representative for every two shareholders. At the plant level, works councils take part in setting rules concerning hours and worker welfare and have the right to be heard on dismissal and work allocation decisions. On purely commercial matters, in companies of more than one hundred employees, works council members serve on an economic committee which is supplied with all information pertaining to manufacturing methods, technical changes, production planning, and financial prospects. Hiring, firing, and promotion must all have the advance consent of the works council.

Other countries have adopted similar measures. In Sweden, for example, the government passed a law in 1973 providing for one representative from each class of worker on company boards. No other European country, however, approaches Yugoslavia in extent of worker control. A workers' council elected by secret ballot exists in every enterprise and holds all the formal power: it approves all important management decisions, appoints management personnel, sets salary scales, decides on hiring and firing, establishes capital investment programs, and carries out long-term planning. The members of the council are elected by their fellow employees to two-year terms, serve without extra compensation, and continue their regular jobs during their terms of service. Council decisions are final; if managers refuse to accept the decisions, the council can force their resignations.

The main purpose of worker participation in management is to guarantee—at least theoretically—that top-level decisions are made with the employees' best interests in view. It does not contribute directly to job satisfaction, although it may enhance the self-esteem of those workers who actually take part in the proceedings. The majority of a work force will gain only the diluted satisfaction of knowing that a few of their own number represent them at the managerial level.

How far in the direction of worker participation should the United States attempt to proceed? This is a question which has increasingly interested me in recent years, and I have discussed it with a great many people in Europe and America— labor leaders, plant managers, experts in industrial relations, government officials, and citizens. I come away from these discussions with a number of rather firm impressions but only one strong conviction.

First as to the impressions. One is that worker representa-

tion on management boards is apt to be more form than substance. "The workers on our supervisory boards," a German
manager told me, "tend to become what your civil rights ac-
tivists call 'Uncle Toms.'" Another impression is that from the
workers' standpoint the most important opportunities for participation are at the plant level. It is at this level—as in the case,
for example, of the Pet Food plant—that worker participation
makes its most significant contribution to work satisfaction. It is
a contribution, indeed, closely analogous to that of political participation in local government. I am predisposed to agree, therefore, with the critic who wrote, "It is not that the level of
workers' involvement should be pushed up, since it is the individual worker's representative who is pushed up and, if he
becomes professional, out of touch, but that the level of decision-
making on an increasing variety of matters should be pushed
down."[26]

Many of the advocates of worker participation use the term
as if it were synonymous with industrial democracy. But the
degree of democracy involved depends, for one thing, on the
manner in which workers' representatives are chosen—whether,
for instance, they are elected by and from the rank-and-file or
designated by the union. And if they represent the union, it
obviously makes a difference how democratically the union itself is run. The Americans who worked at the Saab-Scania plant
in Sweden felt that "the normal activity of an American industrial union seemed to be a more effective manifestation of
worker needs and demands, with a more direct impact on day-
to-day life in the plant than the innovations in worker participation at Saab-Scania." As one of them put it:

> Even given all these situations where workers have par-
> ticipation in what's going on on the floor, it's still a
> situation of benevolence by the corporation . . . something
> that is done *for* you . . . we are taking care of your prob-
> lems, which tends to demean you as a man. . . . A man
> needs to feel that he is doing something about his own
> destiny instead of people laying it out to him.[27]

The issue of participation is a reflection not so much of the
problem of work as of ownership, and hence of control. Nowa-

days, management seldom owns the enterprise. The share-holder's interest in a large, widely held company is so remote and diluted that his fractional share of "equity" does not amount to ownership in any realistic sense of the term. Professor George Cabot Lodge of the Harvard Business School cites this develop-ment in underlining the implications of increasing workers' power in an organization, with specific reference to the self-managed work teams at the Pet Food plant in Topeka. Lodge argues that "a corporate collective works better when the legiti-macy and thus the authority of managers derives from the man-aged." And if managers are answerable to subordinates, "what," he asks, "is to happen to the myth of shareholder ownership and the theoretical tasks of the board of directors?"[28] What, for that matter, is to happen to the unions which have traditionally negotiated with management from the other side of the table?

One possible response avoids these questions by converting workers into shareholders. With the encouragement of tax de-ductions for corporate contributions to employee stock owner-ship trusts, this is a response being heard with increasing fre-quency.* A few companies—Sears Roebuck is the largest—are already under the control of their employees. But this trend, although highly desirable, in my view, from the standpoint of the health of the free enterprise system, leaves essentially where it was the issue of wages and productivity versus the intrinsic satisfactions of work: the only difference is that the worker may be on both sides of the question.

And so, at last, I come to the one firm conviction that I mentioned at the beginning of this discussion: it is that the sub-ject is too new for final judgments. We must, therefore, con-tinue to experiment.

As to the significance of possible experimental results, it is important to keep a steady eye on the one really important

* The employee stock ownership trust, an idea developed by Louis Kelso, a San Francisco lawyer, enables a corporation to finance its capital requirements through the sale of its common stock to the trust. The trust borrows the money to pay for this stock, and the corporation obligates itself to make annual payments into the trust in amounts at least sufficient to service the debt. These payments are tax-deductible.

issue: does the experiment—job redesign or enhanced worker
autonomy or some variant of industrial democracy—enhance
job satisfaction without at the same time costing too much
money or causing a prohibitive loss of productivity? Since work
is inseparably related to self-esteem and an essential contributor
to self-fulfillment, and since the ultimate goals of a free society
are the self-esteem and self-fulfillment of its members, any
measure that adds to the efficacy of work as a contributor to
these goals is valuable to the society. To be convinced that
increased job satisfaction is a good thing, therefore, most of us
have no need for experiments proving that dire consequences
will flow from the failure to provide job enrichment or that
dramatic gains in productivity will result from success in doing so.

The situation is quite otherwise, however, for employers.
While it may not nowadays be entirely clear to whom corporate
managers owe their primary allegiance, I doubt that anyone
would seriously expect them to devote much time or trouble to
job enrichment schemes that offer no real prospect of increasing
productivity or profits merely because it is in the general public
interest to maximize job satisfaction. For purposes of harnessing
corporate energy to this objective, experimental results can be
critically important. If the evidence shows that a given approach
to improving job satisfaction will actually forestall absenteeism
and reduce sabotage and industrial accidents, a management that
does not adopt this approach is ultimately handicapping itself.
And if, in addition, such an approach has been shown to be
genuinely capable of increasing productivity, managers will be
as eager to exploit it as they once were to adopt "scientific
management."

For unions and their members, a proposal put forward in
the name of increasing job satisfaction may look like a shrewd
ploy to get more work for less money—or to make the enhancement of "job satisfaction" a cheap substitute for higher wages.
While material well-being is relatively easy to quantify, intrinsic
rewards like self-esteem and self-fulfillment are inherently difficult to measure. Most American labor union leaders still share
Adam Smith's "money-instrumental" view: wages and fringe

benefits are the only significant form of compensation for work. They regard the unpleasantness of the job, like its hazards or its skill requirements, merely as a factor to be taken into account in fixing the rate of pay. From this standpoint it should make no difference in principle whether the unpleasantness is a consequence of monotony and repetitiveness, noisy machines or noxious odors, extreme heat or extreme cold. Vice-President William P. Winpisinger of the International Association of Machinists feels that programs designed to raise satisfaction levels may saddle workers with managerial responsibilities for which they are not paid. Says Mr. Winpisinger, "If you want to enrich the job, enrich the paycheck."[29]

Notwithstanding this view, the evidence that workers do not live on "bread" alone is likely as time goes on to have an increasing impact on the shaping of worker demands. As this happens, proposals to increase job satisfaction will have to be recognized as a legitimate subject of labor-management negotiations. To the extent that increased productivity is a probable result of putting a given proposal into effect, the question of whether, and how, to go about it will be dealt with in the same way as a plan to speed up an assembly line or install labor-saving machinery. The phasing-in of the job satisfaction scheme, the adjustment of projected manpower savings to normal attrition rates, and the division of the proceeds of increased productivity will become normal subjects of collective bargaining. In situations where job enrichment may not significantly increase output per man-hour but may be an economical means of improving retention rates and reducing absenteeism, the trade-off between the job enrichment plan and a wage increase will also be part of the collective-bargaining process.

But what of the society's more general interest in the improvement of job satisfaction? How is that to be advanced? Not, surely, through some direct form of government intervention. The attempt by government to create incentives for improving job satisfaction seems likely to be clumsy at best, counterproductive at worst, and ineffective in the remaining cases. At least I have not yet heard of—nor can I readily imagine—a governmental role that would not be subject to these disabilities. A tax incentive, for example, would be virtually impossible to administer. What kind of a showing would be sufficient for a company to qualify for the write-off or the credit? That its workers are now more contented than before the job enrichment measure went into effect? No, the general public interest—or, more precisely, the collective interest in individual self-fulfillment— is best served simply by expanding public awareness that it is possible to make the world of work more satisfying without thereby forcing a reduction of everybody's standard of living.

Government has the same reasons for being ambivalent toward increased job satisfaction as do labor unions. The prospect of increasing productivity anywhere near as much as the 40 percent claimed by some advocates of job redesign carries a proportional threat of putting people out of work. And granted that both the prospect of continuing improvement in the American standard of living and the ability of American industry to pay better wages are linked, overall and in the long run, to increasing productivity, the elimination of jobs in the short run cannot help being a matter of public concern. It is a concern which, even though offset by gains in job satisfaction and productivity, is all the more serious at a time of high cyclical unemployment. A slack labor market, in any case, does not afford an auspicious opportunity for job enrichment: a job that does not exist cannot be made more satisfying, and the worker fortunate enough to have a decent job at a time when others are jobless is not apt to risk it by agitating for a more "meaningful" work experience. It is by no means purely coincidental that Sweden, which has taken the lead in job restructuring, has long had a tight labor market.

As a matter of public policy, the desirability of enhancing job satisfaction is thus an important reason for seeking to create full employment. At best, however, it constitutes only a small fraction of the aggregate case to be made for giving job creation, job training, and job placement high priority among domestic social objectives. It is a priority which should be qualified only by a concern for inflation and the avoidance of government domination of the market system. Considered as a whole, the case for a jobs-first policy runs the risk of turning into an appeal for tolerance either of inflation or of a government-controlled economy or both. I regard it, however, as an appeal for ingenuity, resourcefulness, and determination in developing means of promoting full employment that do not inevitably produce these unacceptable side effects.

My own belief in the importance of a jobs-first policy grows directly out of nearly twelve years of social-welfare and law-enforcement experience. Often during those years it seemed that there was no direction in which I could turn without coming up against limitations traceable to the community's inability —or unwillingness—to provide the employment opportunities that could make a difference between creating self-respect and perpetuating dependency. I have previously referred to the discovery during my term as U.S. Attorney General of the inseparability between the hope of successful rehabilitation of criminal offenders and the availability of satisfying employment.* I also remember a visit as Secretary of HEW to a drug-abuse treatment and rehabilitation center in Detroit. The center was run by a group of dedicated black doctors who believed fervently in—and spoke eloquently of—of their ability to free drug abusers of their dependence on chemical crutches and motivate them to become productive members of society. Again and again, however, just when success in breaking the cycle of addiction, treatment, and reversion to drug dependency seemed possible, the doctors were frustrated by their inability to place the ex-addict in a job that would give him self-respect. They pleaded with me to enlist the interest of the Department of Labor in assisting them to stop the revolving door, and I promised to do what I could.

What could be done for ex-offenders and ex-addicts could be done even more effectively and on a much larger scale for all those individuals who are not readily absorbed by the labor market. Their identity is disturbingly apparent in an analysis of the incidence of unemployment: teenagers, black youths, and the aged. For these groups, unemployment ranges from twice to

* See Chapter V.

almost four times as high as unemployment for other groups. And while data demonstrating the causal connection between these high unemployment levels and crime, drug abuse, alcoholism, and welfare dependency are fragmentary, there can be no doubt that the correlation is real. If we assume that a 10 percent reduction in teenage unemployment produces a 5 percent reduction in teenage crime, and if we further assume that the chances that any teenager once adjudicated a delinquent will later be involved in crime are 2 to 1 (the historic pattern), it becomes obvious that society has an important stake in creating job opportunities for teenagers. The return in salvaged lives cannot be measured merely in dollar terms.

But unemployment and underemployment exact social costs far more extensive than those of crime, drug abuse, alcoholism, and welfare dependency. The links between intermittent or prolonged unemployment, desertion or divorce, and welfare dependency are well documented. An extensive review of forty-six studies relating work experience and family life found that "economic uncertainty brought on by unemployment and marginal employment is a principal reason why family relations deteriorate."[30] For me, these facts make unavoidable the conclusion reached by *Work in America*:

> *Thus, the key to reducing familial dependency on the government lies in the opportunity for the central provider to work full-time at a living wage. The provision of this opportunity should be the first goal of public policy.*[31]

Most of my own government service has been concerned with programs designed to cope with the failures of employment policy or the problems of the unemployable—law enforcement, income maintenance, and social services—rather than with the creation of jobs. I do not now believe, however, that attacks on crime, poverty, and dependency can succeed without more powerful support from job-creating policies than we have yet demanded of them. Indeed, our society cannot afford a reasonably adequate income-maintenance program except as a cushion against the failures of an otherwise vigorous job market. The most important social-services objective, moreover, should be to prevent dependency and restore the capacity for self-support.

A clear-cut priority for job creation brings within the realm of possibility a combination of benefits that is not otherwise achievable. This combination embraces both the chance to reduce other costs and the creation of opportunities for positive rewards. On the cost-saving side is the contribution of work to preventing dependency on public support and to avoiding the need for public custody or treatment. On the positive-reward side is the satisfaction of providing for a family and being a source of self-support. On this side also is the satisfaction of work itself. No income-maintenance program, however adequate, and no social-services program, however effective, can supply these satisfactions.

It is one thing, of course, to recognize that the social costs of unemployment are unacceptable and quite another to devise a workable jobs creation policy. And yet the priority attached to the first is the best guarantee that the second will be achieved. On the face of it, there are only three possible ways of maximizing the proportion of the work force which at a given time is actually employed. The first is by pursuing economic policies designed to stimulate a high level of employment. The second is by creating jobs outside the regular labor market. The third is by providing socially useful opportunities that will temporarily withdraw employable people from the labor market. Each of these approaches has its own combination of strengths and weaknesses; none excludes the others.

In the case of the first approach, the problem is not that economic policies do not work but that to rely on these alone is almost surely to exact an unacceptable inflationary price. Only when the economy is expanding at an abnormally high rate does it call upon workers who would be unemployed or marginally employed at other times; in a free economy the conditions which create full employment also create inflation. Even where unemployment is high, the risk of aggravating inflation may inhibit the use of economic and fiscal measures to reduce it, as happened in the mixture of inflation and recession which afflicted the Western democracies in 1974–1975. In the United States, our lowest recent level of unemployment (3.6 percent in 1968) coincided with a new burst of inflationary pressure but still left without jobs many of those whose unemployment exacts the heaviest social costs.

The failure of traditional economic policies to generate full employment in noninflationary circumstances has led economists to conclude that we have a dual labor market. The primary market offers jobs with good wages, pleasant working conditions, and good chances for stability and advancement; secondary market jobs tend to have just the opposite characteristics—low wages, poor conditions, and little opportunity for promotion. Dual-labor-market economists picture economic forces as generating the secondary labor market, drawing the poor into it, and tending over time to lock in even those poor people who initially had traits suitable for the primary labor market.[32]

It seems to me artificial, however, to attribute the duality of the labor market wholly to factors affecting the *demand* for labor. This country also has a dual labor *supply*. Unlike European countries which, until the recent recession, were consistently able to maintain full employment, the United States has had to contend simultaneously with a relatively rapid decline in the proportional demand for unskilled labor and a relatively rapid increase in the supply of such labor. The rural blacks and Puerto Ricans pouring into our large Northern cities (not to mention a yearly influx of an estimated one million illegal aliens, mostly from Latin America)* accumulated a pool of workers which the primary labor market simply could not completely absorb. Programs designed to expand job opportunities for the poor, meanwhile, succeeded mainly in opening up marginal job opportunities, with the result of accomplishing little either to alleviate poverty or to increase upward mobility among secondary employees. The main effect of such programs has been

* General Leonard Chapman, who heads the Immigration and Naturalization Service, has said that the estimate of ten million aliens illegally residing in the United States could be accurate. See *The Washington Post*, September 22, 1975, p. A22.

to recirculate the working poor among the secondary jobs that were, in part, responsible for their poverty.

This effect of manpower training programs has important implications for the second of the three above-mentioned approaches to maximizing employment. Creating jobs outside the regular labor market means, essentially, the public funding of employment opportunities in "public service" tasks that would not otherwise be carried out. And if these opportunities are to contribute to preventing the perpetuation of poverty, they must be of a kind which provides the training necessary for entrance into the primary job market. It is not easy to identify jobs that are at once useful, capable of providing training in a salable skill, and yet not of high enough priority to be done without the benefit of a public subsidy. Conservation and environmental cleanup jobs, for example, do get done when the community cares enough about having them done. If we hold out the availability of federal funds for subsidizing work that might get done anyway, we run the risk of reducing local incentives to raise the money and may end up with no more total employment than would otherwise have existed. If, on the other hand, we subsidize work that would not conceivably otherwise get done (scrubbing the steps of the Statehouse with soap and water, for example), we have increased total employment but may end up paying for tasks that no one cares about having performed.

The line between jobs worth subsidizing and jobs not worth subsidizing may be difficult to draw, but the effort is so important, and the costs of error so comparatively unimportant, that it deserves to be attempted. This is especially true of jobs which equip the worker for the primary job market. As to what these jobs are, there is no substitute for national, regional, and local forecasts of foreseeable manpower shortages. No net gain, plainly, follows from training a marginal worker for a skilled job which the trainee can obtain only by supplanting a worker who already has the requisite skill. And yet it is not uncommon for labor shortages to exist even in areas where the official unemployment level is comparatively high. I recall, for example, being told by a United States Senate candidate in 1972 that he had visited more than two hundred plants which complained of difficulty in finding skilled help notwithstanding the fact that reported unemployment in the state then stood at nearly 8 percent.

The third approach—reducing unemployment by reducing the size of the work force through the temporary diversion of employable persons into other socially useful occupations—can take a variety of forms. The paravolunteer roles discussed in Chapter IV serve this purpose. Higher education, by withholding from the labor market students who would otherwise be employable, performs a similar function. So also does every type of training and retraining program for people who would otherwise be employed.

For the latter group, training in a new skill is a means of escape from an unsatisfying or dead-end job.* It could also be made to serve a counterinflationary purpose. This would be accomplished by encouraging workers in dead-end jobs, or whose skill is in declining demand, to undertake a period of retraining which would qualify them for jobs offering greater prospect of advancement or to practice a skill in higher demand. The impact would be counterinflationary because people in dead-end jobs ordinarily receive pay increases for increased seniority unrelated to any increase in productivity and because employment in skills with declining demand cannot humanely be cut back at a rate commensurate with the reduction in the economic value of those skills. The result is inflation of the wage costs—and therefore of the prices—of the products on which they work. Meanwhile, the skills needed by expanding industries are apt to be in short supply, and competition for qualified workers tends to drive up wages in those sought-after occupations. This too has an inflationary impact. Retraining would reduce inflationary pressures and simultaneously increase overall

* At one time I thought it might be feasible to pay for sabbaticals for workers out of Social Security contributions in exchange for a reduction in eventual benefits. The trouble with this idea, however, is that it conflicts with the function of Social Security benefits as protection against the cessation of earnings.

employment by an amount equal to the number undergoing retraining at a given time.

As one way of reaching these objectives, *Work in America* suggests a "Worker Self-Renewal Program" under which workers with skills for which there is a below-average demand would be eligible for a year's retraining in a skill for which there is an above-average demand. It would be difficult, however, to make this approach work fairly. There would, in the first place, be definitional problems in classifying the relevant skills. Besides, it would be hard to justify letting a carpenter receive training as a draftsman while refusing a television repairman training as an electronic technician on the sole basis that the former occupation has been classified as a skill of below-average demand, while the latter has been classified as having above-average demand. The opportunity, at taxpayers' expense, to acquire valuable training while also receiving an allowance for family support is no small benefit. Eligibility for it should be fair and defensible.

In a speech to the Independent Colleges of Southern California in June 1972, I outlined a proposal for a "GI Bill for Community Service" which, like the original GI bill, would have conditioned eligibility for educational benefits on the past performance of a service—in this case some form of contribution to the community: working in a nursing home, counseling juvenile delinquents, teaching reading to adult illiterates, and the like. I now think, however, that the proposal has two drawbacks: first, its impact on employment would be small (what effect it did have would result from withholding from the labor market individuals who might otherwise have discontinued their educations); second, other sources of financial aid for higher education have all but eliminated the potential of educational benefits as an inducement for community service. Still, the "GI Bill for Community Service" concept does contain the germ of a useful idea. Why not make the rendering of community service —or the willingness to render it—the basis for establishing eligibility for retraining and "self-renewal"?

Two active programs illustrate alternative approaches to the identification of useful community-service activities. One is the Local Initiatives Program started in Canada in 1971 when unemployment reached 6 percent. Under this program the members of a group of unemployed persons, or a community organization acting on their behalf, requests a grant to put them to work for a renewable term of up to six months. Working for some sort of local public need is a prerequisite for making an application. The projects undertaken include a foster-care system, a halfway house, therapy for the handicapped, and school repair. Almost 6,000 projects serving 85,000 people were operating by the winter of 1973.

In 1972, with funds from ACTION, an experiment in the state of Washington undertook to increase employment by means of a voucher plan. In a selected county near Seattle, young people between the ages of eighteen and twenty-five were offered $50 a week for a year in return for finding a sponsor who would accept, train, and supervise them. The plan worked: once the state had created a marketplace and undertaken to subsidize the individual, it spurred 350 citizens and 130 government and private agencies to cooperate in devising brand-new jobs.

Both of these models allow maximum initiative by the unemployed. Both encourage private sponsorship. The results indicate that the people served are those in greatest need; the Washington experiment has also shown that permanent jobs can be created. The psychological benefits deriving from the participants' pride in their own achievements are substantial. The costs, moreover, are within reason: Washington's plan costs about $4,000 per man-year; the Canadian plan costs $2,000 per job and $6,000 on an annual basis. The Canadian model has the additional advantage that employers help meet these expenses; the American model is financed entirely by federal money.

There are, to be sure, certain difficulties with the idea of making community service the touchstone of eligibility for retraining. If the required period of community service is substantial and at a rate of pay significantly lower than the worker has previously been receiving, few workers will be encouraged to participate in the program even though their present skills are in declining demand. On the other hand, to shorten the required period to only a few weeks would undercut the legitimacy of community service as the entrance requirement for retraining in a new skill. Making it of substantial length but increasing the pay would increase the cost.

Properly handled, these apparent difficulties could be turned to advantage. The variables they reflect could be adjusted so as best to meet the needs of the economic situation at a given time and readjusted as the situation changed. If, for example, it seemed important to give priority to shifting workers from declining industries into expanding ones, priority could be given to the retraining function of the program by reducing the required period of community service and increasing the compensation. In a period, on the other hand, of substantial unemployment, the community-service roles would serve the same job-providing function as other forms of public service employment. In this situation the function of community service as a means of earning the opportunity for further training would be subordinated. Indeed, public service jobs for the unemployed could in principle be regarded as earning eligibility for further education or training.

The costs of such a program (let us call it STEP for "Service Training Eligibility Plan") would of course be considerable. Counting training costs, it might amount to as much as $10,000 per worker. If as many as 500,000 workers per year were covered, the total annual cost would be $5 billion. But we shall be spending $1.3 billion in fiscal 1976 on public service employment anyway and an additional $4.5 billion on various forms of manpower training. Most of this money might be used to greater advantage under STEP. The program should, moreover, generate long-term savings in public welfare and social services. If STEP were really successful, the long-term yield on its investment in human resources would more than cover its cost. Given the discouraging history of past failures to cope with the problems of marginal employment and dependency, such an experiment seems to me well worth trying.

THE WORLD OF WORK can never, of course, be made into an earthly paradise. Monotony and noise and dirt can never be banished completely. And yet we have seen vast improvement in the conditions of work and in rates of pay. We now need a comparable emphasis on the satisfactions of work. The combination of job redesign, worker participation, and increasing productivity can bring improvements here also. Understanding, moreover, the soul-destroying futility of prolonged unemployment, we must also do better on behalf of those who seek but cannot find rewarding work.

The achievement of these goals will not be easy. It will take determination and imagination—and *work*. But nothing is more important to the quality of life in America.

VIII

The Loss of Continuity:
Responding to the Need
for Community

NOSTALGIA is a selective sentiment. It is Williamsburg
in the 1750s without the mud, the outhouses, and the
flies. It is Laramie in the 1880s without the heat, the cold, the
vomit, and the bedbugs. It is the New England colonial town
without the censoriousness and the intolerance.

And yet the gentle glow of nostalgia does shed light on
institutions and values that are worth preserving or adapting if
we can. It reminds us that continuity is a satisfaction if not a
duty. The very selectivity, moreover, which nostalgia brings to
the past encourages rejection of the shoddy and meretricious in
the present. And if it is true that we cannot have it both ways,
we can at least make more intelligent compromises between the
compulsions of change and the attractions of continuity if the tug
of the latter is strong.

Nowadays, of course, we have learned to package nostalgia.

Disneyland squeezes together the sights and sounds of the Old Mississippi, the Wild West, and a New England village, but this no more disturbs us than the juxtaposition in a history book of illustrations of different periods and countries. Modern Williamsburg is old Williamsburg minus unpleasantness, plus crowds. Its artisans make real things, but nobody depends on their making them. Williamsburg reminds me of how I used to feel sailing Down East. It was fun to hold a boat on course in a heavy swell and a twenty-knot northwesterly breeze between Cape Elizabeth and Monhegan Island bound for Vinalhaven. But I could not help wishing we had something aboard that the people in Vinalhaven really needed.

I have much the same feeling toward the comfortable, well-groomed exurban clusters that occupy the surviving shells of sometime Colonial townships. The village green, the white clapboarded houses, the barns and fields are lovely to look at—lovelier, perhaps, because better kept than they have ever been—but they are unreal. Their forms have lost their original function. If there is any farming done, it is on a tax-loss basis, not to make a living; the real work is an hour's drive away.

And yet even the bedroom version of the Colonial village serves the need for a sense of community more than most modern settlements. A majority of their inhabitants, to be sure, feel at home in a larger world. For them such places as the Coffee House in New York or the Tavern Club in Boston supply the congeniality and companionship that others find closer at hand in the "local," the corner saloon, or around the potbellied stove of the general store. And yet even the cosmopolite who enjoys wider associations is apt to find a satisfying sense of the familiar in the vicinity of his home. For such an individual, neighbors are a reassuring part of the landscape.

However it may be supplied or discovered, a sense of belonging and continuity is essential to a sense of identity, which is to say a sense of self. For most people, as the previous chapter noted, work and the workplace play a large part in meeting this need. Association with professional colleagues may contribute to it. So also may involvement in a hobby or sport: few fraternities are more closely knit than bird-watchers, Currier and Ives collectors, or bow-and-arrow marksmen. We tend, meanwhile, to be increasingly conscious of belonging to the comprehensive communities constituted by the region in which we live, the nation of which we are citizens, or even—as we begin more clearly to grasp the implications of our collective confinement on a small planet—humanity itself. But these extended associations cannot take the place of closer relationships. On the contrary, as Lewis Mumford has pointed out, the very extension in our time of the range of our consciousness "only increases the need for building up, as never before, the intimate cells, the basic tissue, of social life; the family and the home, the neighborhood and the city, the work-group and the factory."

The need for a sense of belonging and continuity is a powerful one, and if we do not satisfy it one way, we must either find another or pay a price in personal insecurity. I saw this demonstrated during my first days of basic training at Camp Pickett, Virginia, in the summer of 1942. Together with four other basic trainees I was assigned to a pyramidal tent in the Medical Basic Training Center. None of us had known in advance what branch of the Army we would be assigned to. The only two of us who had ever met before were a nineteen-year-old farm boy from East Corinth, Maine, and myself; we had shared the same lower berth in the Pullman car that had taken thirty hours to bring us to Camp Pickett from Fort Devens, Massachusetts. It had been his first train journey. The oldest of us—a stonecutter born in Italy who had spent most of the last twenty-five years in Brooklyn carving gravestones—was forty-five. Another was a second-generation Italo-American from New London, Connecticut—a gentle youth who looked like a model for a Botticelli angel. Murray, the last, was a young man in his late twenties from Lawrence, Massachusetts. Until being drafted he had always lived at home, working—when there was work—in a textile mill and helping his mother take care of the house.

None of us had ever before been so completely uprooted, so completely out of touch with everything that gave us a sense of identity and belonging. It immediately became evident that this was an intolerable state of existence. We soon began to create for each other a set of distinguishing attributes and to improvise predictable relationships with each other. The predictability was important. Just before I entered the army my family had given me as a birthday present an album of Louis Armstrong records. My favorite was "Bye and Bye." I'm not much of a singer, but one of the first nights we were in the tent together I tried to sing what I could remember of it. After that Murray insisted that I sing it every night. To the rest of us the Brooklyn stonecutter was an old man, and he did his best to play up to the part, reminiscing about his childhood in Italy as if it had been seventy years ago. The boy from Maine was the unfooled innocent; the Connecticut youth with the Botticelli look was the ladykiller. I, of course, was "the Harvard man"; we were all very proud of that.

The happiest people I know are those who feel most at home with themselves and the world they inhabit. They are people whose daily lives provide a large measure of the sense of identity and belonging that we in Camp Pickett tried to give each other. Some people acquire during childhood a strong inner core of security that equips them with a solid base of personal stability regardless of the shallowness of their roots in the places where they happen to be. For most of us, roots—attachments—contribute importantly to our belief in our own identity. And although it is true that such attachments can be developed in many ways—professions, hobbies, and so on—nothing more universally or more powerfully evokes them than the associations both personal and geographical that spring from a place. A reason for this, I suppose, is that belonging to a place is a more universally shared experience than anything else a group of people can have in common. Take the weather. Strangers who meet casually talk about it because it is something they cannot help sharing. Second only to weather as a common denominator is the score of yesterday's hometown game. How sharply the field of shared experiences narrows down after that depends on the character of the place. A true community links its inhabitants together through its churches and synagogues, its parent-teacher organizations, its battles over school and sewer bond issues, its public library and its main street stores, its day-care centers, and its community hospital volunteers. A sense of continuity and belonging is woven into the essential fabric of community life.

Democratic processes both depend upon and contribute to a sense of community. As Margaret Mead has said, "The essence of American democracy is the concept of the creative individual in the creative community participating freely in the development of his society."[1] Without the continuing involvement of many people at many levels and in many constituencies, democracy is an intermittent and perfunctory exercise. An occasional plebiscite in the form of a Presidential election is not enough. To be both effective and meaningful, a system of representative self-government must afford the creative individual full opportunity to play a part in developing his society. This is why it is so important to pursue constitution-building efforts aimed at diffusing power and broadening citizen participation. But none of this is possible without a place in which people can be associated, share common concerns, and work together toward meeting those concerns. Such a place is a community.[2]

Communities are disappearing. Swallowed up by urbanization, flattened out by uniformity, overwhelmed by complexity, diminished by distant bureaucracy, and exhausted by the mobility of their inhabitants, America's human settlements are turning into clusters of isolated cells. Within these cells the frustration of community breeds alienation. Lacking in emotional attachment to a society which is indifferent to him, the rootless individual is trapped in a narrow world of ego-centered desires and gratifications. Ceasing to believe in the reality of other people, he can cheat them, steal from them, and hurt them with no fellow-feeling for their loss or pain. At its most extreme stage, the combination of isolation and alienation produces an antisocial predator to whom other people exist only for purposes of exploitation. And while no one knows for sure why crime in the United States has increased so alarmingly in recent decades, nearly five years of involvement with the problems of criminal justice have convinced me that the increase is directly proportional to the decline of community. This interaction, coupled with the concurrent decay of institutional authority, seems to me a sufficient explanation of what has been happening.*

Some of the forces submerging our communities can only be offset by the countervailing efforts and policies discussed elsewhere in this book. Other remedial measures—those which most directly affect the character of the human settlement itself—are the subject of most of this chapter. But before I come to these measures I want first to address the assumption that the American emphasis on individualism stands in the way of the fulfillment of community. How, on the face of it, can the claims of individualism be satisfied except at the expense of the group? Philip E. Slater, in *The Pursuit of Loneliness: American Culture at the Breaking Point*, is a persuasive exponent of this presumed dichotomy. Equating individualism with a belief that everyone should autonomously pursue his own destiny, Slater regards it as implying a denial of the reality of human interdependence. It follows that individualism is incompatible with cooperation, sharing, and thoughtfulness. The expressions of individualism are "free enterprise, self-service, academic freedom, suburbia, permissive gun laws, civil liberties, do-it-yourself, oil depletion allowances."[3]

There is, of course, a certain plausibility in Slater's argument, and yet I think it is fundamentally wrong. Community need not compel conformity. On the contrary, community pushed to the point where it suppresses individuality is not community but collectivism. Individualism need not deny interdependence. Individualism pushed to the point where it overrides due regard for others is not individualism but anarchy. Well short of anarchy, indeed, excessive individualism can stunt indi-

---

* James Q. Wilson points out that "predatory crime does not merely victimize individuals, it impedes and, in the extreme case, even prevents the formation and maintenance of community. By disrupting the delicate nexus of ties, formal and informal, by which we are linked with our neighbors, crime atomizes society and makes of its members mere individual calculators estimating their own advantage, especially their own chances for survival amidst their fellows." (*Thinking About Crime* [New York, 1975], p. 21.) Wilson, however, defines "community" in terms merely of the "observance of standards of right and seemly conduct in the public places in which one lives and moves" (p. 24).

viduality by isolating it. Where the right balance—the creative balance—is struck, individuality gains from community and contributes to it. Indeed, I believe that these aspects of human existence, far from being incompatible, are inseparable.*

The life of a community is enriched by the variety—the eccentricity, even—of its members. In the United States the age of individualism was also the age of community: mourning for the passing of the former is at least as loud as for the latter. Haynes Johnson of *The Washington Post*, in an appreciative essay on Nobleboro, Maine, recently reported that, for all its changes,

> Nobleboro retains a strong sense of place and strong ties of community. It is friendly and open, the kind of place where a stranger is immediately invited to lunch and to dinner; where you can meet old and new all in one day; where you can talk with the Willard Pinkhams and hear about the days of the old country store when butter was 30 cents a pound, eggs a quarter a dozen, and sugar and molasses were dispensed in barrels and hogsheads.

Mr. Johnson's essay ends with an observation by Elizabeth Coatsworth, a writer of poetry, children's books, and sketches of New England who had lived in Nobleboro for nearly fifty years: "If Americans are to become really at home in America it must be through the devotion of many people to many small, deeply loved places . . . people on this backroad retain the independent, self-respecting Yankee tradition."[4]

In the Nobleboros of this country, a strong sense of place and strong ties of community go hand in hand with independence and self-respect. Nor do I think that this combination is exceptional. It seems to me far more likely, rather, that where individualism is suppressed, community also tends to be stunted. If I

* George C. Lodge, in his thoughtful new book *The New American Ideology* (New York, 1975), speaks of a developing transition from John Locke's "atomistic idea of individualism to a new organic, collective idea" which Lodge calls "communitarianism" (p. 163). As I see it, what is happening is a shift of the balance between individuality and community back toward the latter.

am right, the existing societies which enforce collectivism should
exhibit a curtailment of community. And I think they do. The
enforcement of collectivism invariably demands the subordination of individuality to large and remote abstractions like communism, solidarity, and the state. In so doing, it also damages
and distorts the more intimate relationships that are at the heart
of the community. The result, in Robert A. Nisbet's phrase, is
the "radical atomization of every kind of religious, economic,
academic, and cultural association."[5]

Does it make a difference that survival is at stake? In such a
crisis a group of people commonly achieve an extraordinary
degree of cooperation and self-sacrifice. A classic example was
the Long March across China led by Mao Tse-tung and Chu
Teh in 1934–1935. All those who shared with them the suffering of that ordeal emerged from it with a triumphant sense of
comradeship and purpose. Other examples readily come to mind:
Washington's army at Valley Forge, the Battle of Britain, the
Berlin Blockade. It is conventionally supposed that such experiences epitomize the effacement of individuality and the cul-
mination of collectivism. I am convinced, however, that this
supposition is wrong. It is true that in the face of real danger to
a society, most individuals subordinate their personal desires to
the society's need to combat the common threat. But they do this
willingly, even gladly. They are not required to submerge their
individuality. On the contrary, the more clearly those exposed to
a common danger perceive their actions in response to it as freely
chosen, the stronger is their sense of community. It is a commonplace that a company of volunteers shares a livelier spirit of
community than a gang of conscripts.

Collectivism, on the other hand, involves the *suppression* of
individuality. The response to crisis thus has no need for collectivism. The participants in the Long March were highly motivated revolutionaries who shared not only a common ordeal but
a common vision. They were forced to resort to collectivism
only when they sought to impose that vision on an entire society.
This was the aim of the Chinese Cultural Revolution. To maximize the spirit of sacrifice and to minimize the necessity for
coercion, the leaders of the People's Republic have had to gen-

erate an atmosphere of crisis and sustain it by a continual barrage of public exhortation. But it seems to me questionable how long such devices can succeeed. In the Soviet Union the reiteration of slogans seems to be losing its capacity to inspire the new generation. The ferment of demands for individualistic self-expression is pressing against the crust of collectivist solidarity.*

The Soviet experience tells us that when government is authoritarian, when crisis rhetoric is a tool of behavioral conditioning, and when the secret police employ brute force to smother the stirrings of self-expression, people resort to elaborate charades and rituals both to mask the secret stirrings of individualism and to conceal the "counterrevolutionary" spirit of community. And yet the instinct of community, warped, stunted, and driven underground though it may be, is only strengthened —and here is another of the stubborn ironies of the human spirit —by the common sense of crisis induced by harassment.

These manifestations of resistance to repression corroborate a conclusion that I find compelled by everyday observation— the conclusion that individuality and a sense of community are ultimately irrepressible. People will seek out the mutually reinforcing relationship between the two whenever—and to whatever extent—the circumstances permit. To suppress this instinct a despotic government must keep its muscles—its army and its secret police—tensed at all times. But muscle fatigue will eventually, and inevitably, set in, thus releasing the pent-up forces of change. It is happening in the Soviet Union; it will eventually happen in Communist China.

A COMMUNITY is created by people who care about it. To make it work they have to be willing to fight for it. When I ran for Town Meeting Member in Precinct 10 of Brookline, Massachusetts, in 1950, the community leaders who signed my nomina-

* James H. Billington, in his authoritative study of Russian culture, foresaw that this ferment might represent something new on the Soviet scene. See *The Icon and the Axe: An Interpretive History of Russian Culture* (New York, 1970), pp. 584, 594. This forecast has since been corroborated by the "Sakharov hearings" on the repression of the individual rights of Soviet citizens held in Copenhagen in October 1972.

tion papers were all men and women of strongly marked individuality. One was the widow of a Superior Court Judge whose strong-minded leadership of the local School Committee had helped to make the Brookline school system one of the nation's best. Another was a paraplegic who supported himself by conducting a small direct-mail advertising business from his apartment. A third had given up a successful business career to seek a Ph.D. in philosophy. The Town Meeting itself was dominated by as diverse a group of personalities as I have ever known. Any of several could have qualified for commemoration in the *Reader's Digest* as "My Most Unforgettable Character." If I had to choose one it would be Selectman Dan Tyler, Jr., a big, belligerent, loud-voiced man, as kind as he was stubborn, who tracked down every sign of waste in the town government with relentless persistence. He loved to appear unannounced at the motor pool early in the morning just as the men were getting to work or to surprise a policeman dozing in his cruiser during the midnight-to-eight shift. Among the targets of his indignation was the Town Clerk's Eversharp pen paid for by the taxpayers (used to sign marriage certificates at the clerk's home) and the Park Commissioner's free telephone service at his house (for storm warnings). But Dan's detailed knowledge of Brookline government did result in substantial savings, and the town still benefits from his fight for the consolidation of the Highway, Water, and Sanitation Departments into a single Public Works Department.

No one in my memory was a stronger individualist or a stronger believer in community than my uncle Henry L. Shattuck, who for many years represented Boston's Back Bay in the Massachusetts House of Representatives and the Boston City Council. The inspiration for Mr. Parker, the only sympathetically portrayed Yankee in Edwin O'Connor's *The Last Hurrah*, Uncle Harry liked people for what they were; the one thing he could not abide was pretense. He had none of his own. One of his favorite stories about himself told how, hurrying down Charles Street one evening to catch the subway to Cambridge, he was accosted by a bearded old man who, stepping back and surveying him from head to toe, inquired, "The late George Apley, I presume?"

A perception of the importance of cultural identity heightens awareness of the creative balance between individuality and community. Himself a representative of the established "Yankee" tradition in the cultural heritage of Boston, Uncle Harry worked toward healing the historic rift between the Irish and Yankee segments of the community. He understood instinctively that the way to accomplish this was not to subordinate the separate identity of Boston's Irish cultural heritage, but to proclaim and magnify appreciation of it. Such appreciation he felt, would directly enhance the significance of the Irish contribution as perceived by other segments of the community, including the Yankees. It would also increase the value of their heritage in the eyes of the Boston Irish themselves. The result, Uncle Harry hoped, would be to diminish Yankee smugness and to boost Irish self-esteem. In recognition of his efforts toward these ends, including the gift to Harvard of a chair in Irish Studies, the two leading Dublin universities gave him honorary degrees.

Nathan Glazer and Daniel P. Moynihan in *Beyond the Melting Pot* were the first to bring to wide public notice the realization that the melting pot "did not happen. . . . The notion that the intense and unprecedented mixture of ethnic and religious groups in American life was soon to blend into a homogeneous end product has outlived its usefulness, and also its credibility."[6] In a more recent article they delineate the "new saliency of ethnicity" (itself, as they point out, a new term) and examine the questions "Why ethnicity? and why now?" In answer they offer conjectures covering a wide range: "the rise of the welfare state, the clash between egalitarianism and the differential achievement of norms, the growing heterogeneity of states, and the international system of communication."[7] And indeed, they make a plausible case for the contribution of each of these developments to the result that ethnic self-consciousness and self-assertion have become more marked everywhere in the last twenty years. It seems to me, however, that they have left out a contributing factor at least as important as any they have enumerated. This is the role of ethnicity as a bond of community. The affirmation of a distinctive cultural heritage and association with others who share it is one way—and an easily accessible one—of offsetting the forces of modern society which tend everywhere to submerge the sense both of identity and of community. Indeed the "new saliency" of ethnicity has emerged concurrently with the gathering momentum of these forces.

I disagree, therefore, with Glazer and Moynihan's observation—at least as it applies to this country—that "the weight has shifted from an emphasis on culture, language, religion, *as such*, to an emphasis on the economic and social interests of the members of the linguistic or religious group."[8] My evidence is admittedly impressionistic and anecdotal. It comes from the many ethnic gatherings I attended as a political campaign worker and candidate—Polish weddings, Greek picnics, Italian saints' days, Scottish games, Lithuanian Independence Days, Armenian dances, Albanian outings, Lebanese feasts—where I found third- and fourth-generation young people happily celebrating the rediscovery of their ancestral costumes, foods, songs, dances, and literature. It comes also from later years in which I spoke at Pulaski Day in Chicago, talked with American Indians in a Cleveland church basement, listened to Chicano students in San Diego, conferred with representatives of the Puerto Rican community in New York, and met with Chinese leaders in San Francisco. It is not important that the customs being celebrated are sometimes borrowed and sometimes spurious. (Citizens of Eire are uniformly appalled by the picture of the "ould sod" that emerges from our St. Patrick's Day parades, and I take it that the feather bonnets now worn by East Coast Indians at their annual powwows originated with the Great Plains tribes.) Cultures, in any case, are always borrowing, adapting, and improvising. The important thing is that the people concerned are affirming a sense of cultural identity.

As Secretary of HEW I set up an Office of Special Concerns for the specific purpose of responding to groups—blacks, Spanish-Americans, Indians, women—who have historically been the subject of discrimination. And while it is certainly true, as Glazer and Moynihan point out, that the organizations representing these groups devote a large fraction of their energies to asserting economic claims (more government jobs, funds for bilingual education, or support for group-related health services), it is a necessity if not a duty for any organization to re-flect the most selfish interests of its members. The organization represents them, after all, only in a single capacity. Thus it is inevitable that veterans' organizations, labor unions, bar associations, medical societies, rifle clubs, and women's lib groups will tend to ignore the fact that their members are also citizens, taxpayers, parents, husbands, wives, Protestants, Catholics, Jews, Elks, Rotarians, and/or model-train builders.

It does not follow, therefore, from the concentration of ethnic organizations on their members' narrowest interests that the real reasons for the new ethnicity are equally narrow. Nor is it true that the ethnic organizations themselves focus on economic interests to the exclusion of cultural ones. For example, I have asked Puerto Rican or Chicano groups why, when earlier generations of Polish, Czech, German, and Scandinavian immigrants regarded English as good enough for their public-school children, Spanish-speaking parents fight for their children's chance to learn both languages. The Spanish-American answer: that the Spanish language is the most important single element of their culture, and for their children to lose their native language would be to lose their identity. It's a convincing answer, though not, I suspect, a complete one. Another factor, I feel sure, is that most Spanish-speaking people in this country are descendants of people whose territory was annexed by the United States, a fact which significantly distinguishes them from immigrants who voluntarily chose to come here. The great waves of European immigrants occurred before the struggle to preserve—or acquire—a sense of identity had come to seem so important. Indeed, it is indicative of this relatively recent phenomenon that when I headed HEW, the descendants of these very Europeans—the "white ethnics" so-called—had just begun to seek legislation providing federal support for the establishment of "cultural centers" devoted to the perpetuation of their ancestral traditions. This was the only thing they ever asked for my help on, a fact which in itself tends to belie the presumed priority of economic interests.

Where ethnic groups once turned to political organization as an avenue toward security and advancement, political organizations now turn to ethnic groups as sources of marginally decisive support. Politicians will be the last to disregard ethnic self-consciousness. Leverett Saltonstall's campaign for reelection to the United States Senate in 1954 showed why this is so.

Saltonstall is, of course, the epitome of the Massachusetts "Yankee"—a direct descendant of one of the founders of the Massachusetts Bay Colony. His opponent was the State Treasurer, an Italo-American former Congressman named Foster Furcolo. As soon as it became clear that Furcolo was the likely Democratic nominee, Saltonstall's campaign staff got to work on the usual research into the opponent's background. Some surprising things turned up. Although a Catholic, Furcolo had described himself as a "Protestant" in his application to Yale University; he had also been married in a civil ceremony. And although Furcolo is an Italian name, Foster converted it to "Furcolowe," explaining in his application for admission to the bar that this was "to conform to the ancestral spelling." To anyone aware that there is no "w" in Italian, this translated, "to make it look like an English name."

Petty stuff? Yes. Suitable for use in a campaign for the United States Senate? No. Senator Saltonstall characteristically vetoed any use of it. The information circulated, nonetheless, by word of mouth, and one of the Senator's Italo-American supporters saw to it that a few photostatic copies of the underlying documents found their way into the hands of people who would be sure to talk about them.

So matters stood until late in the campaign. By that time it was a horserace. And at that point John F. Kennedy, the junior Senator, in great pain from his World War II back injury, came up to Boston from his Hyannis Port compound where he had been working with Ted Sorensen on *Profiles in Courage*. He had agreed to appear live on WBZ-TV with Furcolo and House Speaker Bob Murphy, the Democratic gubernatorial candidate. Kennedy felt he would be doing a great favor to Furcolo to appear with him at all. This was only in part because of his painful back. Relations between Kennedy and Furcolo had been strained ever since both were junior Congressmen and Furcolo welshed on a joint appeal to President Truman on behalf of executive clemency for Boston Mayor James Michael Curley (who at that time was running the city from his Danbury jail cell).

There had been sharp exchanges over the content of the program: Kennedy, over Furcolo's strong objections, had made it a condition of his participation that none of the participants would attack President Eisenhower or say anything personally critical about Saltonstall. It was agreed that all three would meet at the TV studio fifteen minutes before air time to go over the format. To Kennedy's extreme annoyance, Furcolo showed up with only five minutes left and immediately began to berate Kennedy for his restrictions on program content. For a moment it was doubtful whether the program would go on at all. As it was, any viewer must have been puzzled (I certainly was) as to why, at the end, Kennedy turned to Murphy on his left and said, "The very best of luck to you, Bob," and then, looking straight at the camera and conspicuously avoiding even a glance toward Furcolo on his right, added, "and to the entire Democratic ticket."

A few minutes after I got to my office the next morning (I was Saltonstall's speech and press-release writer), Ted Sorensen walked in and told me what had happened. He was there, he said, on the instructions of his boss to offer all possible help to Saltonstall by the Kennedy organization during the remaining days of the campaign. He also had a specific suggestion to pass on: find two prominent supporters of Kennedy against Lodge in the 1952 campaign which first elected Kennedy to the Senate and get them to sign a letter to be mailed to every person with an Irish name listed in the Greater Boston phone book. The letter would say, in effect, "As supporters of John F. Kennedy in 1952, we believe that he and Leverett Saltonstall have been a great team; let's not break up the team." Saltonstall was reelected by a scant 27,000 votes.

A sense of ethnic and cultural identity has a legitimate place, I believe, in the creation of community. This is true both within and among groups. There may be rivalries, to be sure, or even hostility. But these need not be destructive unless discrimination on the part of the larger society turns them inward and makes them rancid. Rivalries may, indeed, be indispensable to morale, as they are in a military unit: loyalty to each unit is embraced within loyalty to a larger unit. As a member of the Twelfth Infantry Regimental Combat Team, I was convinced that the Twelfth was the best regiment in the Fourth Infantry Division, but I was equally convinced that the "Fighting Fourth" had no equal among Army divisions.

The many-hued tapestry is a metaphor more worthy of America than the melting pot. In such a tapestry each of us—each group—can distinguish our contribution to the whole, and the richness and variety of the whole is enhanced by each group's uniqueness.

So FUNDAMENTAL is a sense of community to the quality of life that its preservation and enhancement should long since have been made an explicit goal of public policy. But even if this were now to be done, as I strongly believe it should be, it would still be important to proceed cautiously in defining the role appropriate for government. We must not lightly allow government rules and regulations to intrude themselves into what Mumford called the "intimate cells" of community life. Government's most constructive—and least intrusive—role, I believe, should be to encourage the design and use of the geographical space in which we live along lines that strengthen a sense of belonging and sharing. No new extension of governmental power is required; government, especially at the local level, is already heavily engaged in matters of zoning, planning, development, and redevelopment. What is needed, rather, is a clear perception of the degree to which the exercise of such powers should be informed and guided by awareness of the ways in which their imaginative exercise can strengthen a sense of community.

Taking as our point of departure the inseparability between a sense of place and a sense of community, we should insist that the planners of physical space take into account the human needs of the people who will occupy the space. It is also essential that the planners keep in view the entire human settlement. Typically, overspecialization finds an architect looking at buildings, a planner at the two-dimensional layout of the city, an engineer at public utilities, and an administrator at local government problems. With little or no coordination among them, the result is overlap at best and counterproductive conflict at worst. The social sciences, anthropology, ecology, and technology should all be harnessed to the task of assembling the resources needed for the creation of the physical settings within which people can build communities.

A first step should be to restrain the planners from policies destructive of the communities that still survive. Just such destruction, ironically, has all too often been the consequence of "urban renewal" projects. In an age which enables demolition crews to raze several stories in a few hours, the appeal of a clean site has too often obscured the merits of alternate courses of action. The "renewal" of Boston's West End is a tragic example. When I first knew the area, it was a close-knit community of Italian families whose associations were constantly renewed by frequent contact in its narrow streets. Mothers kept an eye on each other's children. Old men played checkers together at benches in the small parks. The crime rate was low. When the entire West End was razed in 1958–1960 to make room for high-rise, high-rent apartments, its residents were scattered all over Greater Boston. Their community had disappeared. Many became depressed and lost all interest in life. The best of intentions had produced the worst of results.[9]

It is not only socially but economically important to conserve the investment in existing settlements and to insist that those settlements have served all the purposes for which they were created before they are destroyed. The rush to demolish an area that wears an outworn appearance should be postponed until the question of why it is no longer functional has been answered. The fact that houses have been abandoned, for instance, usually indicates something more than that their structures or facilities are deficient; the chances are that the area's community services, educational systems, or transportation networks are inadequate. In that case, refurbishing the residences themselves will solve nothing. It is the planners' job to develop comprehensive programs both for the improvement of the physical units and for the services that their occupants will need.

Several metropolitan areas have undertaken projects that make imaginative use of existing areas. Among the most promising are the "urban homesteading" programs which permit lower- and middle-income groups to buy dilapidated houses at minimal prices—as low as one dollar in some instances—in return for which the new owners must make them habitable within a specified period of time. A prerequisite for the program's success is a commitment by the city government to augment municipal services in the surrounding area. Minneapolis, Philadelphia, Baltimore, and Wilmington are among the dozen cities that have instituted homesteading, and their preliminary results are encouraging. While HUD officials warn that homesteading is not a panacea for urban blight, it does seem to make a real contribution toward establishing a sense of community. The explanation, apparently, is that "recycling" residences in this fashion requires vigorous participation by homeowners. Washington, D.C.'s Capitol Hill area is a case in point; its residents, many of whom refurbished the townhouses in which they now live, share a stronger sense of community than many older neighborhoods.

Several cities have sponsored projects rehabilitating large areas of historic or cultural value. Alexandria, Virginia, and Philadelphia have resurrected their waterfronts, and these now blend modern commercial functions and sensitively restored architecture. Other cities have focused on ethnic enclaves: in the fall of 1974, for example, Mayor Abraham Beame called for a "risorgimento" that would upgrade the residential and commercial areas of New York City's "Little Italy."[10] The proposed plan calls both for new construction of schools and housing and for restoration of historic stores and residences.

City officials hope that the proposed renovations will induce former residents to return to Little Italy and encourage new immigrants to move in (shades of the West End!). The officials also see the prospect of a new educational and cultural showcase that will be interesting to visitors as well as gratifying to its residents. If Little Italy's rehabilitation does succeed, substantial credit will be due John E. Zucotti, chairman of the City Planning Commission, who is a strong believer in fashioning city planning around local needs and desires. In the case of the Italian area, for example, the Department of City Planning worked with the Little Italy Restoration Association, an organization of community residents. This cooperative approach not only allows but encourages the members of a community to take an interest in the future of their environment. The area benefits from its greatest source of strength—its own citizens—and the resulting plans conform to their ideas, not those of some outside planning body.

Citizen action is undoubtedly the crucial element in revitalizing a community. In *Nation of Strangers*, Vance Packard cites the example of the Park Slope area of Brooklyn.[11] The area contains thousands of old brownstone houses once owned by prosperous Brooklynites, many of whom joined the migration to suburbia shortly after World War II. The residences they left behind went into rapid decline; overall neighborhood deterioration began to approach slum conditions. A group of determined young residents felt sufficiently strong ties to the neighborhood to want to revive it. They formed a Park Slope Betterment Committee, and once the committee had persuaded several dozen "settlers" to purchase and renovate some of the brownstones, a chain reaction of community-building projects had been ignited.

The actual rehabilitation of the Park Slope residences resulted in much neighborly counsel on the problems of plumbing, heating, and wallpapering the old buildings. The comradeship born of cooperation led to discussions of larger community issues as well; joint efforts resulted in the establishment of a cooperative nursery in a local church, Saturday morning street sweeps to cope with the neighborhood's perennial litter problem, and father-supervised touch football games for children too young to negotiate Prospect Park unsupervised. There are gala block festivals and cookouts; residents participate in everything from planting trees to political campaigns. There is mutual dependence based on mutual care for a living place: both result in affirmative action. Federal funds can never take the place of such locally inspired self-reliance.

REGARDLESS of their different methodologies, such students of the urban scene as the late Constantinos Doxiadis, Margaret Mead, and Vance Parkard agree on one overridingly important aim: the necessity of reestablishing human scale in communities. Architecture, whether applied to renovation or new construction, is of primary importance in achieving this goal. The number of needs which architects should address are as numerous as the effects of structural innovations themselves; to appreciate them fully, the complete architect must be not only a designer, but something of a psychologist, anthropologist, and ethnologist as well.

In discussing this point, anthropologist Edward Hall, author of *The Hidden Dimension*, stresses the importance of spatial boundaries as a determinant of human behavior and hence of community. He cites Winston Churchill's remark, "We shape our buildings and they shape us."[12] During a debate on the proposed restoration of the House of Commons, Churchill expressed the fear that abandoning the intimate spatial confines of the House which force opponents to face each other across a narrow aisle, would substantially alter the character of parliamentary government. Expanding on Churchill's point, Hall emphasizes the numerous and varied human needs which should be recognized in designing living areas.

It is Hall's theory, based on an ingenious series of overcrowding experiments with mice, that man has around him, as extensions of his person, zones of space relating to visual, thermal, and tactile perceptions. Violation of these zones can lead to psychological and physical discomfort. Hall asserts that "man's feeling about being properly oriented in space runs deep. Such knowledge is ultimately linked to survival and sanity. To be disoriented in space is to be psychotic." We do not become conscious of the manner in which we define our own "spatial envelopes" until we encounter people from other cultures who define theirs differently. Western Europeans, for example, regularly converse within distances that Americans consider uncomfortably close. Overcrowding violates these spatial territories, and "when stress increases, sensitivity to crowding rises—people get more on edge—so that more and more space is required as less and less is available."[13]

The ability to recognize zones of sensitivity has become increasingly important in a world where builders are packing more and more people into "vertical filing boxes" of houses and offices. Systematic attempts to identify existing deficiencies and define future needs have already shaken the assumptions that replacing slums with high-rise apartments would be visually more pleasant and therefore humanly more habitable. Being intrinsically antithetical to human scale, the high-rise is doomed to disappoint many needs. Writing more than twenty years ago, Robert Nisbet foresaw that the ultimate result of moving residents to "architecturally grim, administratively monolithic" housing projects might be "a new type of slum, one with little hope of culture or community, one in which gangs and violence as well as alienation will be the logical and predictable consequence."[14] The St. Louis authorities who recently ordered the razing of that city's Pruitt-Igoe housing project must wish that they had seen and heeded Nisbet's words. Constructed only twenty-one years ago at a cost of $52 million, the Pruitt-Igoe towers aroused such destructive hostility on the part of their residents that it became impossible to keep them in repair.

Considerations of scale directly concern the determination of proper population density as well. Hall seems to me correct in insisting that in spite of the abstract nature of the notion of scale, it is mandatory that city planners learn more about it in order to establish size specifications for dwelling places, urban areas, and their associated service networks.

A community's composition is similar to an artistic one: remembering the value of silences in a musical score or blank paper in a watercolor, we should avoid filling in all the spaces in a given geographic area. Toronto is one city that American planners would do well to emulate for its appreciation of the necessity of parks and open spaces.* In 1969, a collection of "small 's'

---

* London is another. One-third of the city's area is still free of buildings, and the population density is considerably lower than that of the four larger cities (Shanghai, Tokyo, New York, and Peking).

socialists"—Tory conservationists, academics, and others opposed
to the prevalent "build and be damned" philosophy—gained
power in city hall and decided to take action against encroaching
pavement. Alderman William Kilbourn, a member of the city's
executive, summed up the problem: "In the late '60s, Toronto
was busily destroying its human scale. We were building more
than Los Angeles or New York City. Previous Toronto city
administrations measured the health of the city by the number
of building permits they issued. You can call it growth and progress or you can call it cancer."[15]

Planning during the intervening years has put a damper on
new construction and emphasized retention of open spaces. The
results are pedestrian malls in the city's main shopping area
and shops clustered around courtyards that serve as outdoor
cafés and meeting places. The latest of the city's so-called people
projects is "Harborfront '74," a program designed to transform
a now defunct industrial dock area into an urban activities center.
Old warehouses and loading sheds are to be turned into amateur
and professional theaters, skating rinks, and arts and crafts centers; a concrete dock is now a game surface by day and dance
floor by night; and open spaces between the converted buildings
have been made into playgrounds.

Toronto's city administration has based its strategy on citizen feedback. Tommy Thompson, Toronto's Parks Commissioner, has urged *The Toronto Star* newspaper to solicit the public's suggestions concerning the use of the city's 15,000 acres of
parkland, which comprise 1,171 full-scale and street-corner
parks. "We've got only one rule in our parks," says the commissioner. "If you don't damage property, and don't interfere
with others, you can do whatever you want." Thompson's positive attitude is reflected by one of his first official acts—the placing of signs that read "Please Walk on the Grass" in all municipal
parks.[16]

Toronto's use of pedestrian malls is one means of fencing off
the automobile that is being widely adopted in other cities. And
none too soon. The automobile is the most voracious consumer of
public and private space man has yet invented. In Los Angeles,
an estimated 60 to 70 percent of the entire area is devoted to cars,

either in streets, parking lots, or freeways. A comprehensive approach to the creation of communities must therefore be as much concerned with balanced transportation systems as with parks and green areas. Not only efficient and reasonably priced public transportation but sidewalks and bicycle paths should have a place in the planning. Submerged "deepways" for cars and elevated "skyways" for pedestrians are among the possible approaches to achieving a cohabitable accommodation between human and mechanized traffic.

WHERE EXISTING urban areas are concerned, the planner is never in a position, of course, to correct immediately all the errors of design that have tended to break down the natural clusters of homes and services that might have served as the focal points of community. He can, however, develop a conception of the physical patterns that are most conducive to the building of communities within the urban area and then seek to make sure that the evolving process of change is guided by this conception. High on his priority list should be opportunities to influence the location of community services and facilities; a sense of place grows out of familiarity with streets and buildings, plazas and parks to which there is frequent occasion to return.

There are also the opportunities to get acquainted with other neighborhood residents who are drawn to the same area. Community facilities, moreover, give rise to relationships that are partly associational (the regular users of any facility—bar, bowling alley, public library, day-care center—quickly come to think of themselves as linked by common membership in a group) and partly proprietary (they automatically tend to regard the facilities in question as "theirs"). Even the associations which cluster around a place name add a little to the sense of belonging and continuity: the Loon Lake Branch Library, the Loon Lake Valley Pharmacy, the Loon Lake Child Guidance Clinic, and so on.

Government already has in its hands much of the authority needed for the planner to make sure that locally required services and facilities contribute to the building of community. Most social services are provided by government agencies, and these can be located within walking distance of each other close to the center of other activities. The area served by the local mental-health clinic or multiservice center, moreover, can be laid out so as to respect, rather than ignore, neighborhood lines. Voluntary agencies are likely to want to situate themselves near the public agencies and can certainly be encouraged to do so. The resulting proximity of service providers should help both to enhance the sense of community and to facilitate a coherent response to the needs of the whole person.* And once a community core has begun to take form, new shops and other facilities—day-care centers, for instance—that are not publicly financed or administered can be influenced to locate there by zoning by-laws which reflect the overall community plan.

The most useful single center around which to build other community services is the local elementary school. Its value for this purpose deserves, in my view, to be more widely recognized. I first heard about the idea when representatives of the Flint, Michigan, school system and the Mott Foundation came to HEW in January 1971 to enlist my interest in "community schools." They sold me on the concept, and I have been an enthusiastic advocate of it ever since.

A "community school" builds on the circumstance that in most American cities and towns today the elementary school comes closer to being the unifying element of a neighborhood than any other single institution. Why not, then, use the school building as the center for other activities as well? For example, the Thomas Jefferson School-Community Center in Arlington, Virginia, combines an educational plant with facilities for day-time care of the elderly, adult recreation programs, career counseling centers, a performing arts group, and a joint county-school newsletter. Other community schools embrace a similar, and sometimes even broader, range. There are more than 100 community schools now in operation in the United States; the number would undoubtedly be much larger but for the jurisdictional walls that normally separate education from other community services.

But it takes more than facilities and services, however well

* See Chapter V.

integrated, to make a community. A community has to have a "soul." A theater, an art gallery, a historical museum, musical organizations—some combination of cultural resources such as these can make all the difference between a town that possesses a spirit of community and one that lacks it. And as Margaret Mead once pointed out to me, community colleges may well turn out to be an invention as important as land-grant colleges. With retired admirals teaching mathematics or studying philosophy, women returning to education, and police officers taking courses in community relations, community colleges are becoming increasingly important contributors to the life of the areas they serve.

My first years of law practice in Boston exposed me to a rather different example of what a municipal facility can contribute to a sense of community. Several of us in the law office where I worked used an occasional lunch hour to go to the municipal bath house on L Street in South Boston. This was a place where, on the men's side, you paid a quarter for a bit of cloth worn as a concession to modesty and called, appropriately enough, a "fig leaf." The regulars—local businessmen and politicians, retired policemen and firemen—swam year round in Dorchester Bay, an arm of Boston Harbor. Tanned as leather and almost as tough, they called themselves the "L Street Brownies." Every winter, on one of the coldest days of the year, the Boston papers would run a picture of the Brownies breaking the ice for their daily swim, and every year they had a banquet in a local American Legion Hall. Theirs was part of the sense of community which, far more than racism, accounted for resistance to the Federal District Court decrees ordering the busing of South Boston students to high schools in other parts of the city.

BUT PLANNING which leaves poverty, deprivation, and dependency where they now are may never be adequate. The self-reinforcing circularity of the relationship between dilapidated housing, slum living conditions, poor municipal services, poor health, poor education, and being poor has so frequently been diagnosed that it is by now a sad commonplace. The usual remedy has been to pour resources into the afflicted area in the vain hope that more well-baby care, more counseling for alcoholics, more high-rise housing developments, and more welfare payments will somehow effect a cure. Robert E. Patricelli, former Deputy Under Secretary of Health, Education, and Welfare for Policy Coordination, more recently vice-president for The Greater Hartford Process, Inc., and now head of the Urban Mass Transit Administration, has suggested a reversal of this strategy. Instead of concentrating more resources on sick areas, he proposes policies that will break up and disperse existing pockets of poverty and dependency. If we can devise a strategy that creates neighborhoods and communities that are socially and economically balanced in terms of their resident populations, then many of our other problems will solve themselves. Mr. Patricelli points out that *"low income slums cannot be redeveloped and transitional neighborhoods cannot be conserved unless the suburbs are opened up to receive a significantly larger proportion of the dependent central city poor."*[17] The force of his conclusion seems to me compelling.

Concurrently with this strategy we should also be seeking ways of relieving the pressure on our large population centers. Three-quarters of all Americans live in metropolitan areas representing less than 10 percent of our total land area. At this rate, two-thirds of the population will live in twelve major urban centers by the year 2000. To offset this trend Dr. Peter C. Goldmark, former president and director of CBS Laboratories, proposes imaginative adaptations of communications technology aimed at encouraging a redistribution of population from larger cities to communities of 100,000 or less. "Teleconferencing facilities" would tie the central headquarters of large companies to their small-city units by simultaneous two-way television. A cable TV network would interconnect health institutions and physicians' offices. Satellite campuses would have electronic access to lectures, seminars, and library resources of central universities. New high-resolution color-television signals would relay live performances of cultural and entertainment events for large-screen projection.[18] While I have no knowledge of the economic feasibility of such a network, its objective seems to me clearly valid. The cost, at any rate, would be offset by the lower costs of crime, pollution, transportation, dependency, and other problems that become harder to manage as city size increases.

All of the potential contributions to a sense of community that can be reinforced by public policies bearing on the planning process are doubled in value by the opportunity for citizen participation. This is one of the most important objectives of the "constitution-building" process discussed in Chapter VI. If, in addition to locating social-service agencies in neighborhood centers and defining their service areas on the basis of neighborhood boundaries, steps are taken to give local residents a major role in running those agencies, the result should be a substantial boost for the neighborhood's sense of identity. An even more significant community-building measure would be to give a neighborhood council within a city some of the powers of general government. Meanwhile, "community associations," which came into existence primarily in order to protect property values in residential developments, have gradually been broadening their focus to include better land-use planning and some responsibility for community governance. With new associations being formed at a rate of 4,000 annually, there will be over 25,000 of them by 1976 with about 4 million families as members. A Community Association Institute has recently been formed and is busily telling new associations how to organize and existing associations how to be more effective.

The Community Association Institute, I think, would do well to encourage the kind of community environmental planning pioneered by Lawrence Halprin, a San Francisco-based landscape architect and urban planner. Halprin encourages community residents to explore their neighborhoods looking for answers to questions like the following:

> Are the sidewalks pleasant and clean? Are there places to sit and talk? Where can you tell someone to meet you? Can you see a clock from the street? From the sidewalk? Where can you get a drink of water outside? Where can you find shade in the summer? Protection from the elements during the winter as you wait for a bus? Are the bus stops convenient? What can you smell? Can children play safely within sight of their mothers' win-

dows? What's the noisiest spot? The most peaceful? How
is garbage stored before being hauled away? How far
away is a clinic, a grocery store, a shop, places of worship?
What facilities are there for recreation and learning? What
makes the neighborhood different from any other?[19]

Municipal governments increasingly feel the need for more
citizen participation and more citizen understanding of their
responsibility to make city government better.[20] The Housing
and Community Development Act of 1974, which consolidates
six preexisting HUD community-development categorical programs into a single new block-grant program, specifically undertakes to further these municipal objectives. As part of its application for funds, a locality must provide "satisfactory assurances"
that it has involved its citizens in community development. This
means that the locality must have made available to citizens substantial information about what programs are being considered,
their cost, and the amount of funds available. As part of the
process of establishing the locality's needs and priorities, public
hearings must be held to obtain citizens' views. Citizens must also
be given an adequate opportunity to participate in working out
the subject and scope of the application for block-grant funds.
    As a means of facilitating citizen participation, more and
more cities are setting up citizen assistance offices. There are currently more than sixty of these offices in operation which vary
widely in services. While some citizen assistance offices function merely as mechanisms enabling municipal administrators
to monitor citizen attitudes and reactions, others serve as catalysts
for change in municipal operations. In Fairfax County, Virginia,
where my family and I have lived for several years, the citizen
assistance office publishes a weekly agenda mailed at no charge
to any interested citizen who asks to be put on the mailing list.
It gives information about upcoming public hearings, how to
contact county supervisors, actions taken at the last supervisors'
meeting, and what new services are available. An April 1975
edition, for example, informed readers that the county would
hold an auction of surplus vehicles, that the county police had
stepped up patrols on the Capital Beltway, that the public

libraries were curtailing their hours, and that free diagnostic tests of auto emissions would be available at various locations through May.[21]

Another Washington suburb is carrying out an even more imaginative community-building program through the Takoma Park–Silver Spring Community Foundation, which raises and grants money for useful projects. It has financed a drive to reach elderly people with information about the county's nutrition program, a study to determine the extent of community support for a day-care center in a low-income apartment development, a booklet which lists community resources, and a theater program for teenagers. In reviewing grant applications, the foundation looks for a project that will bring a sense of community to the area, that is well thought out, and, generally, that costs less than three hundred dollars. Residents of the area agree that the foundation's strength lies in its ability to fund small projects quickly.

THE IDEAL OPPORTUNITY to combine all the attributes of community, one would have supposed, would be in the new towns which began to spring up in various parts of the country about a dozen years ago. Here, liberated from the mistakes of the past and enlightened by the wisdom of the present, the urban planner, the architect, and the social engineer could accomplish what Lao-tzu, Plato, and Thomas More could only dream about. Starting with an idea, raw land, and borrowed money, they could end up—in debt. Financial trouble, indeed, seems to be the only common denominator among the fifteen new towns recently surveyed by the Center for Urban and Regional Studies of the University of North Carolina.[22] At their best, however—notably in Columbia, Maryland, and Reston, Virginia—they have made both spatially efficient and aesthetically satisfying use of land.

The best of the new towns have inspired some of the most brilliant architectural innovation in modern America. Their mixtures of apartments, detached houses, and town houses integrated with shopping and office space and interspersed with green areas are attractive and efficient. It is to their credit, moreover, that they have made a conscious effort to provide a substantial pro-

portion of low- and moderate-income housing and to attract a
broad cross-section of the population. The most satisfied residents, according to the North Carolina survey, are blacks, the
nonwealthy, and the elderly.

Some new towns have made the most of their community-
building opportunity. This is what particularly impressed me
about Columbia, Maryland, when I visited it in the spring of
1971. Started in 1963 by the developer James Rouse in the belief
that it ought to be possible, as he put it, "to build a livable city,"
Columbia is composed of neighborhoods of 2,000 to 5,000 people. Each neighborhood is centered on an elementary school, and
all the neighborhood children can walk to school without cross-
ing a major thoroughfare. The neighborhoods also have their own
playgrounds, elementary schools, and multipurpose facilities used
for day-care programs, cooperative nurseries, and general resident
meetings. Two to four neighborhoods make up a village, and
each village has a commercial center with such shopping and
service facilities as banks, supermarkets, pharmacies, and restau-
rants. There will eventually be seven villages, and at their core
the so-called "Downtown" with its plazas, parks, lake, office
buildings, cinemas, hotel, and an all-season mall. A friend who
lives in Columbia has told me that he and his family have found
it much easier to make friends there than it was in the Washington suburb where they used to live.

By and large, however, the resourcefulness and imagination
that went into planning the physical environment of the new
towns have not been matched by the design of their governance.
On the contrary, most are company towns in the sense that the
developer exercises the powers normal to a municipal government. The only means of exerting influence open to their residents is through participation in a homeowners or citizens
association, and while this can be useful as an adjunct to an
elected local government, it is no substitute for it.

In spite of their imperfections, new towns are potentially
the source of a great number of innovative developments in areas
ranging from municipal services to citizen organizations to land-
use planning. Both developers and residents must take full advan-

tage of the opportunity to test new ideas and programs, not only for the success of their particular project but for the benefit of all towns that might benefit from their experience.

FOR SOME PEOPLE, to be sure, all of these approaches rolled into one will not produce a sufficiently satisfying sense of community. For them only a completely communal existence seems to be enough, at least until they try it. And certainly it is true that the atomistic contemporary family does not afford the opportunities for the sharing—the pooling of property, child rearing, and personal relationships—that is a commune's very reason for being. And yet it would appear that the communal impulse is not by itself sufficient to make a commune work. In a perceptive study of American communes written while she was my research associate at the Woodrow Wilson Center, Betty Mansfield, herself a former nun, found that only a carefully selected and homogeneous group of men and women have any chance of building a successful commune: "The groups that have started with and tried to maintain an open membership policy have passed from the communal scene, or are in imminent danger of doing so."[23] The successful nineteenth-century communes were those united by some form of religious belief. Here, I believe, is additional corroboration for the seeming paradox that a durable community can only grow out of the creative tension between individualism and the need for a sense of belonging and continuity. Lacking scope for individualism, a commune, as distinguished from a community, requires for its survival the added dimension of an essentially religious commitment to the importance of subordinating the self to the communal good. And while this is in many respects an admirable form of dedication, it cannot be converted into a general prescription for American malaise.

But just as there are those who do not find even in the most closely knit of ordinary human habitations a sufficient bond of sharing, so there are others who do not acknowledge any conscious awareness of the need for belonging to a geographically defined community. Professor Lyn Lofland, a California sociologist and "unashamed cityphile," has examined the situation of residents in large cities who must face a world of strangers as a permanent home. She does not foresee any retreat from densely urban areas to suburban villages or small towns. She believes, rather, that each individual city dweller must accept a loner's status in attempting to find a sense of inner security.[24]

I suspect, nevertheless, that the very people who would endorse the Lofland view derive a sense of belonging and continuity from some other source than a geographical community. It may be from the world of art or literature, and it is almost certainly—in part at least—from a circle of family and friends which, given today's means of communication and mobility, can extend over great distances. I know that such associations are deeply significant; I am also aware that they may go a long way toward filling the void left by the lack of a sense of community. For most of us, however, the cultivation of private pursuits and personal associations, important though they are, can never be a fully satisfying substitute for community. This is because community calls upon us for giving and sharing within a circle wider than our friends but narrow enough to be compassable by our feelings and imaginations. This call, though not as compelling as that of a commune, is nevertheless considerably more demanding than the claims of a purely private existence.

The satisfaction we receive from joining in an enterprise of common concern to a community may be traceable to generations of ethical teaching; or we may owe it to an intuitive recognition of the dependency of humanity on cooperation for survival. My own hunch is that it derives from both: both, after all, rest on a valid perception of the human condition. Whatever the ultimate explanation, I am convinced that most of us seek instinctively to escape the confines of egocentricity. And surely there is no more rewarding means of escape than some form of community service. We share in building communities both because we need them and because they need us. Nor does it prove the contrary that some people do not seem to care: it is not uncommon, after all, for people to reject the very things which, if they but knew themselves well enough, would give them the greatest satisfaction.

IN THE COURSE of the *Mayflower*'s voyage to North America in 1620, John Winthrop set down a Code of Conduct for the guidance of his small company of Pilgrims:

> Wee must be knitt together in this worke as one man, wee must entertaine each other in brotherly Affeccion, wee must be willing to abridge our selves of our super-fluities, for the supply of others necessities, wee must uphold a familiar Commerce together in a meekness, gentleness, patience and liberality, wee must delight in eache other, make others Condicions our owne, rejoyce together, mourne together, labour, and suffer together, allwayes haueing before our eyes our . . . Community. . . .[25]

Only as individuals, respecting ourselves and each other, may we hope to achieve in freedom this spirit of community.

IX

Equality and Liberty:
The Creative Balance

THE SETTLERS of this country, perhaps because the vision of a society in which they and their children could enjoy liberty was so powerful an incentive to their coming here, had a restricted view of the claims of equality. Our revolutionary forebears, nevertheless, insisted that "all men are equal in their rights." The phrase is from Joel Barlow's *Advice to the Privileged Orders in Europe*.[1] His contemporary Richard Bland added the point that to possess rights is to "imply *equality* in the instances to which they belong and must be treated without respect to the dignity of the persons concerned in them."[2] Equality "without respect to the dignity of the persons concerned" might have seemed to suggest equivalence of status, but even the most radical republicans of the time, as Gordon S. Wood has pointed out, "admitted the inevitability of all natural distinctions: weak and strong, wise and foolish—and even of incidental distinctions: rich and poor, learned and unlearned."[3]

Indeed, John Adams argued, and de Tocqueville later concurred, that the urge for distinction was even stronger in America than in Europe.

Recently, however, there has developed a powerful movement toward greater equality. Growing out of flagrant deprivation, moving gradually through periods of open and then more subtle discrimination, gaining strength as barriers of prejudice were swept aside, it is a movement which is at last beginning to fulfill rights guaranteed, at least on paper, for more than a hundred years. Not only for racial minorities but for all the poor and disadvantaged, affirmative action to assure at least minimum standards of equality is now regarded as a necessary function of government.

What has happened in the last quarter-century to give so much momentum to the movement toward greater equality? One factor, I think, is the growing affluence of the majority. We cannot as a matter of conscience any longer ignore the inequities which, throughout our earlier history, were endured by minorities. A second factor has been a surge of insistence upon respect for the individual that has developed in reaction to the complex, remote, and impersonal forces of modern society. Added to both of these factors is our equally keen awareness of the growing interdependence of all segments of American society; this in itself underscores our claims on each other.

Demands for equality take many forms, of course. Equality of condition or, as it is sometimes called, equality of result, is the farthest removed from our historic attitudes; equality of rights is the most consonant with them. Equality of opportunity and equality of access to government benefits fall somewhere in between. The earliest manifestations of the recent movement toward equality, at any rate, belong to the revolutionary tradition of insistence on equality of rights. Not since the adoption of the first ten amendments of the Constitution has our society seen anything like the swift extension of legal safeguards for individual rights that has taken place in recent decades.

Though we have always insisted on equal rights under the law, the Supreme Court during the Warren years moved rapidly to lay down more exacting standards of legal equality. *Powell, Gideon, Griffin, Mapp, Escobedo, Miranda*—for the poor and the powerless especially, the roll call confirmed Mr. Justice Frankfurter's dictum that "the history of liberty has largely been history of observance of procedural safeguards."[4] The cases showed, too, a developing sophistication about what fair treatment and equal justice mean: where the essential rights of citizens are concerned, it is not enough that the law behave with passive neutrality, insisting on observance of the rules but permitting the citizen to be overmatched by the superior resources of the state. The law now requires that the poor and the ignorant be accorded the same protection of their rights that the well-heeled and the well-informed have always enjoyed. The indigent defendant must be supplied with a lawyer and the resources for conducting his defense. He must be warned of his rights. Unlawfully obtained evidence may not be used against him. And though some of these procedural decisions have aroused protests from law-enforcement officials and others concerned that criminals were being "coddled" at the expense of their victims and of the protection of society generally, it can, I believe, be shown that a scrupulous regard for individual rights is not incompatible with good law enforcement.

Felix Frankfurter, for example, during the year William T. Coleman, Jr. (as this is written, Secretary of Transportation), and I served as his law clerks, never tired of pointing to instances of high professional investigative competence coupled with scrupulous regard for fairness; he had himself absorbed a lifelong commitment to the compatibility of both from his service as an Assistant United States Attorney under Henry L. Stimson in the Southern District of New York. Stimson, Frankfurter told us, used to require his young disciples to accompany government agents on raids to make sure that the agents kept within the limits of the search warrant. So indelibly, indeed, did Frankfurter's teaching transmit to me the standards of his former chief that when I became a United States Attorney myself in 1959, I thought of Stimson as the invisible watchdog of my own prosecutorial behavior.

Many of Frankfurter's examples were British.* I still remember, in fact, his directing me to the report of the Royal Commission on the case of Miss Savidge, whose allegations that Scotland Yard had not treated her with perfect politeness during the course of a four-hour interrogation brought on a storm of public protest. The investigation of these allegations led to the establishment of the Royal Commission on Police Powers and Procedures, whose recommendations are still the basis of British police practice.[5]

Here at home, where Supreme Court standards for the administration of federal justice were for a long time stricter than those demanded of the states by the Due Process clause of the Fourteenth Amendment, the FBI demonstrated that the observance of procedural safeguards could go hand in hand with professional effectiveness. By requiring his agents to rely on up-to-date investigative techniques, J. Edgar Hoover did at least as much as the courts to hasten the end of reliance on such sleazy expedients as the third degree. Even those most prone to point to the great man's clay feet owe him that acknowledgment.

But the Supreme Court's criminal procedure decisions, far-reaching though they were, would not in themselves have warranted the conclusion that a powerful current in the direction of greater equality was gathering headway. Procedural due process was an established staple of judicial business. Concurrently, how-

* One of my first assignments as a Frankfurter law clerk was to look up the decisions in every English-speaking jurisdiction in the world on the question of the admissibility of evidence obtained as the result of an unlawful search or seizure. The outcome of my labors is embodied in a lengthy tabulation appended to Justice Frankfurter's opinion for the Court in *Wolf* v. *Colorado*, 338 U.S. 25 (1948), holding that the Fourteenth Amendment does not forbid a state court from admitting such evidence. *Wolf* v. *Colorado* was overruled thirteen years later by *Mapp* v. *Ohio*, 367 U.S. 643 (1961), on the ground that the total exclusion of unlawfully obtained evidence is the only effective sanction against violations of constitutionally protected rights. And although I now think *Mapp* is right, I am still troubled by the inflexibility of the "exclusionary rule" in situations where the violation was minor or technical. As United States Attorney General I had hoped to find some practical way of giving judges discretion to weigh the importance of the evidence against the seriousness of the violation. And while I have no clear idea of how best to do this, I still regard it as an effort worth pursuing.

ever, the courts began to compel fair treatment and approximate equality in fields beyond the law's own internal processes. Starting with *Brown* v. *Board of Education*, the case which overturned the "separate but equal" doctrine, another roster has been growing—*Shapiro, Goldberg, Baker, Baxstrom,* and *Robinson*. It is fitting that the names of individuals should mark these affirmations of individual rights: the right of blacks to equality of educational opportunity, the right of the poor to fair treatment by the welfare system, the right of the individual to have his vote given full effect, and the right of the mentally ill to a fair hearing.

A S T H E S E C U R I T Y and well-being of more and more Americans have come to depend on some relationship to government, the requirements of due process—an open hearing, representation by counsel, published reasons for the result, and judicial review—have been more widely extended. In a seminal law review article published nearly twelve years ago, Professor Charles A. Reich, better known as the author of *The Greening of America*, pointed out that government benefits constitute a new kind of property. Some of these benefits—particularly unemployment compensation, public assistance, and Social Security—should be regarded as being held as a matter of right:

> These benefits are based upon a recognition that misfortune and deprivation are often caused by forces far beyond the control of the individual, such as technological change, variations in demand for goods, depressions, or wars. The aim of these benefits is to preserve the self-sufficiency of the individual, to rehabilitate him where necessary, and to allow him to be a valuable member of a family and a community; in theory they represent part of the individual's rightful share in the commonwealth. Only by making such benefits into rights can the welfare state achieve its goal of providing a secure minimum basis for individual well-being and dignity in a society where each man cannot be wholly the master of his own destiny.[6]

Reich's article has influenced—or at least foreshadowed—a still-evolving line of court cases. In two 5-4 decisions involving the suspension of high-school students for disciplinary infractions, the Supreme Court recently ruled that school administrators must observe "rudimentary precautions against unfair or mistaken findings of misconduct and arbitrary exclusions from school." The student must at a minimum be given an opportunity to discuss the matter informally and to give his version of what happened. Justice Byron White, writing for the majority in one of the two cases, adopted Reich's reasoning: "The State is constrained to recognize a student's legitimate entitlement to a public education as a property interest which is protected by the Due Process Clause and which may not be taken away for misconduct without adherence to the minimum procedures required by that clause."*

Here again, however, there is no escaping the necessity for balance. Due-process requirements are a means of preventing and correcting the unfair exercise of governmental power. Their effect is not only to constrain but to complicate the exercise of discretion. But without some degree of confidence in the honesty and wisdom of those entrusted with discretionary authority, government would be brought to a standstill. One federal appeals court recently held that a person receiving Social Security disability benefits is entitled to a hearing before the benefits are terminated or reduced; a district court has applied the same requirement to Supplementary Security Income benefits. The Supreme Court has agreed to review the first of these cases, and HEW has appealed the second.[7]

Where the line should be drawn is a matter of practical judgment. The SSI case arose from the discovery of substantial overpayments to a large proportion of the 3.5 million beneficiaries of the program, and HEW contends that it cannot conceivably provide enough administrative judges to conduct a hearing for every affected individual. On the face of it, some mechanism for reconciling the requirements of fairness with the avoidance of unconscionable delays in reducing excessive payments—for

* *Goss* v. *Lopez*, 419 U.S. 565, 574 (1975). The students (all black) had been suspended for disorder touched off by a demonstration against the school administrators' refusal to agree to student proposals for the observance of a black history week.

instance, by applying consistent rules of thumb to the correction of categories of error. The point, in any case, is that due process must not be allowed to become an end in itself.*

Another aspect of the "new property" problem described by Reich—that of equal access to government benefits—has also been the subject of remarkably recent development. In this instance, too, an article started the process. Writing in 1965, Arthur Wise formulated the theory that inequities in educational funding might be unconstitutional.† He started with the fact that the disparities among school districts are indefensible. In most states, even if you eliminate the highest-spending 10 percent of school districts on the ground that they constitute some form of special situations, the ratio between the highest and lowest per-pupil expenditures ranges between 2 to 1 and 3 to 1. By and large, moreover, the school districts which spend the least per pupil are also those which tax themselves most heavily for education: because their taxable resources are meager, they have to squeeze those resources all the harder even to extract minimum sums. And granted that the differences from place to place in the educational value of what a dollar will buy make spending an unsatisfactory measure of educational quality, it is still the only measure we have that is both reasonably accessible and reasonably approximate.

Building on such demonstrations of inequity, legal strategists have formulated a constitutional attack resting on three basic propositions: (1) education is a "fundamental right or fundamental interest" like the right to vote or the right to freedom of

---

* Professor Grant Gilmore, a Yale Law School colleague of Professor Reich, has recently warned that even "the rule of law" can be oversold: "Law reflects but in no sense determines the moral worth of a society. A reasonably just society will reflect its value in a reasonably just law. The better the society, the less law there will be. In Heaven there will be no law and the lion will lie down with the lamb. An unjust society will reflect its values in an unjust law. In Hell there will be nothing but law, and due process will be meticulously observed." "The Storrs Lectures: The Age of Anxiety," 84 *Yale Law Journal* 1022, 1044 (1975).

† Dr. Wise is currently a visiting scholar to the Education Policy Research Institute in Washington, D.C. The article, "Is Denial of Equal Education Opportunity Constitutional?", was published in *Administrator's Notebook*, February 1965.

speech; (2) just as a defendant's right to a fair trial cannot be allowed to depend on his personal wealth, so only a "compelling state interest" could justify making a child's right to education depend on the taxable wealth of the school district in which he or she happens to live; and (3) the interest in local control over the level of spending on education is not this kind of compelling state interest because districts with low property-tax bases have no real freedom to choose a high level of spending.[8]

In August 1971 the California Supreme Court, adopting exactly this line of argument, ruled unconstitutional the state's method of financing elementary and secondary education. Said Mr. Justice Raymond L. Sullivan speaking for the court, ". . . [A]ffluent districts can have their cake and eat it too: they can provide a high quality education for their children while paying lower taxes. Poor districts, by contrast, have no cake at all."[9] There soon followed similar decisions in Minnesota, Texas, New Jersey, Arizona, Wyoming, Kansas, and Michigan, and legal challenges were pursued in more than twenty other states. The Texas case, *Rodriguez* v. *San Antonio Independent School District*,[10] was decided by a three-judge federal court, which meant that the losing side—the state of Texas—had a direct appeal to the Supreme Court. As Secretary of HEW (and an ex-government lawyer), I thought it likely that the three-judge court decision would—and should—be upheld. The United States Office of Education, with my encouragement, did a lot of work on the development of formulas for the distribution of a new federal tax source for the equalization of educational support among and within the states. And I, with White House encouragement, urged the Advisory Commission on Intergovernmental Relations* in March 1972 to explore the question of how federal and state authorities could best accomplish the top-to-bottom overhaul of education financing that would be necessary if the Supreme Court sustained the three-judge court.

* The Advisory Commission on Intergovernmental Relations was created by Congress in 1959 to monitor the operation of the American federal system and to recommend improvements. ACIR is a bipartisan body whose twenty-six members represent the executive and legislative branches of federal, state, and local government and the general public.

In March 1973 the Court handed down a 5-4 decision in the *Rodriguez* case. Contrary to my expectation, it reversed the lower court. In an opinion by Mr. Justice Lewis Powell, the Court ruled that "the consideration and initiation of fundamental reforms with respect to state taxation and education are matters reserved for the legislative processes of the various States, and we do no violence to the values of federalism and separation of powers by staying our hand." All nine Justices, however, were unanimous in recognizing the need for reform. As Mr. Justice Potter Stewart remarked in a concurring opinion, "The method of financing public schools in Texas, as in almost every other State, has resulted in a system of public education than can fairly be described as chaotic and unjust."[11]

And so, although the federal Constitution does not yet compel the states to act, the problem remains. *Rodriguez* does not affect state court decisions invalidating school-financing systems under state constitutions, and new challenges to persisting inequalities are still being brought. The inherent unfairness of the remaining inequalities, meanwhile, stimulates continuing efforts to develop remedial legislation.*

One conclusion made unavoidable by efforts to solve the school-financing problem is that there is no practical way to achieve greater equality except at greater cost. Equalization accomplished by forcing the rich school districts to spend less so that the poor districts can spend more would stand about as much chance as a proposal to confiscate all personal income above $12,000. The state court decisions requiring the more equal funding of education are bound, therefore, to bring about tax increases.

---

* Fourteen states have substantially revised their education finance laws: Arizona, California, Colorado, Florida, Illinois, Kansas, Maine, Michigan, Minnesota, Montana, New Mexico, North Dakota, Utah, and Wisconsin. Expanded state funding, increased per pupil aid, and lowered property taxes are key traits of major new reform. Revised aid formulae, new pupil weighting systems, and geographic adjustments to further equitable dollar distribution have also been instituted as part of the measures adopted by various states. See Gilbert Bursley, "The Political Strategies and Fiscal Ramifications of Educational Finance Reform," a paper presented at the National Conference on School Finance, New Orleans, Louisiana, March 3, 1975.

Concurrently with the school-financing cases there has begun to develop another line of cases involving even more direct judicial demands for increased government spending. These concern the right to treatment of the mentally ill and the mentally retarded. In a series of decisions beginning in 1971, Federal District Judge Frank M. Johnson, Jr., of Alabama broke new ground by ruling that any patient involuntarily committed to a state institution must either be treated or released. How much treatment? What kind of treatment? With semimonthly interviews by one psychiatric social worker at one end of the spectrum and weekly sessions with a trained psychiatrist plus group psychotherapy, occupational training, and miscellaneous recreational activities at the other end, the staffing requirements—and therefore costs—vary enormously. Nothing daunted, Judge Johnson issued an order prescribing detailed standards for adequate treatment.

In 1972 a similar case came before Federal District Judge Sidney O. Smith, Jr., of Georgia. Judge Smith came to the opposite conclusion. Having as Attorney General of Massachusetts helped to draft a legislative "bill of rights" for the mentally ill and the mentally retarded, I came to the Department of Justice in May 1973 strongly committed to the view that a government accepts a moral responsibility to those involuntarily placed in its care. I could easily see, however, that it was going to be extremely difficult to frame and administer court decrees requiring minimal standards of treatment. Assistant Attorney General J. Stanley Pottinger (we had worked together when he was Director of the Office for Civil Rights in HEW) and I agreed that the Department should try to make some constructive contribution toward shaping the evolution of judicial policy. The Department accordingly participated as an *amicus curiae* in the case of *Wyatt* v. *Aderholt*, a case in the series decided by Judge Johnson. In November 1974 the United States Court of Appeals for the Fifth Circuit upheld the Johnson position.[12]

When the *Donaldson* case[13] came before the Supreme Court in January 1975, Solicitor General Robert H. Bork submitted to the Court a letter supporting the position that a patient enjoys "a constitutional right to receive such individual treatment as will give him a reasonable opportunity to be cured or improve his mental condition." In June 1975, the Court deferred the issue by ruling merely that a state cannot confine a "non-dangerous individual who is capable of surviving safely in freedom."

How far is judicial intervention to compel the fairer allocation of public resources likely to proceed? That there is still a need for it in some areas seems to me unquestionable. To help meet it, the Lawyers' Committee for Civil Rights Under Law, formed in 1963 to mobilize support of the legal profession behind the struggle by minorities for civil rights, opened a Government Services Equalization Center on June 1, 1975. The center's aim is to challenge inequities in such matters as the provision of municipal finances and the levying of property taxes; involving community groups and organizations, the lawsuits brought by the center will contribute to the further evolution and refinement of remedies for inequality. Will this process eventually lead to extreme forms of judicially enforced equality of result? To this concern there is no better answer than Justice Oliver Wendell Holmes's retort to Chief Justice Marshall's famous dictum that "the power to tax is the power to destroy": "Not while this Court sits."[14]

IN THE SPACE, then, of twenty years—and especially within the last five—we have seen develop a movement toward equality which started with the objective simply of ending discrimination in equality of access to established rights, swept on to the definition of new rights and the expansion of old ones, and culminated in requiring the dedication of additional resources to the raising of minimum standards. Trailblazing court decisions have been followed up and extended by the Congress and the executive branch. The Civil Rights Acts of 1957 and 1960 hastened the dismantling of the caste system based on race. Subsequent legislation provided remedies against discrimination in public accommodations, voting rights, housing, and employment. Then, in 1965, came President Lyndon B. Johnson's executive order requiring government contractors to take "affirmative action" to hire qualified women and members of racial minorities. Under the impetus of this order the executive branch has been propelled into a highly controversial area with consequences still poorly defined and hard to quantify.

The rationale for affirmative action rests on the proposition that people whose chance at the starting gate has been handicapped by the accumulated residue of past discrimination are entitled to a certain amount of special attention in order to make sure that they are able to overcome this handicap. What kind of "special attention"? Not a job or a contract or a grant awarded without regard to qualifications or fitness to perform: that would be "reverse discrimination," unfair to other claimants. But where a group has, in fact, long been the subject of discrimination—and where this has resulted in its being poorly represented in a trade or profession—one way of protecting qualified members of the group from continuing discrimination, conscious or unconscious, is to make sure that their qualifications are not overlooked by the people who select among the applicants.

This is all, in principle, that "affirmative action" can legitimately require. And this is all that executive orders and guidelines have ever been intended to require. The fact, however, that employers have been obliged for this reason to establish "goals" for minority hiring has led to a considerable amount of misunderstanding and controversy. The "goals" have been consistently—sometimes willfully—confused with "quotas." A legally mandated quota for minority hiring would almost inevitably result in reverse discrimination. A goal, on the other hand, is simply a means of encouraging effort to find qualified minority prospects; if it is pursued in good faith, the fact that an employer has been unable to meet it should carry no adverse consequences.

This distinction, I admit, can at times be hard to explain.[15] At the 1972 Republican National Convention in Miami, Spiro T. Agnew drew deafening applause—the loudest of the convention —for his attack on "quotas." Having long had reason to be concerned about the use of quotas to exclude qualified applicants rather than to admit unqualified ones, the American Jewish Committee and the Anti-Defamation Committee of B'nai B'rith wrote President Nixon a letter expressing their concern. I braced myself for some Presidential directive telling the Departments of Labor and HEW to soft-pedal affirmative action for the duration of the campaign. In order to make the issuance of such a directive as difficult as possible, I decided to use a press conference at Temple University on September 7, 1972, to reaffirm the administration's support for minority hiring programs like the Philadelphia Plan. But first I had to make sure that James D. Hodgson, then Secretary of Labor, was also holding firm. I reached him by phone just a few minutes before the press conference was due to begin. No problem in that quarter: he would stand on the proposition that goals are not quotas and that the Civil Rights Act still required affirmative action. This was the position I took, and although my statement was reported, no complaint or qualification ever came from the White House. The explanation may have been not that my preemptive tactics worked, but merely that the President saw a chance to have it both ways: he and Agnew, each with high visibility, denouncing quotas, Hodgson and I, each with much less visibility, reassuring minority groups.

In fairness it has to be recognized that charges of "reverse discrimination" have in some instances had a real basis. The attempt, moreover, partially to compensate for past low rates of minority admissions to institutions of higher education has raised exceedingly difficult issues. Just how difficult is apparent in the history of the DeFunis case.[16] The plaintiff applied to the University of Washington Law School in 1971. His undergraduate record was good, and it was not disputed that he would have been admitted to the law school but for the fact that the school chose instead to admit a number of minority students (blacks, Chicanos, American Indians, and Filipinos) whose academic records and test scores were less good than his. Not to admit him, he argued, constituted a clear case of reverse discrimination on account of race.

This was a situation, certainly, in which the affirmative recognition of race played a decisive part. From the standpoint of the Department of Justice, however, this was not the troublesome aspect of the case. If race could not be the basis of public policy, no affirmative action program could be justified. The harder question was whether the state of Washington could constitutionally consider factors other than academic achievement,

including the underrepresentation of minorities in the legal profession, in choosing among candidates for admission to law
school.* On this score, I come down on the side of the state. Nor
am I shaken in this view by the awareness that the logic of
affirmative action can easily be caricatured (for example, by
picturing it as being extended to WASPs because they are now
a minority); the wisdom of a policy is not disproved by the fact
that it could conceivably be pushed to a ridiculous extreme.

The affirmative action program has left a lot of room both
for foot-dragging and for excessive zeal, particularly in universities, where a lack of good information on the available numbers
of qualified women and minority group members has complicated the problem of establishing realistic goals. In 1973, just as
a clearer understanding of affirmative action requirements was
beginning to develop, the bottom dropped out of the academic
job market. In nonacademic situations, layoffs have created agonizing difficulties. Since most minority group workers were not
required to show, in order to be hired, that they had been dis-
criminated against personally, no date can be fixed earlier than
the date of their actual hiring when—but for discrimination—
they would have been hired. Seniority rules, therefore, which
normally require that the last hired are the first laid off, can
rapidly undo everything accomplished by affirmative action
efforts.

And yet, on balance, affirmative action has, I think, been a
qualified success. More women, blacks, and Spanish-Americans
are being hired for skilled, technical, and professional jobs than
would otherwise have been likely. Progress has ranged from the
outright abolition of a discriminatory hiring policy in the long-
haul trucking industry to marginal gains for women in university faculty appointments. At Stanford, for instance, one-fifth of
new faculty appointments for the academic year 1973–1974
went to women, and four-fifths of all persons newly hired were

* Other related factors which might also have been taken into account
included consideration of how much the student would benefit from attending
the university, how much he or she would contribute to the education of
other students, and how much each applicant would contribute to society in
later life.

either women or members of minority groups. For the academic year 1974–1975, nearly a quarter of new faculty appointees at the Madison campus of the University of Wisconsin were women. Many other less dramatic examples can easily be found, and though the record is spotty, it reflects gains that would not otherwise have occurred. President Derek Bok of Harvard, where excruciating birth pangs attended negotiation with HEW's Office of Civil Rights of one of the first affirmative action plans adopted by a major university, said in November 1974:

> There is no necessity that targets become quotas. Many individuals and institutions set goals for themselves in order to focus their efforts and measure their progress without committing themselves to achieve these targets regardless of the means employed. With appropriate restraint by the government, there is no reason why the universities cannot do the same.[17]

A real success story is reflected in the enrollment of blacks in college. According to Census Bureau estimates for 1974, black enrollment has increased by 56 percent since 1970 and 248 percent since 1964. During the same period the number of black law students rose from less than 700 to nearly 5,000. By the fall of 1974, more than 9 in every 100 college students were black, compared with 7 in 100 in 1970 and 3 in 100 in 1964. But black enrollment is still less than proportionate to the black college-age population: about 12 out of every 100 Americans aged 18 to 21 are black.

THE MOVEMENT toward equality is a vindication of the courage and initiative of individual citizens. From John Peter Zenger, who successfully resisted prosecution for seditious libel, to Kinney Kinmon Lau, who won the right to bilingual education for non-English-speaking Chinese students,[18] we have always had individuals who championed the rights of others by insisting on their own, often against the pressure of public hostility.

I remember with gratitude several such individuals. Some I

encountered as a young Boston lawyer recruited by the Fund for the Republic to make a survey of the handling of loyalty and security cases in the New England area during the years when Senator Joseph McCarthy of Wisconsin was riding high. I found it heartening to discover how many individuals had been able with the help of their lawyers to prevail against charges of guilt by association. Later, during another brief interval of private practice, my help was recruited by a stubborn old lady named Mrs. MacDonald. Convinced that the Massachusetts Department of Mental Health was exploiting retarded girls farmed out to local nursing homes for substandard wages, she had made herself thoroughly obnoxious to the departmental authorities. Was she, as they insisted, only another "nut"? Realizing that to be regarded as a "nut" is not necessarily to be wrong, I did my best to dig out the facts. Mrs. MacDonald, I found, was at least partly right, and between us we helped get decent compensation for the girls she championed.

With increasing frequency the stubborn crusader and the lonely individualist have been joined by organizations whose very reason for existence is to speak up for the poor, the oppressed, the forgotten, and the friendless. Founded in 1920, the American Civil Liberties Union is the oldest of these, and although it sometimes takes positions which strike me as extreme, it is to the great credit of the ACLU that it has fought just as hard for the rights of reactionaries as for those of radicals.

Another such organization is the NAACP Legal Defense and Education Fund, Inc., not always affectionately known as the "Inc. Fund." Nineteen years younger than the ACLU, the Inc. Fund confines itself principally to discrimination cases, *Brown* v. *Board of Education* is still the most famous of its long string of Supreme Court victories, but the list also includes *Smith* v. *Allwright*, which outlawed all-white primary elections, *Alexander* v. *Holmes County Board of Education*, which ended the "all deliberate speed" doctrine in school desegregation, and *Furman* v. *Georgia*, which sharply restricted the death penalty.[19] As Secretary of HEW I sometimes found myself on the other side of Inc. Fund lawsuits, notably *Adams* v. *Richardson*, which charged HEW with delinquency in desegregating public educa-

tional institutions that were receiving federal funds.[20] And
though firmly convinced at the time that HEW was right in
resisting a court order second-guessing our allocation of priorities
among civil rights objectives, I was much impressed by the thoroughness and skill of the Inc. Fund lawyers.*

The most important recent development in the protection
of the individual against excessive—or merely inert and indifferent—authority has been the enlargement of "standing to sue."
Stimulated by the growth of "public interest law firms," this enlargement of the right to seek legal redress has greatly increased
the impact of conservation groups, neighborhood associations,
minority groups, and consumer organizations. While it is still
necessary for the plaintiff to show that he is in some way adversely affected, the injury need not be economic in nature. Nor
does the fact that an injury may be widely shared foreclose the
right to seek legal redress. One result is to expand the protection
of aesthetic, conservational, and recreational interests.† The adverse effect on any individual member of the class, moreover,
may be relatively slight—a small increase, for instance, in parts
per million of some atmospheric pollutant. The class itself—all
those who breathe the air containing that pollutant—may be very
large.

The value of class suits, clearly, is that they open up the
decision-making process to people not likely otherwise to be
heard or have an impact. A means has been provided of penetrat-
ing the protective layers which insulate the bureaucratic structure, especially where the regulators take on the coloration of the
regulated. And yet there is a real risk that the long-run effect of
the judicial enlargement of standing to bring class actions may be
to *weaken* democratic processes. This, as Judge Learned Hand
used often to emphasize, is the negative side of all forms of

---

* Its President at the time was William T. Coleman, Jr., with whom, as
previously mentioned, I served as law clerk for Felix Frankfurter.

† The current state of the "standing" doctrine is probably best put by the
remark of Professor Kenneth C. Davis quoted in *United States* v. *SCRAP*,
412 U.S. 669, 689, n. 14 (1973): " 'The basic idea that comes out in numerous
cases is that an identifiable trifle is enough for standing to fight out a question
of principle; the trifle is the basis for standing and the principle supplies the
motivation.' "

judicial activism. It was he, I remember, who first impressed on me the wisdom of James Bradley Thayer's warning that "under no system can the power of courts go far to save a people from ruin; our chief protection lies elsewhere. If this be true, it is of the greatest public importance to put the matter in its true light."*

Judicial intervention can strengthen rather than subvert democratic processes so long as it does not undertake to substitute the personal views of individual judges for the considered judgments of the properly constituted legislative and administrative tribunals. So long, in other words, as courts limit themselves to requiring the observance of appropriate standards of fair procedure, scrutinizing factual propositions to make sure that they have some reasonable basis, and restraining arbitrary action, they can help to assure that the other branches of government play their own parts in accordance with the rules of the game. Moreover, the educational impact of judicial opinions and the enforcement of court decrees can combine to bring about significant change in public attitudes.

Doubt on the latter point was widely shared in 1957 when President Eisenhower, referring to the court order which opened the integrated high school in Little Rock, Arkansas, said that "You cannot change people's hearts merely by law."[21] I remember thinking at the time that he was probably right. Since then, however, we have seen that laws and court decisions *can* go a long way toward changing the hearts and minds of men. To a degree not yet adequately appreciated outside the South, the elimination of segregation in public accommodations, the dismantling of the dual school system, and the dramatic increase in the number of blacks registered to vote have contributed to a profound improvement in relations between the races. This in

* I later used these sentences to introduce an article on "Freedom of Speech and the Function of the Courts" published by the Harvard Law Review in 1952. The article ends, "The great battles for free expression will be won, if they are won, not in the courts but in committee-rooms and protest meetings, by editorials and letters to Congress, and through the courage of citizens everywhere. The proper function of courts is narrow. The rest is our responsibility." The next—and final—sentence was from Justice Brandeis's concurring opinion in *Whitney* v. *California* (1927): "The greatest menace to freedom is an inert people" (274 U.S. 357, 375 [1927]).

turn has released an enormous amount of creative energy. During a trip to Mississippi in 1974 I talked with Clarke Reed, Republican state chairman of Mississippi and chief architect of the Republican resurgence throughout the South. "We Southerners fought the courts and the civil rights legislation every step of the way," he said. "We lost, and it was the best thing that ever happend to us."

LOOKING BACK over the past two decades, I think we can see judicial assertiveness on behalf of individual rights as part of a broader development whose unifying force is a growing insistence that the representative institutions of government be equally accountable and equally accessible to all citizens. This has always, of course, been the primary concern of the League of Women Voters, for which I have had great respect ever since 1950, the year after my clerkship with Felix Frankfurter, when I first began to take part in Brookline town politics. More effectively than any other organization, the league publicized candidates' views and qualifications and promoted voter participation. Later, running statewide myself in 1962, 1964, and 1966, I found that the league-sponsored candidates' nights were the liveliest and best attended of any in Massachusetts. In recent years the LWV has expanded its national role, and as Secretary of HEW I was grateful that the intelligent and articulate women who represented the league on Capitol Hill were more often with me than against me.

Since 1968 the LWV has been joined by another effective citizens' lobby, Common Cause. Founded by John W. Gardner and now speaking for approximately 300,000 dues-paying members, Common Cause has concentrated its efforts on reforms designed to make our government institutions more truly representative. And although I do not completely agree with all of these reforms, I wholeheartedly applaud John Gardner's statement of his organization's role: "Common Cause, by linking the long tradition of citizen action with the skills of professional lobbying, is introducing a new ingredient into the political system, a means of assuring continuous accountability to the citizen—a means of voting between elections."[22]

But the best-known citizen activator, surely, is Ralph Nader. Ralph Nader has shown what other citizens could do by demonstrating what he can do. Starting with automobile safety, he has had an impact on a range of issues extending from American Indians to secrecy in government. To many people "consumerism" is only a branch of the larger phenomenon known as "Naderism." In a newsletter Nader himself has set forth the "three basic missions" of his fund-raising vehicle, Public Citizen, Inc.:

> . . . to show that citizens working full-time at the scene of the action can get things done for greater justice, freedom and democracy;
> . . . to show millions of Americans how they can get many other public problems solved at the local, state or national level if they want to learn the skills of citizenship and become part-time citizen activists;
> . . . [and] to help recharge the human spirit with optimism that is nourished not by empty slogans but by solid achievement on the part of people who want to participate more fully in self-government.

If this is "Naderism," I'm for it.*

If politicians were always alert (and honest), government would not have to be goaded by the stings and pricks of nongovernmental gadflies to respond to the "language of just complaint."† But the cumulative sense of frustration with the system

---

* Public Citizen has distributed 150,000 copies of a *Citizens Action Manual* telling people "how to tackle many local problems—from worker safety to deceptive advertising, to unresponsive government, to property tax abuses, to employment discrimination, to starting a citizen action group." Nader's most enduring legacy, however, may prove to be the organization, as of mid-1975, of 58 Public Interest Research Groups ("PIRGs") with 500,000 student members on 135 campuses in 26 states.[23]

† "The language of just complaint, the voice of real grievance, in most cases may easily be distinguished from the mere clamor of selfish, turbulent, and disappointed men. The ear of a righteous government will always be open to the former: its hand with wisdom and prudence will suppress the latter." The quotation is from the Massachusetts Election Sermon of 1780 by Phillips Payson, in *The Pulpit of the American Revolution* (Thornton ed., Boston, 1876), pp. 329 ff. I owe thanks to my Woodrow Wilson Center colleague Professor Charles S. Hyneman for bringing the sermon to my attention.

which has given rise to "Naderism," the emergence of public-interest law firms, and consumerism in general has not gone entirely unnoticed by politicians. Louis Lefkowitz, the perennial Attorney General of New York, made consumer protection his primary cause as early as 1954, and his effectiveness as its champion has helped to reelect him ever since.

The need for responsiveness to the citizen was the central theme of my 1966 campaign for Attorney General of Massachusetts, and I made two specific pledges to do something about it. One was to create a Citizens Aid Bureau to which any citizen with a complaint or a need for information could telephone from anywhere in the state for only a dime. The other was to form a Consumer Protection Division. And I did, immediately on taking office, set up the two new offices. It soon became apparent, however, that I would not be able to deliver on my promise of a ten-cent phone call. The trouble was that from the day the Citizens Aid Bureau opened its door, it attracted more business than its small staff could handle. In fact, had we deliberately promoted a flood of additional phone calls, the infant Bureau would have been completely swamped. A two-to-one Democratic legislature, in any case, wasn't about to give me the money to enlarge it. Questions about the effects of smoking pot, complaints about the inefficiency of the welfare system, inquiries about how to obtain a student loan, tips on organized crime, suggestions for tax law reform poured into the Bureau in a constantly increasing stream. By the end of its first full year it was handling individual problems of all kinds at the rate of twenty thousand a year. In some instances it was enough simply to provide factual information, in others to refer the matter to the right person, but in some we undertook to fight the case on the complainant's behalf. There were a few people, of course, whom we simply couldn't help, including those the Bureau chief called "moon people" because their strange and wonderful delusions flowered in greatest profusion when the moon was full.

Other attempts to penetrate the shell of institutional indifference have evoked responses similar to that aroused by the Citizens Aid Bureau. One of the most successful is "Call for Action." This program, now functioning in forty areas, creates a partnership between television and radio stations and trained volunteers. The stations donate their time and the volunteers take the calls of people who are having trouble with garbage collection, building-code enforcement, police coverage, and a host of other problems. The volunteers have learned what agencies to turn to, how to dig out needed information, and how—and when—to follow up so as to make sure that action has been taken. When official agencies are unresponsive, or when some legal obstacle to an effective response has been identified, the broadcaster begins to mobilize public protest. Use of this technique has made Call for Action an effective instrument of needed change.

In January 1974 the Canadian Broadcasting Company launched an experimental program which takes this approach an important step further. I learned about the experiment in the spring of 1975 when I was interviewed in London by Robert Cooper, the young lawyer who conducts it. Called simply "Ombudsman," the program handles grievances in much the same way as Call for Action. Once weekly, however, on Sunday evenings during prime time, top-level government officials are interrogated by Mr. Cooper about situations of apparent injustice falling within their domains. "The purpose," as he explains it, "is not to attack a Minister. It is to try to rectify an injustice by bringing it to the 'top official's' attention."[24] The good faith of the officials is presumed, and in cases involving the federal government, ten provincial governments, and numerous municipal governments, Robert Cooper has faced an empty chair only once. Most of the time corrective action has resulted. I hope that American television stations are taking note of Ombudsman's success and will find ways of emulating it.

THE LEGAL REMEDIES, the statutory mechanisms, and the voluntary institutions that I have been discussing all evolved as a reaction to growing insistence on respect for the individual. And respect for the individual means respect for *each* individual. Greater equality is therefore both a premise and a product. How far should this evolution proceed? From an equal right to a fair trial, a fair hearing, fair employment opportunity, and fair treatment at the hands of government it may seem but a short step to an equal right to a fair share. But what is a fair share? If it means an enforceable claim to minimum benefits, the step may indeed be short. The school-equalization and right-to-treatment cases illustrate this. So also does income-maintenance and health-insurance legislation. But if a fair share is an equal share, and if the sharing concerns a more nearly equal distribution of property, the case is different—and much harder.

This is a problem that has bothered me all my life, but never more so than since I first began to think about the social and political implications of a world in which per capita economic growth has ceased. Not that economic growth tends in itself to bring about relatively greater equality. On the contrary, most studies indicate that in societies where economic growth has occurred, the gap between rich and poor has grown wider, even though the poor may be better off. It seems reasonable to assume, nevertheless, that the anticipation of growth tomorrow has contributed to social stability and equilibrium today. Discontent is contained by the awareness that the rising tide raises all the boats.

The possibility that growth may not in fact be perpetually sustainable has recently been forced upon our reluctant attention. At the Smithsonian Institution on March 2, 1972, a conference was held to discuss a newly completed report called *The Limits to Growth*. Sponsored by the Club of Rome and based on a study by a group of scientists and economists headed by Dennis L. Meadows of MIT, the report summarized the results of feeding into a computer exponential rates of growth in population, industrial production, pollution, and consumption. Projecting the interaction among these trends, the computer predicted that at some point as early as the first quarter of the next century, and no later than its end, humanity will reach the point of catastrophic "overshoot." The self-reinforcing consequences of increasing strain on the earth's capacity to produce food, the exhaustion of nonrenewable resources, and the choking, pestilential accumulation of human and industrial waste will bring about an abrupt and radical decline in population growth and consumption. Civilization, as we now know it, will have collapsed. Not even the most optimistic assumptions about the potential

for technological innovation—for instance, that an entirely
pollution-free source of unlimited energy will have been developed by the end of this century—can do more than defer the
outcome. The only way to avert catastrophe is immediately to
put into effect policies designed to reach a stage of zero world
economic and population growth at the earliest possible date.

It was possible, I realized, that *The Limits to Growth* might
be mistaken in its apocalyptic vision. To me, as a layman in these
matters, it seemed plausible that technological ingenuity might be
capable of a virtually unlimited response to the problem of scar-
city. And yet, so far as egalitarian pressures are concerned, the
possibility that there may be limits to growth would be likely to
have much the same impact as the probability that there will be
such limits. Once people begin to think of global resources as
finite, they cannot help being concerned about how these resources are distributed. Neither the poor within the United
States nor the poor nations of the world can conceivably be content to accept their present shares of a finite economy.

Speaking at the Smithsonian Institution conference on *The
Limits to Growth*, I pointed out that even if the probability that
its conclusions are correct must be heavily discounted, it was
nevertheless important to face the possibility that the world
might require "political institutions with a degree of sophistication, complexity—and it may be, indeed—power that none of us
have ever seriously envisioned." I concluded:

> It's not easy to visualize a government capable of achieving
> the degree of equalization within a single country, which
> equity under a steady-state economy would require, that
> would not be totalitarian. At least, no such attempt has
> ever been made that did not involve a totalitarian govern-
> ment. And when you extrapolate from a single country to
> the achievement of this result worldwide the mind
> boggles.[25]

The technologists, I believed, were sufficiently aware of the
urgency of developing the innovations needed to offset the trends
projected in *The Limits to Growth*. Intensive efforts were

already being devoted to discovering ways of expanding the capacity of arable land to produce food and of getting better control over population growth. The need for alternative energy sources and better conservation of raw materials was well recognized if not yet adequately addressed. The political and social problems, however, though even more difficult, were scarcely even talked about. These seemed to me deserving of at least as much ingenuity and resourcefulness as the need for technological innovation. Extrapolation of the trend toward equality must otherwise lead to increasing demands for the sacrifice of liberty. Down the road lay Huxley's *Brave New World*—or Orwell's *1984*. If we did not want to wake up in a superhomogenized, superbureaucratized, all-pervasive state—a society in which everyone programmed computers for the automated gratification of everyone else—it seemed to me that we must urgently set about the task of creating the political institutions capable of reconciling liberty and equality.

Was this an exaggerated concern? Its intellectual auspices, at least, are impressive. Goethe said, "Lawgivers or revolutionaries who promise equality and liberty at the same time are either utopian dreamers or charlatans." Such modern thinkers as Russell Kirk, Robert Nisbet, and William F. Buckley, Jr., have expressed the same view with equal force and at considerably greater length. Kirk, Nisbet, and Buckley, to be sure, are "conservatives." Their critics assume that they will resist every proposed use of government on behalf of the poor and the powerless; raising an alarm about some encroachment on individual liberty is presumed to be the standard preface to their usual line of argument. Their views, however, are beginning to gain wide support. Friedrich Hayek's warning in 1944 that well-meaning welfare-statism would lead to the suppression of freedom used to be dismissed by "liberals" and middle-of-the-roaders as shrill, right-wing hysteria.[26] Hayek himself, though a prophet without honor in his own generation, is widely respected in this one: he was awarded the Nobel Prize for Economics in 1974 at the age of seventy-five.

The long-time libertarians are now being joined by the sometime "liberals." Daniel P. Moynihan, for one, in a widely discussed article on the need to resist the redistributive ideology being asserted by the developing countries, concludes:

> The record was stated most succinctly by an Israeli socialist who told William F. Buckley, Jr., that those nations which have put liberty ahead of equality have ended up doing better by equality than those with the reverse priority. This is so, and being so, it is something to be shouted to the heavens in the years now upon us. *This is our case.* We *are* of the liberty party, and it might surprise us what energies might be released were we to unfurl those banners.[27]

Ralf Dahrendorf, who became director of the London School of Economics in the fall of 1974, touched thoughtfully in his BBC Reith Lectures on the underlying reasons for a new emphasis on liberty:

> . . . there is, and must be, plenty of space between the common floor of rights and the common ceiling of private power. For if equality extends further, if the legitimacy of social stratification is questioned in principle, two equally undesirable consequences result. One is that invisible inequalities emerge, much less capable of control, much more dangerous for the majority, the *dachas* of Communist party functionaries, or the brutal personal power often exercised by one or two members of so-called communes. The other result of a false egalitarianism is that greyness and drabness, that absence of any prospect of individual advancement or collective change which makes certain brands of socialism the enemy of liberty. All men are equal in rank and right as human beings and as citizens, but they differ in their abilities and aspirations. To deny such difference is to deny life-chances, thus liberty. Social inequalities do not reflect an inborn differential of human claims to a place in the sun; their justification is rather, if they remain within the limits of citizenship, that they provide an element of hope, and thus of liberty. The new liberty means that equality is there for people to be different, and not for the differences of people to be levelled and abolished.[28]

Among the "liberals" who have come around to Dahrendorf's view of the genuineness of the current threats to liberty are a few who, unlike Dahrendorf, have reconciled themselves to what they regard as the inevitability of subordinating democratic processes to what they see as the paramount necessity for maintaining the governability of human affairs. Harvard Professor Samuel P. Huntington, in a paper written for a meeting of the Trilateral Commission in Kyoto, Japan, in May 1975, argued that "some of the problems of governance in the United States today stem from an excess of democracy." The participation in the democratic process of "marginal social groups," particularly blacks, has created "the danger of over-loading the political system with demands which extend its functions and undermine its authority." The absence of traditional and aristocratic values in the United States "produces a lack of balance in society." Professor Huntington's solution: "a greater degree of moderation in democracy."[29]

Taking a longer-range look at the future, the economist Robert L. Heilbroner combines the Club of Rome's bleak predictions of the limits to growth with a pessimistic outlook toward human capacity for creative cooperation. The combination leads him to despair of the ability of democratic societies to cope with the explosive social pressures generated by a stationary economy. In *An Inquiry into the Human Prospect*, Heilbroner tells us that candor compels him "to suggest that the passage through the gauntlet ahead may be possible only under governments capable of rallying obedience far more effectively than would be possible in a democratic setting." Expanding this view in an answer to his critics, he depicts China as today's closest approximation to "the model of a social order that, however repugnant to us, offers the greatest promise for bringing about the civilizational adaptations that the coming generations must make."[30]

It is not simply my instinctive optimism, I believe, that makes me skeptical both of prescriptions for increased government authority and of the discouraged diagnoses to which the prescriptions are directed. It is ordinarily a mistake to extrapolate the known trends of the visible present without allowing for the unknown counterforces of the invisible future. This, I believe, is the most telling answer to *The Limits to Growth*. As some resources grow scarcer, others will be substituted. Nor will this depend on radical innovations in technology. The use of fiberglass, rock wool insulation, and solar energy becomes increasingly economical as the costs of steel, natural gas, and fuel oil go up. As to natural resources, *The Limits to Growth* bases its projections on "known reserves." But these are only the reserves which are economic to mine at *current* prices. The entire mass of the earth is ultimately at our disposal. Aluminum, for example, makes up 8 percent of the earth's crust. And of course, it is inevitable that new inventions and new discoveries will occur. We should be hesitant, therefore, about precipitating the infringements on human freedom consequent upon strict no-growth policies that could only be enforced by government edict.[31]

When I spoke in 1972 at the Smithsonian conference on *The Limits to Growth*, I supposed that the conflict between the demand for equality and the enjoyment of liberty might prove to be so irreconcilable that only some extraordinary feat of political inventiveness could mediate between them. Since then, largely as a result of reflecting upon what I saw of the Soviet Union in the summer of 1974, I have come to the conclusion that I misconceived the problem. Goethe (and others) to the contrary notwithstanding, it is not true that liberty and equality bear an inverse relationship to each other—that either is enhanced only at the expense of the other. Liberty and equality are not counters in a zero-sum game. The contrary impression arises, I think, from an automatic tendency (one which, when I spoke at the Smithsonian, I undoubtedly shared) to associate "equalization" with the subdivision of some tangible object. In fact, true equality among human beings must embrace every important aspect of human existence—intangible values as well as material things. Once this is understood, it becomes obvious that there is a point beyond which the attempt to achieve equality creates inequality, and to press for more perfect justice is to impose injustice.

The claim to equality must extend, surely, to liberty itself. And if every individual is entitled to an equal portion of liberty, a uniform level of equality in other respects can only be achieved by depriving some individuals of their share of liberty.* But, as history attests, people will fight for the right to liberty. It can be denied or abridged only by a determined exercise of superior authority. This explains why societies committed to the enforcement of equality have to employ large numbers of political informers, thought-controllers, and secret policemen. It also explains why they do not dare to allow free elections. The position of those who hold authority to enforce equality is inherently unequal. Does any major capital other than Moscow have reserved lanes for its official limousines?

Beyond the point at which the attempt to enforce equality produces inequality it makes no sense to subordinate liberty for the sake of equality. This, to be sure, is true only of equality as an inclusive concept. The real question, arguably, is how far to push equality in income, housing, health care, and other material benefits at the expense of other claims to equality, one of which is the claim to equality in the opportunity to take advantage of natural or inherited assets such, for instance, as those in talent, energy, or wealth. If this is the right question, the answer must lie in an examination of the fairness, as well as the collective consequences, of denying that opportunity.

Let us take a look, then, at the theoretically possible ways of making sure that natural or inherited assets neither perpetuate nor result in differences of material well-being. The first step must be to redistribute all existing wealth so that everyone starts out with the same amount. This having been done, there are two (and, so far as I can see, only two) possible ways of preventing new differences in material status from arising. One is to nullify natural advantages by preventing their exploitation. In the case of racehorses this is done by adding weight to the saddle, and the people who do it are called "handicappers." Without pausing to

---

* "There are, to be sure," wrote my former Woodrow Wilson Center colleague Sanford A. Lakoff, now chairman of the Political Science Department at the University of San Diego, "those mock philosophers who claim that equal rights contradict individual liberty, as though there could be a genuine liberty that was not reciprocal, a freedom for one individual to deny to others the rights he demands for himself." *Equality in Political Philosophy* (Cambridge, Mass., 1964), p. 239.

consider the practical difficulties of applying some such system to human beings, I can only say that it would seem to me a strange notion of fairness which empowered some official body to hold the speed of the swiftest human down to the pace of the slowest. What fairness requires, rather, is assistance to the slow in enabling them to make the most of their capacities.

If handicapping is ruled out, the only remaining way of guaranteeing that natural or inherited advantages play no part in bringing about variances in material status is to enforce a uniform scale of rewards which ignores differences in the value of the individual's contribution to the society. Quite apart from the inequalities flowing from the authoritarian measures that the imposition of such uniformity would necessitate, the result would also be to create gross inequalities as between the more and the less fortunately endowed. The former would be making a sacrifice proportional to their gifts; the latter would be reaping a benefit disproportional to theirs. Both groups, meanwhile, would have paid an incalculable price in terms of the loss of liberty.

Any attempt to impose uniformity must exact a sacrifice of equality from many more than half the population. This is because a policy aimed at eliminating inequalities resulting from natural or inherited advantages can be effective only if it imposes a ceiling that holds down all those who attempt to rise higher as well as all those who would rise higher. To flatten out actual differences, it is necessary to suppress potential differences. Many of those who happen, at a given time, to fall below the median line (however defined) are people who expect to rise above it and are striving to do so. The columnist William Raspberry, writing in mid-1975, put the point succinctly: "For if human equality has any pragmatic meaning, it is that people should have the opportunity to establish themselves as superior."[32]

LIBERTY AND EQUALITY are moral values resting on the obligation to respect other human beings. The more wholeheartedly a society honors this obligation, the fairer and freer it will become. It can achieve greater equality before encountering the loss of equality in the degree that it accords equality without coercion.

In a persuasively reasoned exposition of the concept of justice, the philosopher John Rawls has described the link between mutual respect and noncoercive equality in terms of a bond of fraternity among all men which rests on "the idea of not wanting to have greater advantages unless this is to the benefit of others who are less well off." Those who have been fortunate in genetic endowments or social advantage have a moral duty to employ their talents in the service of the least advantaged. Such service, he argues, enhances self-respect, which is not only the foremost "primary good" sought by all men but the basic foundation of a just society: "Properly understood, then, the desire to act justly derives in part from the desire to express most fully what we are or can be, namely free and equal rational beings with liberty to choose."[33]

The effort to act justly and to render service can be a powerful means of self-fulfillment and thus a source of deep satisfaction. And yet it seems to me clear that we cannot safely pin all our hopes for a fair and civil society on the desire of the fortunately endowed to do good. In this, my point of view is closer to Madison's than to Rawls's: self-seeking is the norm, and the public good is a resultant of competing selfish interests tempered by the capacity to take a broader and more magnanimous view. But the issue concerns only the *degree* to which we can count upon disinterested motives to make the society fair while leaving it free. It is clear in any case that without individuals who possess the capacity both for magnanimity and for disinterestedness, a society can scarcely hope to be either fair or free.

The tendency of pressures toward equality to become self-defeating is matched by the similar tendency of pressures toward liberty. In a society in which every individual is unconstrained in the pursuit of liberty—a society in which neither legal constraints nor voluntary respect for other individuals effectively curbs rampant self-seeking—the liberty of a minority is gained at the expense of the majority. The strong flourish and the weak suffer. The historic struggles for liberty have always been waged against oppressors whose own freedom to act as they please deprived the people generally of their just share of liberty. Up to the point discussed in the preceding paragraphs, equality does not diminish a society's aggregate liberty but enlarges it.

Within the limits beyond which to pursue liberty sacrifices both liberty and equality and to pursue equality sacrifices both equality and liberty, liberty is a means to self-fulfillment and equality is a means to liberty. For the society as a whole (though not necessarily, of course, for a particular individual), liberty and equality each achieves its own optimal fulfillment only under circumstances which permit the optimal fulfillment of the other. The relationship is one of tension but not of antagonism. Just as in the case of individuality and community, the task of social policy must be so to adjust the elements of tension as to produce a creative balance. Indeed, I believe that most human striving turns out upon examination to be directed toward achieving a dynamic equilibrium that comes as close as possible to an optimal combination of desired components. To achieve and maintain such a creative balance in a changing situation, an element of discipline is necessary on the part both of the individual and of the society. But the discipline must be largely self-imposed. The law, for example, is a source both of balance and discipline, and the law can be fully effective only when its observance is voluntary.

Discipline is inherent in freedom. This is something I learned in the fall of 1944 when my unit was fighting in the Schnee Eiffel on the border of Belgium and Germany, Almost every night that fall we used to listen to a "liberated" German radio which we kept tuned to the Allied Expeditionary Forces Program of the BBC. One song we heard quite often seemed to me hauntingly to evoke the poignancy of the renunciation implicit in freedom. The refrain went, "I'd rather be here than any place I know." In spite of the blood and the mud and the cold, in spite of the discomfort and danger and death, I knew that I was where I wanted to be. If some higher authority had offered me a dry, comfortable billet somewhere back in Liège or Paris, I would have said, "Thanks but no thanks."

Since then, in the many roles and situations in which for the time being I happened to find myself, I have often been struck anew by the realization that to be free is to have the opportunity to choose, to feel free is to obey the consequences of choice. Woodrow Wilson said it well in one of his campaign speeches:

> We say of a boat skimming the water with light foot, "How free she runs," when we mean, how perfectly she is adjusted to the force of the wind, how perfectly she obeys the great breath out of the heavens that fills her sails. Throw her head up into the wind and see how she will halt and stagger, how every sheet will shiver and her whole frame be shaken, how instantly she is "in irons," in the expressive phrase of the sea. She is free only when you have let her fall off again and have recovered once more her nice adjustment to the forces she must obey and cannot defy.[34]

A SOCIETY that achieves the creative balance between liberty and equality—a balance in which each contributes to the optimal fulfillment of the other—is a just society. This seems to me clearly to follow from all that I have previously said. But how are we to know when the right balance has been struck? This is a question that challenges the wisest philosophers of our own time, as it has challenged those of other centuries. John Rawls's *Theory of Justice* constitutes the most magisterial recent approach to this subject. What help does he give us in reaching a judgment as to the creative balance between liberty and equality?

As his starting point Rawls postulates an "original position" (like Hobbes's "state of nature") in which "principles of justice are chosen behind a veil of ignorance." In this original position no one is advantaged or disadvantaged in the choice of principles by the outcome of natural chance or the contingency of social circumstances. Since all are similarly situated and no one is able to design principles to favor his particular condition, the principles of justice are the result of a fair agreement or bargain. The choice of principles is, however, influenced by awareness of the practical necessity for observing "certain rules of conduct" among which are rules specifying "a system of cooperation designed to advance the good of those taking part in it." To make possible the fair division of the benefits resulting from cooperation, individuals in the "original position" would choose two principles of justice: "the first requires equality in the assignment of basic rights and duties, while the second holds that social and economic inequalities, for example inequalities of wealth and authority, are just only if they result in compensating benefits for everyone, and in particular for the least advantaged members of society."[35]

Considered as moral precepts, these principles seem to me unexceptionable. The process, however, by which Rawls brings them out from behind the "veil of ignorance" raises a number of questions. These have been brilliantly dissected by Robert Nozick, Rawls's colleague in the Harvard Philosophy Department, in a provocative exposition of the virtues of the "minimal state."* Nozick argues that the minimally necessary social arrangements emerging from a "state of nature" can more logically be accounted for by his own "entitlement theory" of justice. This theory embraces three basic propositions. The first, which rests on the "principle of justice in acquisition," concerns "the issues of how unheld things may come to be held." The second, which rests on the "principle of justice in transfer," concerns "the *transfer of holdings* from one person to another"—the processes, in other words, such as voluntary exchanges, gifts, fraud, theft, and the like, by which things are transferred or acquired.[36]

Because the world is not wholly just—because some people have acquired their holdings by theft or fraud or by forcibly excluding others from competing in exchanges—a third proposition is needed. This rests on the "principle of rectification" and employs "information about previous situations and injustices done in them" in order to bring about the approximate distribution which would have occurred if the first two principles of justice had been consistently observed. Nozick's entitlement theory is historical: "whether a distribution is just depends on how it came about."[37]

* "The minimal state is the most extensive state that can be justified. Any state more extensive violates people's rights." Robert Nozick, *Anarchy, State, and Utopia* (New York, 1974), p. 149.

The basic thrust of Rawls's theory is no doubt egalitarian, as Nozick's is libertarian. Such at least are their popular interpretations. And yet neither theory leads us out of the maze of problems that surround us in the real world. On its face, Rawls's theory can as easily be called upon for the purpose of rationalizing existing inequalities as for the purpose of denouncing present injustices. For even if we agree with Rawls that "inequalities of wealth and authority are just only if they result in compensating benefits for everyone, and in particular for the least advantaged members of society," we are still left with the question, what inequalities have that result? How much inequality, for example, could conclusively be shown to be needed in order to preserve incentives to the increased economic growth which, arguably, is the best way of improving the lot of the least advantaged?

Conversely, Nozick's entitlement theory leaves room for state intervention considerably more extensive than would at first seem compatible with the "minimal state." The theory compels Nozick to argue that the subsidy of medical care for the poor (a form of transfer payment) is no more justified or legitimate than the subsidy of haircuts for the poor. Nozick acknowledges, nevertheless, that his own analysis cannot be used "to condemn any particular scheme of transfer payments, unless it is clear that no considerations of rectification of injustice could apply to justify it." Some principles of distributive justice can thus be viewed as "rough rules of thumb meant to approximate the general results of applying the principle of rectification of injustice."

Both Rawls and Nozick thus converge on the real world (and with each other). Having long been in the middle of it, I feel more comfortable starting there. From that vantage point, the effort to achieve equality in some things and to narrow the range of inequality in others seems necessary and important for a variety of reasons. Some of these can be made to fit after a fashion into Nozick's principle of the rectification of injustice. Take, for instance, the situation of people thrown out of work through no fault of their own by a shift in economic demand or a downturn in the economy. Compensating them for their unemployment can be justified as a means of rectifying the injustice consequent upon the inability or unwillingness of the private enterprise system, for internal economic reasons, to guarantee long-term employment. Similarly, cash assistance to the aged can be explained as a way of compensating old people for industry's failure to cover them under some sort of contributory pension plan. The principle of rectification, however, does not reach benefits to handicapped individuals whose disability is not work-related. Neither does it cover white, non-Spanish-speaking mothers whose husbands have deserted them. And yet charity is surely appropriate for such people, and it does not automatically cease to be charity because the money is raised by taxes. To the libertarian objection that no one should be compelled to contribute to the society's collective benevolence, it seems to me a sufficient answer that society can legitimately compel the observance of minimal moral obligations. Not even the most extreme libertarian would deny that society can compel us individually to refrain from acts that cause *slight* harm to others—slander or assault, for instance. No great leap is necessary to justify our being compelled collectively to share in preventing *serious* harm to others—starvation or death, for instance.*

However the case for public charity may be put, once adequately established it becomes the foundation for rationalizing another group of transfer payments. These are payments directed toward preventing dependency on public charity or helping people now dependent on public charity to become self-supporting. These were the aims to which I gave top priority in my HEW departmental strategy for 1971–1972. Somewhat ironically, perhaps, given the necessity for piggybacking their rationale on the underlying case for public charity, programs of this kind are the favorites of "conservatives." A prime example is vocational rehabilitation. Another, though with a longer-deferred yield on its investment, is public education.

---

* "To no matter whom the question may be put in general terms, nobody is of the opinion that any man is innocent if, possessing food himself in abundance and finding someone on his doorstep three parts dead from hunger, he brushes past without giving him anything." Simone Weil, *The Need for Roots* (Boston, 1952), p. 6.

THERE REMAINS one other consideration tending to justify some measure of equalization. That is envy. Any difference among individuals in some desirable attribute—looks, intelligence, athletic prowess, and so on—may awaken envy. And as to most such differences, there is no practical way of equalizing things so as to eliminate or reduce this primitive feeling. Indeed, the awareness of this fact no doubt tends in itself to reconcile people to natural differences. Extreme discrepancies in wealth, however, are not only wider than most differences in human attributes but can much more easily be reduced. Not to do anything to correct them is apt to generate both resentment on the part of the poor and guilt feelings on the part of the rich. Likely results are social alienation, instability, disorder, and fear. To avoid these consequences it is not unreasonable to require the rich, as part of the price of the civilization in which they have such a large proportional stake, to be subjected to progressive taxation in order to pay for minimum benefits for the poor.

Some people, of course, find any system of transfer payments objectionable not on theoretical grounds but on the intensely practical ground that minimum benefits will lead to bigger benefits and these to still bigger benefits until finally all the wealth has been shared and everyone ends up with the same amount as everyone else. And long before that, they argue, liberty will have been destroyed. On the latter point they are certainly right. But so also, as I earlier attempted to show, will equality itself. Indeed, the perception that liberty and equality are not competitive but complementary supplies a powerful rationale for ruling out policies that seek to push either one to an extreme.

The former contention—that the first step inevitably starts us down the slippery slope—is an argument of a kind that has seldom moved me since I learned from Professor Thomas Reed Powell, a masterly deflater of overblown rhetoric who taught constitutional law at the Harvard Law School, that most hard questions are questions of degree. Instead of the slippery-slope assumption, I prefer Lord Nottingham's retort to counsel in *The Duke of Norfolk's Case*: "Where will you stop if you do not stop here? I will tell you where I will stop: I will stop when any visible inconvenience doth appear." Policies that rest on the prevention of suffering and the provision of minimal standards of well-being are not easily convertible into policies calling for the leveling of all inequalities of wealth. In the attempted conversion, moreover, considerable inconvenience *would* appear.

As to where exactly the line should be drawn so that the pursuit of one form of equality does not demand excessive sacrifice either of another form of equality or of liberty, we have no choice, since political philosophy can give us little help, but to rely on the political process. Fortunately, this is just the kind of balance which the political process is constantly called upon to strike. Maximum rates of income taxation are an example, as are minimum levels of income maintenance: both represent a judgment as to the optimal benefits of redistributive mechanisms. A similar balancing requirement is presented by the question of whether or not to invoke wage and price controls and rationing, which necessitate large-scale interference with free markets. In the United States these have been only partially successful even in wartime, when the need for sacrifice in the common interest is most widely understood and supported. This, basically, is why I do not find persuasive John Kenneth Galbraith's arguments for permanent wage and price regulations.[38] Granted that the market does not function perfectly in the case of products whose manufacture and sale is dominated by a handful of big companies, some dilution of competition is preferable to a vast increase in government intrusiveness. In my view, moreover, Galbraith undervalues the efficacy of antitrust enforcement and overstates the degree to which the "planning system" suppresses competition. Be that as it may, how far it is feasible to go in the attempt to enforce equality is a psychological and political, not an economic, question. Liberty is a psychological and political, not an economic, value. And so, indeed, is equality.

In the cause of equality, as in the cause of liberty, there is no escape from the necessity for moderation. I cannot do better than to call once again on the wisdom and eloquence of Learned Hand:

What is the spirit of moderation? It is the temper which does not press a partisan advantage to its bitter end, which can understand and will respect the other side, which feels a unity between all citizens—real and not the factitious product of propaganda—which recognizes their common fate and their common aspirations—in a word, which has faith in the sacredness of the individual.[39]

X

A Sense of Purpose

MANY YEARS AGO at his summer home in Dublin, New Hampshire, the late Grenville Clark showed me a picture of his father, a man of the late Victorian era with handsome muttonchop whiskers and massive gold watch chain. Mr. Clark called to my attention the authority and confidence radiated by the portrait. The elder Clark's face and bearing betrayed no doubt whatever as to the importance of the role he occupied or the ultimate validity of the social order of which he was such an impressive symbol.

Few men today possess a comparable sense of confidence and authority. The father today occupies quite a different role from that of the nineteenth-century father. A contemporary portrait would show a man not too self-assured but too lacking in self-assurance, too prone to believe that the generation gap leaves him not above and ahead but below and behind. With no prospect of becoming the patriarch of an extended family, he yearns to be a companion to his children, not a source of authority.

Mothers are in a better case, but not much so. Parental discipline tends, more often than not, to fall to them. But 35 percent of mothers of school-age children work full time. Divorce—or, in the lowest income brackets, desertion—rates are high. In this increasingly urban and mobile society young people, in any case, are less subject to parental control. Teenage runaways drift from city to city and commune to commune.

The institutions on which society has traditionally relied for authority have suffered a weakening of status. The church, the school, the police, and the courts can no longer rely—any more than parents can—on an exercise of authority which depends on the assertion, "It's so because I say it's so." A scientific age has systematically encouraged the propensity to inquire as to anything and everything: Why? Is it really true? How do we know? On every hand ancient dogmas crumble, conventions weaken, heretofore accepted precepts lose their force. In every area of our lives—the arts, education, sex, other social norms—the established order has been losing ground.

The result has been not only to sweep away the accumulated rubbish of outmoded attitudes and obsolete prohibitions but to undermine the solid and useful standards of conduct enforced by legal as well as by moral sanctions. The national crime rate has increased 32 percent since 1969. In 1974, there were 4,821 crimes per 100,000 people in this country, an increase of 18 percent over 1973. The most disturbing increases were recorded in juvenile crime. Persons under eighteen accounted for 27 percent of police arrests in 1974.

In 1961 I wrote:

> Corruption in its earlier, more innocent phase, such as was depicted by Edwin O'Connor in *The Last Hurrah*, represented the aberration of greed in an environment of firm moral standards. It now tends also to reflect—and to reinforce—the ego-centered, self-indulgent, conscienceless amorality of a fast-buck, expense-account society. In this respect, political corruption belongs in the same shoddy category as the priming of television quizzes, the rigging of commodity prices, and the fixing of college basketball games. Giving impetus to cynicism, cheating begins to seem normal, if not respectable.[1]

Although the examples I used in 1961 are out of date, all too many others have accumulated since then. Watergate revealed a sickening spectacle of amorality at the highest levels. On a pettier scale, the same propensity to cheat is disturbingly widespread: for instance, the Boy Scout Councils which padded their membership rolls to meet recruitment quotas and to justify Model Cities grants, or the American Soap Box Derby winner who was thrown out of the race because his adult mentor had placed magnets in his car. A study cited by Milton G. Rector, president of the National Council on Crime and Delinquency, reports that "there is negligible difference in the amount of delinquency committed by higher status boys and those in poverty areas." College and university student-aid offices, which for generations accepted family financial statements on trust, have had to call upon the College Scholarship Service to provide a nationwide check on cheating. The Scholarship Service has found that the higher a family's income, the more likely the family is to underreport it.

The weakening of our institutions has both contributed to and been reinforced by the other developments discussed in this book. Distrust and cynicism, complexity and the pervasiveness of government, government intrusiveness and citizen vulnerability, centralization and unresponsiveness, work dissatisfaction and the loss of a sense of community, impatience with inequalities and pressures for equality of result—each in its own way has contributed to a loss of confidence and a decline of morale. And though I have outlined what seem to me constructive responses to these developments, it is plain that such responses are not adequate to satisfy the need for more fundamental affirmations. With events in the saddle, a sense of purpose has been lost, and old values seem to have lost their meaning. It is tempting in the circumstances to take up the cry of the preacher in Ecclesiastes: "Vanity of vanities, all is vanity."

IS THAT, then, all there is to be said? Must we resign ourselves to pessimism? My instinct—the instinct of most of us, no doubt —is to say, "No, certainly not," and go about my business. And yet these questions insist upon being taken seriously. The evidence that something has gone wrong is too pervasive, the changes that seem to account for what has been happening are too visible, and the new wave of pessimism is too powerful to be overcome by the simple iteration of "thinking positive."

In seeking answers, the obvious place to begin is with an examination of the implications of pessimism itself. For pessimism, as Ecclesiastes attests, is not new. The struggle against despair, like that against hunger and poverty and disease, has always been with us. If life is not a "tale told by an idiot," it is because man's indomitable spirit has persisted in the search for values that could survive the vicissitudes of transitory events.

What, after all, is pessimism but a subjective attitude of disappointment and frustration? I have little faith in sweeping global judgments about the long-term prospects of humanity at large, civilization in general, or even a particular society. No individual can so far transcend the circumstances of his own historical, social, and geographical vantage point as to be capable of totally objective commentary on the situation he occupies.* I am distrustful, therefore, of "pessimistic" assessments of pervasive trends just as I am of my own disposition to be a "chronic hoper." Given the fantastic complexity of modern society, it is impossible for any finite mind to grasp more than a fraction of what is happening at any time. Depending on one's mood, one can assemble bits and pieces "proving" either that "the end is nigh" or that "this is the best of all possible worlds." The one certain thing is that we are in the midst of an organic process of growth and decay: some lovely and precious things are fading and dying, and with them are also disappearing things that are ugly and ignoble; new things, meanwhile, are taking the old places, some destined to be as cherished, others as detested, as those they replace.[2]

From the standpoint of the individual, in any case, the general direction of profound social trends is largely irrelevant. Once reasonably adequate conditions of subsistence are assured (and most participants in the "postindustrial" society take them for granted), individual happiness is not much dependent on the

* When I was at HEW, we used to express a more mundane version of the same point in terms of "Miles' Law": "How you stand depends on where you sit." The "Law" took its name from Rufus Miles, for many years the senior civil servant in the department.

general direction of the society as a whole. And if, as I believe, happiness lies not in placid contentment but in the fullest exercise of our powers, this opportunity is likely to be greater under conditions of challenge and stress than in easy circumstances. The articulate prophet of doom is happily occupied.

To the extent that the individual is distressed by discouraging social developments, he is wiser to seek reassurance in enduring values than in telling himself that things are bound to look up. That, perhaps, is why most affirmations of value are addressed not to societies but to individuals. We must be wary of sliding from social diagnoses to individual prescriptions. But any affirmation sturdy enough to carry a convincing message must be capable of inspiring a commitment to something beyond ourselves. Lesser values—pleasure, for instance—leave us where we started: they cage us in the prison of our own insignificance.

Affirmations of value transcending a narrow definition of self are distributed along a spectrum ranging from most skeptical to most faith-reliant. But even the most skeptical affirmation recognizes that self-fulfillment demands making some individual mark, leaving a personal imprint. In a passage quoted above in connection with the satisfaction of work, Learned Hand speaks of the "joy of craftsmanship" as including "all efforts to *impose upon the outside world* an invention of our own: to embody an idea in what I shall ask your leave to call an *artifact*." No matter that the result is neither perfect nor permanent; success is measured by the outcome of the effort, and the reward is in the work: "on the whole the best of rewards—let performance fall as far behind conception as it may."[3]

Judge Hand used to credit Oliver Wendell Holmes, Jr., with being the leader, if not the founder, of the school of thought which insists not simply that the pay is in the work but that no other form of pay is worthwhile. But Holmes, I think, can fairly be regarded as occupying a somewhat less minimal position than Hand attributes to him. During nearly a year of combat in World War II, I carried with me everywhere a copy of *The Mind and Faith of Justice Holmes*, a compilation edited by Max Lerner. In part, no doubt, because Holmes spoke from the remembered depths of his own Civil War experience, I found his expressions of faith deeply moving and even consoling. And although some of what moved me then ("the faith is true and adorable which leads a soldier to throw away his life in obedience to a blindly accepted duty") now strikes me as a bit overblown, I still find powerfully impressive the essay on "Natural Law" which, so far as I know, most fully expresses his mature philosophy. These are the key sentences:

> It is enough for us that the universe has produced us and has within it, as less than it, all that we believe and love. ... If our imagination is strong enough to accept the vision of ourselves as parts inseverable from the rest, and to extend our final interest beyond the boundary of our skins, it justifies the sacrifice even of our lives for ends outside of ourselves. The motive, to be sure, is the common wants and ideals that we find in man. Philosophy does not furnish motives, but it shows men that they are not fools for doing what they already want to do.[4]

Somewhat further along the spectrum are those who see man's transcendence of himself, and thus the affirmation of his values, in terms of his membership in the society of his fellows. Plato's *Republic* may well have been the first systematic expression of this view; Richard N. Goodwin's is among the most recent. Goodwin describes as natural and desirable "a social condition wherein common values and shared inclinations are experienced by the individual as his own. Not only does he inhabit society, but society inhabits him." Personal fulfillment flows from serving social goals. Noting the breakdown of community, Goodwin finds that society as presently organized stands in the way of such fulfillment, thus producing the "varied forms of contemporary discontent—grievance without apparent object."[5]

Moving on, we come to those who celebrate the cause of humanity in general. Man's aspirations, man's striving, man's yearning spirit are themselves of value; so also, therefore, is whatever contributes to the realization of man's loftiest conception of himself. Philosophy and art are filled with visions of mankind's higher achievements. Although already capable of infinite subtlety and resourcefulness, the human mind as we now know it is still at an early stage of an evolutionary process that will carry it to undreamed-of heights. The philosopher Bertrand Russell visualizes a "new world" in which the exceptional man "would rise as far above Shakespeare as Shakespeare now rises above the common man."[6] Society as a whole will also see a finer flowering. Russell's contemporary and sometime collaborator Alfred North Whitehead calls upon us to "produce a great age, or see collapse the upward striving of our race."[7]

Such conceptions of humanity's potential are closely linked to the next step in the hierarchy of value: man's awe of the unknowable. Out of his exploratory groping for a rational path to religion comes a profound answer to human despair. In the words of the theologian Paul Tillich, it is an answer "which does not destroy reason but points to the depth of reason; which does not teach the supernatural, but points to the mystery in the ground of the natural, which denies that God is a being and speaks of Him as the ground and depth of being and meaning."[8]

And finally comes the ultimate leap of faith—the leap to a revealed religion. Nothing else so convincingly demonstrates our innate need for a sense of meaning and purpose; nothing else so fully meets it. This, clearly, has been the historic role of the world's great religions. Christianity, Buddhism, and Islam all have in common a perception of man's state as flawed and incomplete. Each undertakes to show the way to overcome imperfection and achieve completeness. Tormented by desire, prone to err, racked by sorrow and suffering, sinful man can be brought through renunciation, repentance, or divine forgiveness to a blessed state—nirvana, a higher rebirth, eternal bliss.

IN SEEKING a refuge from pessimism and the rediscovery of a sense of purpose, we have followed a route that has taken us from the limitations of global judgments about the direction of long-term trends to the affirmative insights that have sustained men of courage and wisdom over the centuries. We come now to a closer look at the footing on which these insights rest. Their basis, I believe, is far more fundamental than personal preference, cultural inheritance, or historic accident. It is nothing less than the human condition itself—man's situation as that is shaped, in Holmes's phrase, by his "common wants and ideals."

Take, to start with, Learned Hand's "joy of craftsmanship": the satisfaction (and hence the value) of imposing "an invention of our own" upon the outside world needs no external standard by which to measure its validity. Indeed, it is not subject to any such standard. The same applies to the values which derive from the individual's relationships to other people. Judge Hand, it is true, enjoyed making fun of the "sense of service." "More cant," he said, "is poured out to youthful ears in the name of serving mankind than would fill the tally of those papers on which Panurge passed his momentous judgment some three hundred years ago."[9] And yet I do not suppose that he intended us to take him literally. The intrinsic rewards of deciding cases and shaping opinions aside, I feel sure he must also have found satisfaction in the awareness that his knowledge and skill were harnessed to the benefit of others—and what is that if not service?

For my part, I firmly believe that the satisfaction of serving, like that of sharing and giving, flows from a basic attribute of the human condition: the inseparability of the individual from other persons. The "self" does not—cannot—exist in isolation. During my senior year at Harvard College I was working on an honors thesis in philosophy, and I had to try to think through the meaning of the concept of "self." At an intense stage of this effort, I went for a walk around the block. It was one of those slaty, late-winter afternoons with a wet wind, not very cold. As I walked, it struck me that no person's identity can be defined in all its essential uniqueness except in terms of others: family, friends, teachers, fellow workers, other members of the same community and the same cultural heritage. We exist in the midst of a web of interconnecting relationships to other people, some of whom are close, others more remote, but none completely disconnected. To be a complete person is to be a part of others, and to share a part of them. This is what we mean by love. This is why sharing is natural. If it were not for our physical separateness—no one else can eat for me or walk for me or see from the same eyes—we would more clearly perceive our psychic inter-dependence.

Hegel had anticipated me, as I later learned, by several generations. But so, for that matter, had John Donne, and by considerably longer. I am still moved by the phrase "for I am involved in mankind" in the celebrated passage from the Donne sermon adjuring us never to "send to know for whom the bell tolls." When I quote it I always bear down hard on the word "involved." It is this *fact* of human existence which, in my view, makes the satisfaction of service—to one's community, country, or mankind generally—so rewarding.

Like the "joy of craftsmanship" and the satisfaction of service, the other enduring affirmations touched on above respond to equally fundamental aspects of the human condition. The faith that mankind will continue to evolve toward a higher level of humanity, the awe of the unknowable that leads to belief in a Supreme Being, the teachings of revealed religion—each is a response to the individual's need for understanding of his place in the universe. Although differing in the degree to which they draw upon—or are inspired by—elements that transcend objective measurement, they have in common the intuitive perception that man has a significant part in a larger scheme of things. These affirmations speak to us from a plane that lies beyond the temporary fluctuations of social history. Their power derives not from exhortation but from truth. At a time of doubt and discouragement in the realm of day-to-day affairs, we have special need to call upon them.

HISTORY AND TRADITION afford both evidence of enduring values and the means of sustaining them. History is the toughest of testing grounds: the ideas that have survived centuries of searching cross-examination, intense political debate, and bitter religious warfare must at the very least have staying power. They must therefore be strongly rooted either in emotional appeal, solid common sense, empirical proof, or some combination of the three. Indeed, the most universally held—and, I believe, the most enduring—ideas are those which combine all three elements.

The ideas that have come down to us through two hundred years of the history of the American Republic demonstrate the persuasive power of this combination. Liberty. Freedom of speech and religion. Respect for the individual. The right to be heard and to be represented. Equal justice. The emotional force of these ideas has not slackened through the centuries. They still command the loyalty of Americans as they still inspire the hopes of countless millions throughout the world. As for the "common sense" of these ideas, was not that the very title of the pamphlet which most persuasively aroused their revolutionary impact? And for empirical proof we have only to look at the cumulative evidence offered by studies of political psychology and surveys of public opinion; this book, in fact, has touched upon such evidence at many points.

Justice Felix Frankfurter summarized the role of history and tradition in his opinion for the Supreme Court in the first "flag salute" case:

> The ultimate foundation of a free society is the binding tie of cohesive sentiment. Such a sentiment is fostered by all those agencies of mind and spirit which may serve to gather up the traditions of a people, transmit them from generation to generation, and thereby create that continuity of a treasured common life which constitutes a civilization.[10]

It is more necessary now than ever before that in our approach to change, we seek to preserve some sense of continuity, some sense of proportion, some appreciation of the old order so fast yielding place to the new. For without an appreciative sense of the old, we cannot properly measure—we cannot discriminately reject or affirm—the new. And yet our society is one that tends to seek escape from continuity. Our commentators parade so-called revolutions before us like so many timeless streakers. Our sense of proportion is lost. Investigative journalists are our new historians. Television anchormen are our historical dramatists. No wonder that we are confused about endings and beginnings.

The late Alexander M. Bickel found in the writings of

Edmund Burke an articulation of the necessity for continuity which seems to me compelling. Referring to Burke's concept of political reason as a "computing principle" which derives "true moral denominations" from "balances between differences of good, in compromises sometimes between good and sometimes between evil and evil," Bickel wrote:

> We find our visions of good and evil and the denominations we compute where Burke told us to look, in the experience of the past, in our tradition, in the secular religion of the American republic. The only abiding thing, as Brandeis used to repeat and as Burke might not have denied, is change, but the past should control it, or at least its pace. We hold to the values of the past provisionally only, in the knowledge that they will change, but we hold to them as guides.
>   This is not, as Holmes once remarked, a duty, it is a necessity. How else are we to know anything? What is the use of empty "rationalists," such as were discovered at many a university some years ago, who being confronted with various demands for instant change, found that they believed nothing and could not judge any change as better or worse than another?[11]

I would add only this: though change is certainly inexorable, and though the values of the past should therefore be held only provisionally, such provisionality does not apply to the values derived from examination of the human condition. If, as I have argued, these values are enduring, their validity must rest on a footing not significantly affected by historic change. And though my belief in them may brand me as a "rationalist" of a sort, I find reassurance in the knowledge that much the same rational process helped to shape the values of the American past. Our "secular religion" is not only consistent with, but part and parcel of, the great traditions of human thought as well as of human aspiration.

SINCE ARNOLD TOYNBEE, awareness of the interaction between challenge and response has become commonplace. We

all know, too (or think we know), that in the interludes between challenges decay sets in. And certainly the secular process
of the rise and fall of civilizations over long periods of time does,
on its face, seem to have a certain sort of organic majesty. Anal-
ogies between the current condition of "Western civilization,"
however, and the onset of the fall of the Roman Empire are
more glib than convincing. The Roman Empire endured at least
four hundred years; its "fall," as recorded by Gibbon, took place
gradually over a period of some two hundred years. And even
with due allowance for the acceleration of change, the relevance
of the Roman example seems to me questionable. The "age of
nationalism" has been with us only somewhat over a hundred
years, and it is only thirty years since "Western civilization"
surmounted the supreme challenge of World War II. The European Community is slowly giving vitality and content to the
concept of European unity. In the United States, as Archibald
Cox has pointed out, we have accomplished during the past
forty years "two social and political revolutions peacefully
within the existing frame of government." One—the New Deal
—revolutionized the theory and practice of government and
brought about a vast transfer of economic and political power.
The other—the civil rights revolution—invalidated "state laws
enforcing a caste system," developed new doctrines to extend
the reach of the Equal Protection Clause, and led to the enactment of new federal statutes "curtailing practices restricting
equal voting rights, denying equal accommodations, denying
equal employment opportunities, and assuring equal housing."[12]

The faltering of a sense of purpose that we are now witnessing is a reflection, I believe, not of the type of long-term
cyclical change recorded by Toynbee but of a shorter-term
phenomenon. The interludes between challenge and response, as
looked at in terms of decades rather than centuries, are characterized less by decay than by boredom. Russell Kirk, in a chapter of *A Program for Conservatives* entitled "The Problem of
Social Boredom," refers to Dean W. R. Inge as having "once
observed that the problem of boredom in society—social ennui
—has never been properly explored." Kirk adds: "It seems im-
perfectly apprehended, indeed, even in its general outlines by

most social planners and students of politics." And although Professor Kirk deals with the subject more broadly (and takes a gloomier view) than I propose to do here, I concur in the correlation he sees between boredom and the loss of a sense of purpose. He writes: "The will flags when it no longer perceives any end, any object, in existence. When the world is obsessed by means and trifles, and the ends of life have declined to no more than a faded memory in most people, then indeed we sink into sloth."[13]

Consistently with this perception of the impact of boredom, it should follow that a strong sense of purpose and a high state of social morale should accompany situations that lift people out of the routine and the humdrum. The new, the different, and the demanding are the obvious antidotes to boredom. A sampling of history reveals that these same ingredients, in one form or another, are invariable components of the cure for a sagging social spirit. As Eric Hoffer, pointing to nineteenth- and twentieth-century examples in France, Germany, and Japan, has remarked, "The reversion of decline is not only possible but may proceed at breakneck speed."[14] A sense of purpose, though commonly a short-term phenomenon, turns out to be not cyclical but circumstantial.

Take, by way of illustration, Frederick Jackson Turner's "frontier thesis" of American history. Turner believed that the distinctive attributes of American society were "the outcome of the experiences of the American people in dealing with the West." But "ever as society on her eastern border grew to resemble the Old World in its social forms and its industry, ever, as it began to lose faith in the details of democracy, she opened new provinces, and dowered new democracies."[15] Not surprisingly, Turner saw the closing of the frontier as foreshadowing the decay of American democracy. And while, happily, he was wrong on that score, he was certainly right in sensing that the challenge of the frontier not only shaped the quality of American life but evoked a degree of commitment and enthusiasm which was bound to lapse when the special effort demanded by frontier life ceased to be necessary.

For others, "the future" has been perceived as performing

the role attributed to the frontier by Turner. Bernard DeVoto perceived Americans as

> . . . realistic, hardheaded men who understood the dynamics of freedom and saw that if they were loosed in an empty continent an augmentation would follow for which nothing in the past could be an adequate gauge.
>
> From then on, not the past but the future has counted in the United States. If it doesn't work, try something else; tomorrow is another day; don't sell America short; the sky is the limit; rags to riches; canal-boat boy to President.[16]

Daniel J. Boorstin has taken much the same perception of challenge that was expressed by Turner in terms of the frontier and by DeVoto in terms of the future and translated it into the language of momentum and growth. In *The Americans: The Democratic Experience*, Boorstin identifies size and speed as the distinguishing dimension of American history. He continues:

> The American boast, and the butt of Old World ridicule, was how big everything was here and how fast everything moved. The United States was a large and speedy nation; Americans knew it, and for the most part, they loved it. Land Promoters, Tall Talkers, Land Hoaxers, and Go-Getters all bragged about the bigger and the faster. You might be a laggard or you might refuse to be a booster, but you still couldn't stop the nation from growing and moving.
>
> Now the American assignment seemed to come no longer from the conscious choice of individual citizens, but from the scale and velocity of the national projects themselves. Growth, ever more and faster, seemed to have become the nation's whole purpose.[17]

The stimulus of the frontier, the future, and of growth, severally or in combination, was bound to lose its inspirational force in time (fifty years, a hundred years?—the period we are discussing is in any case relatively short). Boorstin, however, appends to the above-quoted passage the sweeping observation,

"Man's problem of self-determination was more baffling than ever. For the very power of the most democratized nation on earth had led its citizens to feel inconsequential before the forces they had unleashed."[18] This seems to me to misconceive the situation. If Americans felt inconsequential, it was not because of the forces they had unleashed but because, diverted by an obsession with growth (or the frontier or the future), they had lost sight for the time being of their more fundamental sense of mission.

From the foregoing it follows that a threat to existing values can be at least as effective a means of evoking a sense of purpose as the challenge of the new and exciting. The epitome, of course, is war. "Society," notes Robert Nisbet, "attains its maximum sense of moral purpose during the period of war." The English philosopher L. P. Jacks, Nisbet comments, rightly refers to "the spiritual peace that war brings." The equivalence between the frontier and war is apparent enough: both entail a challenge to survival; both require the sloughing off of nonessentials; both demand maximum effort on the part of those involved. "It is the moral element of war, as William James saw so clearly, that makes for the curious dualism in the response of the average person to war," Nisbet adds.[19] But what James saw, I believe, was not "the moral element of war" but the capacity of war to evoke supreme and dedicated effort; hence, he argued, we should seek "the moral *equivalent* of war"—that is, a moral challenge capable of evoking a response comparable to the response evoked by war.[20]

As a "medic" in World War II, I felt a degree of commitment (and, at moments, of exhilaration) such as I have never felt at any other time. I have ever since beeen intrigued by the question of when hardship and sacrifice cease to be contributors of net gain and become instead sources of true misery. When, therefore, my wife and I visited Israel as guests of Histadrut in the fall of 1968, I was eager to see how the country had adapted itself to the strange interval of neither war nor peace which then prevailed. We, like other visitors, were deeply impressed by the sense of purpose so palpably evoked by the necessity for sacrifice in the cause of national survival. This sense of purpose seemed to explain rates of crime, delinquency, and drug abuse substantially lower than the comparable rates of other countries with similar standards of living but lacking in a similar spirit of sacrifice.

A few months later I became deeply involved as Under Secretary of State in the effort to bring about implementation of the United Nations Security Council Resolution calling for the withdrawal by Israel from the territories seized in the 1967 war and for the establishment of "secure and recognized" boundaries. It was a frustrating endeavor. I came to wonder whether either side really wanted peace—in the case of the Arabs because they could never reconcile themselves to the presence of a new Jewish homeland on what had once been Arab territory; in the case of the Israelis because peace would mean the elimination of the threat whose very existence helped to reinforce the sense of national purpose stemming from their religious and historic heritage. I pressed my curiosity about the latter point whenever I could get the ear of a member of the Israeli embassy. The Israeli diplomats repudiated the idea, of course, pointing to the burdens of national service, cost, and loss of life that Israel was daily called upon to endure. Since then the Yom Kippur war has made it clearer than ever that for Israel the only alternative to peace is the growing danger of ultimate destruction. One must hope, therefore, that Israel will be faced instead with having to adjust to the "spiritual war that peace brings."

Instead of a threat to existing values, a powerful drive to achieve some defined social goal can also serve as a unifying force. More intense than the sense of purpose stimulated by a vague sort of belief in the bigger and better things that tomorrow will bring, the motivation aroused by a social goal tends, in its more compulsive forms, to exhibit all the earmarks of single-mindedness that are evoked in the individual at war. This is the attitude of the zealot, the fanatic, the dedicated revolutionary. The language of warfare comes naturally to such a person, as does the conspiratorial attitude. Indeed, it would be hard to say which comes first: the desire to treat the opposition as the enemy, or the pursuit of tactics that force the opposition to behave like the enemy.

The emotional distance between the conspiratorial cell and the crusading mass can be frighteningly short. In organizational terms, fortunately, the gap is not easily or often traversed; this is one context in which human inertia is a saving attribute. We still recall the lesson taught by the sickening spectacle of Hitler's demonstrations of mass hypnosis. It may also be, as Boorstin has suggested, that the directness of the communication between the political leader and the individual made possible by the broadcast media has given "an unpredicted new twist . . . to the ancient clichés about democracy":

> To be sure, more people than ever could now listen to the voice of their leader. But the people were no longer a "mob," no longer "The Crowd" of the European sociological classics. . . . For the first time each member of the listening multitude had the opportunity and the burden of shaping his own reaction, without visible guidance from the rest.[21]

Despite these reassuring reflections, Yale President Kingman Brewster, Jr., seems to me to have been wise in commending Erich Fromm's *Escape from Freedom* to the incoming class of 1978. President Brewster told the freshmen that Fromm, writing from the perspective of the forties and the war against fascism, had pointed out that "liberation, first from ecclesiastical, and later from political authority, left man standing alone, isolated, afraid, and terribly susceptible to any dogma to which he could surrender his freedom and find purpose in submission." Unlike Stalinism and Maoism, or Hitler and Mussolini, the democratic state grants no release from the burdens of freedom: "It can only provide the circumstances for choice. It may even compound the problem in a sense; for, if public policy is successful, it will multiply your capacities and opportunities."[22]

And yet we must not let our distrust of dogma blind us to visions of a more equitable and more stable world order. At a time, especially, when the prospect of bigger and better tomorrows no longer enlists automatic enthusiasm, force is added to appeals to submerge our egocentricity in a cooperative effort to build a world free from want and fear. "Not merely to save the world, but primarily to save our own souls," exhorted Gunnar Myrdal, "there should again be dreamers, planners and fighters, in the midst of our nations, who would take upon themselves the important social function in democracy of raising our sights."[23] And indeed, from Graham Wallas and Woodrow Wilson to Grenville Clark and Robert McNamara, this century has had no lack of thinkers on a grand scale who have attempted just that. Their visions, it is true, have not yet caught fire, but the interdependence of the world is an increasingly visible fact, and I believe that out of that fact is bound to emerge in due course a compelling—and comparably inspiring—concept of the opportunities for global cooperation.

So MUCH for explanation, rationalization, historical heritage and analogy, and hortatory appeals for a better world. Although each of these approaches contributes something to the affirmation of a sense of purpose, there is more to be said about America and its still unfulfilled potential. The mere fact that we have made mistakes must not cause us to abandon a sense of national purpose. To do so would be as foolish as closing up a store because some of its product lines lost money. Nor should we be discouraged because we have not always lived up to our proclaimed ideals. That too would be absurd—no less so, certainly, than would have been the early abandonment of Christianity because so few of its adherents were successful in emulating Christ. It may be true that America has promised more than any other society, but so too has it attempted more and delivered more.

Comparisons with the comfort, cleanliness, and order of compact, homogeneous societies like Sweden or Denmark are beside the point. The scope of the American undertaking, as well as its shortcomings, is measured by its commitments to groups—the blacks, the native Americans, the Chicanos and the Puerto Ricans—whose forebears, unlike most of the people of our nation of immigrants, were never given the chance to choose to become Americans. In each case they became a part of us because of conquest or enslavement, and so they have twice suffered—first by the act which uprooted or subjugated them, then by the denial of dignity and equality.

"Whom they have injured they also hate," wrote Seneca, and it is true that in America the majority's hatred of those whom they have wronged has been slow to fade. And although we are making progress in righting these wrongs, there is much that remains to be done to redeem the promise of America to all those who have not yet fully shared in it.

If it is a challenge we need, let it be the ever renewed challenge of America's unfinished business. Though the accomplishments of the two revolutions Archibald Cox spoke about are remarkable, both are far from complete. Our treatment of our old people is still a national disgrace. Far too many of those who are able and willing to work are unemployed or underemployed. There is ugliness to be eradicated and pollution to be suppressed. Having come so close to achieving quantitative sufficiency, we now have the opportunity to pursue qualitative excellence in all its forms—in our environment, our culture, our community life, and our self-government. It is a challenge not lacking in excitement; if we do not feel this excitement, the fault is in our failure to use our vision and exercise our imaginations. For certainly this nation's sights have long since been set as high and higher than any goal we could realistically hope to reach.

Americans are a self-critical people. I hope we remain so. I also hope, accordingly, that we never receive from others the ungrudging approval which our self-critical impulses lead us so constantly to seek. And yet it seems to me high time that we gave ourselves credit for having come so far in reducing our vulnerability to the two criticisms that we most frequently direct against ourselves. One is that we are excessively materialistic. The other is that we are excessively conformist.

On the first score, materialism is not now, if it ever was, a dominant American characteristic; indeed, I suspect that we are somewhat less materialistic, by and large, than most Europeans of comparable means. What is distinctive about us is our generosity—our support for the Marshall Plan, United Way drives, community hospitals, and—increasingly—cultural enterprises. Contrary to the forebodings of T. S. Eliot, mass communica-

tions have generated not only mass audiences but mass participation in every form of cultural activity. Orchestras, string
quartets, choral groups, little theaters, dance groups, art classes,
and writing seminars flourish in America today with unprecedented vitality. The National Center for Voluntary Action,
meanwhile, reports that more Americans than ever are engaged
in one form or another of community service.

The promise of America was never a material promise. It
was the promise of a quality of life—a quality of life that would
be characterized by freedom and dignity and participation and
sharing. Americans are working toward the fulfillment of this
promise in greater numbers and with more dedicated decency
than ever before. The trouble is that they either do not know
it or do not believe it.

As to conformity, the truth is that America has been
"greening" at a good clip for quite a while now. We still have a
lot of conformity in our nonconformity, to be sure (I remember my elder son, then about twelve, saying to me once that he
couldn't get his hair cut short because he was "too much of a
conformist"). Generally speaking, however, Americans are
more self-confident in indulging their individuality than they
used to be. The liberation of hair, clothes, and life-styles has
made people freer to choose what they like and what suits them.
The emphasis in postsecondary education on "doing one's own
thing," whatever its impact on the job market, has encouraged
young people to do exactly that. The same spirit is also changing
the world of work, where, as we have seen, the demand for intrinsic satisfactions is diminishing the domination of the "money-
instrumental" attitude. In higher education, leading institutions
are showing the way toward "breaking the educational lock-
step"* for the benefit of individuals who have been penalized
by it.

* The "educational lock-step" is the conventional sequence from secondary
school to college and graduate school without interruption for intervals of work,
childbearing, or child-rearing. Highlighted by the "Newman Report," a report
on higher education submitted to me as Secretary of HEW by a group headed
by Frank Newman, then Assistant to the President of Stanford, the "educational
lock-step" was the target of a number of the report's most useful recommendations.

For better or worse, women's lib, greater sexual freedom, and four-letter words are here to stay. Consciousness III has not dawned, nor is it likely to, but Charles Reich was right in 1970 in noting that young people were nicer to, and more natural with each other than their predecessors. These young people are parents and breadwinners now, but they are still nice and natural, and their successors are at least as much so. Reich's revolution has already suffered the fate of most radical movements in America; it has been assimilated.

THE PROMISE of America! The phrase itself has a bright glow. It has the appeal of the future, but with an emphasis on quality rather than growth; it has continuity with the past, and with the best that America has always stood for; it has the attraction of the difficult and the demanding. The effort to bring it closer should inspire not simply a sense of purpose, but a sense of dedication. But if the words have been overworked, if affirmative goals fail to evoke the required commitment, then let us be stirred by the new urgency of the threats to our society's most important values. These should exert an equally powerful claim on our resourcefulness and determination. Survival is at stake, not of life, but of a way of life.

The corrosive processes described in this book are cumulative and mutually reinforcing. Their compounded effect, as we have seen, is declining confidence in government; a progressive inability to understand, control, and influence the forces that shape our lives; and a diminishing sense of individual identity and significance. Left unchecked, these mutually reinforcing processes will eventually destroy both our capacity for self-government and the human dignity and freedom which are its chief end.

But we are not helpless. We can blunt these trends, perhaps even turn them around and start the spiral in the opposite direction. This book attempts to identify the counterthrusts that could accomplish such a reversal. None, no matter how effectively carried out, can conceivably be sufficient in itself. In combination, however, these counterthrusts can have a compounded impact. To the extent, for example, that we succeed in reducing the number and complexity of the choices that have to be made at the center of government, in pushing responsibility for choice downward and outward to states, localities, and individuals, we shall thereby make the processes of government more accessible and more responsive. To the extent that we also succeed in expanding opportunities for significant individual participation in these processes, we shall make it possible for more people to understand and shape the forces that affect their lives. We shall at the same time have helped to restore a sense of identity and community.

By the same token, we can enhance the value of the opportunity for choice through the honesty and intelligibility with which we confront and communicate the necessity for choice. We can improve, moreover, the likelihood that our choices will be sensible by clarifying the structure of government and reducing the range of alternatives requiring choice. To the extent, finally, that choice is intelligent, the chances are increased that a particular policy for the allocation of available resources (the income strategy, for example) will have enough impact to make a critical difference.

A similar sort of synergistic impact can be brought about through the interaction of measures to strengthen the integrity of the political process. Campaign spending reform, steps to insulate government agencies from political influence, and the adjustments of the executive-legislative balance so as to increase accountability will contribute to strengthening trust in government. So also will the growing receptivity of political professionals to public demands for the politics of openness and candor.

Out of these mutually reinforcing efforts should emerge, in turn, the enhancement of individual dignity and self-esteem. But it *will* take effort, not in a once-and-for-all spurt, but unremitting, year-in, year-out devotion. It will have to be effort, moreover, infused by obligation as well as by interest. For not even the narrowest of the psychological premises on which the framers constructed our constitutional system ever supposed that it could survive without a constantly renewed infusion of civic responsibility.

CIVIC RESPONSIBILITY is only one of the obligations that arise out of the relationships among individuals. Like the others, however, it is unenforceable. Hence the common assumption that obligations are the automatic reciprocal of rights is not strictly true. Obligations transcend rights. The full extent of my obligation to respect my neighbor's right to worship as he pleases cannot be spelled out in any court decree. Obligations imply a moral, and not merely a legal, command. The criminal laws punish stealing, but not a lack of generosity. They penalize the man who uses his hand as a weapon, but not the man who fails to extend it in help. In the case of civil rights, the law can enforce their observance, but not their respect. Where there is true respect for other people—the awareness that each is a unique, sacrosanct individual, equal in dignity to every other human being—there is an awareness of obligation which is higher and more sensitive than any requirement of the law.

Once we accept the full equality and dignity of the moral claim of each individual, we cannot in good conscience assert our own superiority or condone the injustice of a society that denies equal respect to each individual. Conversely, a society committed to such respect is worthy of the best that is in us.

Our society is so committed. We have no need of a higher sense of purpose than to help it come closer to achieving its full promise to a diverse, talented, richly endowed people.

Notes

INTRODUCTION

1. Daniel J. Boorstin, ed., *An American Primer* (Chicago, 1966), Vol. 1, p. 229.
2. Quoted in Catharine Drinker Bowen, *Miracle at Philadelphia* (Boston, 1966), p. 279.
3. Ibid.
4. Alexander Bickel, "Watergate and the Legal Order," *Commentary*, January 1974, p. 21.
5. *The Federalist*, ed. Jacob E. Cooke (Middletown, Conn., 1961), pp. 56–58.
6. Ibid., pp. 352–353.
7. Ibid., p. 378.
8. Richard Hofstadter, *The American Political Tradition* (New York, 1948), p. 4.
9. My source for this quotation is Professor Martin Diamond's thoughtful essay, "The American Idea of Man: The View from the Founding," in Irving Kristol and Paul Weaver, eds., *The Americans: 1776* (to be published in 1976). Madison's statement was made on June 20, 1788, and can be found in Jonathan Elliot's *Debates on the Adoption of the Federal Constitution* (Charlottesville, Va., 1937).
10. Arthur M. Schlesinger, Jr., *The Age of Jackson* (Boston, 1945), p. 509.
11. *Baker v. Carr*, 369 U.S. 186 (1962).
12. James Madison in the Philadelphia *National Gazette*, December 19, 1791. Italics added.

CHAPTER I

1. According to Lyman H. Butterfield, editor-in-chief of the Adams papers, to whom I am indebted for the quoted language, it was drawn by Adams from a tract by James Harrington. See L. H. Butterfield, "A government of laws and not of men," *Harvard Magazine*, November 1974, p. 20.
2. Garry Wills, "The Tyranny of Weakness," *Playboy*, December 1973, p. 118.
3. Ibid.
4. Quoted by Lou Cannon, "The Siege Psychology and How It Grew," *The Washington Post*, July 29, 1973, p. C1.
5. Alexis de Tocqueville, *Democracy in America* (New York, 1961), Vol. 2, p. 144.
6. Jeb Stuart Magruder, *An American Life: One Man's Road to Watergate* (New York, 1974), p. 215.
7. Richard E. Neustadt, *Presidential Power* (New York, 1960), p. 41.
8. Neustadt, *Presidential Power*, p. 2.
9. Ibid.
10. Arthur M. Schlesinger, Jr., *The Imperial Presidency* (Boston, 1973), p. 417.
11. Made by Roland J. Cole, the study is soon to be published by Ballinger Press of Cambridge under the title *Campaign Spending in Senate Elections*.
12. *Katz v. United States*, 389 U.S. 347 (1967).
13. *United States v. United States District Court*, 407 U.S. 297 (1972).
14. As quoted by Solicitor General Robert H. Bork, Remarks to the American Bar Association, Honolulu, Hawaii, August 13, 1974.
15. John Gunther, *Inside U.S.A.* (New York, 1947), p. 475.
16. Edward Weisband and Thomas M. Franck, *Resignation in Protest: Political and Ethical Choices Between Loyalty to Team and Loyalty to Conscience in American Public Life* (New York, 1975).
17. Hearings before the Committee on the Judiciary, United States Senate, 93d Congress, 1st Session, on Special Prosecutor (October–November 1973), pp. 237–318, 383–426. This testimony also deals at length with the jurisdictional issues that I discussed with Mr. Cox and contains copies of all my contemporary notes and memoranda on the subject.

CHAPTER II

1. See Raoul Berger, *Executive Privilege: A Constitutional Myth* (Cambridge, Mass., 1974), pp. 263–297.
2. *United States v. Nixon*, 418 U.S. 683, 705 (1974).
3. *United States v. Nixon*, 418 U.S. 683, 713, 708, 711 (1974).

4. Hearings before the Subcommittees on Administrative Practice and Procedure and Separation of Powers, Senate Committee on the Judiciary, and the Subcommittee on Intergovernmental Relations, Senate Committee on Government Operations, 93d Congress, 1st Session (June 26, 1973), Vol. 2, pp. 239–240.

5. These references to the Task Force on Secrecy report are drawn from Arthur M. Schlesinger, Jr., *The Imperial Presidency* (Boston, 1973), p. 363.

6. *Congressional Record*, March 8, 1973, p. S 4205.

7. See, e.g., Schlesinger, *The Imperial Presidency*, note 5, p. 220; Henry Fairlie, "The Lessons of Watergate," *Encounter*, October 1974, p. 12.

8. As quoted in Richard E. Neustadt, *Presidential Power* (New York, 1960), p. 39.

9. Erwin C. Hargrove, *The Power of the Presidency* (Philadelphia, 1974), p. 307.

10. Remarks of Solicitor General Robert H. Bork, American Bar Association Convention, Honolulu, Hawaii, August 13, 1974.

11. Hearings before the Subcommittee on Separation of Powers of the Committee on the Judiciary, 93d Congress, 2d Session (March 27, 1974), p. 4.

12. Schlesinger, *The Imperial Presidency*, note 5, p. 414.

13. *M'Culloch* v. *Maryland*, 4 Wheat 316, 407 (1819).

14. Thomas Pownall, *Memorial Addressed to the Sovereigns of America* (London, 1783), pp. 52–53.

CHAPTER III

1. These figures are drawn from the tables and graphs in Arthur Miller et al., "Presidential Crisis and Political Support: The Impact of Watergate on Attitudes Toward Institutions" (a paper prepared at the University of Michigan's Center for Political Studies, 1975), and Miller et al., "Social Conflict and Political Estrangement, 1958–1972" (University of Michigan, 1973).

2. *The Works of the Right Honourable Edmund Burke* (London, 1907–1934), Vol. 2, p. 164.

3. Richard M. Cohen and Jules Witcover, *A Heartbeat Away* (New York, 1974), p. 37.

4. Anthony Lewis, "Watergate Aftermath," *The New York Times*, November 28, 1974, p. 33.

5. Dwight D. Eisenhower, *Waging Peace* (New York, 1965), p. 551.

6. *Writings of James Madison*, Hunt ed. (New York, 1910), Vol. 9, p. 103.

7. *Writings of Madison*, p. 103.

8. Russell Baker, "Outasight, Outamind," *New York Times Magazine*, October 27, 1974, p. 6.

9. Mark Harris, "The Last Article," *New York Times Magazine*, October 6, 1974, p. 20.

10. Stewart Alsop, *The Center* (New York, 1968), p. 157.

11. Alsop, *The Center*, p. 159.

12. Douglass Cater, *Dana: The Irrelevant Man* (New York, 1970), p. 155.

13. The quotation is from an internal memo reprinted in *Of the Press, By the Press, For the Press (And others, too): A critical study of the inside workings of the news business*. From the news pages, editorials, columns, and internal staff memos of *The Washington Post* (Washington, D.C., 1974), p. 23.

14. Justice Potter Stewart, "Or Of the Press," Sesquicentennial Address to the Yale Law School, November 2, 1974.

15. *Of the Press*, p. vi.

16. Walter Lippmann, Address to the International Press Institute Assembly, London, England, May 27, 1965. In *Miami Herald* v. *Tornillo* the Supreme Court made the same point: ". . . a responsible press is an undoubtedly desirable goal, but press responsibility is not mandated by the Constitution and like many other virtues it cannot be legislated." 418 U.S. 241, 256 (1974).

17. *Of the Press*, p. 233.

CHAPTER IV

1. From the transcript of President Eisenhower's remarks, November 7, 1956, in *Public Papers of the Presidents: Dwight D. Eisenhower, 1956* (Washington, D.C., 1958), p. 1090.

2. *The New York Times*, January 17, 1957.

3. Transcript of Presidential press conference, January 23, 1957, in *Public Papers of the Presidents, 1957*, pp. 73–74.

4. Lewis Chester, Godfrey Hodgson, and Bruce Page, *An American Melodrama* (London, 1969).

5. *The New York Times Book Review*, May 27, 1973.

6. See Mancur Olson, "An Analytic Framework for Social Reporting and Policy Analysis," *The Annals of the American Academy of Political and Social Science*, March 1970, pp. 112, 117, 123.

7. Elmer B. Staats, "How Can We Increase Confidence in the Management of Federal Programs?", address before the Economic Club of Detroit, November 26, 1973.

8. *Cable: Report to the President*, The Cabinet Committee on Cable Communications (Washington, D.C., 1974), Chapter V, pp. 4–5.

9. Marie Buckley, *Breaking into Prison: A Citizen's Guide to Voluntary Action* (Boston, 1974).

CHAPTER V

1. Paul R. Ehrlich, "The Population-Resource-Environment Crisis" (unpublished ms., 1973).
2. Frederic G. Withington, "Five Generations of Computers," *Harvard Business Review*, July–August 1974, p. 106.
3. Daniel Patrick Moynihan, *The Politics of a Guaranteed Income* (New York, 1973), p. 131.
4. Charles Percy Snow, *The Two Cultures and the Scientific Revolution* (Cambridge, England, 1959).
5. Alice Rivlin, "How Can Experiments Be More Useful?" A paper prepared for the annual meeting of the American Economics Association (New York, N.Y., December 29, 1973), p. 20. For a thoughtful discussion of HEW's New Jersey negative-income-tax experiment (one of several such experiments sponsored by the Department), see Carol Tavris's interview with Donald T. Campbell in *Psychology Today*, September 1975, p. 53.

CHAPTER VI

1. Max Frankel, "Revenue Sharing Is a Counter-Revolution," *New York Times Magazine*, April 25, 1971, p. 28.
2. Amitai Etzioni, "The Fallacy of Decentralization," in Terrence E. Cook and Patrick Morgan, eds., *Participatory Democracy* (San Francisco, 1971), p. 65.
3. The figures are drawn from "The State of the States," the message of Governor Daniel J. Evans of Washington as 1974 chairman of the National Governors Conference.
4. Ibid.
5. "In Some Areas, Today's Temperature is 98.6°," *The New York Times*, August 1, 1975.
6. Robert K. Yin and Douglas Yates, *Street-Level Governments: Assessing Decentralization and Urban Services* (Washington, D.C., 1974), pp. 228–229.
7. Ibid., p. 320.
8. The study was published in 1973 under the title *Citizen Organizations Increasing Client Control Over Services* (Washington, D.C., 1973).
9. Irving Kristol, "What's Bugging the Students," *The Atlantic Monthly*, November 1965, p. 111.
10. Daniel Patrick Moynihan, *Maximum Feasible Misunderstanding* (New York, 1969), pp. 182–183.
11. Staughton Lynd, "The New Radicals and 'Participatory' Democracy," *Dissent*, Summer 1965, p. 328, note 19.

12. Tom Hayden, "The Politics of 'The Movement,'" *Dissent*, January–February 1966, p. 87.
13. Theodore Lowi, *The End of Liberalism* (New York, 1969), p. 247.
14. Harlan Cleveland, "How Do You Get Everybody in on the Act and Still Get Some Action?" *Educational Record*, Vol. 55, No. 3, Washington, D.C., 1974.
15. Cook and Morgan, eds., *Participatory Democracy*, p. 30.
16. See Lewis S. Feuer, *The Conflict of Generations: The Character and Significance of Student Movements* (New York, 1969), pp. 408–412.

CHAPTER VII

1. The example comes from Sar A. Levitan and William B. Johnston, *Work is Here To Stay, Alas* (Salt Lake City, 1973).
2. Learned Hand, *The Spirit of Liberty* (New York, 1952), pp. 260–262.
3. As quoted in Studs Terkel, *Working* (New York, 1972), frontispiece.
4. Terkel, *Working*, p. 222.
5. Ibid., p. 507.
6. Ibid., p. 94.
7. Ibid., pp. 96–97.
8. "Worker Discontent: Where is the Problem?" (A Report to the Ford Foundation, 1974) by Lloyd Ullman, professor of economics, University of California, Berkeley; Robert J. Flanagan, assistant professor of labor economics, Graduate School of Business, University of Chicago; and George Strauss, professor of business administration, University of California, Berkeley, p. ii. In the case of quit rates, the trend disappears after unemployment, relative wages and hours, and—again—the composition of the labor force are taken into account. The report finds similar explanations for the increases in absentee rates, strikes, and accident frequency.
9. Jerome Rosow, ed., *The Worker and the Job* (Englewood Cliffs, N.J., 1974), p. 7.
10. Terkel, *Working*, pp. xxiv, 523.
11. Ibid., p. 31.
12. Ibid., p. xxxiii.
13. Ibid., pp. 108, 119, 294.
14. Frederick Herzberg, *Work and the Nature of Man* (Cleveland, 1966).
15. Adam Smith, *The Wealth of Nations*, ed. Edwin Canaan (New York, 1937), pp. 4–5.
16. Ibid., pp. 14, 81.

17. This information is drawn from the absorbing account of Taylorism in Daniel Boorstin, *The Americans: The Democratic Experience* (New York, 1973), p. 364.
18. *The Wall Street Journal*, February 11, 1975, p. 1.
19. See the Ford Foundation report, "Worker Discontent."
20. Judson Gooding, "The Accelerated Generation Moves Into Management," 1971, as quoted in *Work in America*, a report prepared by HEW task force (Cambridge, Mass., 1973), p. 48.
21. Terkel, *Working*, pp. 451–452.
22. As quoted in *Work in America*, p. 44.
23. Robert B. Goldman, "Work Values: Six Americans in a Swedish Plant" (A Report to the Ford Foundation, March 1975).
24. *The New York Times*, November 12, 1974, p. 31.
25. For a further discussion of industrial democracy, see David Jenkins, *Job Power* (New York, 1973), pp. 1–8.
26. Innis Macbeath, *The European Approach to Worker-Management Relations* (The British-North American Committee, 1973), p. 72.
27. Goldman, *Work Values*, pp. 60–61.
28. George Cabot Lodge, *The New American Ideology* (New York, 1975), pp. 174, 175.
29. As quoted in Rosow, ed., *The Worker and the Job*, p. 181.
30. Frank Furstenberg, "Work Experience and Family Life," in James O'Toole, ed., *Work and the Quality of Life* (Cambridge, Mass., 1974), pp. 341–360.
31. *Work in America*, p. 184. (Italics in original.)
32. See, e.g., Michael J. Piore, "Jobs and Training," in Samuel H. Beer and Richard E. Barringer, eds., *The State and the Poor* (Cambridge, Mass., 1970).
33. See *Work in America*, p. 172.

CHAPTER VIII

1. Margaret Mead and Muriel Brown, *The Wagon and the Star: A Study of American Community Initiative* (Chicago, 1966), p. 15.
2. Richard N. Goodwin has it right, I think: "Community is the form of social existence, the elemental unit through which the individual can express and create the social existence which is essential to freedom. It is the institutional embodiment of shared human purpose, the reconciliation between individual desires and the general well-being." *The American Condition* (Garden City, N.Y., 1974), p. 81.
3. Philip E. Slater, *The Pursuit of Loneliness: American Culture at the Breaking Point* (Boston, 1970), p. 7.
4. Haynes Johnson, "A Last Stronghold of Democracy," *The Washington Post* (April 6, 1975), p. C1.

5. Robert A. Nisbet, *The Quest for Community* (Oxford, England, 1953), p. 217.
6. Nathan Glazer and Daniel P. Moynihan, *Beyond the Melting Pot* (Cambridge, Mass., 1970), p. xcvii.
7. Nathan Glazer and Daniel P. Moynihan, "Why Ethnicity?" *Commentary*, October 1974, p. 33.
8. Ibid., p. 34.
9. For a full account of the social costs of the West End project, see Herbert J. Gans, *The Urban Villagers* (New York, 1962).
10. *The New York Times*, September 20, 1974, p. 1.
11. Vance Packard, *A Nation of Strangers* (New York, 1974), pp. 278–286.
12. Edward T. Hall, *The Hidden Dimension* (Garden City, N.Y., 1969), p. 106.
13. Ibid., pp. 105, 129.
14. Nisbet, *The Quest for Community*, p. xvi.
15. Ronald Koven, "The New Toronto Way," *The Washington Post*, August 25, 1974, p. C3.
16. Ibid.
17. Robert E. Patricelli, "Rebuilding Cities—Population Redistribution and Development Realities," a paper presented to the 1973 Ripon Society Conference, December 1, 1973, Washington, D.C. The emphasis is Mr. Patricelli's.
18. Peter C. Goldmark, "The New Rural Society," 1973 University Lecture Series, Cornell University.
19. "On the Street Where You Live," *Harper's*, September 1974, p. 93.
20. This was one of the findings of a nationwide survey of 1,031 mayors and councilmen by the National League of Cities, which appeared in *Nation's Cities*, April 1974. For a more complete report, see the League's *America's Mayors and Councilmen: Their Problems and Frustrations* (Washington, D.C., 1974).
21. See *The Washington Post*, April 8, 1975, p. A18.
22. *New Communities, USA* (Lexington, Mass., to be published 1976).
23. Betty Mansfield, "The Function of Membership Selection as a Survival Mechanism in Modern Communes" (unpublished paper, 1974), p. 9.
24. Lyn Lofland, *A World of Strangers: Order and Action in Urban Public Space* (New York, 1973).
25. As quoted in Daniel Boorstin, *An American Primer* (New York, 1966), p. 40.

CHAPTER IX

1. As quoted in Gordon S. Wood, *The Creation of the American Republic, 1776–1787* (Chapel Hill, N.C., 1969), p. vii.

2. From Bland's *An Inquiry Into the Rights of the British Colonies,* as quoted in Bernard Bailyn, *The Ideological Origins of the American Revolution* (Cambridge, Mass., 1967), p. 307.

3. Wood, *The Creation of the American Republic,* p. 72.

4. *McNabb* v. *U.S.,* 318 U.S. 332, 347 (1943).

5. See The Report of the Tribunal appointed under the Tribunals of Inquiry (Evidence) Act (1921) (London, 1928).

6. Charles A. Reich, "The New Property," 73 *Yale Law Journal* 733, 783–784, 785–786 (1964).

7. *Weinberger* v. *Eldridge,* 492 F.2nd 1230 (1974). *Cardinale, et al.* v. *Mathews,* 399 F. Supp. 1163 (1975).

8. This summary is drawn from Joel Berke, *Answers to Inequity* (Berkeley, Cal., 1974), pp. 16–17.

9. *Serrano* v. *Priest,* 487 P.2d 1241, 1251–1252 (1971).

10. *Rodriguez* v. *San Antonio Independent School District,* 337 F.Supp. 280 (1972).

11. *San Antonio Independent School District* v. *Rodriguez,* 411 U.S. 1, 58, 59 (1973).

12. *Wyatt* v. *Aderholt,* 368 F.Supp. 1383 (1974); 503 F.2nd 1305 (1974).

13. *O'Connor* v. *Donaldson,* No. 74–8, decided June 26, 1975.

14. John Marshall, *M'Culloch* v. *Maryland,* 4 Wheat 316, 431 (1819); Oliver Wendell Holmes, *Panhandle Oil Co.* v. *Knox,* 277 U.S. 218, 223 (1928).

15. Daniel Bell, for example, apparently found the distinction inconvenient for purposes of developing the concept of "equality of result"; at any rate, he ignored it. See "On Meritocracy and Equality," *The Public Interest,* Fall 1972, pp. 29, 40.

16. *DeFunis* v. *Odegaard,* 416 U.S. 312 (1974).

17. President Derek Bok, speech to the NAACP Legal Defense and Educational Fund dinner, New York City, November 11, 1974.

18. *Lau* v. *Nichols,* 414 U.S. 563 (1974).

19. *Brown* v. *Board of Education,* 347 U.S. 483 (1954); 349 U.S. 294 (1955). *Smith* v. *Allwright,* 321 U.S. 649 (1944). *Alexander* v. *Holmes County Board of Education,* 396 U.S. 19 (1969). *Furman* v. *Georgia,* 408 U.S. 238 (1972).

20. *Adams* v. *Richardson,* 480 F.2nd 1159 (1973).

21. Dwight D. Eisenhower, Presidential press conference, September 3, 1957.

22. John W. Gardner, *In Common Cause* (New York, 1972), p. 20.

23. For more about PIRGs, see Hays Gorey, *Nader and the Power of Everyman* (New York, 1975), pp. 90–94.

24. Robert Cooper, "Ombudsman as an Experiment in Television," speech delivered in Vancouver, British Columbia, 1975.

25. Address to the Smithsonian Institution conference, Washington, D.C., March 2, 1972.

26. Friedrich Hayek, *The Road to Serfdom* (London, 1944).
27. Daniel Patrick Moynihan, "The United States In Opposition," *Commentary*, March 1975, p. 44.
28. Ralf Dahrendorf, *The New Liberty: Survival and Justice in a Changing World* (Stanford, Cal., 1975), pp. 43–44.
29. Samuel P. Huntington, "The United States," paper written for the Trilateral Commission meeting in Kyoto, Japan, May 1975, pp. 60–61.
30. The first quotation is from Robert L. Heilbroner, *An Inquiry into the Human Prospect* (New York, 1974), p. 110. The second comes from a BBC lecture published in *The Observer*, December 29, 1974.
31. The information cited here is drawn from a critique of *The Limits to Growth* published by HEW in January 1973. The author of the paper was Walton J. Francis, a program analyst in the Office of Planning and Evaluation.
32. William Raspberry, "Equality Is the Right To Be Superior," *The Washington Post*, June 13, 1975.
33. John Rawls, *A Theory of Justice* (Cambridge, Mass., 1971), p. 256.
34. Woodrow Wilson, *The New Freedom* (New York, 1913), p. 283.
35. Rawls, *A Theory of Justice*, pp. 12–15.
36. Robert Nozick, *Anarchy, State, and Utopia* (New York, 1974), p. 150.
37. Ibid., p. 153.
38. John Kenneth Galbraith, *The New Industrial State*, rev. ed. (New York, 1972), pp. xii–xiii; *Money: Whence It Came, Where It Went* (Boston, 1975), pp. 308–309.
39. Learned Hand, *The Spirit of Liberty* (New York, 1952), p. 181.

CHAPTER X

1. Elliot Richardson, "Poisoned Politics," *The Atlantic Monthly*, October 1961, p. 77.
2. I do not except the magisterial pronouncements of the authors of "The American Commonwealth—1976," *The Public Interest*, Fall 1975.
3. Learned Hand, *The Spirit of Liberty* (New York, 1952), pp. 260–262.
4. *The Mind and Faith of Justice Holmes*, ed. Max Lerner (New York, 1943), p. 398.
5. Richard N. Goodwin, *The American Condition* (Garden City, N.Y., 1974), pp. 29–30.
6. Bertrand Russell, *Human Society in Ethics and Politics* (London, 1954), pp. 224–226.
7. Alfred North Whitehead, *Adventures of Ideas* (Middlesex, England, 1942), pp. 125–126.

8. Paul Tillich, "Religion and the Intellectuals," *Partisan Review*, 1950, pp. 138–139.
9. Learned Hand, speech at the Bryn Mawr College commencement, June 2, 1927.
10. *Minersville School District* v. *Gobvitis*, 310 U.S. 586, 596 (1940).
11. Alexander Bickel, "Reconsideration: Edmund Burke," *The New Republic*, March 17, 1973, p. 35. Alex Bickel and Richard Goodwin were both Frankfurter law clerks somewhat after my time.
12. Archibald Cox, "Not in Feather Beds," an address given at the annual meeting of the Associated Harvard Alumni on June 12, 1975.
13. Russell Kirk, *A Program for Conservatives*, rev. ed. (Chicago, 1962), pp. 102, 106.
14. Eric Hoffer, "What We Have Lost," *New York Times Magazine*, October 20, 1974, p. 110.
15. As quoted by Hugh Brogan in *The New Statesman*, April 4, 1975, p. 456.
16. Bernard DeVoto, *The Easy Chair* (Boston, 1955), p. 25.
17. Daniel Boorstin, *The Americans: The Democratic Experience* (New York, 1973), p. 558.
18. Ibid.
19. Robert A. Nisbet, *The Quest for Community* (Oxford, England, 1953), pp. 38–41.
20. William James, *The Moral Equivalent of War* (New York, 1910), pp. 12–20.
21. Boorstin, *The Americans*, p. 472.
22. Kingman Brewster, Jr., address to the freshman assembly, Yale University, *The New York Times*, September 11, 1974, p. 45.
23. Gunnar Myrdal, *An International Economy, Problems and Prospects* (New York, 1956), p. 322.

Index

377